EVERY GODDAMN DAY

EVERY GODDAMN DAY

A Highly Selective, Definitely Opinionated, and
Alternatingly Humorous *and* Heartbreaking
Historical Tour of Chicago

Neil Steinberg

The University of Chicago Press

The University of Chicago Press, Chicago 60637
© 2022 by Neil Steinberg
All rights reserved. No part of this book may be used or
reproduced in any manner whatsoever without written
permission, except in the case of brief quotations in
critical articles and reviews. For more information,
contact the University of Chicago Press, 1427 E. 60th St.,
Chicago, IL 60637.
Published 2022
Printed in the United States of America

31 30 29 28 27 26 25 24 23 22   1 2 3 4 5

ISBN-13: 978-0-226-77984-3 (cloth)
ISBN-13: 978-0-226-77998-0 (e-book)
DOI: https://doi.org/10.7208/chicago/9780226779980.001.0001

Library of Congress Cataloging-in-Publication Data

Names: Steinberg, Neil, author.
Title: Every goddamn day : a highly selective, definitely opinionated,
and alternatingly humorous and heartbreaking historical tour of
Chicago / Neil Steinberg.
Description: Chicago : The University of Chicago Press, 2022. |
Includes bibliographical references.
Identifiers: LCCN 2022009764 | ISBN 9780226779843 (cloth) |
ISBN 9780226779980 (ebook)
Subjects: LCSH: Chicago (Ill.)—History—Anecdotes.
Classification: LCC F548.36 .S74 2022 | DDC 977.3/11—dc23/
eng/20220301
LC record available at https://lccn.loc.gov/2022009764

♾ This paper meets the requirements of ANSI/NISO Z39.48-1992
(Permanence of Paper).

For my sons

ROSS & KENT STEINBERG

INTRODUCTION

History is not a place. You cannot go there. The past isn't a field you can run through, admiring the wide sweep of waving grain in one glance, then leaning in close to examine a single kernel on a stalk of wheat.

History is not a thing, either. You cannot touch it. Yes, there are objects, artifacts that you can caress. The solid iron plow, the flapper's beaded dress. You can weigh those in your hand and almost feel the faint vibrations of long ago.

But they are only shells, husks, empty buildings where somebody once lived. You can stand in the room and imagine what the wallpaper must have been like, maybe even find some old shreds. Maybe there is a brass bed; if not, a corner where the brass bed almost certainly stood.

The people from the past are gone, mostly, unaffected by our notice, unmoved by our approval or scorn. And those who linger are not always reliable witnesses. They're just as liable to tell you what they wish had happened as admit what did. Maybe more so.

What remains is the echo of what they might have once done, in words or pictures, written at the time, or later, a confused jumble of facts we can try to sort through, dividing the real from the illusionary, then molding the results into meaningful shapes.

Into stories.

History is a story. Once upon a time this man—and until recently it was almost invariably a man—left his home and went somewhere else, which he then claimed as his own. Voyages and discoveries, wars and treaties, emperors and kings.

These tales are told to explain and justify. Who we are, how we got here, what happened to us when we arrived. Or, increasingly, when the others arrived. To make sense of the world. That's why each generation revisits the past, tells the stories anew, takes the building blocks of events and reassembles them into lessons that resonate now.

Because who "we" are keeps changing, and with it what is considered significant enough to merit understanding. The circle of inclusion expands and contracts as we ask: Who is important to the story? Who is the narrator? Who are the dynamic actors? That evolves, generation to generation.

We winnow the past with our living breath, our values today, blowing away the chaff. Even if we accurately relate what happened before, we *see* it differently than the people experiencing it. Thus history shifts from the perspective of the people on the ships, arriving, to those on the shore, watching them arrive. Nothing more eloquently demonstrates the biases of the past than to read how it conveys history, the blaze of glory we once needed to warm ourselves, marshaling our forebears into a chorus of praise.

History gathers at certain places—battlefields, coastlines, cities—and congeals around certain dates. The arrival of the shock: Dec. 7, 1941. Nov. 22, 1963. Sept. 11, 2001, Jan. 6, 2021. Or even the day a less dramatic event occurred. The calendar serves as a gentle reminder of the past, like a child tugging on our sleeve. "Hey, Daddy. Look at that."

We're obligated to look. It's half responsibility, half recreation. To me, and to many, reading history is part of the joy of being alive, like listening to music or eating good food. Reading history embroiders the present with the designs of the past. It's a regular activity to promote healthy living, like exercise. I write a blog called "Every goddamn day"—the mild expletive a reflection of the grittier corners of life—where I post an essay, true to the name, every single day, usually at midnight. Some are my daily columns from the *Chicago Sun-Times*, some are arguments about current events, or deep dives into etymology, or books, or objects, just about anything. My only requirement is that the topic is something that reasonably intelligent people might want to know more about. Often the blog, like the column, is pegged to the day of the year—a holiday, an anniversary—providing background and context.

Often the essays are about Chicago, a city I've lived in, or near, for more than 40 years. This book breaks the history of the city into 366 entries, one for every day of the year. I have employed several organizing principles: first, what a resident or visitor should know about the city, the most significant parts. But also the most engaging, unexpected aspects. I cover subjects where Chicago affected the world, more than the world affecting Chicago. Thus, the first cell phone call is mentioned but Pearl Harbor is not. I explore transportation, industry, race, labor, finance, culture, architecture, science, sports, music, literature. I try to represent the broad spectrum of people who live in Chicago. "I don't want this to be the white man's history of Chicago," I vowed. I've tried to be expansive, but I know I've been incomplete.

Certain themes had to be sounded: the Chicago River is the key to the city's founding as a portage to the Des Plaines River. Chicago continued growing as a crossroads with the arrival of the railroads. How Chicago appears to others, and how we see ourselves, is another constant refrain. The buildings built here, the books written, the food produced.

And some events have to be in any book presenting the story of Chicago. The Fire of 1871. The World's Columbian Exposition. Certain individuals too. As much as I'd be happy to never hear the name "Al Capone" again, he must be included. Richard Daley too, *pater et fils*. And Michael Jordan. But for me familiar topics should be cast in a new light. The definition of boredom is being told what you already know. Besides, the day will come when readers won't recognize even the biggest names. "Oprah Winfrey? A TV host of some kind. Popular in her day."

I tried to limit the number of gruesome crimes—there have been a lot—and the number of great sports moments. Those are already well covered in books that are readily available. So no Grimes sisters. No Stanley Cup.

History needs a structure or it becomes too vast. I found the vignette to be a challenging, stylized form, like haiku, that focuses and concentrates. For some subjects, the challenge was to find the exact date: Chicago has been the heart of the pinball industry since Gottlieb was founded in 1927. But where to pick up the story? A company's incorporation is a dry event. Chicago is also the capital of the candy universe, or was. But which date should be used to launch the tale?

Some episodes efface others. When Judy the Elephant wouldn't get into a truck in 1943, her handlers decided to walk her from Brookfield Zoo to Lincoln Park Zoo. Judy's journey isn't particularly meaningful; it doesn't speak to a larger truth, beyond the stubbornness of pachyderms. But to me the big gray beast loping along the streets of Chicago symbolizes the wonder of the place. Stand on a street corner in Chicago long enough and an elephant may go by.

Judy left Brookfield on July 2, 1943, and arrived at Lincoln Park in the wee hours of the next day. But if I chose Judy as the vignette for July 2, you would lose Franklin D. Roosevelt becoming the first American presidential candidate to fly in an airplane, arriving to promise a New Deal to the 1932 Democratic National Convention. And if I chose the 3rd, you'd never meet Henry Campbell, age 11, the first defendant in the nation's first juvenile court in 1899.

I was tempted to include a runner-up on some pages. But that seemed the easy path, shirking my responsibility, since an important part of writing history is choosing. To tell this story but not that. FDR or the elephant? The choices we make become history, a tiny fragment of it anyway, and then we choose what stories to present when recounting that history to each other. I hope I made the right choices here.

Sometimes the form required that I finesse when to pick up the story. The evacuation of Fort Dearborn and the bloody battle that followed occurred August 15, which is also the date the Picasso sculpture was unveiled to a disbelieving city. I cherish the Picasso unveiling for its pure shock-of-the-new quality, so I decided to start the story of Fort Dearborn on the 14th instead.

At first that felt like cheating. But I began to notice something. When you start a story changes how the story unfolds. By beginning the Fort Dearborn tale the day before the violence, I include a moment that some renditions leave out: the garrison commander reneging on presents he had promised to give the Native Americans in return for safe passage. Perhaps the reason the Potawatomi gathered in ambush. Beginning the story that way changes the narrative into something more aligned with our current sensibilities, which tend to view all the participants in a story as having integrity and operating on their own moral precepts, which is why we don't call it a "massacre" anymore. It's a fuller, truer story if you start on the 14th, but my original motivation was just trying to fit the Picasso in. That kind of fortune is a reminder that often it is better to be lucky than good, and I consider myself very fortunate in what I stumbled across, sometimes by sheer accident, in searching randomly for *something* on a certain date. Once, as I explain in the acknowledgments, I was directly aided in my research by a kitten knocking over a watering can.

I am a journalist, not a professional historian or trained researcher, and fixing the date something occurred is not always easy. I'm sure *someone* knows when DJ Frankie Knuckles hosted the grand opening of the Warehouse in March 1977, spurring, it is generally agreed, the international phenomenon of house music. There were, supposedly, invitations printed. But I couldn't find them. I even quizzed Robert Williams, the man who opened the club. Nor could I find the date when a cameraman working for the Lumière brothers took a movie of Chicago policeman on parade in 1896, among the first motion pictures made anywhere. Montgomery Ward spurred Chicago's development as the nation's merchandising hub by issuing a single-sheet catalogue in August 1872. But what day, exactly? Damned if I could find out. So I had to work in Ward elsewhere.

Trying to fill those holes, I learned so much. That Chicago quadrupled in size in one day. That the Art Institute of Chicago stuck three Cézanne paintings in a storage closet and they disappeared. That Native Americans, leaving Chicago en masse for the last time, did a ghost dance through the city.

I never realized what an important boxing town Chicago was, that all three great 20th-century champions, Jack Johnson, Joe Louis, and Muhammad Ali, lived here. How important Chicago was to early electronics, to radio, to television.

These stories are not told, I hope, out of mere local pride. Someone was going to publicly demonstrate videotape for the first time; it just so happened to occur here. But Chicago is a place, an attitude, an organizing principle. The book can be read straight through or in daily doses. For pleasure, as complete stories, or as a way to be introduced to events worth further consideration. When I told an old friend what I was writing, she replied, "It sounds like a book that's a lot more fun to research than it would be to read." Ouch. That stings because there is truth to it. I found enormous pleasure in learning about these episodes, researching them, writing about them, honing the result into a presentable form.

But I also struggled to defy her augury, like a curse in a fairy tale. I hope you'll take equal pleasure in absorbing these vignettes. I tried to hide all the spinning-wheel needles of cliché, to banish filler, exile the repetitive, and buff these tales into something that shines; fast-moving, thought-provoking, not just information or nuggets, but stories with a point, a message. Not to merely inform you that such-and-such happened on this day, but make you *feel* it, a little, even at a vast remove of time and space. I had tears in my eyes writing some of these stories, and if you shed tears reading them, then I will have done my job.

Because history isn't about the past. Not really. Those we write about exist in a realm apart, and are not comforted or irked, neither ennobled nor degraded, by how we handle them now. They are out of our grasp entirely. Rather, history is a magic trick we perform in the present, to create the illusion of the past, to conjure up people and situations long gone, and use them to understand and appreciate our worlds, give our lives meaning, scope, and depth, and offer us a yardstick to measure what is going on around us. Chicago is not one of the great cities of the world because of the capital that flows through it, or the steel once produced here, or the corporations headquartered here now, or even the people who were born here, or came here, lived here, and died here. It is a great city because of what happened here, the struggle and surrender, the success and failure, triumph and tragedy, achievement and disgrace, which I am delighted to present to you in 366 individual packages, each a gift, wrapped and ready for you to open and enjoy now.

JANUARY

Jan. 1, 1920

Certain that federal agents are "pursuing a petty, pusillanimous and pussyfoot policy" and may even be tipping off the Reds they believe infest Cook County, Chicago police jump the gun and begin rounding up suspected communists at 4 p.m. on New Year's Day, 12 hours before the national dragnet begins. They raid hundreds of private homes and bookstores, taverns and union halls, including the office of the new Soviet government, and nab 150 suspected radicals. The arrests continue the next day, when federal forces join in, and they hit the Tolstoy Vegetarian Restaurant, at 2609 W. Division Street.

Just before the trap is sprung there, a member of the executive board of the Ladies' Tailors Union, Local 104, one B. Slater, asks the cashier if Mr. Hoffman, scheduled to speak on vegetarianism, has made his appearance yet.

The woman whispers to scram, that the place is full of cops. Too late. One officer tells Slater not to leave, but to stay inside where it's "warm and comfortable." The labor executive is hauled with two other patrons to the West Chicago Avenue Station, where Slater shows a union card and is let go with a warning.

The arrests are the handiwork of Woodrow Wilson's attorney general, A. Mitchell Palmer. Thousands of foreign nationals will be deported for the offense of having opposed World War I, supported unions, cheered the Russian Revolution, or dined in a vegetarian restaurant at the wrong time. These arrests will collectively be known as the Palmer Raids, a low point in the history of American freedom of expression. Not coincidentally, later this month the American Civil Liberties Union will be founded by social activists, including Chicago reformer Jane Addams.

Jan. 2, 1900

There is no ceremony. None planned, anyway. Certainly not the "Shovel Day" of nearly eight years earlier, when work began on a 28-mile artificial channel, the Sanitary and Ship Canal, designed to reverse the Chicago River and carry Chicago's pollution south toward the Mississippi River instead of letting it flow into Lake Michigan, where the city has to drink it, eventually.

Instead, chief engineer Isham Randolph and nine trustees show up with the dawn at the narrow berm of earth near Kedzie Avenue and 35th Street, and order the waiting steam shovel to get busy. When two figures come running, a ripple of concern goes around. Are these legal representatives of the City of St. Louis, carrying an injunction to stop them? No, just newspaper reporters, eager to witness the action.

The canal trustees haven't risked an announcement, certain that St. Louis will resort to law the moment Illinois issues a permit. So the trustees simply skip that step and file a *supra* legal motion of their own, setting Dredge No. 7 to work ripping up the clay between the river and the new canal. The impulse to solemnize the occasion is strong, however. So when B. A. Eckhart arrives with nine shovels—regular shovels, no silver handles—trustees take turns grabbing one and jumping down the embankment to take a few jabs at the earthen berm.

Hours pass. Bonfires are lit to ward off the cold. The steam shovel digs to the limit of its reach. Eight feet remain. Dynamite is driven into holes and set off, to little effect. The steam shovel is moved, and finally claws away the last strip of clay. Water begins flowing. "The Niagara of Chicago!" Eckhart dubs the cascade. The trustees wave their arms and cheer like schoolboys, then have their photo taken before retreating for a celebratory lunch.

Jan. 3, 1974

The concert at the Chicago Stadium is almost over. Bob Dylan's first headline performance in eight years, since he stopped touring in 1966, blaming a motorcycle accident. He has sung his own classics, "Lay Lady Lay" and "The Times They Are a-Changin'." He has played guitar on "Stage Fright" and "The Night They Drove Old Dixie Down," sung by the group backing him, The Band. After their "Rag Mama Rag," Dylan launches into a song never before heard in public:

"May God bless and keep you always," he begins. "May your wishes all come true."

Even the *Chicago Tribune*'s Thomas Willis—a classical music critic in his mid-40s who sometimes lowers his gaze to contemplate contemporary artists—notices. In his generally positive review, he tut-tuts Dylan's use of obscure words. Then dismisses his singing ability. "Dylan will never win any performance prizes." And his harmonica playing.

Finally, Willis gets down to picking apart one specific song.

"He introduced, among others, one presumably titled, 'Forever Young,'" Willis writes. "It is highfalutin' in its diction and full of words like 'courage,' 'truth,' 'righteousness,' and 'joy.' Over and over, in unaccustomed subjunctive, it repeats the line, 'May you be forever young.' Make of it what you will."

Artists make a lot of it, despite that grammatically unusual "may you stay" (which Willis misquotes in his review). The song will be covered at least 75 times, by artists from Joan Baez to Peter, Paul, and Mary, Chrissie Hynde to Diana Ross, Harry Belafonte to Johnny Cash. All seem untroubled by the unaccustomed subjunctive, use of which will not prevent Dylan from winning the Nobel Prize in Literature in 2016.

Jan. 4, 1872

Just because the city burned to the ground three months ago does not mean it is unable to receive royalty. Though Chicago's characteristic unease at being observed by outsiders is magnified by the recent calamity. The mayor all but begged one high-profile guest not to come.

"We have but little to exhibit but the ruins and debris of a great and beautiful city and an undaunted people struggling with adversity to relieve their overwhelming misfortunes," Mayor Joseph Medill had written to Czar Alexander II's fourth son, who came anyway, down from Milwaukee, bearing $5,000 for the city's homeless.

Grand Duke Alexei is six weeks into his American tour, having seen New York City and met President Ulysses S. Grant at the White House. This evening he will be subjected to what the *Tribune* derisively terms a "pump-handle levee," aka a reception whose central activity is shaking hands. "A peculiarly American institution," sniffs the newspaper, still squirming at the memory of "the ungracefulness of the public manners" at a reception for President Grant in Chicago just before the fire. This event is "just as awkward."

"The conglomeration of humanity was mixed and peculiar," it will note the next day, recoiling that some of the hands the grand duke shook were unwashed. "Most of those assembled were laboring men, and persons in mercantile employments."

The story veers from embarrassment that royalty didn't receive its due to regret that any special treatment was offered at all, one subhead itself a rebuke: "Two Thousand Free-Born Americans Wait Upon the Grand Duke."

Jan. 5, 1973

You can't just walk into the airport and go to the gate anymore.
Arriving passengers find velvet ropes, metal detectors, and lines,
thanks to federal guidelines that go into effect today at 535 airports
nationwide, including O'Hare International and Midway airports.
The rules require that luggage carried onto airplanes as well as the
passengers carrying it be checked for weapons, in the wake of a
sensational 30-hour ordeal last November, where three hijackers
forced a Memphis-to-Miami Southern Airways flight to land in a
half-dozen locations across Canada, the United States, and, finally,
Cuba, threatening at one point to crash the plane into the nuclear
reactor at Oak Ridge, Tennessee.

The Thursday before Christmas, the first test checkpoint had
been set up in O'Hare's Terminal Three—long tables where passengers must open their suitcases for inspection before stepping
through a metal detector. American Airlines is also checking visitors, but some speculate that eventually those without tickets might
be barred entirely from the gate section of the airport. Delays run
about a minute, and there are few complaints. Lines begin to grow,
however, and at the end of March United Airlines will bring in a
portable X-ray machine to speed the process along.

Jan. 6, 1970

Illinois poet laureate Gwendolyn Brooks ducks into a coatroom at
Loyola University to consult her notes before speaking to a semi-
nar on "The Current Evolution of Man's Sense of Values." A pair of
attendees tries to hand the Pulitzer Prize winner their coats, and are
slightly miffed when she rebuffs them. Brooks immediately dashes
off a brief prose poem about the encounter, which she reads before
her speech. "Sometimes one does worry about words—about their
fate—about their value," the newborn poem begins, before introducing the duo who mistook its author for the coat-check girl.
"When they were told by me that I was their speaker / one of them
said with some 'miffment of tone': 'They are both honorable occu-
pations.'"

Brooks then launches into her prepared remarks: "Poetry is life.
Life sifted through a strainer. Life distilled."

Jan. 7, 1954

Muddy Waters cuts a record at Chess Records, a studio on South
Cottage Grove Avenue run by a pair of Polish immigrant brothers,
Leonard and Phil Chess.

Like so many, Waters came north seeking better conditions,
bringing the Mississippi Delta blues with him. Here he met Willie
Dixon, who wrote the song they'll be recording today, "I'm Your
Hoochie Coochie Man." First Dixon played it for Leonard Chess,
who said, "If Muddy likes it, give it to him." Waters and Dixon
recently spent 20 minutes working out the music in the good
acoustics of the Club Zanzibar bathroom. If there are two types
of blues songs—bemoaning fate or celebrating triumph—this one
is of the second category, a brag, the singer "boasting and braying,
preening like a peacock" of his success with women, thanks to good
luck and sorcery. Dixon, playing bass with Waters today for the first
time, defines "Hoochie Coochie" as being a kind of soothsayer,
though it is also a term with Chicago roots older than either man:
the name of the shimmy that a dancer with the unlikely name of
Little Egypt used to titillate fairgoers at the 1893 World's Columbian
Exposition.

Jan. 8, 1901

At 3:30 p.m., the first American Bowling Congress National Tournament begins on the second floor of the Welsbach Building, 68 Wabash Avenue, with ABC officials rolling ceremonial balls down the "six new alleys smooth as glass and resplendent with coats of shining lacquer."

The newness of the lanes is significant. The American Bowling Congress was founded in New York in 1895 to establish rules and regulations for the growing sport. But regional tournaments have been riddled with controversy over the condition of the lanes. Up to now, attempts to hold a national competition were scuttled by concerns that local bowlers would have a natural advantage due to their familiarity with the field of play.

Chicago was tapped to hold the event for a number of reasons: its central location, for one. And a local firm, Brunswick, which has two factories in Chicago, is moving from constructing billiard tables into bowling equipment, so was willing to build the alley—whose newness does not squelch complaint, just shifts it: the lanes are now stiff and "sticky as fly-paper." The balls are lignum vitae, a dense, oily, and expensive wood. In five years Brunswick will help the sport reach the common bowler by patenting its rubber "Mineralite" ball.

Jan. 9, 1902

"Dear Sir," today's letter begins. "We are off again at the same old starting post in the race for business during 1902. We enclosed a bunch of new items and they are all GOOD ONES."

The author is William Wrigley Jr., and he is doing what he does best—firing up the troops. Wrigley realized early on, as a child salesman for his father's soap company, that he could either sell one product to one customer himself, or inspire many salesmen—"jobbers," he calls them—to sell many products to many customers, and take a share. The second method pays better. One way to boost sales is with premiums, which also help in identifying hot new products. The boxes of baking powder Wrigley gave away with his dad's soap were so popular he began selling baking powder instead. Chewing gum used to push the baking powder is even more popular. Wrigley's gum becoming famous around the world isn't a reflection of the gum itself so much as an echo of Wrigley the man feverishly promoting his product. In 1915, he'll mail a package of gum to every single address listed in phone books across the United States.

A key lesson is that not everything works: there are a dozen gum packs pictured at the top of the elaborate letterhead conveying this month's pep talk. Some flavors are blood orange and pineapple, vanilla pepsin and lemon cream, Juicy Fruit and Spearmint. Those last two catch on.

Jan. 10, 1836

The charter forming the Galena and Chicago Union Railroad, incorporated by the legislature on this day, deserves careful study. Not only does it authorize construction of a railroad "near the lead mines of Galena, Illinois, and Dubuque, Iowa," but Section 7 provides an out in case all this railroad nonsense proves a bust. "If at any time after the passage of this act it shall be deemed advisable by the Directors of the said corporation to make and construct a good and permanent *Turnpike Road* upon any portion of the route of the *Railroad* then said Directors are hereby authorized and empowered."

Nothing more happens for a year. Then an engineer draws a route from North Dearborn Street to the Des Plaines River. Piles are driven along a stretch of Madison, to support tracks in the sandy soil. That's it. "It soon became evident, however, that Chicago's financial strength was not equal to her ambition," the *Rockford Daily Register Gazette* notes sadly. No train will roll out of Chicago for a dozen years.

Jan. 11, 1873

Harvey L. Goodall, blown into Illinois by the gales of the Civil
War, publishes the first issue of *Drovers Journal*, and it is evidence
of how far we've wandered from our agricultural roots that what
exactly "drovers" are must be explained. For a thousand years
before people drove cars they drove cattle, a usage that lingers
whenever we refer to something coming "in droves." Those who
drove these droves of cattle were drovers, and they will know just
what to expect when they arrive at Chicago's Stock Yards by reading
Drovers Journal, the source of prices for beef and pork and hides,
delivered along with a fountain of upbeat buoyant perspective.
"Chicago's supremacy as a live stock market has long been established, but the record of 1901 gives more emphasis to its greatness
and adds another very interesting chapter to its already wonderful
history," *Drovers Journal* will note. "The magnitude of Chicago's
live stock trade is almost incomprehensible."

Despite those flights of grandeur, there is also a marvelous
specificity to its reports. "Some extensive improvements were
made in the Stock Yards in 1901. Acres of pens have been floored
with vitrified brick, new sewers and water mains laid, alleys paved,
fences constructed . . ."

Drovers Journal continues to this day as *Drovers* ("Driving the
Beef Market"), a monthly publication of Farm Journal Media, based
in Lenexa, Kansas.

Jan. 12, 1949

Tonight's production of a popular local television program is seen by a national audience for the first time, thanks to the coaxial cable hooked up yesterday. *Kukla, Fran and Ollie* is now broadcast to 14 cities along the Eastern Seaboard. The puppets are the brainchild of Burr Tillstrom, a Senn High School graduate who dropped out of the University of Chicago after his first semester, despite a scholarship, to perform puppetry with the WPA-Chicago Park District Theater.

The improvised, chaotic antics of the bald boy Kukla—Russian for "little doll"—and one-toothed dragon Ollie, overseen by a radiant former Iowa teacher named Fran Allison, are ostensibly for children, and among its viewers is an 11-year-old budding cartoonist in Maryland, Jimmy Henson, who will go on to his own fame with

his Muppets. But the show will also draw many adult fans, including John Steinbeck, Adlai Stevenson, and James Thurber.

The overnight sensation—Edward R. Murrow will interview Tillstrom and do a bit with his puppets—has been a decade in the making. In 1939, Tillstrom reluctantly turned down a puppeteer friend who wanted him to sail to Europe on the *Normandie* and assist in his nightclub act. Tillstrom yearned to see Paris, but "I loved my little Kukla," he later explained, "and I had a feeling that the future of my career rested in my own creativity and not assisting someone else's creativity."

The next day, Tillstrom wandered sad and doubtful through Marshall Field's State Street store, ending up on the fourth floor. There he found an RCA Victor demonstration of that new wonder, television: a dozen sets and a small studio. "I have some puppets," Tillstrom said, running to fetch Kukla and Ollie. He turned a card table on its side for a stage and put on a show. RCA invited him to come back the next day. And the next. Unpaid of course, at first. But when the RCA touring demonstration left Field's, Tillstrom left with it. He appeared at the 1939 New York World's Fair and went to Bermuda. During the war he toured hospitals in the Midwest, and in 1942 he began doing occasional puppetry on WNBQ. In 1947, when RCA Victor was scrambling to find something to offer "hours of fun" on all those television sets it hoped to sell, it turned to Tillstrom.

Jan. 13, 1979

It's cold. The coldest winter in 75 years. Ten consecutive days
below zero, tying a record set in 1912. And snowy. Thirty inches
have already fallen so far this year, a foot on New Year's Day alone.
Tomorrow will be among the snowiest days in Chicago history. Plus
it's unexpected: the weather service predicted two inches; instead,
Chicago gets 20. It'll be the snowiest winter on record: almost 90
inches.

Residential neighborhoods won't be plowed for six days, and
when they are, the first two streets cleared are home to Mayor
Daley's widow and to Mayor Michael Bilandic, who sets some
kind of record for poor optics, between ordering police to ticket
stranded cars and allowing CTA trains to run express past Black
neighborhoods. Garbage won't be collected for 10 days.

Chicagoans have a way to register complaint, however. The
Democratic mayoral primary will be February 28. They'll vote
for Jane Byrne, whom Bilandic recently fired as commissioner of
consumer sales, weights, and measures.

Later asked if there was anything he would have done differently,
Bilandic says, "Maybe I should have prayed harder."

Jan. 14, 2014

"No one is above the law," Zachary T. Fardon, US attorney for
the Northern District of Illinois, tells the jury before sentencing
H. Ty Warner. But some do float higher than others, and an
enormous balloon of capital has a way of raising certain individuals
far above the gusty buffeting of the legal system. Had Warner,
billionaire businessman behind Beanie Babies, been a teenager
who held up a liquor store, he'd be lucky to avoid spending a year
in the Cook County Jail. But he is the 69-year-old mastermind of
a wildly popular line of toy animals stuffed with Styrofoam beads.
So, having merely failed to report $24.4 million in income from
the $100 million he had hidden for a dozen years in Swiss bank
accounts, Warner is tapped on the wrist: two years' probation, 500
hours community service at area high schools, and a $100,000 fine.
Which represents the profit his Ty Inc. earns in an hour during a
good year selling small creatures in limited runs that some considered collectible. It may be small comfort that in a separate civil
proceeding Warner will also be assessed $60 million in unpaid taxes
and penalties, or well over 3 percent of his net worth.

Jan. 15, 1984

The sled is heavy, old-fashioned, wood with metal runners. So when it gets away from Terry Tontlewicz as he and son Jimmy tumble down an embankment, the sled shoots onto frozen Lake Michigan. Terry, 35, goes after it. His four-year-old joins him and together their weight cracks the ice. Both plunge in. Terry, a member of a motorcycle club called Hell's Henchmen, comes up. Jimmy doesn't. Passing cross-country skiers form a human chain, but that doesn't work. A WGN cameraman loops a TV cable around Terry. The Chicago Fire Department arrives. "My baby's in there," Terry tells them, a detail he did not mention earlier.

Twenty-five minutes later, when a CFD diver brings the boy up, Jimmy is for all purposes dead: no heartbeat, no breathing. But emergency workers have a saying, "Cold and dead is not dead. Nobody is dead until they are warm and dead." Doctors slowly, gently warm Jimmy over a period of hours, and his heart is shocked to life. Four times. He's put in a drug-induced coma for five days. Over weeks of rehab, the boy fights back. The feel-good aspects of the story collide with the marital conflict that preceded the accident—Jimmy's mom Kathy had complained about Terry being reckless with the boy during visits; he once came home with burns on his hands.

"Why should I be more careful?" Terry asks.

Jan. 16, 1902

Shortly after 5 p.m., Miss Josephine Mullock, of Middletown, New York, stands in the doorway of the dingy baggage room at Dearborn Station.

In her lapel, a white ribbon rosette, the mark by which her beloved will know her.

She left her home yesterday, and is staying the night with a distant cousin who, hearing why Miss Mullock has come—to wed Dr. Andrew S. Hackney, of Kansas City—is unsure of the wisdom of marrying someone she has never met. Maybe Josephine should wait a day or two, to take the measure of the man.

Not necessary, says the 40ish woman, who had been caring for her sick mother up until six months ago, when she died. Miss Mullock had a friend who knew the widower, 56, and his desire to marry again, and suggested they write to each other.

"We have never met, it is true," Miss Mullock tells the press— she sold her possessions before leaving Middletown, and the whole thing somehow got into the national papers before she even boarded the train. "But we have learned much of each other through mutual friends, and one can learn a great deal from corresponding with another."

Arriving that morning, Dr. Hackney secured a marriage license, and arranged for the services of clergy.

Now, a few minutes after 5 p.m., he appears at the baggage room.

They shake hands and give each other a long, appraising look, without speaking. Then they go to dinner.

They are married at 9 p.m. at her cousin's house on Grand Boulevard. The bridegroom is 6 feet tall, given to stoutness, with gray hair and a beard. The bride is dark and slender. They get on a train heading west, and exit history.

Jan. 17, 1920

By extraordinary coincidence, Al Capone's 21st birthday is also the day the 18th Amendment goes into effect, banning the sale of alcohol nationwide. About this time, Capone, the scars on his cheek that will give him his nickname "Scarface" still red and raw, is brought to Chicago from Brooklyn by Johnny Torrio, who runs Big Jim Colosimo's citywide web of brothels and opium dens. Young Al is put to work as a sidewalk shill at a bar/gambling joint/brothel called the Four Deuces at 2222 S. Wabash Avenue.

Colosimo is slow to see the opportunities presented by this constitutional development, however. Come May, he will be murdered by his more ambitious underlings. Some suspect by Capone himself. Colosimo's massive procession will be the first big mob funeral of the Roaring '20s. Capone won't stand for very long in the cold of Wabash Avenue, steering passersby into a whorehouse. His name will become welded, more than any other, to the global reputation of Chicago, an uncomfortable set of conjoined twins, the gangster and the ambitious city. Passage of a century will scarcely uncouple the two.

Jan. 18, 1896

Thorstein Veblen takes a piece of stationery from the University of Chicago's *Journal of Political Economy*, which he edits, and writes to graduate student Sarah Hardy, on her way to Hawaii to recuperate after suffering a breakdown. The book he is struggling with, he tells the object of his unreciprocated affection, is not "approximately up to grade. It disappointments me and puzzles me." Veblen adds that he will persist, though "it is very doubtful" the book will be published.

The Theory of the Leisure Class will indeed be published, three years later. A groundbreaking rumination on money and status, it coins the term "conspicuous consumption" while mystifying and disappointing Veblen's colleagues. "Have you thought about having it translated into English?" one will taunt him, to his face. University president William Rainey Harper will invite the assistant professor to his office and say, "Dr. Veblen, much as we appreciate you and your work, I would not stand in the way of your going should you be called to another institution." Veblen ignores the unsubtle hint and stays for another decade. The book remains in print and widely influential for 125 years, with fans including Albert Einstein and John Kenneth Galbraith, who calls it one of only two economics books written in the 19th century still worthy of study.

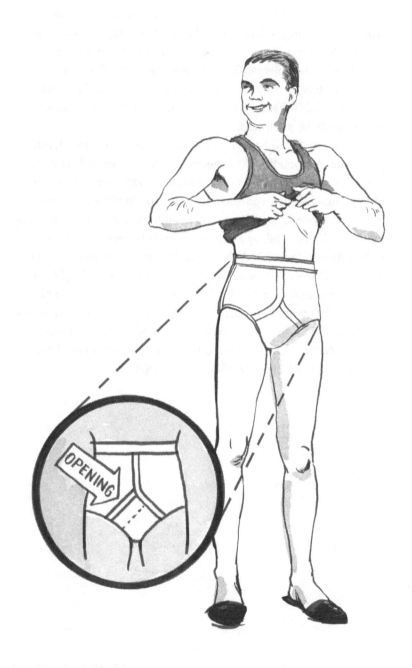

Jan. 19, 1935

A display window at Marshall Field's on State Street is filled with underwear, briefly. The handiwork of Arthur Kneibler, an executive at Coopers, a Wisconsin manufacturer of men's socks and undergarments, which in these days consist of either boxer shorts or union suits—those full-body long underwear with the flap in the back. In 1934, Kneibler received a postcard showing a man on the French Riviera wearing a high-cut bathing suit. The garment strikes him as athletic; he dubs the style "Jockey shorts." Despite the Great Depression ravaging the city, 50 cents is a luxury that shoppers can afford, and by day's end all 600 pairs are sold, including those in the window.

Jan. 20, 1984

If it sounds as if it were made in a bedroom, it was: Jesse Saunders's bedroom at 7234 S. King Drive. Someone had stolen his copy of Mach's "On & On" bootleg disco megamix—a mash-up of Space Invader blasts and marching crunches, car horns, and looped Donna Summer exclamations set to a 4/4 beat.

His signature record, and the loss is huge, like someone stealing your nose. Without it, Saunders can't be himself, working as a DJ. So the 22-year-old tries to create his own version, with friend Vince Lawrence. Starting with Mach's bass line, adding their own original lyrics—"Just dance until the beat is gone, just say you must go on and on"—using a motley array of electronic equipment: a Roland TR-808 drum machine, a Korg Poly 61, and a four-track recorder.

Over a period of days, the two friends struggled to capture that lost sound, as well as the relentless, driving, heavy dance beats spun by guys like Frankie Knuckles at places like the Warehouse, which supposedly gave house music its name. They end up with a recording more complicated, nuanced, satisfying, and original than their model. Except for the title, which remains "On and On."

Precision Record Labs cut 500 12-inch EPs on the newly minted, hand-drawn Jes Say label which, officially released today, starts passing from hand to hand, party to party, circling the globe, played at full volume for thronged sweaty ecstatic dancers bobbing in dark, cavernous, strobe-flashed rooms, scratched in DJ booths, borrowed, lost, and, yes, sometimes stolen.

Jan. 21, 2017

There are too many marchers to march. Some 250,000 stream downtown for the Women's March on Chicago. Not a protest *per se* against Donald Trump, inaugurated as president the day before. Rather, an organized cry of outrage, across the nation, across the world, against the tottering patriarchy of white privilege, racism, bigotry, and sexism that Trump embodies at its most shameless and ugly. The women wear pink knit "pussyhats" and carry signs reading "Resist" and "We are greater than fear" and "Women's rights are human rights," "Our rights are not up for grabs," and "Stay nasty," those last two references to the new president's admitted assaults and his tendency to hurl that term at any female bold enough to challenge him. The protesters stand and chant and listen to speeches, too many to actually move.

"There is no safe way to march," an organizer says. "We are just going to sing and dance and make our voices heard here."

Jan. 22, 1914

"Peaches sweet," Theodore Dreiser begins, in a letter to Kirah Markham, his "delicious, forceful, pagan girl," who has left their love nest at the center of the world, New York City, and gone home to the wilds of Chicago over Christmas, then lingered to work in local theater.

"You are a flower of art, sweetest kiddie," coos Dreiser, to a woman who was nine years old in 1900 when he published his field guide to seduction through middle-class materialism, *Sister Carrie*. He tries to lure her back with flattery. "Life for you should be lived with your equals—your peers."

Otherwise, she'll be doomed to mere existence in Chicago, without him; "to have to live it with your inferiors adds nothing save a disgust and memories you would rather not have."

Still, even the gods sometimes descend from Mount Olympus.

"I wonder how long you will be in Chicago?" Dreiser ventures, contemplating a trip to the boondocks. "I thought I would take a little vacation."

Markham is an accomplished artist who will marry Lloyd Wright. Dreiser suggests that he can see the naughty sketches Markham has been drawing without her running risk of prosecution for sending obscenity through the US mail. "Why not put them in a perfectly plain envelope without word of any kind save the address on the outside & mail them? They could not be identified as being either solicited or sent."

Jan. 23, 1951

"It was a freak," Clint Youle, "Mr. Weatherman," explains to the few Chicagoans—only 5,000 even own a television—who tune in to his program on WMAQ. "It was just a local thundershower, except it came in winter."

What had happened is this: Youle told viewers that it would not snow in the Chicago area, which prompted a general rush to the telephone. Over the next dozen minutes, 72 got through the NBC switchboard to say that not only might it snow, it *is* snowing, right now, so heavily they couldn't see across the street.

Youle is not a professional meteorologist. He takes reports from the National Weather Service, then writes a script for a 10-minute show running twice each weeknight, at 5:50 and 10:05, with visits to the national broadcasts Wednesdays and Fridays. Do the math. That's 100 minutes of live television a week; plenty of room for error, particularly broadcasting from a windowless studio.

The first weatherman on national TV offers the kind of personality that will be tied with standing before a map — a store-bought, Rand McNally map, covered with plexiglass — telling folks what the weather might be like outside.

"As much as any TV show in Chicago, the weatherman has become a household habit," Jack Mabley will write in the *Daily News* tomorrow. "Listening to his nightly report is as automatic as putting out the cat and brushing your teeth."

Why?

"His secret is his complete lack of pretense. He is a normal, immensely pleasant man whose job is to tell what the weather is going to be. He does so without salesmanship, without theatrics and, naturally, without rehearsal."

Fittingly, Youle's stardom came by accident. He was an editor in the newsroom and overheard the news director saying they were having a hard time finding a weatherman.

"I'm a weatherman," he said, stretching the truth a bit: he took a course in meteorology in the army.

Jan. 24, 2020

"This is a single travel-associated case, not a local emergency," Chicago Department of Public Health commissioner Dr. Allison Arwady is quoted saying in today's *Sun-Times*. "We obviously take emerging viruses seriously and there are still many unanswered questions."

Arwady is referring to a Chicago woman in her 60s, who returned from China on January 13 and has been diagnosed with COVID-19, the first person in Illinois and the second in the United States to be found carrying the virus, contracted the month before while caring for her elderly father in Wuhan province.

Right now, Arwady says the risk to public health is "low at this time both nationally and in Chicago," and there is no need for anyone to change their behavior.

There will be. By the middle of March, ordinary life will come to a skidding halt as Gov. J. B. Pritzker shuts down all the bars and restaurants in Illinois. Two years later, more than 12,000 Cook County residents will have died of the virus, making it the second most deadly pandemic to hit the city, after the 1918 Spanish flu.

Jan. 25, 1890

"Apathy leads to stagnation," T. Thomas Fortune tells the 141 delegates from 23 states meeting today to form the National Afro-American League, one of the first civil rights organizations in the United States. "It is a narrow and perverse philosophy which condemns as a nuisance agitators," who in fact will be essential to establish "Afro-Americans"—a term he championed—as proud, free, equal, and valued American citizens. "The old idea and the new idea, the spirit of freedom and the spirit of tyranny and oppression cannot live together without friction."

Fortune, an East Coast newspaperman, has deliberately picked "the free soil of Illinois" to start his organization. Listing the reasons for gathering, the first is "The almost universal suppression of our ballot in the South," though his model is as much Napoleon as Lincoln. Fortune sees progress through the laws and courts and public opinion, but also believes that violence should be met with violence. "It is time to fight fire with fire," he says. "We shall no longer accept in silence a condition that degrades our manhood and makes a mockery of our citizenship."

The league itself will be short-lived—just four years—but its example will inspire longer-lasting groups to come, like the NAACP.

Jan. 26, 1986

The Chicago Bears don't just beat the New England Patriots in Super Bowl XX in New Orleans. They smash them to splinters. Seven sacks leading to six turnovers. At the end of the first half, the Patriots haven't advanced a yard, but instead lost 19 in the face of the Bears' brick-wall defense. Starting Patriots quarterback Tony Eason doesn't make it that long—he throws six incomplete passes and is benched five minutes before halftime.

Of course, not all is perfection: the Patriot defense focuses on Walter Payton, the greatest running back of all time, limiting his effectiveness. But that distraction allows six other Bears to score, including 310-pound oddity William "The Refrigerator" Perry. Payton, whose nickname is "Sweetness," will bitterly complain that coach Mike Ditka should have tapped him to run that one-yard touchdown in instead of the Fridge. But Payton had already fumbled once and might not have blasted through the Patriot line the way Perry did. Not that the Bears will need the points. They'll win 46–10: up to then the most points scored and the largest margin of victory in Super Bowl history.

Jan. 27, 1967

Babies don't know from snow. So when 23 inches falls—two-thirds of what Chicago usually receives all winter—over 29 hours, bringing the city to a standstill, the babies keep coming. Dozens are born into "a desolate scene of colossal snow drifts, abandoned cars and roads clogged so badly that many areas are virtually isolated," as the *Chicago Daily News* describes it.

Drifts so deep snowplows get stuck in the snow. The babies don't know that, so are delivered at home, with neighbor women helping, as if Chicago were a 19th-century Siberian village. Doctors guide men through deliveries over the telephone. Babies are delivered in cars on the way to the hospital: one frantic father-to-be wades through drifts to Columbus Hospital, collars nurses and a physician eating their dinner, and leads them back to his wife, in the backseat of their car, marooned on Lake Shore Drive, in time to welcome his son, Charlie.

Some babies manage to be delivered at hospitals, but not at the hospitals their parents had set out for, hours before. A Summit mother-to-be is carried to the hospital in a snowplow. Patients are ferried by bobsled.

One doctor arrives to work on skis. A nurse goes home by snowmobile after a 36-hour shift. Other staffers can't make it to the hospital at all, but stranded motorists can. Sixteen who seek refuge in Holy Family Hospital in Des Plaines are put to work folding laundry and taking trays of food to patients. At Hines VA Hospital, patients wash dishes. This spirit of helpfulness is common, though some are moved to help only themselves, and a 10-year-old girl is killed in cross fire between police and looters.

For most children, however, the Big Snow of 1967 is an unforgettable holiday, with their parents unexpectedly on hand. Irvin Goldberg does not go to work at his metal tube-bending business, but spends the day building a curved igloo against the side of their Bellwood home that his youngest daughter will remember fondly 50 years later.

Jan. 28, 1910

"There's leprosy in Oak Park," an excited woman tells the *Chicago Examiner*, one of a half-dozen concerned citizens to phone in the tip today. "A Chinaman is dying of it and a girl in the very best white society has got it."

The story, as it is teased out, is as follows: about two weeks ago a girl was walking home, supposedly, when she hurt her elbow. A clean handkerchief "newly laundered by a Chinaman" was applied to the wound. Leprosy ensued.

Digging further, the reporter finds that Oak Park Chinese laundries are being boycotted, chop suey shop business is ebbing "to the vanishing point," and children are fleeing in terror at the approach of a Chinese person, a rare sight in 1910, when there are 1,713 Chinese men and only 65 Chinese women living in Chicago.

Baseless hostility, including the fear that, like all foreigners, they carry exotic diseases that would survive a thorough laundering, severely constrains the prospects of Chinese Chicagoans. Restaurants and laundries are about the only businesses permitted them, provided no mass hysteria stifles even that.

The same periodic rumor and widespread fear is driving the community's Chinatown from its central location at Clark and Van Buren to the hinterlands of Wentworth and Cermak. A lucky break, it turns out, as there it will have room to grow, allowing Chicago's Chinatown to become one of the most vibrant and extensive in the country, the rare enclave where Chinese Chicagoans could live without facing abuse.

What about the girl? The *Chicago Examiner* could not find her. Oak Park speculation runs that she had already been removed to a leper colony. The police are consulted, and they confirm that "a girl did hurt her elbow." Beyond that, they have nothing else to add. No, they don't know her name. Nobody does.

Jan. 29, 1968

Mrs. Beatrice McGill, Mrs. Edith Joyce, Mrs. Eleanor Gross, Mrs. Irene Frymire, and Mrs. Jennie Drakas work too slowly.

Okay, not the Police Censor Board itself—they are required by law to view a film within three days of receipt, according to the Chicago movie censorship ordinance of 1907, the first in the nation, banning "exhibition of obscene and immoral" moving pictures. Rather, they are part of a system where it might take almost two months to appeal their decision. The US Supreme Court rules that the ordinance allowing from 50 to 57 days for appeal is not the "specified brief period" required by law.

For decades, the board has interposed itself as a kind of human shield between the citizens of Chicago and troublesome reality, from banning Paul Muni's *Scarface* in 1932 because it implies there is organized crime in Chicago, to forbidding newsreels in the late 1930s that suggest something is amiss in Germany. In 1939 an educational film called *Birth of a Baby* was banned for being true to its title, and "because menstruation, pregnancy and childbirth are not considered fitting subject for an entertainment medium such as the screen."

Not that any court ruling will stop the board from meeting at the Traffic Court Building tomorrow to pass judgment upon the movie version of Truman Capote's *In Cold Blood*.

"As far as we're concerned, we're still in business," says Sgt. Robert Murphy, the cop in charge of the board, explaining that they take their orders from the Chicago Corporation Counsel's office. The order dissolving the board will not come until 1984. Making Chicago not only the first American city to have police censorship of movies, but also the last.

Jan. 30, 1931

Paul Robeson was an All-American football star at Rutgers who dabbled in pro athletics. He first performed in Chicago 10 years ago, in the role of left tackle for the Akron Pros when they faced the Chicago Cardinals. The Pros won, 23–0.

Robeson didn't want to be a professional athlete, however. He wanted to be a lawyer. But the legal community had limited use for Black lawyers, even those with a law degree from Columbia University.

So Robeson tried the stage, starring in Eugene O'Neill plays, where in one scene he was required to whistle. But Robeson could not whistle—the story goes—which would make whistling one of the few skills not in his repertoire. So instead he sang, which is what brings him to Chicago tonight, in front of 2,205 Chicagoans, mostly white.

"There is not a more beautiful voice to be heard in this country," the *Daily News* notes.

"Here is one of the great voices of the world, regardless of race," adds the *Tribune*, casting doubt on the whistling story. "Whether he sang, whether he merely spoke to announce a song, that voice rolled out with an effortless vitality that filled the hall and carried every syllable to the remotest corner."

Hearing him sing Negro spirituals, raves the *Tribune*, not typically a fan of Black culture, is "the experience of a lifetime."

Robeson will become an unflinching voice in the civil rights movement before tiring of the glacial pace of racial progress in this country and moving to Paris.

Jan. 31, 1910

There are hundreds of open brothels operating in Chicago's Levee district, a swamp of depravity between 18th and 22nd streets on the near South Side. The most notorious, the Everleigh Club, prints brochures, with photographs. Something must be done.

Tonight, clergy representing 600 churches meet at the Central YMCA Building to discuss the "Social Evil Problem in Chicago." Walter T. Sumner, dean of Chicago's Chapel of Saint Peter and Paul, reads a resolution from the mayor that "men and women who command the respect and confidence of the public at large" should thoroughly investigate "conditions as they exist." Though the mayor will later emphasize that the situation in Chicago "is exactly like that in any other American city" and worry that trying to address it will only create the impression that Chicago has a problem worse than others. He nevertheless welcomes any effort toward "a slow and partial solution for these questions, pending the perfection of the men and women who make up society." Despite this less than ringing endorsement, the Levee district will indeed be shut down by police in 1912.

FEBRUARY

Feb. 1, 1900

Gold covers a multitude of sins. So the Simms sisters of Virginia, Ada and Minna, apply it liberally to what is still a brothel, albeit a classy one. The Everleigh Club opens its doors for the first time at 8 p.m. in a twin brownstone at 2131-33 S. Dearborn, in a former bordello at the heart of the Levee, beginning an 11-year run as the most celebrated of Chicago's 500 or so houses of assignation, most festering with unseen degradation and misery.

Not here, not on the surface anyway, which glitters. Each room has a gold-plated spittoon. The Gold Room has gilt furniture, a gold-rimmed fishbowl, and a $15,000 piano covered in gold leaf.

With champagne the only alcoholic beverage served, at $12 a bottle, a night here can easily cost a month's wage for a working man, not that a working man could pay the $10 fee just to be admitted, nor the $25 to go upstairs. In these pre-income-tax days there is no shortage of rich men lining up. Marshall Field Jr. will be a patron (and, it is whispered, will be fatally shot here in 1905 before hurrying home to die); Theodore Dreiser visits too, when he doesn't have a young admirer fluttering in his web. As will poet Edgar Lee Masters, who preserves Minna's trademark greeting to customers, "How is my boy?"

The Everleigh Club's visibility will be its undoing. At first the sisters will pretend the nosy reformers are touts providing customers. "We're glad for the business," says Minna—the public face of the club; Ada keeps the books—after a reformer leads a mass sidewalk prayer vigil in front of the brothel, "but I'm sorry to see so many nice young men coming down here for the first time."

The pamphlet the Everleigh Club publishes, promoting the bordello, falls into the hands of Mayor Carter Harrison II, who orders his police to close it down. The Simms sisters will tour Europe for six months, then take their money and their gilt piano and live in comfortable, anonymous retirement in New York City.

Feb. 2, 1925

At 8:30 a.m., Sears & Roebuck opens its first retail department store at Homan and Arthington in Lawndale, ballyhooing it as "Chicago's Most Centrally Located Department Store," with a full block of free parking. The company has ridden the coattails of Montgomery Ward to even greater success. "That's the game I want to get into!" Richard Sears had said, seeing his first Ward catalogue. This time Sears leads the way—Ward will race after, opening its first store in 1926, with 500 more in the next five years.

The first Sears store is near the company's 40-acre West Side merchandising center, built in 1906, with a 14-story tower, where it will be headquartered until moving downtown into the Sears Tower in 1973. Advertising is key to Sears's success—the year before, Sears debuted its own radio station, to better reach the countryside, called WLS, for "World's Largest Store." Despite pretensions of modernity, print ads running today have a whiff of the old world. "Never before such a bargain" reads the headline over a $16.95 mattress, redolent of Maxwell Street *Yiddishkeit*. The drugs on sale are for the most part forgotten: Hinkle's Pills, Nux and Iron tablets, California Spirit of Figs. Though some are familiar nearly a century later: Listerine, Vicks VapoRub. Sears appeals to the prairie frugality that low-cost merchandise will do much to efface, offering custom-ers bolts of cloth and pillowcasing, urging them to "Make your own pillow cases at great savings."

Feb. 3, 1876

Albert Spalding and his younger brother Walter open a store at 118 Randolph Street selling "all kinds of baseball goods"—the first sporting equipment store in the United States.

Their initial product line offers uniforms and guidebooks— Spalding is a pitcher and a good one, lately for the White Stockings, shutting out so many opponents that being held scoreless is called being "Chicagoed." Later in the year the Spalding brothers introduce an item that does well: the first regulation baseball, which Spalding will provide exclusively to the major leagues for a century. Spalding also prints the first annual baseball rule book and guide.

Balls are already a necessity. Next year Spalding will truly revolutionize the sport. Playing in an era when teams boast only one pitcher—in 1874, Spalding appeared in every game the Boston Red Stockings played—Spalding's hands became terribly bruised. He saw a mitt on the hand of first baseman Charles C. Waite, who colored the glove to match his skin so people wouldn't notice it and think him a sissy. Baseball pros are generally aghast at the idea of protective equipment. The first wire catcher's masks are dismissed as "babyish" and "cowardly."

But Spalding is a star, and a fine specimen of a man—6'1", with a thick mustache and dark hair. His endorsement of the first commercially manufactured baseball mitt helps it catch on.

Feb. 4, 1977

A switching problem sends the Evanston Express to the elevated station at State and Lake, where it doesn't belong. A Ravenswood train then stops east of the station, waiting for the express to leave.

As a northbound Lake–Dan Ryan train approaches the sharp Lake Street turn, its driver, Stephen A. Martin, who has a string of safety violations in his eight years, sees the flashing red light on his control panel and thinks it means "Go slow." It doesn't. It means "Stop." At 5:27 p.m., his train hits the Ravenswood train, "a quiet thump" to passengers in the back four cars, which stay on the tracks. The front four cars do not.

This is no high-speed crash, but a "slow-motion horror."

The first and third cars end up on their sides on Wabash Avenue; the second and fourth are hung up by girders of the elevated superstructure.

For a moment, Agnes McCormick fears the train is going to come right through the window. The 59-year-old secretary is sitting in the Lakeview Restaurant, 179 N. Wabash, drinking coffee, when she hears a cracking noise. She jumps up to see the packed train plunge 20 feet to the slushy street.

McCormick and others rush outside to help those pinned under the train cars. Eleven people are killed, 180 injured.

Feb. 5, 1924

She forced him to keep track of his money. She bought him new clothes that make him look less fat. She even convinced him—*him*, Louis Armstrong—to take trumpet lessons. They wrote a song together too, "Cornet Chop Suey."

Shortly after Lillian Hardin, "The Hot Miss Lil" professionally, joined King Oliver's Creole Jazz Band, she found a lawyer to get herself and Armstrong divorces—both were married, she to a singer named Jimmy, he to Daisy Parker, an unstable New Orleans prostitute.

Today's fancy wedding—Hardin wears a Parisian gown of white crepe with rhinestones and silver beads—is part of her program, though Armstrong sees it differently, as husbands tend to. "We felt so sorry for each other we decided out of a Clear Skies to get together for good," is how he'll later put it.

Next on Hardin's agenda is Joe Oliver, the overbearing bandleader who often jokes that he is Armstrong's father. Oliver is there, at the reception at the "chic and colorful" Ideal Tea-Room on South Michigan Avenue. But he won't be around long, nor will his band have its spectacular second horn.

"You can't be married to Joe and me," Hardin will tell her husband. "Play second trumpet to no one. They don't come great enough."

Armstrong listens to his wife. After finding out that Oliver is skimming his pay, he'll strike out on his own.

Feb. 6, 1984

It is every actor's worst nightmare. Opening night in his hometown, the American debut of a major play, David Mamet's *Glengarry Glen Ross*.

Joe Mantegna forgets his lines.

In the first act, where Mantegna's Ricky Roma, in a long speech, pours out his tortured morality to the mark who's about to buy real estate he doesn't want. "What I'm saying, what is our life? It's looking forward or it's looking back."

Only it doesn't pour out. Mantegna goes blank. Silence, for maybe 30 seconds. The audience stirs, wondering if this is a bit, part of Mamet's realistic dialogue. But the cast and crew know better, and start feeding him lines from the wings, harsh whispers, loud enough that everyone in the 135-seat Goodman Theatre studio space can hear.

Mantegna just sits there, "having an out-of-body experience," according to William L. Petersen, the actor on stage with him. Mantegna fumbles for another half minute, until he finally gets through the scene and flees offstage. He feels humiliated, certain he has ruined both the performance and his career.

But that isn't what happens.

Lindsay Crouse, married to Mamet at the time, comes running into the dressing room "like Mike Ditka on speed." She grabs Mantegna and starts shaking him.

"This is going to be fabulous and don't you worry about a thing," Crouse insists. "You're going to be phenomenal in the second act and you're going to New York and win the Tony."

Which is exactly what happens. The play goes on to Broadway, where it runs for 378 performances, and Mantegna does win the Tony Award for best actor. He also learns something.

"God had found out that I was unprepared for opening night and He was going to teach me a lesson," Mantegna said, years later. "I really hadn't learned that speech all that well. I thought I could wing it a bit and get it right eventually. Now I study every word, and nothing like it has ever happened since."

Feb. 7, 1968

Bernard DeYoung's fifth and final stop of the day, delivering fuel for the Hartigan Oil Company. Just past 4 p.m., he pulls his tanker truck into the alley alongside Mickelberry's Food Products plant at 49th and Halsted. Everyone knows Mickelberry's: they make sausage, ham, corned beef, olive loaf.

Maneuvering in the alley, DeYoung somehow shears off the truck's outlet valve. Gasoline pours out, flowing directly down a basement stairway and into the boiler room of the factory.

That's one version; another is that he somehow accidentally pumps the gasoline into the basement instead of the underground tank.

Either way, a fire breaks out, engulfing the truck and a nearby car. DeYoung runs to a pair of policemen, who call the fire department. The fire trucks arrive, and the firemen begin climbing ladders to rescue employees, driven to the roof by thick black smoke billowing out of the basement. There are two small explosions.

Drawn by the sirens and the noise, kids come running—there are houses all around the plant in the Back of the Yards neighborhood. What kid doesn't love a fire?

Kevin Burian, 11, pauses from delivering newspapers to watch. "Fires interest me," he'll later explain.

About 10 minutes after the fire department arrives, a third, massive explosion—caused by vapor from the burning gasoline— levels the entire factory, shattering windows three blocks away. Nine people die, four of them firefighters, and 70 are injured, mostly by flying bricks and broken glass. Half of the injured are children.

"I'll never forget it," whispers an eight-year-old at one of the 11 hospitals handling the victims. "Four twenty-eight on the afternoon of Wednesday, Feb. 7, 1968. It's something I'll always remember."

Feb. 8, 1959

The Winter Dance Party does not stop. Yes, Buddy Holly, along with 17-year-old Ritchie Valens, J. P. "Big Bopper" Richardson, and pilot Roger Peterson, had been killed February 3 in a plane crash after playing the Surf Ballroom in Clear Lake, Iowa. The famous "Day the Music Died" immortalized by Don McLean in "American Pie." Only the music didn't die; just the musicians. The tickets were sold, and the shows must go on—the promoter won't pay the surviving performers otherwise—including the gig in Moorhead, Minnesota, the night of the crash. In Chicago, tonight's concert at the Aragon Ballroom is performed by Waylon Jennings, singing Buddy Holly songs. Jennings is the bassist in Holly's band—he learned the instrument the month before, at Holly's request, to join the tour. He would have died along with the others. But the Big Bopper was called that for a reason; he weighed 300 pounds, and had a bad cold. He asked Jennings for his seat on the plane, and the future country-music star gave it to him.

Feb. 9, 1947

You probably do not want to attend the first annual meeting of the American Academy of Oral Pathology. There is a snowstorm, so only 17 dentists—and, *mirabile dictu*, 24 guests—show up at the Stevens Hotel on Michigan Avenue. In the morning, election of officers. In the afternoon, papers on topics such as salivary gland tumors and myxomas of odontogenic origin. Last to speak is the academy's newly appointed second vice president, James Roy Blayney, discussing his work feeding fluoride to dogs.

The University of Illinois scientist is feeding the element to more than just dogs. He is also spiking the drinking water for the town of Evanston, using Oak Park as a control. It will be 15 years before Blayney publishes his landmark study, "Evanston Dental Caries: A Study of Fluoride Deposition in Bone." Spoiler alert: fluoride prevents tooth decay. In 1954, Chicago will become the first major city to decide to fluoridate its water, despite a public outcry against "illegal mass medication." The practice spreads. So if your teeth are real and in your mouth, and not false and in a glass on the night table, you might want to thank James Blayney. Fluoridation of water will become important not only as successful public health engineering, but as a classic conspiracy theory among the American lunatic fringe, who will continue to argue that it is poison, despite being safely consumed by hundreds of millions of Americans every day for more than half a century.

Feb. 10, 1969

Federal Judge Richard B. Austin delivers his ruling that the Chicago Housing Authority has illegally discriminated on the basis of race when it comes to the construction and assigning of its 30,848 units of public housing. Since 1954, the CHA has built 98 percent of public housing in predominantly Black neighborhoods, a choice "no criterion, other than race, can plausibly explain."

Judge Austin gives the CHA a month to work out a plan with the American Civil Liberties Union, which filed the suit, and orders the CHA to build its next 700 units in census tracts that are less than 30 percent Black, and after that to build three of every four apartments outside predominantly Black areas. That doesn't happen. What does happen is a near-complete halt to CHA construction. Rather than building public housing in white areas, it builds no public housing at all. Over the next 10 years, only 117 new apartments will be built, a reduction of almost 99 percent.

Feb. 11, 1952

"The Hog Butcher of the World had a queasy stomach last week," chuckles the new issue of *Life* magazine. "The citizens of Chicago, who are wont to accept with blasé equanimity their gang wars, blizzards, the smell of their stockyards, the over-chlorinated drinking water, were shaken to their vitals by some news about their victuals."

Yes, we were. Nor is it the only bad news. Lately, the city has been vivisected by the national press. Last month, the *New Yorker* keelhauled Chicago in A. J. Liebling's contemptuous three-part dismissal, the first installment's title, "Second City," branding that term into the public mind.

It is not a compliment.

To Liebling, Chicago is where sloshed conventioneers are beaten in alleys outside dreary bump-and-grind clip joints, its downtown a painted theatrical drop, a "Radio City set among a vast Canarsie." Its public voice is the *Tribune*'s doddering Col. McCormick, blasting his prairie xenophobia and characteristic Chicago grandiosity across the endless cornfields of the Midwest via his radio station, WGN, which stands for World's Greatest Newspaper, another empty boast.

One of the few calumnies not in Liebling's backhand—uncovered too late—is the horse-burger scandal drawing snickers from *Life*. Turns out organized crime is greasing the palms of agricultural inspectors to look the other way as they sell hamburger that is 40 percent ground horseflesh. Millions of pounds were sold, and even the famous Blackhawk restaurant is forced to close, temporarily. The adulteration stops, but the city is left with a sour taste in its mouth, and the image lingers of Chicagoans, napkin bibs around our porcine necks, obliviously gobbling up Old Nellie. For the past three years. For dessert, the city is treated to its private distress drawing raucous national ridicule.

Feb. 12, 1901

She's late.

A dozen policemen hold back waiting crowds. It's 8:20 p.m. when the train bearing the terror of Kansas finally pulls into the Van Buren Street station.

Chicago has been expecting her for a week.

"AX HEADING THIS WAY," the *Daily News* announced, on its front page.

"Her feeling toward the liquor interests may pass the limit of fanaticism and approach outright insanity," observed the *Tribune*— indeed, not only was she jailed in Topeka, but authorities there tried to commit her to an asylum.

The black-shrouded figure of reverence and ridicule has been breaking up Kansas saloons with her hatchet, aided by devoted followers, who sent a warning postcard to Chicago saloonkeepers ordering them to "abandon immediately the sale of intoxicating liquors, to close up your present premises and destroy every and all vile intoxicant in your possession," or suffer the consequences: a visit from Carry A. Nation, the Lord's avenger, herself, who now steps down from the train.

Nation heads directly to Willard Hall, where 125 of the curious paid 50 cents apiece to hear her rail against liquor. She then makes the rounds of Loop bars, not smashing them—she promised Mayor Carter Harrison II she would not—but pelting their denizens with words. The toughs at Alderman Michael "Hinky Dink" Kenna's headquarters, the enormous Workingmen's Exchange saloon at Clark and Van Buren, are neither persuaded nor amused.

"You ought to be ashamed of yourself to run a hellhole like this!"

Nation shouts at a barman. "You are sending scores of persons to hell every day."

"Oh, shut up and get out of here!" he replies.

Nation gets a warmer reception at Riley & Edwards Saloon, 290 State Street.

"Hello, Grandma, don't you know me?" says a young man, inviting her in. "I am Riley White, the son of Josie Nation." They sit holding hands while hundreds of people jam around them, some climbing on tables to get a better look.

"What strange things happen to one," Nation sighs. "To think I should find my grandson tending a bar in Chicago. How pathetic life is after all."

She urges him to get out of the business.

"Oh come on, Grandma," he replies. "Don't talk like that."

Feb. 13, 1882

Two thousand Chicagoans come to hear "the great esthete," Oscar Wilde, talk about decorative arts.

Understand, Wilde has not yet written any of the plays that will make him famous. Rather, he is one month into a yearlong speaking tour from New York to California and back, based entirely on his ability to shock. More performance artist than poet, he is capitalizing on his transatlantic reputation as the orchid-sniffing apostate of a manly age. Asked if he had really pranced down Piccadilly carrying a lily, he replies, "It's not whether I did it or not that's important, but whether people believed I did it." Andy Warhol could not have said it better.

Wilde likes to work local references into his talks. His infamous remark about the Water Tower, still charred from the Great Fire 11 years earlier, is not a quip, but scripted provocation. The beloved civic landmark, in his eyes, is "a castellated monstrosity, with perforated pepperboxes stuck all over it." Seeing it, Wilde says, he "felt amazed and grieved, that you should so misuse gothic art, and that when you built a water tower you should try to make it as unlike a water tower as possible, to make it look like a medieval fortress."

That draws raucous laughter in Central Music Hall, at State and Randolph, though with "not the slightest suggestion of rowdyism or ridicule," the *Tribune* notes with relief. Informed that he has "wounded the pride of our best citizens" with his slurs, Wilde replies, "I can't help that. It's really too absurd. Your city looks positively too dreary to me."

Feb. 14, 1929

The details are so familiar that the jarring violence of the moment is blurred into something almost quaint. Seven men—five mobsters affiliated with the Moran-O'Banion gang, a dentist who likes to hang out with thugs, and a bystander mechanic—are lounging around at North Clark Street garage. Four men enter, two dressed as police, line them up against the brick wall, and mow them down with machine guns.

The culprits are never nabbed, and the story is offered up as the apex—or, rather, nadir—of 1920s gangland Chicago. Which is too bad, because though this crime is never solved, the attempt to sift the evidence will lead to other crimes being solved. Within a day, the idea is floated.

"This is a day of specialization. We need specialists in crime detection," says Alderman John Massen. "This suggests the organization of a Scotland Yard here."

Unlike most aldermanic pontification, this notion bears fruit: the creation of the Scientific Crime Detection Laboratory, the nation's first independent forensic-research facility, at Northwestern University. The FBI won't follow their lead until 1932. Northwestern's crime lab will be purchased by the Chicago Police Department in 1938. Forensics would eventually suggest that ultimate responsibility for the massacre lies with Al Capone: a pair of Thompson machine guns recovered in a raid at the home of one of his hit men will be shown to be those used in the murders.

Feb. 15, 1933

Two immigrants are waiting for Franklin D. Roosevelt tonight in Miami's Bayside Park, where he will give a speech.

Well, more than two, in the crowd of 25,000. But two who figure into what happens next.

One is Anton Cermak, the first, and to this day only, mayor of Chicago born outside the country, his birthplace 50 miles from Prague.

The other is Giuseppe "Joe" Zangara, an unemployed New Jersey bricklayer who moved here six weeks ago. A bitter, disturbed man, he considered seeking solace by shooting President Herbert Hoover. But then he read about Roosevelt coming to Miami after a 12-day fishing trip and decided to shoot him instead. He went to a pawnshop and bought an $8 pistol.

FDR delivers his brief remarks, then sees Cermak among the well-wishers surrounding the car where he is perched.

"Hello, Tony," the president-elect says, beckoning him over, fatally.

At that moment Zangara empties the pistol, six shots that hit five people, none of them Roosevelt. Cermak, shot in the stomach, is raced to the hospital in Roosevelt's car. "I'm glad it was me instead of you," a *Tribune* reporter who wasn't there quotes the wounded mayor as saying. Also unsubstantiated is talk back in Chicago that Cermak was the true target. Neither seem true.

Five days later, Zangara will be sentenced to 80 years in prison. FDR is sworn in as president on March 4. Then, on March 6, Cermak dies from gangrene in his right lung. Zangara, now a murderer, will go to the electric chair exactly two weeks later, the wheels of justice—if that's what this is—spinning faster back then. His noble-if-improbable line to FDR is engraved on Cermak's tomb at Bohemian National Cemetery.

Feb. 16, 1912

"Capital punishment is barbarous and brutal and should be abolished" reads the sign Isaac Maron, 25, carries as he leads a group of hundreds on South Halsted Street, approaching the Cook County Jail where five men await their appointment on the scaffold—the most ever executed at one time in Illinois.

Police arrest Maron and charge him with disorderly conduct. Meanwhile, the condemned men receive the usual jail breakfast of coffee and a roll because it is up to them to purchase anything more lavish as a last meal, and they've spent all their money on cigarettes. In court, their lawyers present their last, desperate arguments.

The first four men executed are members of the gang who in October robbed and murdered a truck farmer, Fred Guelzow Jr., on his way to market in 1911. Two are brothers, Ewald and Frank Shiblawski. They are hanged together. At which point a breathless bailiff arrives from Judge McKinley's court with a request that the proceedings be delayed. The chief deputy sheriff and the jailer confer and decide that a request is not a court order and the process has already begun. So, the other two are hanged.

The fifth man to hang, Thomas Jennings, broke into a house and . . . well, let's wait till September to talk about him.

Charges against Maron are dropped later that day at Maxwell Street court, after a brief interrogation by Judge Isadore H. Himes.

"What did you mean by carrying a sign of that kind?" the judge asks.

"I don't think capital punishment should go on," Maron replies.

Himes says that every man is entitled to his opinion, but that every man is not entitled to paint it on a sign and parade it with a crowd in the streets of Chicago. He will let Maron off with a warning if he promises not to do it again. He promises.

Feb. 17, 1989

"What is the Proper Way to Display a U.S. Flag?" by Dread Scott goes on display at the School of the Art Institute. A simple conceptual art installation featuring a store-bought American flag, made in the USA, costing $29.95, spread out neatly on the floor against a wall. Above the flag, a black-and-white photomontage of flag-covered coffins, a burning flag, and protests, plus the name of the piece. On the wall between the silver gelatin print and the flag is a ledger where visitors can record their thoughts. They don't have to trample the flag to do so. But they can; it's easier to comment if you step on the flag. And some do. Others stretch to write something without stepping on the flag. Their choice.

That's too much freedom for veterans groups, which will hold tumultuous, flag-waving protests that shut down Michigan Avenue. The school receives bomb threats from defenders of the flag, and closes, briefly. Putting a flag on the floor is un-American, apparently; threatening violence against students is not.

In March, President George H. W. Bush will condemn the artwork. The city council and Illinois legislature pass laws to punish flag disrespect. A woman who steps on the flag will be arrested by two off-duty Chicago police officers. The US Senate bans the display of flags on the floor, 97–0. That October, however, the US Supreme Court, considering cases arising from several flag burnings, including one participated in by Scott, will rule that desecrating the flag is free speech, protected under the First Amendment. Of course it is. If setting flags on fire were the real issue, then VFW posts could be arrested for burning worn-out flags, which veterans groups consider the proper way to dispose of them. It isn't the burning of flags that upsets some, it's the idea being communicated. To them, freedom means being free to think just like they do.

Feb. 18, 1970

Judge Julius J. Hoffman clears the courtroom. No relatives, no friends, no curiosity-seekers. Just the defendants: Lee Weiner, John Froines, Rennie Davis, Abbie Hoffman, David Dellinger, Thomas Hayden, and Jerry Rubin—known collectively as "The Chicago Seven"—their lawyers, plus prosecutors and members of the press.

"We'll dance on your grave, Julie," Anita Hoffman shouts as she is dragged from the courtroom.

No wives either.

Assistant US Attorney Richard G. Schultz has asked for the room to be emptied because of "miniature riots that have occurred in the past." That is only a slight exaggeration. This has been a 148-day circus of a trial. Hoffman—Abbie, not 74-year-old Julius—playing with a yo-yo. Judy Collins singing until a bailiff clapped his hand over her mouth. Witnesses ranging from Mayor Richard J. Daley to Norman Mailer.

The jury is brought in.

All seven are found not guilty of conspiracy, the most serious charge. Five are guilty of inciting a riot at the 1968 Democratic National Convention. Eventually all the convictions will be overturned.

Feb. 19, 1909

Jake Block, Nathan Wolf, J. H. Ferris, B. Munstock, and S. Van Ron-
kel are Chicagoans who make their living showing silent pictures for
a nickel.

At least they try to make a living that way—the police refused
to grant a permit for a pair of popular Westerns, *James Boys* and
Night Riders, claiming they are not fit to be displayed to the public
because of their glorification of crime.

The nickelodeon operators sue. Among their various arguments
is that Chicago's ribald vaudeville and melodrama theaters do not
need police approval for each new show. Yet a story that passes
unnoticed when performed on the stage is banned when told in a
moving picture. That isn't fair.

Yes it is, according to the final ruling in *Block et al. v. City of Chicago*, issued by the Illinois Supreme Court today. The court explains
that movies can be held to a stricter standard because it would be
too difficult to check everything that happens on every stage.

Or, as Justice James H. Cartwright puts it:

There is also a radical difference between the burden imposed by
the exhibition of films and pictures to be exhibited in the moving
picture show and a requirement that a large number of actors shall
go through a dramatic performance before the chief of police.

Besides, the judge points out, kids go to the moving pictures:

The audiences include those classes whose age, education and
situation in life specially entitle them to protection against the evil
influence of obscene and immoral representations. The welfare of
society demands that every effort of municipal authorities to afford
such protection shall be sustained, unless it is clear that some constitutional right is interfered with.

Feb. 20, 1967

A front-end loader piles several tons of snow into an insulated boxcar at the Chicago, Burlington & Quincy yard in Cicero. Nothing unusual there. For nearly a month, after the big snowstorm of January 27, railroads, trying to find somewhere to put all that snow blanketing their switching yards, have been loading it onto empty trains to melt as they roll south.

But this particular load is bound for a particular customer: Terri Hodson, 13, of Fort Myers, Florida. She saw news of the snow-filled trains and wrote to William Quinn, president of the Chicago, Burlington & Quincy railroad. "I was born here in Florida and have never seen snow," she writes. "If you have an empty car coming this way could you please send me some snow." Dotting her i's with circles but forgetting that last question mark, as kids sometimes do.

Recognizing a good PR stunt when he sees one, Quinn complied. When Terri's parents sat her down to deliver the news, she at first thought, "I'm in trouble." Snow, alas, will be a disappointment, at least in the form it assumes after the two-day, 1,200-mile journey. "It wasn't quite what I pictured," Hodson later recalls. She expected it to be soft and powdery. It was hard and icy. Still, she gamely sticks a shovel into it for the photographers, then a mass of Sunshine State kids hold an impromptu snowball fight.

Feb. 21, 1947

French writer Simone de Beauvoir arrives at Union Station with 36 hours to kill before the Super Chief leaves for the West Coast. She checks into the Palmer House, "the most monstrous of the hotels I've seen," she'll note in her diary, finding it hard to breathe in a lobby "permeated by a stifling heat and the thick scent of dollars."

She seeks refuge in the Art Institute, then walks the streets, admiring buildings "built at a time when the skyscraper had won the game and needed no more excuses for itself." Her friends gave her the names of two people to look up, a writer and an "old lady." She phones the writer first. Nelson Algren growls "wrong number" and hangs up. She calls him again; he hangs up again. And a third time. Then she tries the old lady, but nobody answers. So she calls Algren a fourth time, first going through the telephone operator, who keeps him on the line long enough to hear the name of their mutual friend. His attitude changes. They meet half an hour later at the fake French cafe in the lobby of the Palmer House. Algren takes her to a dive bar on West Madison populated with "bums, drunks, old ruined beauties." They drink whiskey and talk. Though de Beauvoir misses half of what Algren says, what she does understand she likes enough to go home with him to Wabansia and Bosworth. De Beauvoir doesn't get back to the Palmer House until the next morning.

Feb. 22, 1983

So how did Chicago, despite being the most segregated city in America, riven by fear and prejudice, manage to elect a Black mayor? One who defeated not only the sitting mayor, Jane Byrne, but a future mayor and current state's attorney, Richard M. Daley. How does that happen? What changed?

The short, hard answer: nothing.

Yes, he is charming, charismatic, larger-than-life. Ebullient. The son of Roy Washington, a minister and big shot in the treacherous Third Ward, Harold Washington grew up in politics, and brings the church into his campaign; he announced his candidacy for mayor surrounded by clergy.

None of which explains how Washington wins the Democrat primary today. The most significant factor is that Jane Byrne hates Rich Daley, and Rich Daley hates Jane Byrne, and neither would drop out and let the other win. Insiders hint that Byrne was angling for a Black candidate, deliberately provoking the community, trying to draw one out to blunt the threat of Daley. Washington's candidacy was seen as a godsend, allowing Byrne to whip up support, insisting that only she can win, and a vote for Daley is a vote for Washington. In a column running today under the headline "Racist finale," columnist Mike Royko suggests that Washington's campaign is virtually an election maneuver orchestrated by Byrne. "Their warning cry to white neighborhoods was, 'The blacks are coming, the blacks are coming!'" Royko writes.

When the smoke clears, Byrne gets 34 percent of the vote. And Daley gets 30 percent. And Washington squeaks past them both to victory with 36 percent.

Typically, in Democratic Chicago, the winner of the Democratic mayoral primary waltzes into the fifth floor of City Hall in the general election. But that won't be how it works for Washington. He has another hurdle to clear. Nothing makes the Republican Party suddenly more appealing to many Chicagoans than a Black Democratic mayoral candidate. The racism that Washington in theory overcomes today will be waiting for him this spring, ready to try again.

Feb. 23, 1905

Chicago is certainly a more exciting place to set up a law practice than tiny Wallingford, Vermont. But Paul Harris misses the small-town neighborliness that you just can't find in the crowded nickel lunchrooms and dizzying 12-story skyscrapers. So he invites three associates to form a club with him. They meet today in room 711 of the Unity Building. The club doesn't have a name, at first, it has an intention: to provide members with fellowship and perhaps, eventually, to forge business contacts in the indifferent commotion that is Chicago.

It makes sense to rotate each meeting from office to office, which is how they'll get their name, the Rotary. By year's end, it'll have 30 members. In 1908, the second club opens, in San Francisco. Within a decade and a half, the Rotary is a significant enough national presence to draw ridicule, most notably in Sinclair Lewis's 1922 novel *Babbitt*, whose International Organization of Boosters' Clubs ("a world-force for optimism, manly pleasantry and good business") is a direct parody.

To its credit, Rotary will take pride in such criticisms, or at least pretend to, noting that Lewis is the first American winner of the Nobel Prize in Literature, and even claiming to learn from him, lauding Lewis for doing them a favor.

The organization is aided in its quest for self-improvement by the courts. Rotary will be an all-male operation for its first 82 years, and also in many communities all-white, particularly in the South. But in 1987, after fighting the move for a decade—self-improvement apparently has its limits—and losing in the Supreme Court, it'll begin admitting women. The Rotary now has 1.2 million members in 30,000 clubs around the world, and the Chicago branch is designated Rotary/One.

Feb. 24, 1870

Wilbur F. Storey is taking his evening stroll with his wife on Wabash Avenue when they are confronted at 12th Street by a group of thespians.

"Is this Mr. Storey?" demands Alexander Henderson, manager of a burlesque troupe.

The editor of the *Chicago Times* admits that he is indeed himself.

A woman steps forward.

"I am Lydia Thompson," she announces, "and have come here to obtain satisfaction for a scurrilous article which appeared in your paper and written, I understand, by you."

The publisher of the *Times* is not apologetic.

"I believe you are a whore," Storey says, prompting Thompson to produce a horsewhip from under her shawl and cut him across the neck with it.

The subsequent brawl—complete with brandished pistols and blackthorn walking sticks plus a squad of police—can unfold unseen while we review some background.

Thompson's show opened February 14, to less-than-glowing reviews.

"Wretchedly bad songs and simply grotesque dancing," the *Tribune* summarized.

Storey is the classic combination of public moralist and secret sinner. "He lived a debauched life of whiskey and women and nightly orgies" is how one historian put it, suggesting that Storey might have been insane from syphilis and his wife a prostitute. Whatever his private tumult, Storey went on the warpath in print, damning "the glare of cheap tinsel, the luxury of rouge" offered by "large limbed, beefy specimens of a heavy class of British barmaids," turning Crosby's Opera House into "a Wells Street Bagnio."

Thompson will later explain that she whipped Storey—a more common form of public reprimand in that equine age—because she didn't want her touring schedule interrupted by court cases. But she'll find herself in court anyway after the publisher sues her for assault. Leading, eventually, to a fine of $100.

"It was worth it," she will tell a reporter.

Feb. 25, 1861

Work begins promptly at 10 a.m. Hundreds of men manning thousands of jackscrews around and under the Tremont House, an imposing six-story hotel covering an acre on Lake Street. At the toot of a whistle from George Pullman, the men turn their iron screws and the building begins to rise.

A growing city needs a functioning sewer system, and that requires help from gravity. Chicago is built on a swamp. Pipes laid in a swamp won't drain. So the council ordained that buildings be raised from 4 to 7 feet, so their sewers will work. Pullman, who moved buildings with his father to get them out of the way of the Erie Canal, came to Chicago two years earlier for the specific purpose of raising buildings.

By 6 p.m. the Tremont House has gone up a foot, without either a crack in the walls or a pause in the guests coming and going. Five more feet to go. Meanwhile, masons hurry to keep up, laying the new foundation underneath as the building slowly rises.

Feb. 26, 1987

A basketball player as good as Michael Jordan gets fouled a lot—it's the only way to stop him. He also knows how to draw the foul. The average player takes about five free throws in a game. Today, Jordan steps up to the free-throw line 27 times against New Jersey. He makes 26 of them, 19 in a row. Overall, he scores 58 points, the club record at the time. Then he does something that doesn't go in the record books.

"Take me out," he says to coach Doug Collins, with 2 minutes and 44 seconds left. The fans, who want to see him make 60 or even 70—there is enough time—begin to chant, "Michael! Michael! Michael!" Jordan, on the bench, bows his head and smiles.

"I didn't want to be selfish," he says after the game.

Feb. 27, 1979

He is backed by most businessmen in the city. By 49 of the 50 Democratic ward committeemen. Endorsed by all three major daily newspapers. The city's largest labor unions. Then again, backing the sitting mayor, even one as anemic and inept as Michael Bilandic, is usually good business.

But it's a warm day, for February. Sunny, perfect weather to come out and vote for Jane Byrne, who has no organization to speak of, nor much money. Who was fired by Bilandic from her job as commissioner of consumer services 18 months ago. The same Bilandic who, initially asked for reaction to Jane Byrne running for mayor, had snapped, "Of what? Peoria?"

Come out for her they do. In the lakefront wards. In the Black wards. On the Northwest Side and even making inroads in the Southwest Side.

Byrne defeats Michael Bilandic, 51 to 49 percent. Not by a lot. But enough.

"I beat the whole goddamn machine single-handed," she exults.

Not exactly. She had help. Besides January's paralyzing snowstorm, there was the hapless Bilandic, who when criticized, wallowed in self-pity and compared himself to Christ crucified. His wife Heather did her part, appearing in TV ads that were regal and tone-deaf.

"Now," Byrne, the candidate whom columnist Mike Royko labeled "Little Ms. Sourpuss," vows, "I will do one thing everybody has asked me to do: smile."

And she does.

Feb. 28, 1984

"Willie the wimp was buried today," the song begins. *"They laid him to rest in a special way."*

Yes, yes they did.

White organized crime is celebrated. *The Godfather. The Sopranos.* Black gangsters, not so much. The glorification of rap, true. But those are Black artists singing about a life they know, in theory. "Willie the Wimp" will be written by a Texan, Bill Carter, who saw the news story and was fascinated. It'll become a minor hit for blues rocker Stevie Ray Vaughan.

"Southside Chicago will think of him often | Talking about Willie the Wimp and his Cadillac coffin."

Maybe the street-level carnage, the tragic effect on ordinary Black lives, is just too great to pretty up. Italian American kids are not being cut down every day in every city by the mafia. Drug dealers like Willie do too much damage, take too many lives. He's easily, gratefully forgotten. And yet, what a sight he was.

"With hundred dollar bills in his fingers tight | He had flowers for wheels and flashing headlights."

The funeral happens today, just as the song says. Willie "the Wimp" Stokes Jr., the 28-year-old son of drug kingpin Flukey Stokes. At the South Side's A. R. Leak Funeral Home. In a pink suit, propped up behind the wheel of a coffin made to resemble a Cadillac Seville, down to its wire-spoke wheels, and authentic grill, put on at a body shop. The headlights and taillights work. Enormous wide-brimmed gray hat on his head. To some, the effect may be more of a toddler's play car than anything that would seem elegant to anyone who isn't high on the drugs he sold.

To others, however, there is a pride in the ostentation, a definite respect. *Jet* magazine gives the funeral three pages and is not critical. It ends pointing out that his mother finds comfort in the send-off. "I think he would have really liked it because that's the way he was," she says. "He was flashy and he believed in style."

And this is definitely style, of a certain sort.

"He been wishing for wings, no way he was walking | Talking about Willie the Wimp and his Cadillac coffin."

Feb. 29, 1960

Seven years have passed since Hugh Hefner, unhappily employed at a children's publication, borrowed a thousand dollars from his mother and started his own magazine, *Playboy*. The John Baumgarth Calendar Company received $800 of that seed money, for a dozen old cheesecake calendar photos, including one of Marilyn Monroe. The girlie aspect was supposed to be temporary, until the magazine found its audience for quality fiction and fashion advice. But it didn't work out that way.

No matter, an entire lifestyle, an attitude, a pose, a cool, is conveyed, along with the naked women. Hefner isn't a pornographer; he is an advocate of the First Amendment. He certainly believes that, and other people do too, sometimes.

Plus, he is a really good businessman.

In 1959, *Playboy* published an article about the Gaslight Club, a Chicago establishment where waitresses wear corsets and patrons buy yearly memberships and are given keys. Thousands of readers wondered how to join, and Hefner saw an opportunity for his own business, selling the right to patronize an expensive restaurant.

It's a cold night, but would-be patrons line up for the opening of the first Playboy Club on Walton Street. Keys cost $25, and 50,000 are sold this first year, giving members access to the club—and nothing else. There is none of the seediness, none of the danger of the low-class strip joints that pepper the city's more downtrodden streets. No Mickey Finns here, no worn bar girls cadging drinks.

"We are looking for very pretty girls, 18–25, whose attractiveness is matched by their charm and refinement" read the classified ad in the *Daily News*. "ALL girls will wear one piece brief bunny outfits supplied by club."

Bobby Short is on piano for the first night, Professor Irwin Corey tells jokes. Eventually there will be 33 Playboy Clubs all over the world. Chicago's will remain open for 25 years.

MARCH

March 1, 1784

The state of Virginia, since 1609 the nominal authority over the region that will become Chicago, formally abandons its rights to the land, a move promptly accepted by the Continental Congress. Not that it had control the entire time; "Illinois County" was a part of British Quebec before it was seized in 1778 by George Rogers Clark leading 150 volunteers. Chicago might yet become a city in southern Wisconsin—Illinois's northern border is originally a westward continuation of Indiana's, cutting off lake access. But Nathaniel Pope and the savvy Illinois delegation will see the start of the Erie Canal and grasp what it means for a portage between the Chicago River and the Des Plaines River at the southern tip of Lake Michigan. They'll also see the slave/free fracturing that will lead to the Civil War and want Illinois commerce tied to the Northeast and New York through the Great Lakes, and not just linked to the South through the Mississippi River. Thus bringing "addition security to the perpetuity of the Union," as Pope will put it, they'll successfully press Congress to push the Illinois border a crucial 60 miles north when the state's outlines are formally set in 1818.

March 2, 1908

The man at the door looks strange. He says he has a letter for Chief
George Shippy. But those hollow cheeks, those wild, deep-set eyes.
Just last week, a priest in Denver was killed by an anarchist. Who's
to say this is not another assassin? The police chief grabs his visitor's hands and yells to his wife, "Mother, see if he has a gun."

Sadie Shippy feels the lump of a revolver in his right coat pocket,
she later says. The chief of police draws his own gun and shoots the
stranger in the head, killing him. Shippy's driver and son, rushing to
help, are both shot and wounded.

Coroner's physician Dr. Otto W. Lewke examines the body and
declares that his head and hands "showed signs of the utmost degeneracy." The coroner agrees that the head is "of peculiar formation."
The official police bulletin concludes, "He may be a Russian Jew."

He is, or rather, was. By the name of Lazarus Averbuch. City
officials immediately start talking about the need to identify, arrest,
and deport anarchists.

"Every known anarchist or malcontent in the city would be
arrested or driven from Chicago," a mayoral aide hopes. The mayor
is urged to ban all street meetings, but hesitates, as this would also
ban the Salvation Army and religious organizations.

At the inquest, Averbuch's sister testifies that he never owned a
gun, and a troubling alternate scenario takes shape: that Averbuch
had gone to the police chief's home to deliver a letter and Shippy
shot his own wife and son, firing blindly in a panic at a scary
stranger. He resigns two months later and dies in 1911, of syphilis.

No matter. The passion against anarchists, foreigners, and Jews—
and really, in the minds of many, what's the difference?—burns
brighter.

"Every crank and fanatic in Chicago may now get up in a public
street and decry our form of popular government and it is time that
a stop is put to it," one of Mayor Busse's advisers tells the press.
"The men who are not satisfied with our government should get out
of the country."

March 3, 1914

Production begins on Model T automobiles at Henry Ford's first Chicago factory—the sixth outside Detroit. Dedicated to cutting costs and making cars more affordable, Ford focuses on streamlining production: at first cars were assembled on skids pushed through the plant. He also sees his factory employees as potential customers, and two months earlier began offering them $5 a day, twice the going rate, certain that some of that money would be coming back to him in the form of car purchases.

He also has to pay more because he has trouble holding on to workers, who hate the repetitive drudgery of the assembly line, an idea spawned by flour mills and the cables carrying animal carcasses at the stockyards.

"The idea came in a general way from the overhead trolley that the Chicago packers use in dressing beef," Ford will say in 1922.

Ford's Chicago operation won't stay at 39th and Wabash for long. By 1920, the company will be looking to expand, purchasing 66 acres on the Calumet River, dredging a channel and dumping the tailings on the triangular site. Ford runs a rail spur south to the Nickel Plate Railroad so that up to 56 freight cars at a time can roll into the plant, which covers 11 acres. The building at 12600 S. Torrence Avenue will be a quarter mile long, begin operations February 24, 1924, and turn out automobiles for the next century, even during World War II, when it makes light armored cars for the military. In later decades, it will struggle to reclaim auto manufacturing from the Japanese. Because storing inventory costs money, Ford adopts a just-in-time production system where parts arriving on trucks in the morning are installed on new cars in the afternoon. Using industrial robots, the need to shut down production for months to retool for new models is eliminated: different models can be assembled at the same time on the same line. Although some money saved by using robots will be lost because of an unavoidable side effect: robots don't buy cars.

March 4, 1837

"AN ACT to incorporate the city of Chicago" is long. The city charter signed today begins with perhaps the most protracted and unromantic description of a place ever committed to paper, a long list of numbered tracts. Then straight to the first order of business: enabling litigation. "The inhabitants of said city . . . may sue and be sued, complain and defend in any court . . ."

Six wards and 12 aldermen who meet at least once a year in common council. They can dole out jobs whose titles offer a Whitmanesque tour of early Chicago: "A clerk, treasurer, city attorney, street commissioner, police constables, clerk of the market, one or more collectors, one or more city surveyors, one or more pound masters, porters, criers, cartmen, packers, beadles, bellmen, sextons, common criers, scavengers, measurers, surveyors, weighers, sealer of weights and measures, and gaugers."

Certain ancient crimes warrant mention. The city may prevent and punish forestalling and regrating (buying from merchants on the way to, or at, a market and underselling them) as well as "all playing of dice, cards and other games of chance . . . with or without betting, in any grocery, shop or store."

Brothels, billiard tables, and bowling are suppressed in a single breath. The city will "prevent the running at large of dogs, cattle, horses, swine, sheep, goats and geese." Chicago, a killjoy at its conception, empowers itself "to prevent the rolling of hoops, playing at ball, or flying of kites, or any other amusement or practice having a tendency to annoy persons passing in the streets or on the sidewalks of said city."

Despite the 1837 city charter's 92 sections, when it comes time to mark a centennial, the impatient elders of a far larger Chicago will jump the gun, and use its incorporation as a *town* in 1833 to mark its Century of Progress.

March 5, 1962

The *Daily News* describes them as "a beaming family," but if you actually look at the photo, Ellerine Weston has a dubious, almost grim, expression. She is looking, not at Mayor Richard J. Daley thrusting a symbolic key at her husband James, but away, as if sizing up the place and thinking, "I'm living *here*?"

It's not a bad apartment: first floor, two bedrooms, conveniently located at 3919 S. Federal. A shared kitchen, yes, but brand spanking new, the first of 4,415 apartments in an expanse of twenty-eight 16-story buildings that will line State Street from Pershing Road to 54th Street and be known collectively as the Robert Taylor Homes.

"This is a great thing for the city," says Daley. "It provides decent housing for fine families."

For a while. Then Robert Taylor becomes a symbol of urban blight, segregation, compartmentalized crime, poverty, and despair. Daley's son will tear the whole thing down by 2007. By then the Westons will be long gone, having moved out in 1967.

March 6, 1940

Why *that* book?

Of all the stories that could have been written, why did Richard Wright have to come up with *Native Son*? And why would America embrace it so enthusiastically? Book-of-the-Month Club success? Two thousand copies–a-day success?

Is Bigger Thomas an honest-if-stark portrayal of real "negro life" on the South Side in Chicago? Or a grotesque stereotype? Black Americans are proud that a novel about Black people written by a Black man is getting attention—Richard Wright is the first best-selling Black author in American history. And horrified by what they are reading. By what white folk are reading.

"Last Sunday's *Times* carried a page on *Native Son*," Shirley Graham writes today to her mentor and future husband, W. E. B. Du Bois. "That book turns my blood to vinegar and makes my heart weep for having borne two sons. They say it is a great book. Why?"

Du Bois tries to explain. "It is a great piece of work and the only kind of thing that compels action just now," he writes back. "Wright too is a nice fellow. I met him in Chicago. I think he will go far."

March 7, 1918

"The first important thing is to get a good, square look at Billy Sunday, who in a few days will be dusting off Chicago's soul and giving it a chance to shine pure and spotless upon the world," writes Ben Hecht, on the front page of the *Chicago Daily News*.

In public memory, Billy Sunday will endure primarily in a list of local attractions in the classic anthem "Chicago"—"The town that Billy Sunday could not shut down." But in life he's an annoyance to those elements who pride themselves on their reprobate ways. No lesser vivisectionist than the future co-author of *The Front Page* is dispatched to the wilds of Indiana to dissect the man.

Hecht doesn't like what he finds.

"Billy Sunday is, in his own words, no spring chicken. He has a white, colorless face, lined, seamed, somewhat dusty looking. He has been shouting his gospel across tabernacles and circus temples for twenty-two years, and it has made him serious. He walks with his shoulders hunched together, his head lowered a bit. He looks like a businessman worrying over some deal all the time. But when he unlimbers and cuts loose with his curious phrases, evidently plucked at random from his texts and sermons, a change comes over him. . . . His voice has little power, but his words grate and crackle across the room."

Maybe Sunday just needs a bigger audience. When he arrives a few days later at his Chicago revival, the police will designate 24 patrolmen, four mounted officers, three sergeants, a dozen detectives, and a lieutenant to keep watch on the gathered faithful. Fifty streetcars will be waiting to ferry them to salvation.

March 8, 1963

Today is Friday. Which means AM radio powerhouse WLS publishes its Silver Dollar Survey of Top 40 hits in the Midwest. No. 2 is "Walk Like a Man" by the Four Seasons on Vee-Jay Records, a Chicago outfit. The Vee is Vivian Carter, a disc jockey on WGRY in Gary. The Jay is her husband, Jimmy Bracken, who runs their record store. Black groups that Carter plays on the radio can be hard to track down for Bracken's store—mainstream labels won't distribute them. So in 1953 the couple took $500 from a pawnshop loan and started Vee-Jay, which actually has two songs on WLS's list.

The Four Seasons are also big in Britain, where they caught the eye of record giant EMI, whose American affiliate, Capitol Records, recently turned down a new group doing well for EMI, citing their harsh Liverpool accents and risqué lyrics. So EMI offered the group to Vee-Jay, which has had success with edgy race musicians like John Lee Hooker and Elmore James.

Two weeks earlier, on February 25, Vee-Jay released the single that Capitol spurned, which people whisper is about s-e-x. Overwhelmed—trying to keep up with monster hits will wreck them—Vee-Jay misspells the group's name on promo 45 records, which is how the station lists their first single, making the band's American chart debut, 11 months before they play the *Ed Sullivan Show*: "No. 40, Please, Please Me, by the Beattles."

March 9, 1943

Bobby Fischer is born at Michael Reese Hospital to a troubled single mother who is homeless. The future deeply disturbed chess champion will live briefly at 2840 S. Lake Park Avenue while his mother works as a typist for Montgomery Ward. But soon they move to Brooklyn, and Fischer's connection with the city of his birth ends. Though he represents a certain class of famous person whose story begins in Chicago but then unfolds elsewhere without circling back. Walt Disney is another. The movie star Harrison Ford was born at Swedish Covenant Hospital and grew up in Park Ridge, as did Hillary Clinton. Raymond Chandler wrote noir mysteries about Los Angeles but was born here. Choreographer Bob Fosse was born in Chicago and first performed professionally here before joining the navy and moving to New York. The model for this breed is Ernest Hemingway, who grew up in Oak Park, served as a Red Cross ambulance driver in Italy during World War I, came back to Chicago, lived at several locations near Rush and Division, got married here, then left for France and lived in, bonded with, and celebrated a number of locations around the world, from Paris to Key West, Idaho to Cuba, even upstate Michigan and Kansas City. Chicago is not among them.

March 10, 1894

Countless thieves have appeared in Chicago courtrooms for a broad spectrum of brazen acts. But perhaps none can match Frank Louboski, whose case is set to be heard before Judge C. J. White today, charged with a most singular theft: stealing a two-story house from 611 N. Elston, moving it 14 blocks to an empty lot on Dudley Avenue, then selling it for $165 to Joseph Piszazek and his wife.

The crime was uncovered when the house's true owner, Jesse M. Furst, who lives across town, went to see if the place was worth the cost of paint and repairs to get it into rentable shape. He found only a cellar open to the sky and debris. Rawson Street station officers Schultz and Hunning were put on the case, which they cracked by the discovery of a shingle in the street, and by interviewing residents and finding some who, yes, did see a house go by. The officers knocked on the door and informed the astonished residents that they were living in stolen property. They produced a bill of sale from Louboski, who was arrested and charged with obtaining money under false pretenses.

March 11, 2016

The UIC Pavilion is filled with thousands of Donald Trump supporters, and hundreds of protesters who snuck in with them. Security
leads the protesters out one by one as they manifest themselves,
including a group of Muslims United Against Trump. Whether this
amounts to legitimate protest against a loathsome racist, or the
un-American squelching of the freedoms of a disliked candidate
and his locally unpopular followers, depends on which side of the
widening national schism you choose to stand. Either way, when the
scheduled starting time for the rally arrives, the candidate decides
not to show his face.

The rally is postponed, officially, though Trump will never attempt
another public event in Chicago, where some residents of his namesake tower refer to their homes as "401 North Wabash" to avoid the
stigma of being associated with him. Instead Trump will use the city
as a dog whistle to excite his fans. Asked if his divisive rhetoric might
have had something to do with the heated pre-rally atmosphere,
Trump sounds a favorite theme: "I don't take responsibility."

March 12, 1906

A letter arrives at the White House.

"I am glad to learn that the Department of Agriculture has taken up the matter of inspection, or lack of it, but I am exceedingly dubious as to what they will discover," Upton Sinclair writes to Theodore Roosevelt. "I have seen so many people go out there and be put off by smooth pretenses."

The author of the muckraking novel *The Jungle* then gives the president a tip on how not to be gulled by the folks at Armour & Company: "A man has to be something of a detective."

Another long letter in a correspondence that flourished in the half year between publication of Sinclair's gut-twisting literary exposé of life in Packingtown, and passage, at the end of June, of the Pure Food and Drug Act. Which would be enough to satisfy most young novelists. But Sinclair had his sights on larger game: he had hoped to draw public attention to the cruel exploitations of the capitalist system, not the problem of spoiled meat.

"I aimed at the public's heart," he later said, "and by accident I hit it in the stomach."

Roosevelt will eventually grow exasperated with the relentless 27-year-old, writing his publisher: "Tell Sinclair to go home and let me run the country for a while." At a speech a month later, Roosevelt will say that muckrakers who do not know "when to stop raking the muck and look up at the celestial crown . . . are not a help to society" but rather "one of the most potent forces for evil."

Chicago knows what to do with evil. That same day, the Chicago Public Library will explain that its three copies of *The Jungle*, though "unsuitable for promiscuous circulation," are not being suppressed, since they can be read by anyone within the confines of the reference room.

"Many books with realistic matter of an objectionable nature within their covers are not for general circulation," head librarian Frederick H. Hilo explains.

March 13, 1913

Jeremiah O'Connor is not merely a sergeant in the Chicago Police Department. He is also the city's official art censor. His arrival at Fred D. Jackson's art store at 44 N. Wabash is no accident. He has been here before, buying a print of *September Morn* by Paul Chabas to personally show to Mayor Carter Harrison.

He returns today to charge Jackson with "exhibiting and offering for sale a certain indecent picture of a nude woman." The young woman is shown ankle deep in a lake, covering herself demurely—or out of cold; the distinction will be debated a week later at trial, while the press, the public, art critics, and artists pile on.

"Nude?" says sculptor Lorado Taft. "Oh yes, Paul Chabas's figure is nude. But indecent? Never. It is art, pure art." He wonders when the raid on the Art Institute is coming, a common refrain from art's defenders in Chicago.

A jury—all married men, it is noted—will take 30 minutes to find Jackson not guilty. By fall, millions of copies of *September Morn* will be sold, songs will be published, musicals performed. Even Peoples Gas will run a winking newspaper ad of a toddler in a bathtub. And Chicago politicians, apparently with nothing better to do, will weave an even tighter net of obscenity ordinance to better catch the next unclothed maiden testing the waters of public morality.

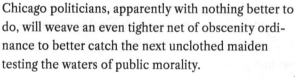

March 14, 2012

The Encyclopædia Britannica, a Chicago institution for almost 80 years, announces it is no longer publishing physical volumes of its famed reference set, but will exist entirely online.

The revered reference work didn't start in Chicago, of course. Before there was a Chicago, even before there was a United States of America, there was an Encyclopædia Britannica. Founded in Scotland in 1768, the idea was to compress world knowledge into three convenient volumes. But information, once gathered, tends to aggregate, bursting any frame built for it. The second edition had 10 volumes. The same problem manifested itself. The third had 18 volumes. The world is always discovering new stuff.

In 1928, Britannica is taken over by Sears, which for a dozen years had been publishing a cut-rate version for American readers and infusing money into the company. Britannica moved to Chicago in the mid-1930s, with offices in the Civic Opera Building. The addition helped Chicago establish itself as a reference capital: World Book is here too. And Rand McNally. And Replogle Globe. Most phone books are printed by R. R. Donnelley. In Britannica's peak year, 1990, more than 100,000 sets were sold.

Then the internet happened, providing a frame that smoothly expands to fit whatever is put within. Wikipedia is boundless, instantly adaptable, and free.

The Encyclopædia Britannica's last print run was in 2010: 12,000 thirty-two-volume sets costing $1395 apiece. After it is announced today that there will not be another, they sell out within weeks.

Is the internet version of the Britannica just as good? It is bigger, more adaptable. However, there are certain things that only a physical book can do. When the *Endurance* was locked in Antarctic ice in 1915, Ernest Shackleton's crew used their 11th edition of the Britannica for entertainment, and for practical information—such as treating scurvy and amputating toes. Eventually they realized its fine paper could be used for rolling cigarettes and lighting pipes and, as it was put with British discretion, also "good for other things."

March 15, 1937

Perhaps no other doctor can claim being a pioneer in two fields as divergent as those tilled by Dr. Bernard Fantus, a Hungarian immigrant who spent his career at Cook County Hospital.

Before World War I, Dr. Fantus studied ways to make medicine more palatable to children, perfecting the sugar tablet—*tabellae dulces*, he suggested calling it, grasping for a bit of Latin gravitas. He noted previous experiments with cod liver oil chocolate creams in his 1915 booklet *Candy Medication*, where he declares his intention to deprive "childhood of one of its terrors, namely nasty medicine," by rendering it into "perfectly delicious sweets."

The list that Dr. Fantus, a medical man of his time, compiled of medicines that could be readily given to children in candy form includes morphine, cocaine, and heroin, the last one being good for coughs.

The horrors of World War I changed everything, and Dr. Fantus shifted from sulfur taffy and flavoring cough syrup with balsam to trying to preserve blood. Battlefield doctors learned that blood can be transfused, if there is a donor of the proper blood type on an adjoining cot. The procedure would work so much better if they could preserve blood so it can be stored and transported outside of a person.

By the late 1930s, that becomes possible. Before blood can be transfused, however, it has to be collected. So Dr. Fantus created what he initially calls, with medical directness, the Blood Preservation Laboratory. But shortly before it opens its doors today, the doctor who spent years trying to make medicine more palatable to children comes up with a more digestible name that better reflects the interplay of deposits from donors and withdrawals for those in need, dubbing it the "Cook County Hospital Blood Bank," the first in the world.

March 16, 1900

The National League plays dirty. Ban Johnson doesn't like that. Spitting, swearing, and drunkenness drive away families. Bad for business. So the president of the failing Western League is forming a new league, an *American* League. Meetings have been going on for weeks, in New York, in Cleveland, as gradually the upstart major league arises from the old. At noon, he convenes a meeting at the Great Northern Hotel in Chicago with Connie Mack, of Milwaukee, and Charles Comiskey. The outlines are laid out. Eight teams: Buffalo, Cleveland, Detroit, Indianapolis, Kansas City, Milwaukee, Minneapolis, and Chicago, that last team being Comiskey's St. Paul Saints, relocated. The Saints will move to the South Side and take the nickname "White Stockings," discarded by a West Side baseball club, called several names—rigorously referring to a team by a single name is a very 20th-century practice—on its way to moving to the North Side and becoming "The Cubs." Which is why, in one of those delightful if somewhat confusing paradoxes of baseball, though the White Stockings were founded 25 years before the Cubs, it is the Cubs who are 25 years older than the White Sox. The first game by the new White Stockings will be played a little more than a month later, April 21, against Mack's Milwaukee Athletics on a former cricket pitch at 39th and Wentworth.

March 17, 1864

Chicagoans love a beginning. At 10:45 a.m., some 100 gentlemen assemble where Chicago Avenue meets the lakeshore to hear Mayor Sherman give a short speech about water. It is an enormous challenge, providing clean water to a growing city, but this plan ought to solve everything.

The problem is well known to every Chicagoan: the sewage produced by the city, its tanneries and slaughterhouses, printing plants and lumberyards, washes into the Chicago River, which empties into the lake, which the city then drinks, or tries to.

The plan is audacious and unprecedented: dig a tunnel two miles beneath the lakebed, out to where fresh water can be drawn through an intake and piped back. The work will be done by workmen wielding shovels, 24 hours a day. They'll be aided by two small mules, lowered into the shaft to live there.

The speech given, a ceremonial shovelful of earth is turned. Eventually, a pumping station and water tower—the Water Tower—will be built nearby.

The contract states that the work will be done in two years, but the engineers are confident they can complete it in one. It takes three.

March 18, 1957

Frank Lloyd Wright, 89, arrives at Robie House with newspaper reporters, preservationists, and neighbors in tow. Two weeks earlier, the Chicago Theological Seminary announced plans to tear down the Wright masterpiece to build a dorm. Wright designed the home in 1908 for Frederick C. Robie, a 28-year-old assistant manager at the Excelsior Supply Company on the South Side. It is considered the apex of his Prairie School architecture.

The Robie House—incidentally, one of the first homes in the United States to have a garage integrated into the main structure— remained a family home for less than 20 years before the seminary bought it, for use as a student residence and dining hall, with an eye toward eventually replacing the building—plans they've kept secret for a year. Demolition is to start in September.

Wright circles the building in a light rain, using his cane to point out areas in need of slight repair. "To destroy it would be like destroying a great piece of sculpture or a great work of art," Wright says, with characteristic immodesty. "It would never be permitted in Europe. It could only happen in America, and it is particularly sad that professional religionists should be the executioners."

The day is saved by two fraternities on the block. Zeta Beta Tau, next door, and Phi Delta Theta, which Wright belonged to at University of Wisconsin, next to that. Their chapter headquarters are in non-historically significant buildings. They offer to vacate their houses to make room for the new dorm. The seminary accepts the offer.

March 19, 1928

They play ne'er-do-wells on the radio. But Freeman Gosden and Charles Correll have big ambitions for themselves. National ambitions. So when WGN rebuffed their idea of syndicating *Sam 'n' Henry*, the radio program they created there in 1926, the pair walk over to WMAQ, where tonight they debut a new version, renamed *Amos 'n' Andy* since their old station retains the rights to the original show.

If you flinch just seeing the words *Amos 'n' Andy*, there is good reason. Gosden and Correll are white comedians playing Black characters in dialect, an American tradition of expropriation and mockery that has gone on for more than a century.

Nevertheless, the two have created the first situation comedy. At the show's beginning, Amos Jones and Andy Brown are farmhands in Georgia when—like so many in the real world—they abandon hopeless southern toil and head toward a better life in Chicago, taking with them four ham-and-cheese sandwiches and $24 in cash. They settle on State Street and, eventually, form the Fresh Air Taxi Company.

The sensation caused by *Amos 'n' Andy* is hard to exaggerate. It is not only the most popular radio program of its time, but some argue that it's the most popular broadcast program of *all* time. It will run for 32 years on radio, and two years on television. At its height, 40 million Americans, a third of the country, will tune in five days a week for the 15-minute update. Movie theaters stop their features in the middle to broadcast *Amos 'n' Andy*. President Calvin Coolidge is a fan—Louisiana's governor Huey Long takes his nickname, "Kingfish," from a character.

Black protest is immediate: *Amos 'n' Andy* is the last gasp of the blackface minstrel shows that tried to put a shiny gloss on the horrendous institution of slavery. Yet it has Black fans. Gosden and Correll are feted at the 1931 Bud Billiken parade the *Chicago Defender* puts on for children.

How can that be? The show is crude caricature, yet the sitcom also delivers "all the pathos, humor, vanity, glory, problems and solutions that beset ordinary mortals and therein lies its universal appeal," according to journalist Roy Wilkins, who will later head the NAACP (and reverse his view of the program). Scholars have argued that as repugnant to modern tastes though it certainly is, the lives, hopes, schemes, and doings of the Mystic Knights of the Sea Lodge are also a shift away from even more vile racist stereotypes, and they encouraged the white public to warm toward fellow citizens they usually dismiss and despise. As with Jewish comics in the 1950s, *Amos 'n' Andy* offers mainstream America a chance to open their homes—and, just a little, their hearts—to a distorted vision of people who otherwise they'd never welcome at all. Like Elvis, *Amos 'n' Andy* is a crack in the wall, one through which authentic Black culture and representations will trickle then, someday, pour.

March 20, 1975

First deputy police superintendent Michael Spiotto admits to reporters that, yes, the police intelligence unit spied on community organizations. Five of them. The groups are benign do-gooders: the Organization for a Better Austin, the Metropolitan Area Housing Alliance, the Citizens Action Program, People United to Save Humanity—better known as Jesse Jackson's Operation PUSH—and the group that busted the cops, the Alliance to End Repression. None are hotbeds of crime. But they could nourish the kind of social unrest that marked the 1960s, and the CPD's subversive activities section is keeping an eye on them.

Speaking of anachronism, it's still sometimes called the "Red Squad," a nod to its sniffing out commies after World War I; the group itself was first formed to go after anarchists following the Haymarket Bombing in 1886.

"It's a thing of the past," says Spiotto, of the secret police unit. "In the past decade we were going through turbulent times. Recently things have been more tranquil."

He's lying. It's not a thing of the past. What the police do instead of disbanding the unit is destroy more than 100,000 individual and group files collected on law-abiding Chicagoans, in the trademark Chicago cop notion that a thing cannot be wrong if nobody finds out about it. The Chicago Police Subversive Activities Unit will exist for another decade.

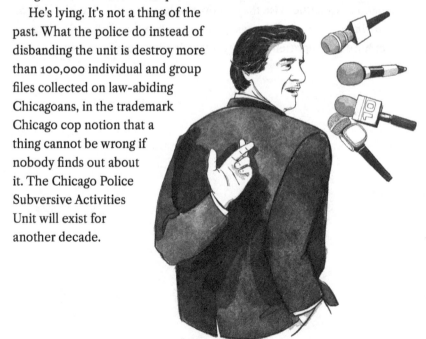

March 21, 2000

Only about 50 supporters show up at the Ramada Inn at 49th and Lake Shore Drive. Why would they? Nobody wants to hang around with a loser.

"I confess to you, winning is better than losing," Barack Obama tells them. "I thought maybe we could pull this off."

"This" refers to unseating four-term Congressman Bobby Rush, the 1960s Black Panther leader who pivoted into politics. Illinois state senator and University of Chicago lecturer Obama thought he had a chance of winning.

He didn't. In Obama's defense, it had always been a long shot. At the start, Rush had 90 percent name recognition; Obama, 9 percent. Obama rang doorbells and shook hands on freezing "L" platforms, but it wasn't enough. Rush's son, Huey, was killed by robbers in October, ramping up a sympathy vote. Not that it was needed; Obama kept tripping over himself. He was aloof, condescending, long-winded, impatient, boring, thin-skinned, arrogant, and, oh yes, he "wasn't Black enough," a charge that opponents like Illinois state senator Donne Trotter—also running—had no problem saying out loud, calling him a "white man in blackface."

Rush phrased it only a little more delicately: "He went to Harvard and became an educated fool." Rush wins by slightly more than a 2-to-1 margin, 61 to 30 percent.

Obama is anything but a fool, and certainly can learn outside of Harvard. This will be not only the first election he loses, but also the last.

March 22, 1958

"Fair and sunny," Henry Darger writes in his daily diary of Chicago weather. "Low 29, high 46." Which might seem terse, coming from the man who at the same time is writing and illustrating a 15,000-page fantasy novel, "The Story of the Vivian Girls, in What Is Known as the Realms of the Unreal, of the Glandeco-Angelinian War Storm, Caused by the Child Slave Rebellion." A pious hospital janitor living alone for 40 years in a one-room apartment at 851 W. Webster, Darger will never show his writing to anyone, nor the hundreds of watercolors he produces to illustrate his tale of adventurous little girls leading an army through macabre battle.

The weather diary is kept for 10 years, and his autobiography, "My life history," runs 580 handwritten pages, recounting his Dickensian upbringing, for a time downstate at the Illinois Asylum for Feeble-Minded Children. It returns again and again to the weather. "I would not even stand for a snowless winter," he writes, saying how he could remain by the window all day, watching it snow. "I cried once when the snow stopped falling."

In 1972, a year before his death, Darger, 80, will move into a nursing home and tell his landlord to keep the contents of his densely packed apartment. After Darger dies, the landlord begins throwing the mounds away, but stops, recognizing an imaginative, if disturbing, world. Darger today is considered among the most important "outsider" artists, his works featured in museums and commanding hundreds of thousands of dollars. Darger artifacts are assembled into a tableau evoking his cluttered Webster Street room at Intuit: The Center for Intuitive and Outsider Art on Milwaukee Avenue.

March 23, 1901

Chicago's "First Annual National Automobile Exhibit" opens at the Coliseum, a former Civil War prison at Michigan Avenue and 15th Street. Admission is 50 cents. Dealers come from around the country, and Chicagoans are proud that our auto show is larger than the one in New York. The public is "filled with curiosity and anxious to ride in the strange vehicles," according to the *Tribune*, which notes with approval "a liberal sprinkling" of society people attending. "It promises to rival the horse show as a society event."

The cars on display are guided with tillers, which direct the front wheels toward the left or right. Steering wheels won't become popular for a few more years. No gasoline engines either; the automobiles are electric or steam-powered. A wooden ¹⁄₁₀-mile track rings the exhibition hall. Visitors taken for a spin are usually riding in a car for the first time. The track is intended to show potential dealers that the vehicles actually work and "would neither fall apart nor kill them." The various models are also raced on a sort of treadmill, their freely spinning wheels attached to a speedometer. An electric gets the best time of the show, completing a mile in 57 seconds.

March 24, 1981

City crews are busy at Cabrini-Green. Workers sweep broken glass from parking lots. Garbage trucks haul away bags of trash. Streets and Sanitation workers patch potholes around 1160 N. Sedgwick. Stray dogs are chased down, abandoned cars towed away. Inside, painters and plumbers are busy. All of this is routine.

"We do this on a daily basis," Cabrini housing manager Elton Barrett tells a gaggle of reporters. "The press just happened to catch us at work. You should come by more often."

They will, starting in one week, when Chicago mayor Jane Byrne moves into apartment #416. Residents scoff at claims that this is ordinary public-housing upkeep. "If the mayor wasn't coming, those cars would be here until doomsday," one says.

What is Byrne doing? Drawing attention to a neglected part of Chicago, she says. Demonstrating with her own body that she cares. Drawing attention away, her critics suggest, from racial problems in the city, particularly the two Black members of the School Board she replaced with whites.

If it is a PR stunt, it's a bad one. Security takes up residence on either side of her apartment, meaning that Chicagoans who actually need a place to live are displaced. It may be a war zone, but families still wait for years for a chance to move here. "She got in here so fast it hurt," a resident observes.

Byrne speculated beforehand that she might stay six months. She stays three weeks, then moves back to her luxury apartment on Chestnut, eight blocks away.

March 25, 1967

Martin Luther King leads 5,000 anti-war demonstrators down State Street as last-minute Easter shoppers toss them a glance. Counter-protesters, mostly teenagers, chant, "We want white power!" Members of the American Nazi Party yell "treason," and a few grab signs calling for an end to the war and throw them in the Chicago River. There are no arrests.

After the march, King speaks at the Coliseum, calling the war "a blasphemy against all that America stands for."

He opposes the war, he tells the crowd of 4,000, "because I love America. . . . I speak out against it, not in anger, but with anxiety and sorrow in my heart, and above all with a passionate desire to see our beloved country stand as a moral example to the world."

Mayor Richard J. Daley, at a luncheon, condemns "people not from this city" who feel compelled to come to Chicago and hoist protest signs for their own grubby political ends.

"Poverty, urban problems and social progress generally are ignored when the guns of war become a national obsession," King says at the Coliseum. "Our arrogance can be our doom. It can bring down the curtains on our national drama. Ultimately, a great nation is a compassionate nation."

It is King's first anti-war march. There will, he promises, be more.

March 26, 1905

"Sometimes I think the materialism we talk so much about in America amounts to just this: we do take the boots and the shoes and the dresses, which industry and invention have made cheap and deck ourselves out in them, but we don't have any sympathy, any communal feeling with the people at whose sacrifice they are, many of them, made," Jane Addams tells a New York meeting of the Women's Trade Union League, formed two years earlier after the American Federation of Labor refused to admit women. The League pushes for the eight-hour workday, and fights child labor.

"I don't believe anyone here would buy sheeting made in a Southern mill, by a child under ten years of age, if he knew the particular piece of sheeting the child made," Addams says.

She is joined by Samuel Gompers, president of the American Federation of Labor, an ally in raising awareness of problems of the workingman and, eventually, working woman.

"Not to see the moral problems which belong to our particular age, is, of course, the great dodge of everybody," says Addams. "To say that the condition of working women is not a moral but an economical problem, or none at all. Sometimes, when I see a self-complacent audience, I think that we are all down in the pit together."

Even so, they have each other.

"We used to say that it was so hard for the Chicago mind to understand [the poetry of Robert] Browning that we had to pool our intelligence in clubs. So in this movement we must pool our interest," Addams says. "There are 11,000 Trade Union women in Chicago, already organized. In going into this movement we are going to stand with them, to share their blunders with them as well as their successes. No moral movement has been without its perplexities."

March 27, 1997

Quaker sells the Snapple Beverage Company for $300 million, which might sound like a lot if you don't know that they bought the trendy juice drink business just 28 months earlier for $1.4 billion. The sale marks the end of one of the great business fiascos of the 20th century. The Chicago hot-cereal maker, which also owns the sports drink Gatorade, not only paid $1 billion too much for the quirky bottled tea company, but then turned around and quickly sold it for half its real value.

What happened?

When Quaker bought Snapple, it was a hot brand with a devoted following stirred to passion by TV commercials where fan letters were read by real-life Snapple employee Wendy Kaufman. But the brewed iced-tea bubble burst just as Quaker bought it. Cheaper teas were becoming popular. The day the sale was announced, Quaker stock fell 10 percent.

There was also a clash in cultures. Quaker's chief was the sort of guy to call customers reaching for his product "thirst occasions." Quaker failed to understand Snapple's distribution system, botching it so badly that product backed up, went bad, and had to be dumped. They fired longtime spokeswoman Kaufman, whose neighborly warmth had been intrinsic to the brand, instead running commercials that were laughable failures. "They killed themselves," Kaufman will later say. "Coming in with such egos. I never saw anything like this. Who can deal with people who don't listen to anything you have to say?"

March 28, 1980

There is no warning. Wisconsin Steel, a huge 105-year-old South-east Side steel plant that employs nearly 3,500 workers, simply goes out of business.

Well, not so simple. Quite complicated, actually. International Harvester, Wisconsin Steel's former longtime owner and principal customer, is having its own financial woes, dealing with a strike that has gone on 145 days. Worried that it will lose the coal and iron-ore mines held as collateral on loans to the steelmaker if Wisconsin Steel's parent, Envirodyne Industries, goes bankrupt, IH seizes the properties. Prompting Chase Manhattan to freeze Wisconsin Steel's inventory and stop its shipments. With no steel going out, or money coming in, the company ceases operation. Stunned middle managers go around the factory telling workers, many who have worked there 30, 40, even 50 years, to go home and not come back. There is hope that the shutdown won't be permanent, but it is. Their health insurance will stop in one month. Their last paycheck bounces.

March 29, 1675

The wind finally shifted, bringing a thaw from the south. But the welcome warmth also broke up the ice on the river, which started to rise, quickly.

"We had barely time to decamp as fast as possible, putting our goods in the trees, trying to sleep on a hillock," Father Jacques Marquette writes in his journal.

He and his men are the first non-natives to pass the winter at what would be Chicago. Today, with the water navigable again, they set out "with great joy" for the village of the Illinois, causing the French Jesuit to reflect on their experience here:

> The blessed Virgin Immaculate has taken such care of us during our wintering that we have not lacked provisions, and have still remaining a large sack of corn, with some meat and fat. We also lived very pleasantly as my illness did not prevent us from saying holy mass every day.

The rising river reminds us that the Chicago River is the central motivating fact of Chicago. It is the reason the Native Americans are here, at the portage between it and the Des Plaines River. Their presence drew Marquette, to preach the Gospel to them. And it will be the reason the federal government will build a fort on this spot, where a great city will eventually rise. Debate over whether "Chicago" means onion or wild garlic misses a far more important point about the name: it was attached to the river first. Chicago is named, not for any plant, but for the river, not the other way around. There is a Chicago River long before the place where it meets Lake Michigan will be considered worthy of a name.

March 30, 2003

They came in the dead of night. Bulldozers, with a police escort to keep away the curious and the media. They carve a big X at the north and south ends of the single runway at Meigs Field, for 45 years the little lakefront airport next to the Adler Planetarium. A firetruck points a spotlight at the internet camera on the Adler, to blind the world to what they are doing. Guiltily, without warning; illegally, without approval. Without informing the FAA, stranding 16 planes parked at the field. The planes will have to be towed away. The city will pay a million-dollar fine.

Richard M. Daley had tried closing the airport before—he wants parkland there, and perhaps dislikes Meigs as the place where Republicans from downstate show up to cause trouble. It isn't like you could ask Daley and expect an honest answer—a year and a half after 9/11 he mutters something about securing downtown from aerial attack. As if Cessnas had brought down the Twin Towers. Richie Daley never actually says, "I'm the mayor; fuck you." He doesn't have to. It's implied.

March 31, 1952

Frederick Rex, the municipal reference librarian, estimates that the population of Chicago is 3,665,792.

The highest count in Rex's career as city librarian, a post he'll hold for 48 years, from 1907 to 1955. He's a well-known figure, given to releasing this sort of information. When "Big Bill" Thompson announced that Chicago was the sixth-largest German city, he wasn't just making it up, for once, but using figures supplied by Rex. It was said Rex could quickly find any particular passage among the 200,000 books and pamphlets on his shelves on the 10th floor of City Hall. He also prepared civil-service tests for librarians throughout the country.

It was also the peak population of Chicago—census figures cite 1950, but population counts are part art, part science. The population will steadily slip: in 1984, Los Angeles will surpass Chicago to take the "Second City" title after almost a century. In 2020, Chicago's population will be 2.7 million, a million below its peak, with Houston closing in fast.

APRIL

April 1, 1918

A few minutes after 10 a.m., 113 defendants are brought in. Their handcuffs are removed and tossed in a pile in a corner of the courtroom.

That process alone takes half an hour, under the watchful gaze of 30 armed constables and deputies, who consider the accused, in the words of one, "a collection of unwashed maniacs." In the hallway, marshals keep an eye out for bomb throwers.

At 11 o'clock, court is called to order in the trial of 165 men and one woman indicted on charges of sabotage and trying to overthrow the government, though only 115 could be found and arrested. All are members of the Industrial Workers of the World, founded in Chicago in 1905, now facing justice before Federal District Judge Kenesaw Mountain Landis.

A. K. Kimball isn't here—ill in Columbus Hospital. Italian poet Arturo Giovannitti—who already caught snickering press attention by kissing an associate on both cheeks and then the lips—is here, and objects that his name hasn't been called. He is told the case against him has been dropped. "I wish I'd known this 48 hours ago," Giovannitti mutters. "I came from New York to be here . . ."

"We will continue this case against William Haywood et al. tomorrow," Landis says, and starts quizzing the 72 potential jurors. Jury selection will go on for a week when charges of tampering are raised—it seems someone connected to the IWW has been quizzing prospective jurors about their politics outside of the courtroom. Judge Landis dismisses all the prospective jurors and starts anew.

The largest federal trial ever held will wrap up August 17. After 18 weeks of testimony, the jury will require a little over an hour to reach its verdict, less time than Landis spends instructing them: all defendants guilty on all counts. It turns out that freedom of speech is a peacetime prerogative. "Once war is declared, this right ceases," says Landis, who the next year will become the first commissioner of baseball.

The convicted IWW members will be sentenced to between 5 and 20 years in prison. "Big Bill" Haywood will famously flee, spending the rest of his life in the Soviet Union. The rest will be shipped on a special train to Leavenworth, though many see their sentences commuted before Franklin Delano Roosevelt pardons the rest as part of a Christmas Eve 1933 mass amnesty of a thousand World War I draft dodgers and violators of the espionage act.

April 2, 2019

All 50 wards. Seventy-three percent of the vote. Almost a 3-to-1 margin. Lori Lightfoot doesn't just win, she crushes her opponent, the once formidable Cook County Board president Toni Preckwinkle, now brought low in part by her misguided push for a wildly unpopular tax on soda, a cash grab she tried to disguise by telling her constituents they were too fat. These are Dad Daley numbers—the same percentage of the vote, as it happens, that Richard J. received in 1967.

However, Lightfoot is not Bridgeport Irish, but African American lesbian—Chicago's first openly gay mayor, the "openly" both a quiet nod to certain question marks and recognition of her style, which is not down low in the slightest.

"I sure wouldn't have made it without my wife Amy and our daughter Vivian," she says at her victory party at the Chicago Hilton, after the crowd chants Amy Eshleman's name. "I want to thank you both for your endless inspiration, your support at the toughest times, and your undying love. You are my all, my everything."

April 3, 1979

Jane Byrne wins the only elective office she will ever hold, mayor of Chicago, beating Republican Wallace Johnson with a staggering 82 percent of the vote, the biggest win in a mayoral race in modern Chicago history.

Of course in Democratic Chicago, the spring general election is a formality. The trick was the Democratic primary in February, when she defeated Michael Bilandic, who became the first candidate slated by the Democratic machine not to win since 1927.

Byrne could win, but she couldn't govern. During her first three months in office, the transit worker, teacher, and firefighter unions each will go on strike, boom boom boom, one after the other. Hampered by rampant sexism, adrift and overwhelmed, with a tendency to make decisions and phone calls to the newspapers after tossing back a few cocktails, she will quickly embrace the very machine hacks she thought she had defeated.

"An erratic and stormy person, she kept the city quaking during her first administration," Nobel laureate Saul Bellow will conclude. There will not be a second.

April 4, 1917

The Chicago City Council unanimously adopts a municipal flag: two horizontal blue bars flanking two six-pointed red stars on a field of white. The banner originated in 1915 with a contest proposed by writer Wallace Rice. In a classic Chicago move, Rice suggested the competition, wrote the rules, judged the entries, and decreed himself the winner.

In his defense, the rules he devised are excellent, including "The municipal flag should be beautiful," and demanding both simplicity and originality.

Rice worked up hundreds of designs, arranging and rearranging them on the floor of his Lincoln Park home. The blue stripes signify the north and south branches of the Chicago River. They define three white stripes, which represent the north, west, and south sides of the city.

"White," Rice mused, "the union of all the colors, to symbolize the union of all the races in the City of Chicago." A racial harmony that will be more celebrated in theory than honored in practice. The flag's two distinctive, sharp-pointed stars were also designed by Rice, a lifelong student of vexillology, or the study of flags, and bunched toward the staff, representing the Great Fire of 1871 and the Columbian Exposition. Two more will be added, for the 1933 Century of Progress and for those lost at Fort Dearborn.

Chicago's mayors will be energetic boosters of the municipal flag. In the early 1950s, Mayor Martin Kennelly will keep postcards of it on his desk, handing them out to visitors. In the late 1960s, Richard J. Daley will send city flags to Chicago soldiers serving in Vietnam.

There will also be continual suggestions to add a fifth star, marking everything from the first nuclear fission at the University of Chicago to the founding of the Special Olympics. In 2020, Lori Lightfoot will twice declare that the city's reaction to COVID-19 should be so laudable as to "truly warrant a fifth star on our flag." Though it is uncertain whether this is a general rallying cry or a sincere proposal. If the former, it worked, more or less. If the latter, it didn't.

April 5, 1955

The weather is perfect. Seventy degrees. Sunny. Which bodes well for the Republican candidate, progressive Hyde Park alderman Robert E. Merriam. He's hoping to mobilize every Republican, plus convert enough Democrats who in the February primary vainly backed the current mayor, Martin Kennelly, or that son of Polonia, Benjamin Adamowski. The strong turnout dwindles as the day progresses, however. Chicago is its usual election day self—the bars are closed, to keep ward heelers from corralling barflies and herding them to the polls, though bottles of wine are spotted being sold out of the trunks of cars. Republican hopes melt away like snow in April.

"I promise no miracles, no bargains," Richard J. Daley, the victor with 55 percent of the vote, tells supporters at the Morrison Hotel. "But with unity, cooperation, and teamwork, we will continue to build a better city for ourselves and our children."

Alderman Charlie Wheeler, of the Forty-Fifth, puts it more bluntly: "Let me tell ya, this Daley—he's going to be one tough sonofabitch."

April 6, 1915

Oscar De Priest, former county commissioner, is elected alderman of the Second Ward, the first African American to sit on the city council. He serves a single two-year term but goes on to bigger things. In 1929 he will be the first African American to join Congress in the 20th century, and the first ever from north of the Mason-Dixon line. De Priest will reform Congress just by being there—a white representative from the South threatens to move rather than endure De Priest occupying the office next to his. While De Priest will be allowed to eat in the House dining room, alone, some of his colleagues will flee to avoid "the embarrassment" of eating alongside him. In 1934, the new member will create "a national sensation" by trying to integrate the House restaurant for Black Americans other than himself. He will not succeed.

April 7, 1968

Jennie Robinson takes her seven-year-old son Donald to Our Lady of Sorrows Church, as usual.

"We go to church every Sunday," the post office clerk explains. "We couldn't let this Sunday be any different."

But today *is* different, and not just because it's Palm Sunday. The smell of smoke hangs in the air. Hundreds of soldiers from the US Army's Third Division patrol the streets of the West Side. Rev. Martin Luther King was killed Thursday in Memphis, and for two days Chicago, like cities across America, was seared by riots. Twenty-eight blocks of Madison Street are a charred ruin, a scar that will remain for decades. The seed is also planted for this summer's cataclysm at the Democratic National Convention. Later today, Richard J. Daley will fly above the riot zone in a helicopter. When he comes down, he'll air two false conclusions. First, that the schools are to blame, as he'll claim, in an incoherent news conference where he imagines girls being slashed while principals shrug. And second, that part of the problem is police being too soft on rioters. A week later he'll say he thought he had instructed the police to "shoot to kill" any arsonist and "shoot to maim or cripple" any looters. Though that might be his way of distracting public attention from what actually happened. Nine people were killed Friday, all Black men, some under circumstances that suggest they were arbitrarily gunned down by the police. Claiming police were too soft is an attempt to forestall scrutiny of that. For Daley, the best defense is always a strong offense.

April 8, 1889

It was the epic road trip of all time. Half publicity stunt, half curve-ball imperialism. The Chicago White Stockings base ball team—still two words in those days—left Chicago six months earlier and played their way across the country to San Francisco against All America, a composite rival team. Then A. G. Spalding's squads got on a ship and kept going. Why? "To establish the National Game of America upon foreign soil," according to a participant. Visiting Hawaii, they were received by the king but didn't manage a game, then on to Japan, China, the Philippines, Ceylon. Up the Suez Canal to Egypt, where they tossed baseballs at the Sphinx. Through Europe, Paris, London. And finally back to the United States.

Now days from home, a welcome to crown all their previous receptions is held. A champagne testimonial banquet at Delmonico's in New York City, the most famous restaurant of its era. A four-hour dinner in nine innings, featuring fare from the lands they had visited. About 250 men pack the second-floor ballroom: three former New York mayors are here, a US senator, and Theodore Roosevelt, then a lowly state legislator.

And Mark Twain, who of course speaks, envying "the glories they have achieved in their march around the mighty circumference of the earth." Comedians Hopper and Bell recite "Casey at the Bat," a poem that became popular the year before. Dinner won't break up until 2 a.m., leading sportswriters to detect a certain sluggishness in the game played in Brooklyn that afternoon.

April 9, 1969

About 150 observers jam the 23rd-floor federal courtroom; another 200 wait in the hallway outside. The charges are conspiracy and crossing state lines to cause a riot. One defense lawyer asks for six months to file motions, noting that the grand jury took that long to indict the eight. Judge Julius J. Hoffman gives them 30 days. David Dellinger raises a fist as an act of defiance, and tries to make a speech. Hoffman cuts him off, several times, and he settles with pleading, "obviously not guilty; the guilty parties have not been indicted," for which he is admonished again.

Abbie Hoffman, Jerry Rubin, Tom Hayden, and the rest are less dramatic, pleading not guilty, a development the *Tribune* will summarize in a headline the next day as "8 DENY GUILT IN RIOTS AT CONVENTION," which is not quite the same thing. Black Panther leader Bobby Seale is there. Judge Hoffman will later order him bound and gagged in open court, and his case separated from the rest, which is how the Chicago Eight becomes the Chicago Seven.

April 10, 1928

Sen. Charles Deneen, whose house was bombed last month, is accompanied by four armed guards as he goes to cast his ballot. He is pushing for a slate of reformers, and Mayor "Big Bill" Thompson and his mob pals are pushing back, hard.

Ballot boxes are stolen and votes cast illegally. There are numerous kidnappings of election judges, who are beaten and held captive, sometimes 20 at a time, in remote apartments until election day is over.

Poll workers are also arrested by police who otherwise tend to step out of the room just before attacks begin. Chief Justice Harry Olson has to call the police commissioner to court and threaten charging him with contempt before he produces four poll workers who are in jail but haven't been charged.

"This is not Russia," Olson says.

Police may have done worse. A candidate for ward committeeman, Octavius Granady, is boldly murdered. Granady, a Black World War I vet, is in a car chased through the crowded streets of the "Bloody 20th." The pursuing car has banners advertising his opponent, Morris Eller. Granady crashes his car and is riddled with bullets.

"Someone is going to hang for this," the coroner promises. Pretty to think so. Though there will be a trial, of several gunmen and seven Chicago policemen—for providing protection to the killers—before charges are dropped.

In the Great War, hand grenades were called "pineapples," and today comes to be known as "The Pineapple Primary." Though that creates a lingering misperception. The 60 or so bombings associated with the election do not all take place today, but over the previous six months. With such regularity that one paper refers to "Chicago's daily bomb."

"In no case has a bomb thrower been apprehended," says a Democratic Party leader.

What gets overlooked in all the mayhem is this: the bad guys lose anyway. Chicago voters turn out at double the expected number—more than 800,000—and deliver a stunning rebuke to Thompson and his gangland thugs. His state's attorney, Robert E. Crowe, is crushed by Deneen's candidate, Judge John A. Swanson, whose home was also bombed. Thompson promised to resign if Swanson won, but nimbly changes his mind.

April 11, 1973

Four men are working on a platform in an express elevator shaft at the Sears Tower: Larry Lucas, Robert Wiggins, Leonard Olson, and William Walsh, employees of Westinghouse's elevator division. The building's frame is nearly complete; it'll top out in a month.

The men, ages 20 to 52, are in a blind shaft, meaning there are two ways out: the bottom entrance at the 33rd floor, 100 feet below where they are now, on a temporary platform at the 42nd floor. And at the top, the 44th floor, 20 feet above where they use turpentine to scrub away oil the foundry used to coat the elevator tracks to keep the steel from rusting.

A spark must have set off the fumes. Workers on the 42nd floor hear screams, and desperately tear a hole in the drywall, trying to get to them. But it's too late.

Three of the men are found at the bottom of the shaft, horribly burned. The other is still on the platform. Damage to the building is estimated at $1,000.

The four are not the first to die building the Sears Tower—that was welder Walter Kettleston, who fell to his death in October. His work partner, who was also his son, slid down two stories of steel beam to cradle his father's head as he died.

Nor are they the last. Just four days later, Jack De Klerk, one of many workers going "12/7"—12 hours a day, seven days a week, racing to get the job done—will be knocked off the 109th floor by a stray cable. He falls 35 feet before landing on the 106th floor. Not that far, but far enough.

Members of a grim fraternity that Chicagoans seldom think about—the human toll to create these soaring towers. Almost every tall building has cost a life or two. Or more. Four workers fell to their deaths constructing Marina City in the early 1960s.

They are remembered by those who love them. Three weeks after his death, De Klerk's widow Jo Ann will crash the Sears Tower topping-out ceremony, sneaked in by her uncle Ronnie. On the ground, she'll boldly sign her husband's name in the middle of the celebratory white beam, then go up to the 109th floor, open to the air, and put one foot out on a steel beam like the one her husband fell from, the wind howling around her. The beam was narrower than her foot, she'll later recall, adding that it was one of the scariest things she has ever done in her life.

April 12, 1983

Historic, certainly. Joyful to the city's Black population too long shut out of the corridors of power. Absolutely.

But it should not have been that close. Buoyant Harold Washington receives 51.8 percent of the vote today, while bland Republican Bernie Epton gets 48.3 percent. Epton, who championed civil rights for his entire career in the state legislature and thought he would be running against Jane Byrne when he first entered the race, found himself the "great white hope" against Washington. A role he allowed himself to slide into. He later claimed to be surprised that his campaign slogan, "Epton for Mayor: Before it's too late," was viewed as a racist code, explaining, "If I had known that it was going to be interpreted that way, I would never have approved it."

Yeah, sure. Epton supporters blanketed the North Side with racist literature such as the new seal for the city of "Chicongo," showing a pair of thick lips, or the job applications for Washington's staff asking "How many words do you jive a minute?" Or the popular buttons showing a slice of watermelon with a slash through it. Loathsomeness done in his name that Epton didn't denounce during the campaign with a fraction of the vigor he directed at the media for reporting it, calling newspaper reporters "just slime" who should resign "en masse" for the crime of holding a mirror up to his supporters.

"Harold," as he is known, is embraced by the Black community as a sign their time has come. But victory will ring hollow when the new mayor tries to wield the power he supposedly won, thwarted by a city council divided 29–21 purely on racial lines.

The mayor will die of a heart attack early in his second term (followed closely by Epton, ironically, three weeks later), replaced immediately by David Orr, Chicago's shortest-serving mayor—in office less than the week it takes while the powers-that-be find a suitable placeholder in the form of affable nonentity Eugene Sawyer, his inauguration held privately, in a parking lot, to cut down on protests. After two years, a special election will be held to fill out Washington's term. Sawyer will lose the Democratic primary to Rich Daley. While Washington will linger in the hearts of Black Chicago, a lost, beloved figure, a tantalizing might-have-been. The mayor's office, another birthright stolen from them.

All that is four and a half years away. It will be about 1:30 a.m. tomorrow morning when a jubilant Washington meets his supporters at McCormick Place.

"Harold! Harold!" they chant.

April 13, 1992

Chicago was warned. In September, a crew from Great Lakes Dredge & Dock Company was replacing rotten pilings in the Chicago River near the Kinzie Street bridge and drove a timber into the river bottom, opening a crack in the network of early 20th-century freight tunnels below the river that most Chicagoans didn't know existed.

In January, a videotape showing men in thigh-deep water inside the tunnel under the river was given to the city. The Department of Transportation put the repair job out to bid.

But water is relentless, and doesn't respect the formal bidding process. At dawn today, the crack becomes a hole the size of a Buick. The Chicago River starts pouring through 47 miles of underground tunnels into the basements of Loop office buildings and businesses.

Streetlights go out. Water cascades over open electrical circuits in subway tunnels, so the CTA cuts power. Telecommunications and compressors and power supplies across 24 square blocks short out. Elevators stop working, and employees scurry down darkened stairways. At 7:14 a.m. the famous clock outside Marshall Field's stops. It won't start again until after Labor Day.

The Chicago Board of Trade, the Chicago Board Options Exchange, and the Chicago Mercantile Exchange suspend trading as the city's wet basement problem sends waves of consequences rolling across the globe. The First National Bank of Chicago dispatches traders to its office in London. They won't return for three months.

With the courts at the Daley Center closed, lawyers race to the Skokie courthouse to file the first of a river of lawsuits—so many that by summer, flood lawsuits will have their own biweekly journal, the *Chicago Tunnel Litigation Reporter*.

The Loop Flood is the oddest disaster—a flood where almost nobody gets wet, where few ever see floodwaters, a catastrophe without casualties, whose damage is extensive but hidden, in basements submerged, inventory ruined and business lost.

It'll take five days for the city to fill the breach, and the Army Corps of Engineers five weeks to pump 134 million gallons from Loop basements. Most of the tunnels will be sealed off, but the city still employs an engineer whose No. 1 priority is to keep an eye on them. The disaster's cost will be about $2 billion. The job to repair the initial leak, had it been done promptly, might have run $10,000.

April 14, 1956

The Saturday before the National Association of Radio and Television Broadcasters formally kicks off its 34th annual meeting, 200 CBS affiliate owners and managers gather at the Conrad Hilton. At a lectern, CBS engineering vice president William Lodge hints at a big technological breakthrough. When he finishes speaking, he takes a few questions while engineers operating a hidden Ampex Mark IV VTR prototype rewind the two-inch tape.

Television monitors come alive with the speech the group has just heard, the first videotape replay ever seen in public. There is shocked silence, then the room erupts into cheers and whistles.

Up to this point, TV programs can only be recorded by creating kinescopes—films of a program shot by a camera bolted in front of a TV screen. They're expensive, take time to produce, and the picture quality isn't good. Plus viewers know they're watching a recording.

The Ampex breakthrough has drawbacks. The machines cost $45,000, they are the size of a stove, and there are a grand total of two in the world. To read the videotape, the recording heads spin at 14,000 revolutions per minute.

Ampex researchers estimate that the global market for video-recording machines might be a dozen and plan to produce five for evaluation by government agencies in 1957. By the Monday after the convention ends, they will have taken orders for 82.

April 15, 1955

There were problems. Beginning with where to put the first one. Near his office on LaSalle Street downtown? That turned out to be "impossible for a number of reasons." The little red-and-white-tile hamburger stand opening today was also designed for Southern California, where the first eight are located. In sunny California, potatoes can be stored out back in a chicken-wire bin. That won't work in inclement Illinois. Room inside the tiny building must be found to put the potatoes. And a furnace.

Ray Kroc has solved each problem. He picked Des Plaines for his first McDonald's restaurant because it's 15 minutes from his heavily mortgaged home in Arlington Heights. The furnace and potatoes are relegated to a basement.

Each problem solved, however, leads to a new problem. The basement could not be constructed until the McDonald brothers sent a registered letter permitting its addition, according to their overly rigid franchise agreement. They dallied. Once built, the fans for the fryer and griddle kept blowing out the furnace pilot light. Plus, the French fries taste like bland mush, no matter how carefully the McDonald brothers' procedure is followed. Oh, and the siblings sold the rights to franchise their name in Cook County to the Frejlach Ice Cream Company for $5,000. They forgot to mention that.

"It was a hell of an ordeal," Kroc will later recall.

Kroc consults with the Potato & Onion Association. They finally figure out that storage in a chicken-wire bin in the desert air lowers the moisture content of potatoes, making them taste better. So a big electric fan goes in the basement to dry the potatoes.

The Frejlach Ice Cream Company agrees to part with the rights for five times what it paid. It'll take a year to work out these and other problems at that McDonald's restaurant, the first link in a chain that would grow to span the globe. But that's okay. The place makes money right away.

April 16, 1913

At 4 p.m., students of the School of the Art Institute jam the museum's south portico to hold a mock trial.

"Henry Hair Mattress" is accused of "artistic murder, pictorial arson, artistic rapine, total degeneracy of color, criminal misuse of line, general esthetic aberration, and contumacious abuse of title."

It is the end of the Armory Show's 24-day run at the Art Institute of Chicago, and the "monsterpieces of art" are bound for Boston.

In February, when the landmark show opened in New York at 69th Regiment Armory—hence its nickname—Chicago newspaper critics hurried to take a peek at Futurists and Neo-Impressionists, Postimpressionists and Cubists, including Marcel Duchamp's multi-image *Nude Descending Staircase*.

"Art Show Opens to Freaks" read one headline.

William M. R. French, the director of the Art Institute, of course went as well, finding the work ranging "from madness to humbug." Paintings that are "mere unmeaning assemblages of form, with gay color conveying no idea whatsoever." The whole circus leaves him depressed; Matisse's work is "a joke" and "without merit," yet still better than Van Gogh's, whose paintings are "actually unbalanced and insane."

Although credit where due: Director French didn't stop the show from coming to his museum. Though he arranged to be absent, lecturing in California, during its entire run. So he misses the sensation. Chicagoans flock—200,000 visitors come, though many are aghast. "Our splendid Art Institute is being desecrated," howls the *Chicago Examiner*.

The students find Matisse guilty as charged, burn three reproductions of his paintings, and are poised to burn him, too, in effigy, when police step in. If the Art Institute seems unusually tolerant of their antics, remember the school was founded first; the museum began as the school's gallery, to show off student work. In a rare reversal of generational roles, Walter Pach, one of the show's organizers, chides the students, noting that the teacher who riled them up had hated the Impressionists too. "Ten or twenty years from now," he says, "some of these students will be eating crow."

April 17, 1943

It's after midnight. Charles Kikuchi's eyes are drooping. But he's
a diarist, and so takes a blue pen and sets down an account of his
"most busy day." Yesterday, he and two of his seven siblings, sisters
Emiko and Bette, arrived in Chicago from the Gila River internment
camp in Arizona.

They were met by Travelers Aid, who directed them to the
Friends Hostel, one of two run by Quakers for the 20,000 Japanese
who will relocate to Chicago during the war.

Kikuchi finds the city "windy and dirty."

He meets many fellow Nisei—"bewildered, confident, anxious,
hopeful"—like himself, who just arrived from the West and are
looking for a place to live. Frankly, they bother him. "They seem to
lack a hospitable attitude or something. . . . I never met so many in-
quisitive people in my life as among the Nisei. They do not hesitate
to ask the most detailed personal questions."

To his vast surprise, the next day he finds an apartment, after
taking the "L" through the South Side. "Going through the Negro
section was a little depressing," he writes. "300,000 Negroes or $\frac{1}{10}$
of the city population live in a restricted area consisting of 5 percent
of the total housing of the city. The Negro area is dirty and we
passed by the back ends of the houses which were filthy beyond
description. Nobody can ever convince me that the Negroes are
happy to remain cooped up in this area. The color line is very sharp
and the Negroes just are not able to expand."

The Friends don't want to settle Japanese there, Kikuchi
believes, because the government worries about the two groups
finding common cause. "Could this be a tacit acknowledgement that
the whites fear the fraternizing of two minority groups that have
been grossly mistreated?" Kikuchi ponders. "This is a hell of a way
to solve any problem. Suppression by force only breeds fraud and
greater barriers."

April 18, 1950

The US Patent Office issues Patent #2,504,679 to Chicago inventor Eddy Goldfarb. Glance at the paperwork and it might seem some kind of dental appliance—those are certainly teeth in the patent illustration, seen in profile, set in their gums. But what about those gears? And the wind-up key? The category is "Novelty and Amusement Device," and the invention's purpose, the patent explains, is "simulating the opening and closing of the teeth of the mouth in rapid succession and creating the amusing illusion of a person who is jabbering."

Chattering teeth are only one of many classic gag devices to come out of Chicago, a hub of toy design for more than a century. Fake rubber vomit is another, conjured up in 1959. Goldfarb will go on to invent 800 toys and games. He soon leaves for California, but his partner, Marvin Glass, establishes a company that turns out a series of 1960s classics: Mouse Trap, Rock 'Em–Sock 'Em Robots, and Operation, created in 1962 when University of Illinois industrial design student John Spinello is assigned to design a toy. He develops a game using electric probes, then shows it to his grandfather, who works for Glass.

Earlier classic toys came from Chicago and environs. The Flat Iron Laundry on Halsted Street attracted business by giving away small white zinc charms to children of customers—cars and ships for boys, Scotty dogs and thimbles for girls, who wear them on bracelets. The company that made them, Strombecker Toys, manufactured trinkets that go into Cracker Jack boxes, and repurposed laundry charms—that flat iron, a top hat, a shoe, a cannon—became tokens moved around Monopoly boards.

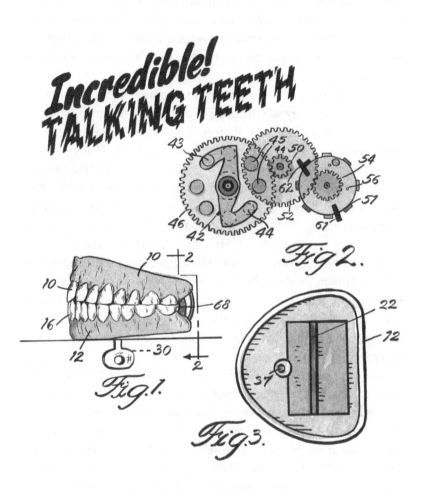

Incredible!
TALKING TEETH

43 45 44 50 54 56 51 61 52 62 46 42 44

Fig 2.

10 2 10 68 16 12 30 2 22 12 37

Fig.1.

Fig.3.

A. GOLDFARB

NOVELTY AND AMUSEMENT DEVICE

INVENTOR.

Adolph Goldfarb

April 19, 1861

The call by Gov. Richard Yates for 6,000 volunteers in response to the Confederate bombardment of Fort Sumter ignites Chicago. "The entire mass of the people are swollen with a sense of duty," notes this morning's edition of the *Tribune*, which has been an enthusiastic advocate for war. "They are alive to the fact that we are in a struggle for national existence."

All is noise and commotion in the city, drums and fifes and young men hurrying this way and that, desperate to find a company to join. Captain Sherman's "splendid" Battery of Flying Artillery marches to the train "as true as steel to the cause and in fighting trim." That evening Captain Charles Barker drills his 120 Chicago Dragoons at the Armory; 80 members of the Lincoln Rifles go through their paces as well. The Highland Guards' roster is full, so they declare that it is now "Company A" and start taking volunteers for Company B. Crowds of men watching the maneuvers are so thick they are told to "fall in or fall back."

Three and a half years later, with black crepe draping many doorways for fallen fathers, brothers, and sons, the city will have dramatically changed its attitude. In the face of new draft quotas, there will be mass protests and hundreds of men fleeing Chicago, many to Canada. *Tribune* editor Joseph Medill will petition Abraham Lincoln to excuse the city from its military obligation.

"Gentlemen," the president will reprimand, "Chicago has been the chief instrument in bringing this war on the country. . . . It is you who are largely responsible for making blood flow as it has. You called for war until we had it. You called for Emancipation and I have given it to you. Whatever you have asked for, you have had. Now you come here begging to be let off from the call for men, which I have made to carry out the war you have demanded. You ought to be ashamed of yourselves. I have a right to expect better things of you. Go home, and raise your 6,000 extra men. And you, Medill, you are acting like a coward. You and your *Tribune* have had more influence than any paper in the Northwest in making this war. You can influence great masses, and yet you cry to be spared at a moment when your cause is suffering. Go home and send us those men."

And they do.

April 20, 1951

Would you buy a car from a madman?

Earl "Madman" Muntz has already demonstrated the answer to that question: a resounding yes. The Elgin-born used-car dealer moved to Los Angeles before the war and became famous with billboards showing a cartoon of himself, cross-eyed, wearing a Napoleon hat and red long underwear.

His TV commercials—Muntz claims to have coined the term "TV," and named his daughter "Tee Vee"—feature him saying things like "I want to give them away. But Mrs. Muntz won't let me. She's CRAZY."

He didn't say which Mrs. Muntz; there were seven.

Now Muntz enters a new branch of the car industry, challenging consumers to buy a car *made* by a madman.

"EVANSTON AUTO PLANT TURNING OUT A CAR A DAY" reads a headline in today's *Tribune*, the story noting his latest caper. The car-a-day pace, if ever true, could not last long—only a few hundred Muntz Jets were manufactured from 1951 to 1954.

Yet the used-car salesman manages to turn out an attractive, high-tech, American sports car with ahead-of-its-time safety features. A padded dashboard, for one (extra important, perhaps, because the car comes with a built-in bar option). Since the car is called the "Jet," Muntz outfits it with a device that up to this point is only found in jet airplanes: seat belts. They were considered something of a joke.

Large carmakers notice the Jet, and other homegrown sports cars, and recognize a market. The year Madman Muntz will stop making sports cars, 1954, is the year Chevrolet will start, with its first full year producing Corvettes.

April 21, 1855

Sticking it to immigrants is nothing new. Levi T. Boone was elected mayor in March, heading up a coalition with the hard-to-argue-against official name "The Law and Order Party." But they really are the "Know-Nothings," an anti-immigrant, anti-Catholic, anti-liquor movement (as well as anti-slavery; even the most misguided are rarely entirely mistaken). They sweep into office thanks to low voter turnout—most Chicagoans are too busy working to vote—and because the objects of their scorn often are not yet citizens. Boone promised to use the law to cut back drinking, which might at first seem puzzling because he likes his glass of grog. What is unvoiced was the "among the Germans" part of his promise. Cut back drinking *among the Germans*. A good Protestant Chicagoan enjoys his brandy at home, in the parlor, as God intended, while rough Germans and even more loathsome Irish Catholics profane the Lord's Day by gathering in beer gardens and taverns and other low haunts. (This bias was not unique to Chicago; in 1851, the Illinois legislature banned the sale of less than a quart of wine or liquor, as well as the sale of alcohol for consumption on the premises.)

Boone and his city council hiked liquor-license fees from $50 to $300 while shortening their terms from one year to three months. He tripled the police force, hiring only native-born cops, and put them in uniform for the first time. Then he began to enforce the Sunday closing law.

Today's trials of tavern owners are before Judge Henry L. Rucker, itself a bad sign. Rucker is a member in good standing of the Washington Temperance Society. A crowd of several hundred brewers, tavern owners, and patrons gather to hear incendiary speeches, then march toward the courthouse, led by a fife and drum. Some are armed with cleavers or muskets.

They pack Rucker's courtroom. The judge prudently decides to adjourn for the day, and Boone tells the police to clear the building and the square. The mob repairs to the near Northwest Side to make use of the imperiled taverns, then returns about 3 p.m., now swelled to perhaps several thousand. Boone orders the Clark Street bridge swung open (the bridges then did not raise but pivoted on a central pier).

The bridge is eventually swung back, and the angry throng swarms across to the courthouse. About a dozen shots are fired at the police, none too accurately, except a double-barreled shotgun, which shatters the left arm of a police officer, George Hunt, requiring amputation. The gunman, Peter Martens, is shot down as he flees, on orders from Chicago's de facto chief of police.

Boone declares martial law, activating several volunteer militia groups, who clear the square with fixed bayonets and set up a pair of cannons on either side of the courthouse. There are 60 arrests.

Imbibers of all nationalities do not back down, and the city reconsiders the wisdom of its recent changes in policy. In June, an attempt at a temperance law will be soundly defeated, in part due to German and Irish Chicagoans awaking to their civic duty and voting.

April 22, 1872

Life is a long time, if you do it right. And though Alexander Robinson, who dies today, is not the 110 years old claimed on his headstone—more like his mid-80s—he is without question bound up in the origins of Chicago. The child of a Scottish trader and an Odawa woman, he spoke English and was friendly with settlers before the Battle of Fort Dearborn, helping convey survivors to safety. In gratitude, the 1829 Treaty of Prairie du Chien grants Chief Robinson, also known as Che-Che-Pin-Qua, or Winking Eye, two square miles by the Des Plaines River, in what is now Schiller Park. Part of his longevity is no doubt due to his rejection of alcohol, and he spoke at temperance meetings, where he would smash a bourbon bottle with a hatchet. His descendants will live on that land, in a home built by Native Americans with wooden pegs, until May 25, 1955, when it burns to the ground. To this day the 265-acre Robinson Woods is part of the Cook County Forest Preserve, and the remains of Robinson are buried there along with members of his family.

April 23, 1884

Before the nation began recoiling in horror at contaminated meat made in Chicago, it was frightening itself with tales of bad candy. Just how much of this was based on Victorian disapproval of sweets, journalistic sensation divorced from fact, or ignorant shock at benign artificial ingredients and standard industrial processes, and how much was based on actual adulteration, is hard to tell. But modern historians believe that headlines like "Candy Kills a Little Boy," "Poison in Christmas Candy," and "Candy Caused Death" do not necessarily prove the existence of actual victims. An 1888 *Tribune* story under the headline "Poison in Cheap Candy" is based entirely on the opinion of an "up-town confectioner" who seems to have his own motives. "I wouldn't let a child of mine eat a bit of candy that sold for less than 75 or 80 cents a pound," he confides. Nobody in the story has ingested or detected any poison.

Often these claims are from moralists, and it is difficult to imagine anyone eating the candies they describe: half clay, half machinery grease, spit, and the scrapings from workers' shoes.

As a hub where raw goods come in and finished goods go out, Chicago has been "the center of the candy universe" since the Civil War. Sixty-nine candy manufacturers gather today to form the National Confectioners Association, whose primary purpose is to sweeten the sour reputation of candy. Though ironically, their efforts to counteract the libels against their product also disseminate and preserve them. The NCA is still based in Chicago.

April 24, 1933

It is supposed to be a silent march. Five thousand teachers, stealthily advancing upon City Hall, which has been paying them for a year, not in cash but in nearly useless scrip. A partial cash payment April 15 does little to stop the gathering crisis.

The scrip are "tax warrants"—basically IOUs to large corporations, such as banks, which are not making good on them. Adding to the already steaming public hostility.

At noon, the mass of tight-lipped teachers, to the surprise of the line of police facing them, suddenly split into five groups, each heading in a different direction. Soon their destinations become clear: banks. The First National. The Harris Trust and Savings. City National, Northern Trust, and Continental-Illinois.

They are silent no more.

"Pay us! Pay us!" the teachers chant, swarming past guards, rampaging inside the cool marble interiors. Desks are overturned, inkwells dashed against walls. At City National, teachers union president John Fewkes demands to see the chairman of the board—and former US vice president—Charles Dawes.

"Hey, Charley, give us our money!" one teacher cries. Dawes comes out, and is heckled "so unmercifully that he exclaimed, 'to hell with troublemakers!'"

When school begins next week, the teachers will be paid. Not all they are due. But something. In cash.

April 25, 1917

Letters pour into the newspaper office in advance of May 15, which the *Chicago Defender* has dubbed the official day of the Great Northern Drive. The paper is urging a million Blacks to leave the brutality of the South and escape to the North, to freedom and dignity. Those eager to do just that write in seeking encouragement and information. One letter, from a young woman in Mobile, Alabama, seems to imagine train cars are being sent to fetch them:

"Sir," she begins.

I was reading in that paper about the Colored race and while reading it I seen in it where cars would be here for the 15 of May. . . . Will you be so kind as to let me know where they are coming to and I will be glad to know because I am a poor woman and have a husband and five children living and three dead one single and two twin girls six months old today and my husband can hardly make bread for them in Mobile. This is my native home but it is not fit to live in just as the *Chicago Defender* say it says the truth and my husband only gets $1.50 a day and pays $7.50 a month for house rent and can hardly feed me and his self and children. I am the mother of 8 children 25 years old and I want to get out of this dog hold because I don't know what I am raising them up for in this place and I want to get to Chicago where I know they will be raised and my husband crazy to get there because he know he can get more to raise his children and will you please let me know where the cars is going to stop to so that he can come where he can take care of me and my children. He get there a while and then he can send for me. I heard they wasn't coming here so I sent to find out and he can go and meet them at the place they are going to and go from there to Chicago. No more at present. Hoping to hear from you soon from your needed and worried friend.

The South claws at the workers it has terrorized for so long, trying to stop them from leaving, arresting them on train platforms, warning them they would freeze up north, where the reception is indeed sometimes chilly. "Black Man, Stay South!" reads the headline of one *Tribune* editorial. Too late. "The Exodus" has begun—seven million Blacks leave the South between 1916 and 1970, the era of the Great Migration. Half a million come to Chicago.

April 26, 1973

Two hundred traders from the Chicago Board of Trade crowd its windowless members' lounge next to the trading room on the fourth floor, a collection of "speculators, hopeless optimists, and dyed-in-the-wool entrepreneurialists." A bell rings, and the Chicago Board of Options Exchange begins trading options on 16 equities, the first trade being on the price of Xerox in July. Seats on the CBOE that cost $10,000 yesterday cost $25,000 today.

They are trading what used to be referred to as "puts"—the ability to sell a certain stock at a certain time for a certain price—and "calls," the right to buy one.

Their inaugural day is welcomed officially by Gov. Dan Walker, and unofficially by a lawsuit filed in federal court by the Department of Justice. Not for what the CBOE does, but for its fee structure, which fixes commissions from $25 to $65 on each block trade. The feds feel this is restraint of trade. The start is slow—banks are reluctant to enter the options market. There are 911 calls on 16 stocks that first day. You can invest not only in how a certain stock will be doing in a year but in whole indexes, buying shares in the Dow Jones going down, for instance. Eventually the practice grows. The CBOE—called the Cboe Global Markets since 2017—will see the wisdom of the Justice Department perspective. Transaction fees are now closer to $1 per trade, which still works out, since there are over a billion trades a year.

April 27, 1959

Les Ballets Africains begins its run at the Blackstone Theater. At first Lt. Edward O'Malley, head of the Police Censor Board, said the dancers from Guinea who perform bare-chested, both male and female, may do so on opening night while he and two experts observe and form their conclusions. "It isn't our privilege to pre-adjudicate matters of this sort," he said. "Nudity of itself does not constitute obscenity."

But his boss, police commissioner Timothy J. O'Connor, over-rules him, pointing out that he has already written a letter to the show's producers demanding they adhere to community standards during their 17 performances. Those standards require that "a definite, adequate attire should be worn, which includes that the breasts of the females be covered."

The *Sun-Times* promptly sends a reporter to the Cabana Club, the Silver Frolics, and the 606 Club, which seem to be located in a different community, as their dancers routinely expose on their stages what cannot be exposed onstage at the Blackstone.

"How come?" the paper wonders, with casual glee. The police hedge, the dancers perform in net bras, and the show is well received. In Chicago's defense, New York City made the same demands. Boston, however, manages to let the dancers perform undraped. Yet somehow the city does not crumble.

April 28, 1919

"Does anyone in this congregation accuse me of disloyalty?" Rabbi Emil G. Hirsch is quoted asking, from the pulpit at Temple Sinai, 46th and Grand Blvd., in today's *Tribune*. He stepped back, folds his arms. Silence from 2,000 people. "Under the false and malicious accusations made against me, I spent many nights without a wink of sleep. I walked the streets of Chicago, looking back of me, wondering whether I would see a mob which would put a rope around my neck and string me up to a lamp post."

What has the rabbi done? It's complicated. Like many German Americans, Hirsch supported Germany early in World War I and tried to bring his people along with him.

"Jews all over the world, with the exception of the Spanish Jews, are with Germany in this war," he had said in December 1914. That made the pivot Americans took when the United States entered the war in 1917 a little harder for Hirsch. As did his fluency in German—he speaks 16 languages and teaches at the University of Chicago—and his nine relatives currently serving with the German military.

By war's end, Temple Sinai was flying a "service flag" out front, with a star for every member in uniform. American uniform, that is.

But as war fervor grew, calls from Hirsch's own congregation for him to resign continued, especially from parents with boys in the service. Dissent that lingered past the Armistice last November.

The story in the *Tribune* today is headlined "HIRSCH DEFENDS LOYALTY FROM TEMPLE PULPIT." It's running on a Monday because the sermon was given on Sunday, the rabbi having previously canceled Saturday services. Hirsch is a leader in the Reform movement, which hopes that worship on Sundays will help Jews fit in better with American society. They do, but assimilation thins their ranks with an efficiency oppression could never approach.

April 29, 1983

"Every mayor begins anew," says Harold Washington, in his inaugural address, wishing it weren't so, wishing the first permanent resident of Chicago, Haitian-born Jean Baptiste Point du Sable, "had written a book about how to be a Mayor of a vast city like ours, a repository of wisdom that had been handed down from Mayor to Mayor for all these years."

Maybe then, Washington says, he'd have something to go on. Otherwise, "there is no blueprint for the future."

Of course, du Sable wasn't actually mayor. There wasn't anything to be mayor of. He operated an isolated trading post in a sandy swamp in the late 1700s, surrounded by Potawatomi, the economics of which are fairly simple. As valuable as his memoirs no doubt would be, historically, it's not as if his insight would be of immense practical value to those running the modern metropolis.

Rather, Washington is pointing out that the first non-native resident of Chicago was, like him, a Black man facing new challenges without much guidance. Like every mayor to follow, Washington starts his administration in a deep hole, worse than people know. The school system is not $100 million in the red. It's double that. The transportation system is also facing a $200 million shortfall next year with no solution in sight.

Beginning Monday, he promises, there will be a freeze in all city hiring and raises. Executives will take pay cuts, including the mayor's office.

The only comfort is that things have been worse in Chicago, at least once before. "The only greater challenge in our history in Chicago was 110 years ago when Mayor Joseph Medill looked over a city burned to the ground," Washington says, "and called for an enormous outpouring of civic spirit and resources to make the city new." That worked then. Maybe it'll work again.

April 30, 1916

"Can't come in!" shouts the sweaty doorman about 2:30 Sunday morning, as dozens of members of the Anti-Saloon League try to descend upon a boisterous 31st Street dive called Schiller's Cafe. "Wait till some of the others come out."

They eventually get in, but there is little chance to preach to the damned. "It was impossible for anyone to be heard," the *Chicago Herald* will report, because "the shriek of women's drunken laughter rivaled the blatant scream of the imported New Orleans Jass Band which never seemed to stop playing."

This may be the first appearance in a newspaper of the name of a new type of music being played in Chicago. Next February, the band will record "Livery Stable Blues," labeled a "Fox Trot" but considered the first jazz record. The word will start to appear in ads. "Jass Band Records for the First Time on Victor Records," offered by the George R. Bent Company, 214 S. Wabash, which sells records "on approval," meaning, if you didn't like them, you could mail them back.

By fall 1917, "jazz," with two Zs, is both a word and a craze, and in headlines on the front page of the *Chicago Daily News*, reporting on a sheet music copyright infringement lawsuit: "DISCOVERER OF JAZZ ELUCIDES IN COURT." Dominic LaRocca, "The Jazz Kid," and leader of the New Orleans Jass Band, resplendent in patent leather shoes, a purple striped shirt, and green tunic, lays claim in federal court to the authorship of "Livery Stable Blues."

"May I ask," Judge George A. Carpenter will inquire, "what are the blues?"

"The blues is jazz," LaRocca testifies. "The jazz is blues."

The judge will take to heart the testimony of former bandmate Alcide Nunez, who tells the court: "Nobody wrote the 'Livery Stables Blues.' Naw. Nobody writes any of that stuff." Using that logic, the judge decides that the song is in the public domain and cannot be copyrighted, since it doesn't represent an original work.

May 1, 1893

Dawn brings dark clouds and "cheerless drizzle." A massive opening day crowd nevertheless braves the fog and muddy pathways at the fairgrounds, where everything is not quite ready. At 12:10 p.m., just a little late, President Grover Cleveland presses a golden telegraph key, perhaps causing fountains to jet and flags to unfurl, steam whistles to sing and 200 white doves to be released. (It was either him pressing the key, or the man nearby waving his hat at the exact same moment.) The sun breaks through, luncheon is served, then Cleveland and his entourage enter the enormous Manufactures Building at the newly opened World's Columbian Exposition. They head directly to the Russian section, where all they see is a sign reading "RUSSIA EXHIBIT DELAYED ON ACCOUNT OF THE ICE BLOCKADE IN THE BALTIC SEA."

Meanwhile, an older white-haired gentleman is spied walking alone down Columbian Avenue: Frederick Douglass, born into slavery.

The fair will run six months, draw 26 million visitors, and be the transformative event in the history of Chicago, second only to the Great Fire, 22 years earlier. It introduces the world to marvels from the Ferris wheel—the idea being "Let's make an Eiffel Tower that spins"—to the moving walkway to Cracker Jack. Like Douglass, the future doesn't always draw much notice. In a corner of the Transportation Building, lost amid the giant steam engines and massive dynamos and model steamships and bridges, is a spindly Daimler quadricycle, the first four-wheeled, gasoline-powered automobile to be displayed in public in the United States.

The newspapers have fun with the indignities suffered by Mayor Carter Harrison that first day—arriving to the ceremony "conspicuously late," stuck in an elevator, nudged aside from the presidential party, then chasing Cleveland across the fairgrounds. At one point Mayor Harrison has the president cornered at the Administration Building, according to one account too delicious to be consumed without a grain of salt.

"Which way did President Cleveland go?" Harrison pants at a guard.

"Up beyant there," the guard replies.

"Then I want to get up beyant there," demands the mayor.

"Who might you be?"

"Carter Harrison."

"Who's he?"

"The mayor of Chicago!" yells Harrison.

"Then ye can't git in," concludes the guard.

May 2, 1950

The story in today's *Sun-Times* is brief, an AP report noting that the musical *South Pacific* has won a Pulitzer Prize, as has the *Chicago Daily News*. Samuel Flagg Bemis won for his biography of John Quincy Adams. Editorial, cartoon, and photographic winners are also noted. The last sentence: "Gwendolyn Brooks, for the best poetry, 'Annie Allen.'"

Almost as if they didn't *know*. Which is odd, because the future Illinois poet laureate was phoned last night by Jack Star, a *Sun-Times* reporter.

"Congratulations," Star said.

"On what?" Brooks replied.

"You've just won the Pulitzer Prize for poetry," Star told the first African American to win the honor.

"I didn't!" screamed Brooks, who is then sick to her stomach—she had just finished dinner. Brooks backed out of plans to take her son Henry to the movies, instead headed to her parents' house to listen to the news on the radio. Arthur Godfrey mentioned her name!

She couldn't listen to the radio at home because the power was out at 9134 S. Wentworth Avenue, a modest residence in the Princeton Park homes. Her husband Henry Blakely, a skilled poet himself, is having trouble at the auto shop where he works.

Brooks worried about the press arriving to find her lights out. The shame of it. But this morning, when the world comes knocking at her door—such as the telegram from Dwight D. Eisenhower, president of Columbia University, telling her she has won—the power is back on. Like magic. Like a miracle.

May 3, 1932

"You'd think Mussolini was passin' through," quips Al Capone, seeing the crush of newspapermen and photographers—some of whom light up the sky with aerial flares—as he leaves the Cook County Jail for the last time.

"You got a bum break, Al!" someone calls from the crowd. "Good-bye, Al!" others shout. Capone, chewing gum, dressed in a dark blue three-piece suit and new light hat, tries to smile, but is visibly crestfallen as he's hustled into a car and the motorcade takes off, speeding up California to Ogden, down Jackson to Clark, then south to Dearborn Street Station, sirens shrieking, pedestrians leaping out of the way.

At the station, between his 255-pound bulk and his leg irons, Capone has trouble getting out of the car.

The most famous mobster ever is handcuffed to Victor Morici, a frightened young auto thief. They pass hundreds of onlookers, including a few of his criminal associates, jostling to catch a glimpse. His family said their good-byes at the jail.

"Damn it, c'mon, let's get out of this," Capone says to Morici, urging him forward. Capone keeps his hands in his pockets, so the cameras won't see the handcuffs.

Capone's transfer to Atlanta instead of Leavenworth to serve his 11-year sentence on tax evasion is supposed to be a closely guarded secret. So of course everyone in Chicago knows.

"I'm glad to get started," says Capone, climbing aboard the train, along with guards, police, treasury agents, and newsmen. Asked if he is feeling down, Capone shrugs and grimaces, replying, "How would you feel if you had 11 years staring you in the face?"

Promptly at 11:30 p.m., the Dixie Flyer pulls out of the station, as scheduled, taking Al Capone away from Chicago for the last time. Though, of course, Chicago will never really be rid of him.

May 4, 1886

Nobody sees who throws the bomb. Or at least nobody who will ever tell. Just as well, because the arbiters of justice do not actually care. Revolution is to blame. Radicalism is to blame. The hand that pens the explosive word and the hand that throws the dynamite bomb are one and the same.

Plus, those guilty of putting incendiary words to paper are easier to apprehend.

Someone led the unrest that has roiled Chicago for days, as thousands of workers went on strike, demanding an eight-hour day. Bloodshed the day before at the McCormick Reaper Works. Police fired into the crowd, as is their habit. A protest was called for today. "REVENGE! WORKING MEN, TO ARMS!!!" reads the notorious flier. "Your masters sent out their bloodhounds, the police; they killed six of your brothers at McCormick's this afternoon."

Mayor Carter Harrison instructs the police to hold back and let the workers meet. He is there himself, on horseback, after 9 p.m., making sure his police behave. He hears August Spies, author of the "REVENGE!!!" screed and editor of the German labor paper *Arbeiter-Zeitung*, talk to the 2,000 gathered at Haymarket Square. Albert Parsons climbs atop the hay wagon next, giving what strikes the mayor as "a very timid speech." The mayor heads home.

With Harrison gone, the police move in to break up the crowd. The bomb explodes in their midst: 60 are wounded; eight die. The labor movement is also hurt. Labor meetings are banned. The newspapers thunder against foreigners. Hundreds of suspects are arrested. Without any clue who threw the bomb, authorities accuse Spies, Parsons, and six others of causing the bloodshed through their words, which certainly are tinged with calls for violence. Eight radical lives in exchange for eight policemen. That's justice.

Seven are condemned to die. Four will hang on November 11; one will cheat the hangman, killing himself by setting off a blasting cap in his mouth. In 1893, newly elected Gov. John Altgeld will pardon the two surviving condemned men and the man sentenced to prison. He'll do so knowing it will make him, as he told Clarence Darrow, "a dead man politically." He will be excoriated in the press, which views Altgeld, born in Germany, as a dangerous radical himself. The *Tribune* will thunder the governor had not "a drop of true American blood in his veins. He does not reason like an American, does not feel like one, and consequently does not behave like one." Altgeld will not be re-elected.

May 5, 1905

Three hundred issues roll off the presses, at a cost of $13.75—on credit. Produced in an office with room enough for a card table, a borrowed kitchen chair, and a secondhand typewriter. By a man named Robert Sengstacke Abbott, who is publisher, editor, and circulation manager. And reporter, having spent his last quarter on a pencil and notebook. The failed lawyer is certainly no businessman: selling every copy at 2 cents an issue would mean a loss of $7.75, the difference being made up by paid advertising.

In theory.

Nobody thinks to save a copy—that won't happen until the fall. But the story of its name is preserved: Abbott said he wants this newspaper to take African Americans and "wake them up" and to stand between a racist nation and its would-be prey, to be "a defender of the race."

Call it the *Defender*, then, a friend suggests, and Abbott does. For more than a hundred years, the newspaper will not only report on, comfort, scold, document, celebrate, and mourn an enormous community that the white press is generally blind to, but be crucial to building that community. The city that Chicago will become owes a great deal to the *Defender*. Many Blacks escaping the Jim Crow South in the Great Migration will come to Chicago instead of Cleveland or Detroit or Milwaukee because the *Defender* is here, calling them home.

May 6, 2004

Jim Loewenberg, 68, is a longtime real estate developer. He built the identical quadruplets of Presidential Towers as well as some 35,000 units worth of similarly nondescript high-rise apartments. Lately, he's commissioned five of the six planned buildings for the 28-acre Lakeshore East development downtown.

Jeanne Gang, 40, has a growing reputation in architectural circles despite the fact that exactly one building she has designed has been constructed: the Starlight Theater in Rockford.

Fate seats them together tonight at the Mid-America Club, where Harvard alumni have gathered to hear star architect Frank Gehry speak—his Pritzker Pavilion, with its billowing stainless-steel mane, will open in July. Beforehand, the oldish developer and the youngish architect make conversation.

"We talked about architecture," Gang will later recall.

In six months, Loewenberg will ask Gang if she'll take a crack at that last Lakeshore East building, maybe come up with something a little out of the ordinary.

She does.

Condos are sold by their location, like all real estate, but also by their view. Gang realizes that if she bulges out the terraces, she can greatly expand what residents can see from their balconies. Plus, the irregular balconies will break up the wind. Gang's Aqua Tower is celebrated for its undulating surface, a visual effect evoking cascading water, all accomplished by playing with the same concrete balconies adorning 100,000 buildings whose architects aren't visionary geniuses. And Loewenberg's career of building profitable if soulless structures is capped with a magnificent finale.

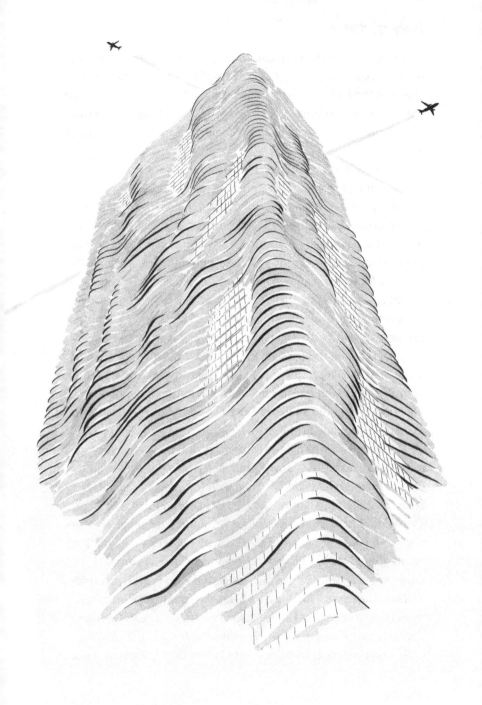

May 7, 1902

The *Yakima* is stuck. At 11 a.m., the coal-carrying steamship, one of the largest vessels plying the Great Lakes, grounds itself on the crown of the LaSalle Street tunnel—built 30 years earlier, the tunnel rises so quickly to street level it leaves a hump in the river bottom just beyond the riverbank, a threat to navigation. The ship cannot move.

Chaos ensues. The bridge at Wells Street pivots on a center pier, meaning that not only is traffic on a major street downtown utterly cut off, but 150 people are trapped in mid-river on the open center span. It can't close to release them. Meanwhile, boat traffic has trouble passing; it too snarls, between the small boats ferrying those stranded on the bridge to shore and tugs trying to move the *Yakima*. A switch engine on the riverside Chicago & Northwestern freight tracks adds her might to the effort, the train's huge driver wheels spinning uselessly, spraying sparks. The Clark Street bridge becomes clogged with gapers, delighting as the emphatic language of the men trying to aid the *Yakima* drifts through the heavy springtime air. The ship is finally freed, only to immediately ground again. The problem radiates outward. Navigation is delayed as far as Lockport, where the locks are closed to raise the river level, hoping to float the grounded ship.

This goes on for two days. During which time the Sanitary Board meets and decides the path of prudence is to replace all center-pier bridges on the river's south branch with trunnion bascule bridges: at Lake, Washington, Madison, Adams, Jackson, and six other streets. These are short, hardy drawbridges ("trunnion" is French for cannon; both pivot on similar stout pins) with counterweights sinking below ground level. Chicago will eventually have 32 bascule bridges, more than any other city in the world. And zero center-pier bridges.

Their inspiration is Chicago's first bascule bridge, which will open in three weeks at Cortland Avenue. It's still there. Another ship eventually comes along and yanks the *Yakima* free. It will cruise as far north as Division Street before becoming stuck again.

May 8, 1921

Today is the first Sunday that the Field Museum of Natural History is open and so, because it is a Sunday, the museum is free to all Chicagoans. It's also free on Tuesdays and Thursdays. Otherwise, it costs a quarter to marvel at the wonders within.

But the Field—so named thanks to an $8 million bequest from department-store magnate Marshall Field—does more than show off dinosaur bones and Egyptian mummies, stuffed birds and Eskimo kayaks, a whale skeleton and a Roman bathtub. Its scientific staff scours the globe for treasures.

The doors first opened Monday, "marked by no formality or celebration," something of a tradition—when the original Field Columbian Museum opened in 1894, it was done simply because "Chicago had had quite enough of glory" after the World's Columbian Exposition. It was decided that the collection should not scatter after the fair, though finding a home was a 12-year struggle. The Field came so close to being built in Jackson Park that the steel and marble were delivered to the site. An Illinois Supreme Court ruling kept it out of Grant Park proper. The idea of putting it on an island in the lake was briefly considered. The museum ended up at the base of what was then 12th Street on "made land" on the lakefront, aka landfill—a legal dodge sidestepping the clause in the municipal code that the lakefront be kept "forever free and clear." Construction started in 1915, was supposed to take three years, but took almost six.

The building, modeled on the Erechtheum at the Acropolis, was constructed of Georgia marble. The collection had been transferred to the new building at what would be Roosevelt and McFetridge in an unusual fashion: the Illinois Central Railroad laid spur tracks connecting the two buildings to their lines: 321 boxcars and flat cars, plus another 350 loads on five-ton trucks.

While controversy will attend specific depictions of peoples, over the next century the Field will be doing Darwin's work, nudging humanity into the realm of rocks, plants, and animals, wedding the study of anthropology to the fields of botany, zoology, and geology.

May 9, 1937

So how did gospel music ever make it out of church? Radio helps, with shows like WSBC's *Quest for Choirs*. Then there are public appearances, like today, as the Progressive Community Church Choir, Miss Edna Winters, directress, sings at the big labor rally at DuSable High School, at 49th and State.

Speaking on the National Labor Relations Act, sit-down strikes, and how they relate to Black workers is A. Philip Randolph, president of the Brotherhood of Sleeping Car Porters, the first Black union chartered by the American Federation of Labor. The Brotherhood and Randolph are important in the rise of civil rights, not only providing good-paying jobs to Black workers, but helping them organize throughout the country (and, not incidentally, distributing the *Defender* by hand in southern towns that bar it from the mail).

Randolph is in the midst of negotiations with the Pullman Company that will finally, finally bear fruit this August, with a signed contract offering improved working conditions and a raise. And it only took 12 years of constant effort, since the Brotherhood first got a foothold in Pullman in 1925.

May 10, 1894

The pair of lions guarding the entrance to the Art Institute of Chicago are unveiled. They are similar but not the same: the lion north of the entrance is "on the prowl," according to sculptor Edward Kemeys, while its companion is "in an attitude of defiance," which is harder to render. "The most difficult I have attempted," says Kemeys, America's first professional "animalier," or artist who specializes in animals. The Civil War vet honed his craft by traveling out West, where he shot and dissected animals to better understand their bones and muscle structure. His work was shown in Paris and at the Art Institute at its earlier location at Michigan and Van Buren.

The two felines, cast in Chicago at the American Bronze Founding Company, were considered symbolic of the city in the 73 years before the Picasso was unveiled. They also became de facto PR representatives for the museum, which will drape them in Christmas wreaths, or crown them in Bears or Blackhawks helmets or baseball caps (during crosstown battles, having a pair oriented the way they are comes in handy: the north lion sporting Cubs blue, the south lion rooting for the Sox). During the COVID-19 pandemic, the lions will wear city-flag surgical masks and, this being Chicago, one of the masks will be promptly stolen. These decorations would invariably make the papers, TV, and other media—the lions have their own twitter account, @ChicagoLions.

May 11, 1988

It is supposed to be a private, invitation-only show, a three-day fellowship exhibit before David K. Nelson receives his degree in painting from the School of the Art Institute. Half a dozen paintings, hung in a hallway for 72 hours.

One painting doesn't make it to lunch, however. "Mirth and Girth" depicts Harold Washington, Chicago's late mayor, who died the previous November, in lingerie. A white bra, panties, garter, and stockings.

It conceivably could have gone unnoticed. But today is Wednesday. The city council meets on Wednesdays, which means an elite group of the most entitled and judgment-impaired individuals in the city are assembled seven blocks away. Someone drops a dime on the painting.

The city council immediately passes a resolution threatening to cut off funds to the Art Institute, which had no role in the display. Unsatisfied, aldermen storm the school. Alderman Ernest Jones takes the painting down and turns it to face the wall. A student rehangs the painting.

A trio of aldermen—Bobby Rush, Dorothy Tillman, and Alan Streeter—arrive. Screaming ensues. Tillman, famous for her large hats, threatens to burn the painting on the spot. Streeter, demonstrating a tenuous grasp on the concept of offense toward groups other than his own, declares to the media that the painting is obviously the work of a Jewish artist. It isn't.

At one point nine aldermen crowd into school president Anthony Jones's office. Police superintendent LeRoy Martin orders the painting taken into custody, and the 20th century wanes the way it waxed in 1913: with City of Chicago officialdom convulsed over a painting, with ascendant racial sensitivity stepping in for dwindling sexual prudery.

The aldermen guarantee that, instead of being relegated to the obscurity of Nelson's garage, the painting becomes known around the world, making it literally into a federal case. The trio will argue that they were trying to avoid a riot. That won't fly.

"The aldermen cannot be permitted to defend their actions by reference to such unrest within the black community as their own lawless, provocative, and publicity-mongering actions may have stirred up," Judge Richard Posner will conclude, ruling against them.

The city will hand over $95,000 to end the case. Which might seem not a bad payday for a 23-year-old novice artist who gets to keep the painting. But Nelson will give the money to the American Civil Liberties Union to help cover its litigation costs.

May 12, 1926

The *St. Joseph* goes first, rattling down the cinders at 6:05 a.m. The *Chicago* follows, rising into the sky shortly before seven. Of course airplanes have names, like ships; a general air of the nautical suffuses the new industry of aviation.

Though "industry" is a tad grandiose for what is going on here. Right now the primary commercial user of aircraft is Uncle Sam. The two Curtiss Carrier Pigeons making their debut runs are designed to post office specifications to carry the US mail, with holds capable of carrying a thousand pounds and gas tanks big enough to make the flight from Chicago to New York without refueling.

Not an issue today. The two planes are inaugurating airmail service from Chicago to Dallas, with eight stops on the route between "the Maywood flying field" and Love Field. (In 1926, places where planes land tend to be called "fields" because many are little more than that. "Airport," like "port," often describes a general area, as in businessmen "boosting Chicago as an air-port.")

Congratulatory letters from Mayor William Dever to the nine other mayors are carried within the 445 pounds of mail, roughly 20,000 letters, aboard the two planes. At St. Joseph, Missouri, Mayor Louis V. Stigall will be waiting to christen the *St. Joseph* with a bottle of champagne, again following maritime tradition. In 1931, the owner of these four mail planes, National Air Transport, will change its name to United Air Lines after merging with Boeing and Pratt & Whitney. But Congress will pass a law barring companies that make planes from also running airlines, and they'll break apart. United Airlines will stick around. Boeing will depart for the West Coast, but will eventually tire of life in rainy Seattle and return its headquarters to Chicago in 2001, Boeing executives saying that one reason they chose Chicago over, say, Dallas, is because of the quality of the opera here.

May 13, 1894

"Half a loaf is better than no bread," Rev. E. Christian Oggel, the pastor at the beautiful Greenstone Church, tells his flock. "No strike for higher wages should be undertaken without reasonable hope for success."

It is not just the wages, lowered during the brutal depression winter of 1893–1894, that caused workers at the Pullman Palace Car factory to set down their tools two days ago. They live in houses and shop at stores owned by George Pullman, who slashed their wages 20 percent while keeping rents and prices the same.

Still, a strike is ill advised, Oggel insists, "precipitated by outsiders," and will not win public sympathy. He points out that he, like they, saw his wages cut. And he is as disappointed as they are that Pullman didn't cut rents as well. But these are rational decisions made by heads wiser than their own.

"This is not a matter of sentiment but of business," he says, noting that therefore, "any hope for higher wages is doomed for disappointment."

Nothing keeps them here, Rev. Oggel continues. They could look elsewhere. But they will never find a more welcoming home than their Pullman idyll. Never. "There is no industrial community in the world where men can do better than here."

The world is now connected—that's what railroads do—and this strike is not just local workers at a sleeper car factory. They are also members of the American Railway Union, which will support the strike by refusing to handle Pullman cars, and by sending their dynamic president, Eugene V. Debs, to join the fight.

May 14, 1912

Ed Burroughs never set eyes on Africa. He never saw a lion or a gorilla. What the stationery salesman did was visit the Chicago Public Library, where he read about Stanley and Livingstone's African adventures. Not much, but enough to pen this "damn-phool tale," as he later put it, for which he holds scant hope. But a man with two young children needs money.

So he sits in his Near West Side apartment and finishes his improbable story, writing in black fountain pen:

> "I don't know," said Tarzan quietly. "My mother was an ape, and of course she couldn't tell me anything about it, and I never knew who my father was."

> The End.

He underlines the last two words, then signs his name, the date, and the time, 10:25 p.m.

Edgar Rice Burroughs will send the tale off to *The All-Story Magazine*, which accepts it, paying him $700 and featuring "Tarzan of the Apes" on the cover of its October issue. Publication in magazine form first allows Burroughs to correct certain gaffes—there are no tigers in Africa—before publication as a best-selling book in 1914. Burroughs will eventually see at least one living gorilla: Bushman, the famous resident of the Lincoln Park Zoo, whom he'll visit in 1939.

May 15, 2006

It wasn't the first choice. That was Jeff Koons's 150-foot steel and glass playground slide, which proved too difficult to construct. Nor is it in the original location: that was Lurie Garden, to the southeast. Plus, it's nearly two years late—the park around it opened in 2004. Buffing was more time consuming than originally thought. More expensive too. The thing ends up costing $23 million, way over its $9 million initial estimate.

Chicagoans casually discard its given name—the airy "Cloud Gate"—preferring to call it something earthy, literal, and midwestern: The Bean.

Still, this second-place, dislocated, late, over-budget, misnamed blob nails the most important quality when it is officially unveiled today at 11 a.m.: it's perfect, framing the city and its visitors in one undulating, 100-ton, highly polished icon. Even the artist is surprised.

"I didn't know how powerful it would be," says Anish Kapoor, at the dedication of the sculpture that is immediately embraced, beloved, and symbolic of the city today. The Picasso sculpture has been in that role for 40 years; now it is nudged to the side, where it joins the Art Institute lions and the 1893 World's Fair statue of Columbia as former Chicago icons now half sunk in the bog of the hazy past.

May 16, 1988

There was no gun. No note. No bundles of cash plucked from drawers. In fact, the First National Bank of Chicago isn't even aware that it has been robbed until about 8 a.m., when someone in the finance department, reviewing computer printouts, notices "a substantial overdraft" in one account. Then another. Then another.

Three accounts, belonging to United Airlines, Merrill Lynch, and Brown-Forman, totaling $69.1 million, were transferred using stolen security codes from First National to two New York banks, on their way to accounts in Austria. Another day, prosecutors will later say, and the conspirators might have gotten away with it. As it was, they didn't get a cent. Seven men will be arrested, including two bank employees. The New York banks will send the money back and mastermind Armand Moore will be sentenced to 10 years in prison.

May 17, 1900

L. Frank Baum had great success last year with *Father Goose: His Book*, illustrated by W. W. Denslow. But the George M. Hill Company, like all publishers, is out to make a profit. It isn't about to take a bath paying for full-color printing plates for the duo's latest effort, *The Wizard of Oz*.

Undeterred, Baum and Denslow foot the full-color printing bill themselves. Which is why, two days after his 44th birthday, the author is personally pulling the first pages that come off the presses and sewing them together, creating a debut copy he will present to his sister.

The book will go on sale in August and be a huge success. Two years later the first adaptation, a musical, will be staged in Chicago. Baum and Denslow are splitting proceeds 50/50, but quarrel over the production, and generally over which of them is responsible for the book's popularity. The 13 sequels Baum writes will be illustrated by others.

May 18, 1860

Convinced that gathering in an eastern city would "run a big chance of losing the West," Republican officials picked Chicago for their 1860 national convention—the first of 25 political conventions from both major parties that will be held here. The city is seen as a symbol of "audacity"; its population of 109,000 is triple what it was 10 years earlier. After two days of speeches and formalities, 500 delegates, 900 journalists, and thousands of the curious converge on the Wigwam, an enormous log hall erected at Lake and Market Street, now Wacker Drive, for today's key nomination battle.

Abraham Lincoln is not among them. "I am a little too much a candidate to stay home but not quite enough a candidate to go," Lincoln supposedly tells his friends in Springfield. New York senator William Seward leads the first two ballots, but favorite sons keep him from securing the nomination. As they drop out, the thwarted candidates throw their loyalties to Lincoln, thanks in part to a flurry of quid pro quo deals that Lincoln had flatly forbidden. The rail splitter's savvy backers simply ignore him. On the third ballot, boosted by supporters "recruited for their lung power," Lincoln creeps within two votes of Seward.

"If you can throw the Ohio delegation to Lincoln, Chase can have anything he wants," *Chicago Tribune* publisher Joseph Medill tells the head of the state delegation, who immediately stands up and announces a shift of four votes for Lincoln. There is a moment of surprised silence—you can hear the scratching of pencils and the click of telegraph keys. Then pandemonium. "Imagine all the hogs ever slaughtered in Cincinnati giving their death squeals together," an Ohio journalist writes.

"City wild with excitement," one supporter telegraphs Lincoln.

"Do not come to Chicago," another insists.

"Don't come here," warns a third.

They are afraid, were Lincoln on the scene, he might learn of their under-the-table maneuvers and try to undo them. They don't want Honest Abe's honesty to ruin his election chances. Perhaps they worry unnecessarily; as president, Lincoln will be good to their word, making Ohio powerhouse Salmon P. Chase first his secretary of the treasury, then chief justice of the Supreme Court. Not a bad return for an investment of four votes.

May 19, 1875

A delivery boy carrying eight pairs of lace curtains—total cost $549.83—arrives at the Grand Pacific Hotel, at LaSalle and Jackson, and steps into an elevator. Along with the hotel manager, Samuel Turner, two policemen, and Leonard Swett, an attorney and former adviser to Abraham Lincoln, bearing a warrant for the arrest of Mary Todd Lincoln, the president's widow. The five arrive at her door and knock. The policemen wait in the hall.

She is surprised to see them, and worries about the state of her hair.

"Never mind your hair, Mrs. Lincoln," says Swett. "I have some bad news for you."

She grasps what this is about.

"You mean to say I am crazy, then, do you?"

"Yes, I regret to say, that is what all your friends think."

"I am much obliged to you," says Mrs. Lincoln. "But I am abundantly able to take care of myself. Where is my son Robert? I want him to come here."

It is Robert Lincoln who that morning convinced a judge to sign the papers. The hearing is at 2 p.m. "I have no doubt my mother is insane," young Lincoln will say in court. "She has long been a source of great anxiety to me."

Of course being trouble to your son and being mentally ill are two very different things, and historians will long discuss whether Mary Todd Lincoln was indeed deranged, or suffering from a physical malady. The assassination of her husband is not the only trauma she has suffered over the past decade; she was also in Chicago during the Great Fire of 1871. No question she is deeply unhappy, complaining bitterly, "purchasing trunkloads of drapes to hang over nonexistent windows." Mrs. Lincoln will be committed to Cook County Hospital but allowed to stay at a private sanitarium in Batavia.

May 20, 1882

Amateur productions do not, as a rule, enter history.

Especially plays performed in a blend of Danish and Norwegian.

But Helga Bluhme Jensen is the daughter of an actor and theater manager in Denmark, where she had great success on stage in the 1870s. In 1879, she divorced her husband, remarried, and moved to Chicago, where she started a restaurant.

Today she stars as Mrs. Alving in the Norwegian-Danish Society's production of Henrik Ibsen's *Ghosts*, leading a band she describes as "skilled dilatants" at the Aurora Turner Hall at Milwaukee and West Huron for an audience of over a thousand. It is the world debut of the play, and the first performance of Ibsen in the United States.

Ghosts—Gengangere in Danish, the language Norwegian Ibsen wrote his earth-shaking plays in while living in Italy—is about the family baggage we are saddled with, as represented by congenital syphilis, adultery, incest, and assisted suicide, themes not then sounded in public, never mind hurled from the stage. The play had been published six months earlier. While Ibsen's work is eagerly reviewed and debated—his previous play was *A Doll's House*—this one wasn't. Nobody wanted to even mention the "repulsive pathological phenomenon" it focuses on, according to the censor at the Royal Theater in Copenhagen, who rejected *Ghosts*, as did every other dramatic venue in Europe to consider it.

Scandinavians were reluctant to be seen possessing the published script. Sales were poor at Christmas. Swedish actor August Lindberg described the reception in Stockholm.

"The book vanished in silence. Absolute silence," he wrote. "The newspaper said nothing and the bookshops sent the book back to the publisher. It was contraband. Something which could not decently be discussed."

In America, however, the cup of art that dropped from the trembling hand of professionals was snatched up by enthusiastic novices, performing in Dano-Norwegian.

"Ibsen shines the torch of doubt over everything once accepted," Bluhme writes, in Norwegian, explaining the production in the daily *Skandinaven*, which called *Ghosts* Ibsen's gloomiest drama.

It certainly sparked the greatest criticism—Ibsen's next play, *An Enemy of the People*, is a reaction to the vituperation he received for writing *Ghosts*. Not here. After today's Chicago debut, the production will tour other midwestern cities with large Scandinavian communities. *Ghosts* will not be performed in Norway until the end of next year.

May 21, 1924

They know him.

In all the notoriety to come, the glare over the "Crime of the Century," the media circus, and the famous defense by Clarence Darrow, that salient fact can be overlooked. Nathan Leopold and Richard Loeb are University of Chicago classmates who spent six months planning "the perfect crime," an elaborate kidnapping and murder scheme. Today they go hunting for someone to kill, just for the thrill of doing so and getting away with it, because they are so brilliant, in their own estimation.

But instead of a stranger, as planned, they impulsively pick Bobby Franks, 14, not only because he is walking through their Kenwood neighborhood, but because they're familiar with him. He's Loeb's second cousin and has played tennis at Loeb's house. Still, Franks at first refuses the offer of a ride. But he's enticed into the rented car with talk of tennis rackets. There he's killed with a chisel, purchased for that purpose, wrapped in tape to protect their hands.

The two teenage criminal geniuses—Leopold is 19, Loeb, 18— prove to be anything but. Leopold leaves his prescription eyeglasses behind when they hide the body in a watery ditch in Hammond, Indiana, and the police quickly trace the expensive spectacles back to him. He must have left them during one of his bird-watching expeditions, Leopold explains. Besides, he has an alibi: his good friend Loeb. The Underwood 3 portable typewriter used for the ransom notes might have been smashed and sunk to the bottom of Jackson Park Lagoon, but the school study sheets typed on it are available, and after the pair become suspects, two *Daily News* reporters dig the papers up and compare them to the ransom note. They match.

Darrow convinces the two to plead guilty, in an attempt to save their lives. It works. Though harsh punishment finds Loeb, who will be slashed to death with a razor in prison in 1936. Leopold will live to be released in 1958, having spent 33 years in prison, 14 more than he had spent on earth before going in. He moves to Puerto Rico and dies there in 1971.

May 22, 1935

A wreath is sent by the king of the hoboes—or the International Itinerant Migratory Workers' Union, as they are formally called—to thank her for letting them use a room to hold meetings when no one else would. The arrangement becomes part of a vast bank of flowers, lilies of the valley and roses, surrounding the body of Jane Addams as she lies in state at Hull-House.

Her body is brought this morning from Passavant Hospital, where she died last night, having never been told that she had cancer. Asked by a doctor how she felt, she said, "Swell. You can't kill an old woman." A rare departure from the truth, no matter how stark, for Addams.

Beginning about 2 p.m. and all the next day, a sea of grieving Chicagoans from all walks of life arrive. Workmen in coveralls pay respects, carrying their lunch boxes. Thousands of schoolchildren "in an almost endless line." Immigrants in shawls hold up babies so they can see her face. Girls from nearby factories. Mexican and Japanese, Italian and Jewish.

The next day, at her funeral, Dr. Charles W. Gilkey, dean of the University of Chicago's Rockefeller Memorial Chapel, will use a phrase to describe her that will echo with anybody who ever tried to lubricate the gears of social change: "The patient collector of facts."

John Vitullo, a neighborhood man, puts it another way: "She got lots of fellows jobs."

May 23, 1895

Today's edition of the *American Bee Journal*, published in Chicago, founded in 1861 and thus "The oldest Bee-Paper in America," is 16 handsomely illustrated, densely packed pages. As befits a publication "Devoted Exclusively to the Interests of Honey Producers," there are articles with titles such as "Facts About Bees and Strawberries" and "The Length of Life of the Bees" and "Automatic Swarming—Queries and Comments." There is a "Southern Department" and an entire page on "Canadian Beedom," whose challenges hardly need to be mentioned. ("The first special features to be considered about Canadian beedom are the length and severity of the winter.")

Chicago remains an excellent place to keep bees, simply because there is no agriculture, so nobody is spraying pesticides. Plus all those forest preserves and parkways, flower boxes and backyard gardens, not to forget the lake and river. The mint in Millennium Park's Lurie Garden is particularly popular among bees. The *American Bee Journal* survives to this day. Not in Chicago, alas; it moved to Hamilton, Illinois, in 1912. The hives are gone from the City Hall roof.

May 24, 1955

Willie Dixon is having a good week.

Today he plays bass on "Mannish Boy," recording with Muddy Waters at Chess Records. Three days earlier Dixon backed Chuck Berry on "Maybellene"—yes, named for the brand of mascara.

While the lyrics of "Mannish Boy," which becomes Waters's signature song—"I'm a man. Spell that M . . . A . . . N, man"—might at first seem standard bluesman boasting, there is also a political overtone, answering the question "Am I not a man?" posed for the past 100 years, first at abolition rallies, recently at civil rights marches.

But political significance does not negate a sense of fun. "Mannish Boy" is also an answer song, replying to Bo Diddley's "I'm a Man" recorded 11 weeks earlier at Chess's delightfully named secondary label, Checker Records, and now on the charts. Borrowing the "M . . . A . . . N . . ." refrain, it's a not-so-subtle poke at Diddley's relative youth: Waters is 41, Diddley, 26. "I'm a Man" was answering Waters's "Hoochie Coochie Man," which, to come full circle, Dixon wrote. He will continue being the behind-the-scenes backbone of a string of classic 1950s hits to come out of Chicago: in three years he'll play on Chuck Berry's "Johnny B. Goode." All told, Dixon will write 500 songs, recorded by everyone from the Grateful Dead to Led Zeppelin.

May 25, 1979

"Damn."

The last word caught by the McDonnell Douglas DC-10's flight recorder, uttered by its co-pilot a few seconds after American Airlines flight 191 takes off from O'Hare International Airport.

Then silence.

The left engine has fallen off, and the plane goes into a slow roll. The tower sees it all.

"All right, ah, American, ah, one ninety-one heavy," says traffic controller Edward Rucker. "Heavy" is tower-speak for laden with fuel; the plane is bound for Los Angeles. "You want to come back in to what runway?"

Too late for that. A DC-10 can, in theory, fly on the remaining two engines. But one engine tearing out of the wing severs the hydraulic lines inside and the pilots lose control of the aircraft. The plane nosedives into a field and explodes, killing all 258 passengers, 13 crew members, and two people on the ground. One member of the recovery crew compares the human remains to black lumps of coal.

The National Transportation Safety Board will determine that American Airlines cut corners during maintenance, removing the engine and pylon holding it onto the wing together as a single unit to save time, instead of separately, as they're supposed to do. This, coupled with the fact that a regular forklift was used instead of a more precise crane, created a crack in the pylon. American also ignored warning memos from mechanics. It remains the deadliest airplane crash on US soil, the toll higher than the passengers lost aboard the four planes hijacked on September 11, 2001, combined. American Airlines will stop designating a flight 191, and make changes to flight procedures. Laws are passed too, including an Illinois statute requiring that dentures be marked with the name of the wearer.

May 26, 1934

The railroad tracks between Chicago and Denver pass countless rural crossings, lonely stretches of nowhere lucky to have an "X" sign. For today they are lonely no more, populated with local police bearing red flags, ready to stop any motorists who might appear. Or American Legion volunteers in their jaunty service caps. Even Boy Scouts, doing their duty. Joined by townsfolk, who climb off their tractors and leave their kitchens to stand trackside, arms crossed, waiting for the modern world to come tearing by at up to 112 miles per hour.

The Burlington Zephyr, a sleek aluminum engine and two cars, making its "Dawn-to-Dusk Dash," leaves Denver at 6:04 a.m., bound for the Century of Progress Fair, to cap off opening day, its second. The fair was such a hit in 1933, Chicago is extending it for a second season.

The Burlington Railroad is taking no chances. It diverts all other trains and spikes the switches along the route so that some careless rural trainman won't divert the streamlined wonder onto a dead-end siding by accident. The train flashes across the country, a straight thousand-mile shot never done before or since, carrying railroad officials, newsmen, and a burro named "Zeph," a present from the mayor of Denver to the mayor of Chicago. After averaging 77 miles per hour, the train pulls into Chicago at 7:10 p.m. and arrives at the fairgrounds 59 minutes later. Right on time.

May 27, 1933

"The main drag's all set to go," says Nat D. Rogers, impresario, showman, and chief of the amusement division at the Century of Progress exposition. "I'll tell you it's the greatest show on earth. I've seen many fairs and many midways, but this one takes the cake."

The former circus owner and native Texan waves his cane at the Midway—the term comes from the World's Columbian Exposition, where the tawdrier carnival aspects were crowded onto the Midway Plaisance. "It makes the culmination of a long series of Midways in America, dating from the original one at Chicago's first world's fair in 1893. Never has the present century seen a Midway like the ones we've got here. Everything's new and fresh and unique."

What is on it? What *isn't?* There is an Old South showboat and "The World a Million Years Ago." Thrill rides—the Lindy Loop, Bozo, Hey-Dey, and Cyclone—shooting galleries, the Palace of Living Wonders, featuring the smallest couple in the world and the world's tallest man. Ripley's Believe It or Not Odditorium. If the "Midget Village," with houses scaled to size, isn't small enough for you, there's also a flea circus. The Temple of Mystery, where Carter the Great puts on shows. A painting of the Fort Dearborn Massacre augmented by sound effects. A German beer hall, the Old Heidelberg Inn, a Belgian Village, and the Streets of Paris.

Fairs were conceived as monuments to civic pride, but all the civic booster hoopla of this one will be eclipsed by a five-foot-tall platinum blonde named Sally Rand, who took her name from the Rand McNally Road Atlas, imported all the way from the Paramount Club on East Huron Street, dancing apparently naked behind her flashing ostrich fans. The rest of the Century of Progress pales in memory beside her.

May 28, 1950

"Adventure! Education! Entertainment! A show for the whole family," promises an ad for tonight's episode of *The Zoo Parade*, the Lincoln Park Zoo's weekly Sunday evening foray into television starring its lanky director, Marlin Perkins.

Actually, two shows are produced every Sunday, one local on WNBQ, sponsored by Jewel Supermarkets, which offers Animal-of-the-Week trading cards to shoppers, and another national, going out on NBC and sponsored by Quaker Oats. The performers simply do the show twice, though with live animals, surprises must be expected. Such as the timber rattlesnake that twisted in his grasp and bit Perkins. It did not do so on camera, as viewers would later insist they saw. But the extraction of the venom was televised. Perkins ended up in the hospital for three weeks. He cleverly packages his program to appeal to kids: he might do one show on animal ears, another on animal feet. By fall the Chicago Public Schools will declare *Zoo Parade* one of only five programs on television "of educational value," shows that teachers may work into their curricula.

But being educational doesn't mean that it can't also be fun.

"His demonstration a week ago of the feeding of tigers and lions had more entertainment value than five hours of Berle and Godfrey," *Daily News* columnist Jack Mabley wrote that February.

Mutual of Omaha will take over sponsorship in 1955—the year Chicago Park District officials will demand that Perkins choose between his job at the zoo and this TV distraction. Perkins quits the zoo, which immediately comes to its senses and decides he can keep both jobs after all. The show will be renamed *Wild Kingdom* and run until 1988.

May 29, 1962

Prior to today, John "Buck" O'Neil could not sit on the dugout bench once the games began, not when the Cubs were visiting other ballparks. Not unless the home team gave special permission, and on a recent road trip, a few National League clubs wouldn't.

Which might gall another man. But O'Neil had picked celery in the South—his grandfather came to this country on a slave ship. So O'Neil doesn't take offense. He played on the Kansas City Monarchs in the old Negro American League. Then he became their manager. When he heard about a hot prospect in Amarillo, Texas, and saw Ernie Banks with his quick wrists and sure hands, he signed him up. What Banks liked most about O'Neil is the friendly way he gives advice, in a tone of "please let me help you." Three years after signing Banks, O'Neil took him in a cab to Wrigley Field, walked him into the office, and basically gave him to the Cubs. "I patterned my life after Buck O'Neil," the Cubs legend will later say. O'Neil became a scout: he recently signed Lou Brock. When not on the road, O'Neil hangs around, giving advice. Which is technically a coach's job. So today, the Cubs sign him up, assigning him No. 53 to wear. This makes O'Neil the 11th coach on the Cubs roster and the first Black coach in the history of major league baseball, free to sit in the visitors' dugout in any major league park, whether the home team likes it or not.

May 30, 1937

Mayor Kelly assured the striking workers at Republic Steel they would be allowed to peacefully picket.

That's not what happens.

US Steel recognized its employees' right to unionize in March, and signed a deal: $5 for an eight-hour day plus overtime. But its competitors, dubbed "Little Steel"—Bethlehem, Youngstown Sheet and Tube, American Rolling Mill, and especially Republic—refused. At Chicago's Republic plant, half the workers walked out and tried to set up a picket line earlier in the week, twice. And twice the police chased them off.

That's why Paramount knows to be here today, the only newsreel company present—the rest are off covering the Indianapolis 500. Orlando Lippert sets his movie camera up on a sound truck at the steel plant gate at 117th and Burley, the perfect vantage to see the thousand strikers, in shirtsleeves and hats, carrying signs and flags, walking across the field, the line of 200 policemen in dark coats, tapping their hickory batons, waiting to greet them.

The official police version of what happens next is simple: an armed mob of dangerous radicals led by outside communist agitators attacks a police line with guns, clubs, and bricks. The police defend themselves. The press will fall in line behind them.

"RIOTS BLAMED ON RED CHIEFS," the front-page headline in tomorrow's *Tribune* will read, describing "the mob attack on the police who were guarding the company's property rights."

But there are certain inconsistencies. Forty strikers are shot, most in the back. Ten die. No police are shot, or even seriously injured.

And there is that newsreel.

Nobody sees it, at first. Fearing "crowd hysteria," Paramount simply shelves the footage. But Wisconsin senator Robert LaFollette subpoenas it to show before his Civil Liberties Committee, which faults the police.

After the hearing, Paramount releases a newsreel of what will be called the "Memorial Day Massacre" into theaters. Except of course in Chicago, which bans the film.

May 31, 2020

Angelo Bronson isn't from Chicago. He lives in Washington, DC, where he installs solar panels. But he has family here, and frequently visits. That is what he is doing when, shortly after midnight, standing on the 6800 block of South Laflin, in Englewood, a vehicle pulls up and someone shoots him in the chest and leg. The 36-year-old father is pronounced dead an hour later at the University of Chicago Medical Center, making him the first of 18 people murdered in Chicago today—another 67 are shot and survive—the highest 24-hour toll since daily statistics began being kept in 1961. No one is arrested for the crime.

This happens after a long evening of rioting, looting, and arson after protests over the police killing of George Floyd in Minneapolis. Mayor Lori Lightfoot raised the bridges into downtown, an echo of the Beer Riot of 1855, a move later condemned by the inspector general as counterproductive, sparking violent clashes as police tried to clear the bridges first, trapping rioters in the Loop as much as preventing more from coming. The violence is the result of festering resentment and righteous indignation boiling over. Or of lawless opportunists with little to lose taking advantage of a moment when the rules governing society seem to no longer apply. Either way, the city trembles and the downtown, already a ghost town due to COVID-19, becomes a ghost town of plywood-covered windows and parked police SUVs.

JUNE

June 1, 1970

Hamlet complains of the law's delay. But it moves briskly for Barry and Merle Gross. The party of the second part, eight months pregnant, spurs the party of the first part, a lawyer, to sue in federal court to be allowed into the delivery room with her, despite a 1933 Chicago Board of Health rule clearly stating "no lay visitors including relatives shall be permitted in the delivery rooms or nurseries." The fear is germs and, the Chicago corporation counsel will argue, fainting fathers who later sue.

Merle Gross testifies that it would be "reassuring and crucial" to have her husband in the room for the birth of their second child, to guide her through the Lamaze training both have undergone together.

Judge Alexander J. Napoli rules today that the 1933 law is "overly broad and goes beyond that which is reasonable and necessary." Barry Gross may witness the birth of his son, Daniel, who will be born the day before Father's Day. Though Lamaze has not in fact familiarized the father-to-be with every aspect of the process. "As much as I was prepared for what was going to happen, I was unprepared for the emotional response to being present for the birth of a child," Gross will recall half a century later. "I was awe-inspired."

To end the story here, however, would suggest that such changes are sudden, seismic, and permanent. When often they're incremental, tentative, and subject to backsliding. Seven years later, another father-to-be will want to be in the delivery room—the complication being that this is for a C-section—and the same Board of Health, headed by the same commissioner, Murray C. Brown, who tried to bar Barry Gross, will again say no, insisting the Gross case was only "applicable to a single individual and to a specific hospital on a single occasion of childbirth." And so the struggle continues.

June 2, 1928

Who decided that Mexicans are a degraded race, meant to leave the place of their birth and go to a foreign land to work in misery until their death? What if they are instead destined for greatness? What if their diaspora is no less noble than the wanderings of the Jews?

"Mexicans, let us never forget or cease to show interest in our country and in the land in which we first saw the light of the day," José Vasconcelos says to a group of about 50 gathered at Hull-House. "For if we are here, working hard and suffering, it will not always be so. We are but the children of Israel who are passing through our Egypt here in the United States, doing the onerous labors, swallowing our pride, bracing up under the indignities heaped upon us here."

Vasconcelos is a professor at Northwestern University, teaching Latin American studies. By year's end he'll quit and return to Mexico to run for president. He won't come close to winning but will continue the struggle as a writer and philosopher—his ideas about "The Cosmic Race," *La raza cósmica*, stressing how ultimately all ethnicities and races must blend together, having particular significance. Though it is ironic that he holds the Jews up as an example since Vasconcelos will veer into racism and antisemitism— he'll nuzzle up to Franco and take money from the Nazis—ending up with a legacy that is complicated and contradictory.

June 3, 1863

At 5 a.m., soldiers from Camp Douglas—two companies from the 65th Illinois Infantry—march to the office of the *Chicago Times* and shut down its presses. Too late. Knowing they were on their way, the newsmen had hurriedly printed up 8,000 copies and bundled them out the door. The soldiers find only several hundred papers still in the pressroom, and destroy them.

The *Times*'s fiery owner, Wilbur F. Storey—who once said, "It is a newspaper's duty to print the news and raise hell"—supported Abraham Lincoln until the Emancipation Proclamation. The white-supremacist publisher thought ending slavery would ruin both South and North, and afterward found the president's prosecution of the war "imbecilic."

Two days earlier, Gen. Ambrose Burnside, chafing at the chain of Union defeats and looking for some kind of victory, decreed that "declaring sympathy for the enemy will not be allowed." He ordered the closure of the *Times*, officially for "repeated expression of disloyal and incendiary statements." Though perhaps the paper's characterization of Burnside as the "Butcher of Fredericksburg" was also a factor.

Storey quickly got a restraining order, prompting Burnside's extralegal measure.

Though Storey is generally loathed—the Board of Trade refused to allow *Times* reporters at its meetings, the Galena and Chicago Union Railroad briefly banned the newspaper from its trains—Chicagoans like being under the thumb of the army even less than they like bullying bigots. That night, some 20,000—by Storey's highly unreliable count—gather at Court House Square to protest the "spectre of military despotism." Whatever they think of the *Times*, they don't want their news spiked on a bayonet. The next day, Lincoln will revoke Burnside's order.

June 4, 1927

Jelly Roll Morton and his Red Hot Peppers record four songs, two takes each: "Hyena Stomp," "Billy Goat Stomp," "Wild Man Blues," and "Jungle Blues," at the new Victor Talking Machine Company studio at 952 N. Michigan.

Morton's people had been in New Orleans since before the Louisiana Purchase. He left when the US Navy shut down Storyville, the red-light district where he played piano in a brothel. Morton headed north but found St. Louis prejudiced and Kansas City worse. "It was like St. Louis except it didn't have one decent pianist and didn't want any," the father of jazz will tell Alan Lomax. In Chicago, "you could go anywhere you want regardless of creed or color." His trademark song, "Jelly Roll Blues," will become so popular he'll decide to rename the song in honor of the city that welcomed him: "The Chicago Blues."

Of course, you trust the boasts of a blues man at your peril. One historian will describe Morton's claims to Lomax as "sometimes accurate." Maybe Mr. Jelly Roll played in Storyville; maybe he originated jazz; maybe his "Jelly Roll Blues" is a completely original work. Maybe not. Hard to tell at this point.

June 5, 1946

Just after midnight, patrons at the Silver Grill Cocktail Lounge in the LaSalle Hotel smell smoke. They notice flames peeking between the walnut wall panels. Someone goes at the fire with a seltzer bottle. Then sand. Ten minutes pass before anyone thinks to phone the fire department.

Battalion chief Eugene Freemon is first to arrive. He sees fire in the lobby of the 22-story luxury hotel at the corner of LaSalle and Madison and sends his driver running—literally—down the street to the nearest signal box to tap out a 2-11 alarm on the telegraph key inside.

Meanwhile, the fire races up the stairs; the fireproof doors that were supposed to be guarding each floor were never installed. The open stairway acts as a chimney. There are no sprinklers, no alarms of any kind. There are, however, fire escapes on the sides of the building, and most of the 900 who exit the fully booked hotel get out that way, many alerted by hotel telephone operator Julia C. Berry, who sits at her post, calling room after room, waking the guests.

Night manager D. H. Bradfield sees Berry at the switchboard and tells the widow to go. "No," she says. "I'm going to stay at my station. We've got to give those folks on the top floors a chance."

She will be among the 61 who die. Chief Freemon is another.

In the postmortem it will be realized that many guests died of smoke inhalation—they might have survived if, like Lt. Col. Ralph P. Weaver, they had just stayed in their rooms. He will emerge the next morning, freshly shaved and dressed. So Berry's sacrifice saved some and doomed others.

After this fire, the Chicago Fire Department will start putting radios in all trucks, and the city council will pass an ordinance that hotels must have a central alarm, and that each room should have a card instructing occupants what to do in case of fire. AT&T will award Berry its citation for heroism and give her 16-year-old son a thousand dollars.

June 6, 1901

The *Chicago Record-Herald* prints one of the more significant letters to the editor in Chicago history, from Edward P. Brennan, a bill collector for the Lyon & Healy Harp Company, suggesting that the city's chaotic streets be put in order.

Navigating Chicago is confusing even to those who have lived their whole lives here. There is a Michigan Street, Michigan Avenue, and Michigan Boulevard—none, incidentally, where North Michigan Avenue will eventually be located; that's Pine Street. Many roads have several names along a single length, and numbering is haphazard, thanks in part to the fact that Chicago has absorbed surrounding municipalities such as Irving Park, Kenwood, Hyde Park, and Pullman.

Brennan recommends a baseline be set at the intersection of Madison and State—that should be 0/0. Then addresses assigned in most of the city will be 100 to the block, 800 to the mile, so if you are at 800 W. Madison, you know you are a mile from State Street.

The letter is not Brennan's lone effort but part of a lifelong campaign to rationalize the street grid. After the requisite years of debate, the city council will adopt his idea, and it goes into effect in 1909. When Brennan dies in 1946, the council names a two-block street in his honor.

June 7, 1857

The infernal heat keeps Rhode Island botanist Edward L. Peckham in his hotel room most of the day. The day before had been enough for him to form a judgment that he has alighted in "as mean a spot as I was ever in." The sidewalks are uneven, with some structures at grade level, others raised three to eight feet above. "How persons can navigate this dirty city in a dark night without a broken arm or neck is a mystery to me."

The city is a rare mix of wretched AND expensive. "Nothing in Chicago costs less than 10 cents, called a dime," Peckham writes. South of the river he finds the "wealthy and enterprising," while north "Germans and Irish and other foreigners" laze in their miserable hovels.

Today he tries to walk again, but is driven back to his room by the heat, where he strips down, reads the paper, and misses New England. After dinner, two friends urge him to explore north of the river, where he casts a disapproving Presbyterian eye on whom he finds there.

"Although it was Sunday, the shops were all open, and everywhere seen groups of Germans, smoking, jabbering, and drinking Lager beer to their hearts' content."

June 8, 1893

"Of course we saw the Princess," May Bragdon notes in her diary, "a good looking blonde, most animated and gay—dressed in gray and big red roses—her husband, handsome, dark, blasé, with pointed beard."

A secretary from Rochester, New York, Bragdon, 28, has already spent four days at the World's Columbian Exposition. She almost skips going again today to instead take a wagonette ride with a young man. But the prospect of laying eyes upon the Spanish Infanta Eulalia draws her back for a fifth day, which she describes in a breathless rush.

Mayor Harrison (in his first silk hat, Lew Jones says.) and Mrs. Potter Palmer, gray haired and conspicuous. The Dahomies, opposite, set up a howling song & bowed to the earth, the Chinese played their pandemonium band in our ears and the Old Vienna let go their cannon & everybody cheered & waved their handkerchiefs . . . I came up thro' the Transportation—all thro' the Machinery, where we saw looms working—cloth—brocades—ribbons, badges &c and clothes cut by machinery—potter's wheel—cigar making—grinding lenses— the big switch-board—the 3000 horse power engine—the rows of boilers, the immense travelling crane. etc. etc. Then went over to the mining—we saw them washing out Diamond dirt & cutting diamonds (Tiffany exhibit) and all guarded by big half-naked Africans—like the Dahomies—only worse. It was all behind plate glass. Listened to the bands in the bandstands awhile, and then went over to Baker's Cocoa place and had 2 cups of cocoa each—served by "La bonne chocola-tiere." Walked thro' the Peristyle & Agricultural . . . Then sat on the steps of the Agricultural Landings a long time. It was beautiful—about sundown—till 8, when we met Guy & Claude at the Administration. The interior of this at night is pretty fine—Palms & yellow light & color & motion & vastness! Claude took me right back to the Agricultural where . . . the Crowds were not so thick & we saw the finest display of fireworks I ever witnessed. They would searchlight on the smoke from the rockets—had magnificent bombs—bouquets—jewels &c &c. of fire & the whole lagoon ablaze with the colored lights & snakish wheels—the universal crowd—the music—the Princess on the balcony—and all made it a scene never to be forgotten. We left just as they set off the "set pieces"—circus of Spain & US & Eulalia's picture & managed to get a train home before the crowd.

June 9, 1930

It is a lovely spring day, and *Chicago Tribune* reporter Jake Lingle decides to shirk his duties and have some fun. He buys a racing form at a newsstand and heads into the pedestrian tunnel under Michigan Avenue, on his way to take the train to the Washington Park racetrack. There, in an appropriately underworld setting, Lingle is shot dead, a single bullet in the back of the head.

The *Tribune* will reflexively thunder that its reporter—a "leg man," meaning he hoofed around town, digging up details and phoning them in to rewrite men at the paper who would craft them into stories—is a martyr to the newspaper's bold attack on organized crime. But that calliope of self-praise comes to a wheezing halt as it is revealed that the diamond-studded belt buckle Lingle was wearing when a man dressed as a priest shot him is a gift from Al Capone, and that he had become something of a powerhouse in organized crime, influencing everything from the appointment of police captains to the protection of rackets. His murder is not because of what he has reported, but due to what he might tell federal investigators as an organized-crime insider.

June 10, 1971

The "R" is for Richard Melman, whose father opened a cafeteria across from the Civic Opera as cover for a dice game he ran there. The "J" is for Jerry Orzoff, a real estate broker who imagines a restaurant will be a good place to meet women. Thus their first restaurant is "R. J. Grunts," the "grunts" being a tribute, of sorts, to Jerry's girlfriend, who makes guttural pig noises when she eats.

The doors swing open at 11:31 a.m.—the time afterward immortalized on the menus, goofy in a Grateful Dead meets Robert Crumb cartoonish fashion.

The two partners are young, and so do things differently—no uniforms for the waitresses. Just normal street clothes. Hipper, and costs less too, as does decorating the walls with photos of the good-looking people who work there. And no elevator music: rock music. There is also a feature not found anywhere else in the continental United States: a salad bar. Melman read about the concept being tried at restaurants in Hawaii, and put one in. His has caviar. And cream cheese with chocolate chips.

This is no high-end joint. There is a lighthearted comfort to the place: the company the two form has a pun for a name, "Lettuce Entertain You Enterprises," and each new restaurant is christened in that jocular 1970s vein: Fritz That's It, the Great Gritzbe's Flying Food Show, Jonathan Livingston Seafood (a twist on a then wildly popular book of smarm).

By the time they open Lawrence of Oregano, they'll have purchased the Pump Room, the famed place-to-be-seen in the Ambassador East Hotel. At the end of the 1980s, Lettuce Entertain You will own 90 restaurants and have created a variety of successful national chains: Wildfire, Ed Debevic's, Joe's Seafood. In Chicago there will come to be so many successful Lettuce restaurants that realizing you're eating at another one and not an independent effort is almost a letdown. They're so good at what they do that at times it almost seems unfair to the other restaurants.

June 11, 1964

The Rolling Stones finish their second day of making music at Chess Records, "hallowed ground" to guitarist Keith Richards. In what he considers the "perfect sound studio, in the room where everything we'd listened to was made." Over two days, they'll record 14 songs, including their first No. 1 hit, "It's All Over Now," plus several songs from the Chess catalogue such as Muddy Waters's "I Can't Be Satisfied," which bears scant resemblance to the song they will write themselves and return to Chess to record next year, "I Can't Get No (Satisfaction)." They also record a blues jam, the only instrumental the band will ever release, heavy on organ and harmonica, which they call "2120 South Michigan Avenue," the studio address. While they are here, they notice Waters himself, in coveralls, painting the ceiling. When they've finished recording, the king of the blues—it's printed on his business card—helps the band load their equipment.

June 12, 1920

The three strong candidates—Sen. Hiram Johnson of California; former army chief of staff Gen. Leonard Wood, and Illinois governor Frank Lowden—are deadlocked. In four ballots over four days in the 100-degree heat at the Chicago Coliseum, no one can gather the 493 votes needed to become the Republican Party candidate for president. No one can win, and no one is willing to drop out.

Something has to be done.

The obvious solution is to pick a fourth that all can agree on. But who? Finally, about 2:34 a.m., the senator from Ohio enters a suite at the Blackstone Hotel, the original "smoke-filled room" that would go down in political lore as the epitome of insider machination.

Sure, he did miserably in the primaries. Sure, he has 61 votes. Sure, he is bland and affable, "the essence of conciliation and compromise." That's what makes Warren G. Harding the perfect pick. Harding is also handsome, often compared to a Roman senator or an Indian chief. He looks like a president. He takes instruction well.

Harding is asked one question: "Do you have any dark secrets?" No, he lies, ignoring his mistresses and his illegitimate child, less than a year old. And to be honest, from a historical perspective, his extramarital dalliance will not besmirch his name half as much as the carnival of corruption he'll overlook among his pals.

The powerful agree: it will be Harding, and the word is put out. By 6 p.m. the nomination falls to Harding, and in the hall, "a cheer rose that shook the earth." One of the greatest mediocrities ever elevated to the presidency will be elected by the biggest plurality in history. Though you might say that Woodrow Wilson, now stricken and paralyzed, elected him. "After an eight-year audience with an arch-bishop," Alistair Cooke will write, "America wanted nothing so much as a quiet, long drink with a crony." Which is exactly what they'll get.

June 13, 1986

In the 1960s and 1970s, the soldiers returned home to deserted airport terminals. Now Chicagoans line the streets, offering handshakes and kisses, and thumbs-ups and cheers. "L" cars blow their horns.

Organizers expect 100,000 marchers but at least 200,000 show up. Vets and their families walking in the big "Welcome Home" parade they were denied when the bitter, divisive Vietnam War finally ended in 1975. The parade starts at Olive Park next to Navy Pier, named for Milton Olive, an 18-year-old Congressional Medal of Honor winner, a Black soldier from Chicago who saved his buddies by throwing himself on a live grenade in 1965. When the marchers turn in to the canyon of LaSalle Street, they get a surprise: a sea of confetti, brokers tossing torn-up computer printouts and shredded phone books, an echo of the ticker-tape parades of old. They head to Grant Park, where in the summer of 1968 rioters clashed with police, trying to shout down the war.

Children in wagons and legless vets in wheelchairs. Joe Hertel dug out his old jungle fatigue jacket, the one he wore in Bien Hoa and Long Binh in 1967 and 1968. "The time has come," he says. "The nation must be healed."

The parade lasts nearly five hours.

"It's a long parade, daddy," a little girl tells her father.

"It was a long war, honey," he replies.

June 14, 2018

Electric car and commercial spaceflight entrepreneur Elon Musk and Mayor Rahm Emanuel gather the press to a subterranean bunker beneath Block 37 to announce plans for the "Chicago Express." Musk's amusingly named Boring Company, the duo promise, will drill a train line. "12 MINUTE SERVICE FROM DOWNTOWN TO O'HARE AIRPORT," a slide claims, which would put the average speed at 85 miles per hour. A newspaper reporter bets a mayoral aide a steak lunch that nothing will come of this, not a single teaspoon of dirt will ever be turned in earnest. Which is exactly what happens or, more precisely, doesn't happen.

Big plans often don't come to fruition, despite high-powered participants. From Richard M. Daley's 2016 Olympics squib to Mayor Ed Kelly's lakefront Coney Island, Chicago's stillborn projects deserve remembrance, just because there are so many, and together they offer a cautionary tale: the Miglin-Beitler Skyneedle, a 1,999-foot, 125-story skyscraper, never built, but whose design influenced the Petronas Towers in Kuala Lumpur. Daley's $5 billion Lake Calumet airport, that would have required leveling most of the Hegewisch neighborhood. Ground was actually broken for the Spire, a 2,000-foot-tall drill bit of a structure that would have been the tallest building in the Western hemisphere, but ended up a deep circular hole. Best of all: the Chicago–to–New York zeppelin line announced with front-page fanfare in 1923 by a partnership of Marshall Field, William Wrigley, and Franklin Delano Roosevelt.

Musk and Emanuel claim work will begin soon. But what is instantly dubbed "the rich folks' underground railroad" remains a pipe dream. Within the year, Rahm has shifted from city administration to TV punditry. His aide never bought that lunch.

June 15, 1921

Lots of jawboning goes on in a barbershop. Lots of idle talk, waiting for a shave or a haircut. Chatting up the pretty manicurist in the window. Teasing her.

"You Chicago girls don't know shit," one former doughboy said, or words to that effect. "Now those French girls, they know where it's at. There are French girls who know how to *fly*."

Usually this kind of thing leads nowhere. Not this time. Right then, Bessie Coleman made a decision. "That's it!" she said. "You just called it for me."

She has always wanted to make something of herself. That's why she was in Chicago, doing nails, and not back home in Waxahachie, Texas. If French girls can fly, so can she. There are airfields in Chicago and flying instructors, but nobody who is going to teach a Black manicurist how to pilot a plane. Coleman studied French. She saved her money. She got some help—a manicurist holds the hands of many rich men. Maybe from Jesse Binga, the banker. Maybe from Robert S. Abbott, the publisher.

Today a French official fills out her license from the Federation Aeronautique Internationale. She is the first Black woman to hold a pilot's license, and returns to this country a star, performing acrobatic stunts. It will be 17 years before a Black woman earns a pilot's license in the United States.

June 16, 1996

Winners. Not once-in-a-century flukes, like the Super Bowl shuffling Bears, with their stupid headbands and their punky QB. Not the Cubs and Sox, whose victories are sunk so far in the historic—1908, 1917— that they might as well be fossilized between layers of shale with the trilobites. Not that niche Canadian import, hockey, where the Blackhawks last took the Stanley Cup during the Kennedy administration.

The Chicago Bulls win the NBA championship, again, fourth time in six years. It would have possibly been the sixth championship in six years had not Michael Jordan, the best there ever was, the best there ever will be, not decided to exert himself in 1994 by retiring from the sport he so thoroughly mastered to try his hand at professional baseball, just because he could.

But now he's back. Where he belongs. With Scottie Pippen and Dennis Rodman and the rest, "arguably the greatest team ever," winning 72 games, the best NBA season ever, up to that point—it'll take 21 years for the Golden State Warriors to top that by a game, and then they'll lose the championship to the Cavaliers.

Nor are the Bulls blasé about it. The Seattle Supersonics lost the first three games, rallied, and are handily defeated today in game six, 87–75. When it's all over, Michael Jordan rolls in the middle of the United Center floor, clutching the game ball and weeping. This was the Bulls' first championship since Jordan's father, James, was murdered. He had always been there to celebrate. And today is Father's Day. "I know he's watching," Jordan says, when he's composed himself. "This is for Daddy."

The team will go on to win two more NBA titles. More than winners. Champions.

June 17, 1918

An ordinance is passed by the city council to change German street names—Berlin to Canton; Frankfort to Charleston; Coblentz to Carver; Rhine to Coyne. The idea is to placate Poles, who have been tearing down these street signs in an expression of patriotic fervor.

Mozart and Goethe are spared, with Chicagoans arguing that their genius makes them citizens of the world and negates the stain of their national origin. Besides, Mozart is Austrian, which is not quite as bad. (The ladies who will form the "Use Nothing German" club at the South Shore Country Club next month similarly exclude Wagner and the poetry of Henrich Heine, reasoning they were exiled from Germany and thus acceptable.)

German language classes will disappear from public schools as the culture recedes during World War I, so much so that it becomes easy to forget what a prominent role Germans once played in Chicago civic life. At times in the late 19th century they made up 20 percent of the population, 40 percent of foreign-born Chicagoans. They created their own world.

"A consciousness of common origin led them to prefer German-made goods, German hostelries, German churches and theaters, German trade unions, and even patent medicines wearing a German label," historian Bessie Louise Pierce will write in 1937. "It was, therefore, the better part of wisdom for native business organizations to employ German clerks, to carry German goods, and to advertise their wares in the German language. In some way this subservience to group consciousness laid open the way for Germans to proclaim that they were 'the most energetic, most enlightened and cultivated citizens of the union,' and the 'counterpoise against the corrupting influence of American materialism and its excrescence.'"

But pride goeth before a fall, and after two horrific world wars the German cultural presence in Chicago dwindles to a handful of restaurants, a massive monument to an idealized Goethe at the northern tip of Lincoln Park, a bust of Schiller, and Oktoberfest. The 1985 Von Steuben Day parade does appear in John Hughes's love letter to Chicago, *Ferris Bueller's Day Off.* Significance of a sort.

June 18, 1959

Otto Preminger's *Anatomy of a Murder* with Jimmy Stewart and George C. Scott is screened in Chicago for the police film censorship board—known colloquially as the Police Widows—and found lacking or, rather, overburdened with stark, unacceptable reality. Chief censor Sgt. Vincent Nolan demands five cuts.

In early July Preminger will fly to Chicago directly from the world premiere in Detroit, where they had given him the key to the city. His reception in Chicago is chillier: Richard J. Daley, for whom prudishness is both personally satisfying and politically expedient, won't see him. Preminger does see police commissioner Timothy J. O'Connor, who allows that the film can be shown with only two cuts of "obscene, immoral" dialogue: the words "rape" and "contraception."

Instead Preminger and his attorney visit Federal Judge Julius Miner, who gives them a warmer welcome. "I do not regard this film as depicting anything that could reasonably be termed obscene or corruptive of the public morals and found that the censorship exceeded constitutional bounds," Miner says.

June 19, 1984

"We wish he were 7 feet, but he isn't," says a disappointed Bulls general manager, Rod Thorn. "There just wasn't a center available. What can you do?"

Shrug and sigh and apologize, apparently, then draft Michael Jordan, whose raw talent, incredible drive, and limitless potential are clear to anybody who isn't in Bulls management. There is enough doubt, when it comes time to pick, that the crowd watching the NBA draft on television in the Conrad Hilton ballroom feels obligated to chant "Jordan! Jordan!" by way of encouragement.

The Bulls take the hint, and view this setback philosophically.

"We picked him because you can't pass up a great player," says Thorn. "If we were a great team, we could have drafted for need. We need a center; we're going to have to get one. There just wasn't one there."

No one, the Bulls caution, should get his hopes up. "Jordan isn't going to turn this franchise around," says Thorn. "I wouldn't ask him to."

That's the thing with Michael Jordan. You don't have to ask.

June 20, 1966

Jose Cruz is not his real name.

Anonymity is in order when your life is splayed out in the newspaper in detail, from what you earn as a punch-press operator ($2.22 an hour) to the rent you pay for your second-floor West Side walk-up ($25 a week) to the fact that you purchased your refrigerator and television on the installment plan ($27.18 a month).

"They belong to me," Cruz tells the *Daily News*, jumping the gun. They will belong to him *if* he makes his payments, the kind of detail that can trip up an immigrant.

The story in today's paper is notable for its ordinariness. Cruz is not a criminal or a victim; he has no complaints and the most modest of dreams: "I would like to move out someday to a larger place."

But the profile does appear in an extraordinary context; a city suddenly waking to its Puerto Rican community. The week before, 100 police and 1,000 Puerto Ricans clashed on the Northwest Side. A police car was overturned and burned, firemen pelted with rocks, their trucks looted. The shock came not so much from the episode's violence but because it happened at all.

In 1950, there were 255 Puerto Ricans living in Chicago. That number rose to 32,371 by 1960. Now it's 65,000, and, during the riot, "to the police it seemed all of them were on W. Division St. between Damen and California."

In the ensuing handwringing, the *Daily News* runs a front-page editorial, in Spanish—"Puerto Ricans must not be strangers in our midst," it says, translated. "Their culture—the oldest in the Western hemisphere—and their language—revered in world literature— must become part of the life in Chicago. This cannot be done by violence."

Why the riot? Some blame is placed on a failure to communicate. Charles H. Percy, Republican candidate for US Senate, suggests teaching police Spanish. Then there is the difficulty of the scale of life in Chicago: 85 percent of Puerto Rican immigrants come from small rural towns.

"The Puerto Ricans come here with an inability to cope with the problems of the city," Rev. Daniel Alvarez, head of Casa Central, a social service agency, tells the *Daily News*. "They don't find the proper services, they run out of money, they lack the ability to find employment, and they get trapped. . . . They borrow money, they risk everything they have for the $106 one-way ticket to Chicago."

That ticket is significant. Puerto Ricans are "the first ethnic group to come to the United States predominantly by airplane." The suddenness of the transition—no long voyage, no wait at the border—adds to the shock. Despite difficulties, Puerto Ricans are on their way to becoming the second-largest Latino group in the city.

"All these things bring problems, problems that did not exist at home," says Alvarez. "We are trying to solve them. But it will take time—and understanding."

June 21, 1920

Ruth Wanderer, eight and a half months pregnant, is walking home with her husband Carl after seeing *The Sea Wolf* at the Pershing Theater in Lincoln Square. Arriving at 4732 N. Campbell, she is surprised by a stranger in the darkness of their inner hall. "Don't turn on the light," the man commands.

Passersby drawn by the gunshots find Carl, a decorated World War I veteran, using a pistol to pummel the face of a poorly dressed man, who is dead. He tells them the man shot his wife. She is taken upstairs, where she dies in a bed next to the new bassinet, decorated with ribbons.

The police begin digging into what becomes known as "The Case of the Ragged Stranger." *Chicago Daily News* reporter Ben Hecht notices that the gun, a Colt M1911, is not only a fairly pricy weapon for a Skid Row bum but also identical to the gun Wanderer used to kill him. Another reporter, the *Herald-Examiner*'s Charlie MacArthur, learns that the assailant's gun was sold to Wanderer's cousin several years earlier.

Wanderer will confess, eventually, and be sentenced to hang. The $300 the *Herald-Examiner* pays him for his life story is supposedly won in a poker game by another reporter, a few hours before the doomed man's date with the noose.

What is unquestionably true is that Hecht and MacArthur use this and other experiences to write their classic 1928 comedy *The Front Page*, borrowing the lucky poker-playing reporter's distinctive name, Hildy Johnson, for their hero.

June 22, 1937

Joe Louis, in purple trunks and a robe trimmed in blue and red, makes his way to the boxing ring at the center of Comiskey Park. He is moved by the thousands of Black faces he sees in the crowd.

They must have saved real hard to get that money together, the challenger will remember thinking. *Lord knows what they sacrificed to see me. I have a responsibility to them.*

A responsibility that does not end in the eighth round when Louis delivers a left to the body and a right to the chin that practically lifts Jim Braddock off his feet and sends him crashing to the canvas like a sack of meat as 41,675 fans at Comiskey cheer.

Louis is now the heavyweight champion of the world. The *second* Black heavyweight champion of the world.

"We got another chance," neighbors call out to him in the street. "Don't be another Jack Johnson."

Johnson won the title from Tommy Burns in Australia in 1908. The flamboyant champion so horrified Edwardian America, with his high living, white chauffeur, and white wives, that Louis had feared he'd never be given a shot at the title.

But the handlers of the "Brown Bomber" are savvy, making sure he is never photographed with a woman other than his wife, Marva, who listens to the fight on the radio from their home at 4320 S. Michigan.

If Johnson was unapologetic and loathed, Louis is apologetic and loved—a source of pride among Blacks and accepted by whites, particularly after he knocks out Nazi champ Max Schmeling next year and enlists in the army after Pearl Harbor. It will take the boldness of Muhammad Ali to eventually blend those two qualities into a new type of Black celebrity: unapologetic and loved. Once American culture catches up with him, that is.

June 23, 1960

Civil War veteran Gideon Daniel Searle was a druggist who, having found success with a chain of stores in Indiana, began selling pharmaceuticals in Omaha in 1888, moving to Chicago in 1910. He died in 1917, but his namesake company kept on, introducing several long-standing products—Metamucil, the first commercial bulk laxative, in 1934; then in 1949, Dramamine for motion sickness. In the 1950s, its scientists experimented with synthetic progesterone, to treat gynecological troubles. They weren't interested in creating a form of birth control, under the assumption that the government won't allow a drug to be sold for that purpose, religious authorities would forbid it, and besides, women have no interest in taking a pill every day if they aren't sick.

But nothing G. D. Searle ever produced had an impact anywhere near that of the drug it puts on sale across the country today: a small white pill, an oral contraceptive taken by women. Officially called Enovid-10, but so monumentally significant to the sex life of the world that everyone simply calls it "The Pill."

June 24, 1942

Hans Haupt takes his son Herbert to a near Northwest Side car dealership, looking for a good used car for his boy. After considerable haggling, the elder Haupt puts $10 down on a $1,045 black 1941 Pontiac. The next day, Hans pays an additional $405, and Herbert drives the car off the lot.

The purchase is no ordinary rite of passage. Lane Tech graduate Herbert Haupt, 22, is a Nazi spy. A week earlier a U-boat had landed him on a Florida beach with three other conspirators. He took a train north and is staying with his folks at their third-floor apartment at 2234 N. Fremont Street. This will prove a costly homecoming for all involved.

Before Herbert steps off the train, his cover is blown. Four other saboteurs had landed at the same time in New Jersey and were reported to the FBI, which began tracking them. The FBI watches as Herbert tries to get his old job back at Simpson Optical— manufacturer of parts for the top-secret, highly accurate Norden bombsight.

The FBI will soon arrest Herbert Haupt. The press speculates that the eight spies might escape death in civilian court—they hadn't actually done anything yet—prompting the government to put them before a secret military tribunal, arguing that justice will be swifter.

It is.

Two of the group are pardoned because they went to the authorities before the FBI closed in. The other six are electrocuted on August 8, only 52 days after landing on American shores. Herbert Haupt is first. That autumn, his parents, Hans and Erna, are found guilty of treason, the purchase of the Pontiac being their central act of war. Both are stripped of their citizenship. Hans is sentenced to death, Erna gets 25 years. She will be deported in 1946; he receives leniency on appeal, and is deported 10 years later.

June 25, 2011

Until recently they were simply *Poetry Magazine*, nearly a century old, their glory days of T. S. Eliot and Carl Sandburg long behind them. A staff of four, sequestered in an 850-square-foot office on the second floor of the Newberry Library, space loaned to them for free, part collegiality, part pity.

Now they are the Poetry Foundation, which today begins two days of festivities to celebrate the opening of its $21.5 million black zinc-clad building at the corner of Superior and Dearborn, a block west of Holy Name Cathedral. Twenty-two thousand square feet, not counting the 4,000-square-foot public garden. A two-story library of blonde wood, a gorgeous public space for readings.

Consider it a lesson in the value of rejecting aspiring writers gently. In the 1970s, budding poet Ruth Lilly sent some of her efforts to *Poetry*. They weren't published, God knows, but she received a kind handwritten reply, which made her feel warmly enough that when she died, Lilly, heir to the Eli Lilly pharmaceutical fortune, left $100 million in stock to *Poetry Magazine*, a figure that doubled thanks to the surging market. Like the humble green bud in springtime opening into a glorious red rose, the magazine morphed into a foundation, with a vast, comprehensive, and quite well done website devoted to poets and poetry, plus this magnificent office/performance space/shrine. It doesn't top publishing "The Love Song of J. Alfred Prufrock" in June 1915. But it ain't bad either.

June 26, 1833

Arriving by boat the previous month from Michigan's Upper
Peninsula, Rev. Jeremiah Porter was deposited at the mouth of the
Chicago River, "a wide, wet prairie, as far as the eye could reach,
on a muddy river winding south over a sand-bar to the Lake with a
few scattered dwellings." He had been preaching at Sault Ste. Marie.
Having persuaded the soldiers at Fort Bradley to give up the vices
of drinking and dancing, or at least convincing himself that he had
done so, Porter accompanied garrison troops relieving soldiers sta-
tioned at Fort Dearborn in Chicago, still not officially incorporated
as a town.

Disappointed to find John M. I. St. Cyr, the first Catholic priest
permanently assigned to Chicago, already busily at work, having
arrived the month before, Porter knelt beside St. Cyr's church and
prayed for its downfall, setting the tone for interdenominational
relations in Chicago for the next century. Not to be outdone by any
papist, he organized early prayer efforts into the First Presbyterian
Church of Chicago, its articles of faith adopted today, at the corner
of State and Lake—seven moves later, today it is at 6400 S. Kimbark
Avenue. Porter will leave Chicago in 1835; during the Civil War he'll
bury the dead from the battle of Vicksburg. He'll keep following the
advancing frontier, and be ministering to soldiers in Wyoming at the
end of his life.

June 27, 1970

There are no floats, no bands, certainly no politicians. The parade is just another event of Gay Pride Week, sponsored by Chicago's Gay Liberation Front, along with workshops and a gay dance at the Aragon Ballroom. The march marks the first anniversary of New York's Stonewall riot, on June 28, 1969, an event not covered at all by Chicago newspapers, which tend to view homosexuality as private illness and public problem. ("Experts Doubt They're Dangerous" reads the subhead on a June 1966 four-part series in the *Daily News*, "unearthing the secrets of this tormented twilight world.")

"The homosexual's greatest dread continues to be exposure and ruin," the *Daily News* writes, an attitude not conducive to participation in parades. But a lot has changed since 1966. Today 150 men and women gather, not in twilight but daylight, to listen to speeches at Bughouse Square. Waving flags and carrying banners, chanting "Gay power to gay people!" they march to the Water Tower, then over to the Civic Center, now Daley Plaza, where they dance around the Picasso sculpture. Same-sex dancing in public is still a crime in Chicago. But police merely watch and there are no arrests.

By marching a day before the actual anniversary, Chicago beats out a much larger New York effort as the first gay pride parade in America. The parade will relocate to the North Side and eventually draw a million onlookers who overwhelm the neighborhood. Acceptance makes the parade celebratory rather than defiant, and it becomes a mainstream civic ritual, with floats from automakers and Commonwealth Edison. Richard M. Daley will be the first sitting mayor to ride in the parade. He'll also allow the city's Gay & Lesbian Hall of Fame to be established during his administration.

June 28, 1940

Last January, Chicago ad man Louis G. Cowan was sitting in his office, gazing at Lake Michigan, chewing on a pencil, and trying to dream up a new radio show. His thoughts strayed to his expectant wife. A bright kid, he hoped. Proud parents of bright kids, showing off their prodigies. On the radio . . .

A dozen sponsors consider his Quiz Kids program, then pass: too many quiz shows already. And a game tossing hard questions at gifted children, drawing their clever replies? Nobody would believe it wasn't rehearsed.

Finally Alka-Seltzer bites. But they have a concern: the name. There is already a show in Minneapolis with a similar name, *Kiddie Kwiz*. What if they sue? Efforts to brainstorm a new name fail, and with airtime hours away, producers think to call the Minnesota show's owner and just ask: Will you sue? No. A cable attesting to that is sent. *Quiz Kids* debuts today with a ringing school bell at 9:30 p.m. on WMAQ and is an immediate sensation.

The show will run for 13 years on radio and five on television. *Quiz Kids* contestants who go on to great success include James Watson, who co-discovers DNA's double helix and wins the Nobel Prize. Others will struggle with their moment of youthful fame and its subsequent lifelong absence. Gerard Darrow, at seven the youngest of the original five kids, will be featured on the cover of the September 29, 1941, *Life* magazine, gazing at one of the birds he adores. He will spend his life at menial jobs and be profiled by Studs Terkel in his epic examination of American employment, *Working*, under the name "Bruce Fletcher"—the book uses pseudonyms to encourage candor. "I grew old at a very early age," Darrow will say. "I wish it had never happened."

June 29, 1889

In the span of a few hours, Chicago quadruples in size. Saturday
morning the city fills out 43.5 square miles. By nightfall it will be 174.

What happened?

The *Daily News* is practically giddy as it lists the haul: Oakland,
Normal Park, Union Stockyards, Oakwood, Central Park, Kenwood,
Cloverville, Moreland, Hyde Park, Center, Pullman, Kensington,
South Chicago, Colehour, Hegewisch Park Manor, Riverdale,
Cummings, Englewood, Auburn Park, Argyle, Irving Park, and
Ravenswood.

But how?

Yesterday, Chicago was the fourth-largest city in the United
States, behind New York City, Philadelphia, and Brooklyn, which
will remain separate from New York until 1898. Today, and for the
next 95 years, until Los Angeles surpasses it, Chicago is indeed
America's "Second City," right behind New York.

How?

Annexation, via the ballot box. Voters went to the polls—
Saturday was selected for election day so more workmen could use
their half day off to cast their ballots—and voted to fold their towns
into Chicago.

Which leads to *why?* A number of reasons. At a packed meeting
at Grand Crossing in Hyde Park last night, L. A. Bisbee outlined
them. Not only are Chicago taxes cheaper, but "the Chicago water
was purer. The schools were better managed." Annexation would
also give Hyde Parkers access to the Chicago Public Library.

Plus there is another reason, one that will resonate with every
suburbanite who ever, while traveling, tried to tuck his home into
the charmed circle of Chicago. Just for brevity's sake, of course,
for clarity, to save trying to explain where someplace like Arlington
Heights or Northbrook are located to those who neither know nor
care. A reason articulated Friday by Frank Walker at a meeting up in
Lake View during its last hours as a separate town.

"After tomorrow," he said, "we won't have to write ourselves
down as liars every time we go away from home and register as
from Chicago so as the clerk will give us a good room."

June 30, 1870

Ada Kepley graduates from the Union College of Law of Chicago University, the first woman in the United States to earn a law degree. That doesn't mean she can practice law, however. She will be "very politely and [with] many apologies refused."

"Women might be cooks, wash women, floor scrubbers, and do any sort of menial labor at that time," she later recalls, "but they were barred from the so-called 'learned professions.'"

Kepley claims the news of her achievement will go around the world. "America which boasted to the rest of the world to be 'the land of the free and the home of the brave' gave no freedom to her women." Her husband, Henry, who had urged her to go to law school, drafts a bill in the Illinois Senate "that any women, whether married or unmarried, shall have the same right that men have to follow and engage in any business, trade or profession." It meets with "every sort of ridicule and sarcasm and objection." But it passes, and becomes law in 1872.

She does not practice, however, being caught up in the temperance movement. But Kepley will apply to the Illinois bar and be easily admitted in 1881.

JULY

July 1, 1910

The new ballpark is finished just in time. At 1 p.m., as the first of 24,900 fans stream through the turnstiles, they pass the last straggling workmen, filing out.

Right now it is simply "White Sox Park." But there are intimations of what is to come. In a pre-game ceremony, Mayor Fred A. Busse presents team owner Charles Comiskey with a banner that reads "The City of Chicago Congratulations Comiskey." The ballpark at 35th Street will officially take his name three years later.

In the 80 seasons it stands, Comiskey Park will see highlights and lowlights—1917 offering an example of the former, as the Sox win three games here against the New York Giants on the way to their sole Comiskey World Series championship. A much-cited example of the latter is the July 12, 1979, "Disco Demolition Night" radio stunt, the explosion of a crate of dance records that turned into a riot, forcing the team to forfeit the second game of a doubleheader.

But there is one aspect of that first game in 1910 that endures for over a century and might very well last as long as baseball is played: on the mound is Sox pitcher "Big Ed" Walsh. If you look in the record book at pitchers with the lowest career earned run average, No. 1, with an ERA of 1.816, is Ed Walsh. Maybe today's heat, in the mid-90s, gets to him, however, because today he does a little worse than average and lets the St. Louis Browns score twice, shutting out the White Sox in the first game in their new home.

July 2, 1932

"Four One Five H," radios Municipal Airport. "Chicago calling."

"We're over Napoleon, Ohio," replies pilot Ray Wonsey, assistant operations manager at American Airways. "Wait a minute. I have an important passenger with me. How do you like the trip, governor?"

"Fine, it's my first trip in a big cabin plane like this," says Franklin Delano Roosevelt. "When I was in the navy department we had only open planes."

The big cabin plane is a silver Ford Trimotor. It can carry 13 passengers, but two seats were removed so FDR can stretch his paralyzed legs during the eight-hour flight from Albany to Chicago and into history. Two firsts: FDR is breaking protocol by showing up to accept the nomination for president in person, and he's arriving via airplane.

An act of courage. Beloved Notre Dame football coach Knute Rockne died last year in an airplane crash. The danger is real. Traveling at 130 miles an hour, FDR's plane is buffeted by storms, and must refuel twice, at Buffalo and Cleveland, where it has to circle for 10 minutes while the waiting crowds are pushed back from the runway. Someone in the welcoming throng calls for Roosevelt to make sure to meet with Al Smith, the failed Democratic candidate in 1928, who is in Chicago already in a futile attempt to become the 1932 nominee. A meeting would prove impossible. While Roosevelt is still in the air, Smith checks out of the Congress Hotel and heads home by train. He won't be in the Chicago Stadium tonight to hear Roosevelt apologize for being late. "I have no control over the winds of heaven," he'll say, then promise a "New Deal" for America.

July 3, 1899

The official opening is not until Wednesday. But Henry Campbell, 11, is here now, on Monday. So Judge Richard Tuthill, showing the flexibility essential in juvenile court, convenes the first in the world two days early.

Campbell, of 84 Hudson Avenue, is accused of stealing. The complainants are his parents, Frank and Lena Campbell. They are present. Along with a crowd of reformers.

As with most social change, the Illinois Act to Regulate the Treatment and Control of Dependent Neglected and Delinquent Children did not happen quickly or by accident, but required years of effort. The idea is to keep children under 16 out of Chicago jails and downstate prisons, where they are housed with hardened criminals.

Henry's teary mother doesn't want him in an institution. "Judge, Henry isn't a bad boy at heart," she says. "I know he's been led into trouble by others." She urges that her son be sent to live with his grandmother in upstate New York to "escape the surroundings that have caused the mischief." Judge Tuthill agrees.

Before hearing the next case—four boys "of tender years" incarcerated at the poorhouse at Dunning—Tuthill, a Civil War vet, reads aloud the last part of the new act.

Officers finding a wayward or neglected child, Tuthill says, should not use undue haste in hurrying little ones into court, but should confer with parents or clergy, using every effort to set youthful offenders right without resorting to an arrest, save as a final measure.

He urges that the law, when applied to children, always be "liberally construed."

July 4, 1909

"Make no little plans," Daniel Burnham said, famously. And *The Plan of Chicago* is no little plan, but a hefty volume two feet tall, containing 142 illustrations. Nor is publication on the Fourth of July an accident. "The *Plan* was a declaration of independence from what its framers saw as a self-imposed tyranny of unregulated development," historian Carl Smith writes. It lays out the future for the lakefront, the parks, for thoroughfares that will radiate from downtown, striking a deliberate blow against "the formless growth of the city."

But time has a way of cutting big plans down to more modest size. The future is a headstrong beast, and will not gallop along the course Burnham sets for it. His boosterish predictions—"This city will be larger than London: that is, larger than any existing city"— will be mocked by subsequent events.

London today is more than twice the size of Chicago, measured at their borders. And cities such as Tokyo, or Sao Paolo, or Bombay, are not just bigger than either London or Chicago. But bigger than *both* put together.

Certain recommendations do become reality: the development of a shoreline parkway called Lake Shore Drive. "Municipal Pier No. 2" becomes Navy Pier, complete with stunning circular ballroom. The two-level Wacker Drive and the Michigan Avenue Bridge are indeed built.

Municipal Pier No. 1, however, remains notional. Most of the Chicago Plan's suggestions are only partially achieved. Union Station is built, but the consolidation of railroads never happens— Ogilvie and Union stations are still across the street from each other, which makes no sense from a planning perspective.

Burnham's idea of a comprehensive vision also ages poorly by completely overlooking key aspects of city life. Before the year is out, a Chicago health commissioner will denounce the plan "as lacking sufficient provisions for the comfortable housing of the poor and for bettering their living conditions."

Not true, Burnham replies. Benefits to the poor "consist chiefly of playgrounds where not only children but adults may get out and exercise in the open air near their homes." He considers that an adequate defense.

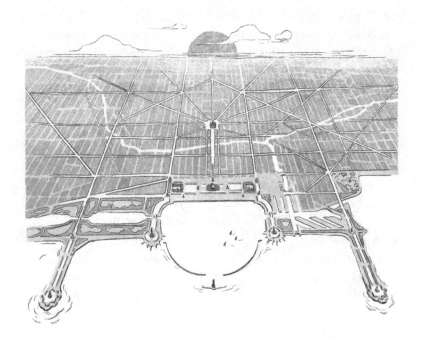

July 5, 1894

"HAVE YOU SHOT THE CHUTES?" ask ads for Paul Boyton's Water
Chute, "a novel and . . . fascinating pastime for everybody" at the corner
of 63rd and Cottage Grove. Admission to the grounds is 25 cents, including one ride and music by the Second Regiment Band.

The Water Chute, open today from 10 a.m. until midnight, the evening lit by electric lamps and spotlights, is the first permanent modern
amusement park in the United States, the first to charge admission
to an enclosed area where mechanical attractions are offered. "Flags,
illuminations, music, etc. will make the place look brilliant," promises
the *Chicago Record*, "and everything conductive to public comfort
is promised by the manager." Aquatic daredevil Boyton—who styled
himself "The Frog Man," braving frigid waters in his custom-designed
inflatable suit—is inspired by both the Ringling Brothers' and Barnum
& Bailey Circus, and the Midway at the 1893 World's Columbian
Exposition, which closed the previous fall.

The park debuted July 3, and welcomed 3,000 people on the 4th,
most braving the Water Chute. The ride requires climbing to the top of
a long wooden ramp and entering a small boat, eight at a time. The boat
is then sent racing downward at 40 mph, splashing into a small pond,
traveling some 300 feet.

"You forget to hold your breath or grab your neighbor," the *Inter
Ocean* reports, summarizing both late 19th-century anxieties and the
universal appeal of thrill rides. "You forget the price of coal and potatoes: you have no knowledge of the bill collector and the first of the
month: you are hopelessly oblivious to strikes or troubles or a scarcity of
chewing gum or cigarettes in the market, but you do know you are sail-
ing through space in a great hurry and it is a most delicious sensation."

The car then splashes into the water and cruises another 300 feet.
Such rides convey an element of real peril, though today's *Tribune* story
notes, "it is entirely safe. There was not an accident yesterday."

The Water Chute will close in 1907, supplanted by Riverview, the
Northwest Side mecca of roller coasters and games. Paul Boyton has
one more trick up his sleeve, however: he'll move east, and start another
amusement venue: Sea Lion Park at Coney Island, begun in 1895.

July 6, 1959

Queen Elizabeth II arrives, fittingly, on the royal yacht *Britannia*, which anchors in the harbor. The nautical entrance is appropriate since she is visiting Chicago to commemorate the opening of the Saint Lawrence Seaway, a series of canals and locks that alllow oceangoing ships such as hers to enter the Great Lakes via the Saint Lawrence River.

The royal barge puts the queen ashore by Buckingham Fountain. Mayor Richard J. Daley welcomes the monarch, a sea change from his predecessor "Big Bill" Thompson, whose 1927 campaign was an absurd tilt against British royalty that saw his minions weeding British books out of the library. What constitutes savvy politics has changed in 32 years.

The queen tours the Museum of Science and Industry, where she sees herself on color TV, supposedly for the first time, and notices the Supermarine Spitfire hanging from the ceiling—one that saw combat in the Battle of Britain. "Oh look, a Spit," Her Majesty says. Before formal dinner at the Conrad Hilton, she stops by a dentist's office in the Drake to have the filling that has fallen out of a royal tooth replaced.

July 7, 1931

Acting Mexican consul general Adolfo Dominguez enters Judge Thomas A. Green's municipal courtroom. Not in relation to the case being heard, vagrancy charges against a Mexican immigrant found sleeping in an alley. But for an upcoming case, in support of two women attacked at Calumet Park beach.

What happens next depends on whom you believe.

The judge will accuse Dominguez of "boisterous and improper actions, and using abusive language" after his vagrancy ruling, in which he referred to Mexicans as "idlers" and wondered why the consulate doesn't so something about them.

Dominguez's lawyer will insist that the moment the consul walked in the courtroom and Green was informed of his presence, "the judge leaped to his feet, and began an amazing and incoherent tirade in which he said the consul was no good, the Mexican government was no good. . . . Senor Dominguez tried to remonstrate, but he was outyelled, the judge shouting, 'Shut up or I'll throw you in the can.'"

Which Green does, sentencing the consul general to six months in the Cook County Jail, vowing that nothing short of an order from President Hoover will get him to back down. In reality, all it takes is a complaint from the Mexican government to the State Department, and a telegram from the State Department to Gov. Louis Emmerson, who does the rest. Green relents, voiding his order—Dominguez will spend about four hours behind bars—while insisting to the press that he is in no way apologizing.

"I still believe I'm right," the judge says.

July 8, 1926

Railroad rules prohibit a train from moving unless there is sufficient pressure in the brake lines of the last car. As a 116-car New York Central train—62 loaded boxcars, 51 empty—builds up steam in the Englewood yard, conductor A. M. Jellison asks engineer J. E. Nelson to give him more air in the line. Normally this would be done with hand signals, or a lantern, or even sending someone hurrying the mile and a quarter between the caboose and the engine.

This is not a usual trip, however, but the official first test-run of a new system: shortwave radio, designed by the Zenith Radio Corporation. In a passenger car are newsmen and officials from Zenith, plus officials from the Rock Island, the Nickel Plate, the Michigan Central, the Lehigh Valley, and other railroads.

At 10:15 a.m., the brakes charged and ready, Engineer Nelson, at the controls of the Mohawk-type engine, No. 2561, opens the throttle and says into the transmitter, "We're moving."

July 9, 1893

James Cornish does not seem like a man poised to make medical history. A railroad package handler, he is relaxing in a bar, enjoying a whiskey, when a fight breaks out around him. He stands up, and is stabbed in the chest by a stranger.

Cornish is rushed to Provident Hospital, where he comes under the care of Dr. Daniel Hale Williams. Williams sews him up. But the next day Cornish's heartbeat grows fainter, and Williams decides the knife must have nicked his heart. Williams makes a six-inch incision and, lifting a rib, sees a tear in the pericardium, the sac surrounding the heart. He sews it up.

Williams achieved many firsts in his career. Though sent to be a shoemaker's apprentice at age 11, he became the first African American to graduate from Northwestern University's Chicago School of Medicine. He was one of the founders of Provident Hospital, a mecca for healthcare to the Black community. But those crediting him with "the first successful open-heart surgery" are simply wrong, because a) repairing a nick in the pericardial sac isn't open-heart surgery, and b) the identical procedure was performed almost two years earlier in St. Louis. That said, he's certainly the first surgeon in Chicago to open a man's chest and operate on his beating heart. More importantly, it works. James Cornish lives until 1931.

July 10, 1926

Lester J. Wolf is only 19, one of the youngest people in the country to hold a commercial broadcaster license. He still lives in Homewood with his parents and works as assistant operator at the transmitter for WOK. Tonight he's working the late shift.

At 40 minutes past midnight, Al Katz and his Kittens are playing the Moon-Lite Gardens at the Chicago Beach Hotel in Kenwood, 20 miles away. The crowd calls for "Valencia! Valencia!"—the dance craze of the moment—and the group swings into the number. "Its exotic rhythms sent gilded heels gliding across the glistening floor," *Radio Digest* notes, after the tragedy.

WOK broadcasts the fun "throughout the Middle West into homes where lonely hearts were hungry for happiness and joy." During the thunderous applause that follows, a fuse blows at WOK's transmitter and the signal goes dead. In his eagerness to get the station back on the air, Wolf reaches for the blown connection without first cutting the power. The Thornton High School graduate receives a 6,000-volt shock and falls to the floor. He quickly stands up, tells the studio director he is okay, but a few seconds later collapses and dies. *Radio Digest* calls him "the first martyr in the field of broadcasting for public entertaining," as if there will be many more. "A MARTYR TO RADIO" is inscribed on his tombstone in Homewood Memorial Gardens.

July 11, 1985

Senior Cook County circuit court judge Richard LeFevour is a cheat. For 14 years, Assistant US Attorney Candace Fabri assures the jury, he "cheated the people of the state of Illinois" of the right to a fair judicial system, not one where the chief judge of traffic court takes cash bribes to let drunk drivers go free.

No, Patrick Tuite counters for the defense at the close of today's six-hour session, it is the three government witnesses against LeFevour, all police officers, who are "a pathetic drunk . . . a con man and a snake oil salesman," all three "liars and cheats who made deals and would say anything."

The dramatic eight-week trial is the capstone of Operation Greylord, a federal probe into corruption in Cook County.

LeFevour is the biggest fish of the 15 judges, four court clerks, 13 police officers, and 50 lawyers convicted in a massive investigation. The probe saw the FBI stage fake robberies, concoct drunk-driving arrests and false illegal weapons cases, result-ing in fabricated charges that LeFevour and others could be bribed to dismiss. That way, no actual lawbreakers were let off the hook.

Tomorrow the case will go to the jury, which ponders eight weeks' worth of testimony over seven hours before finding LeFevour guilty of 59 counts of racketeering, plus mail- and income-tax fraud. US District Judge Charles Norgle Sr., an honest jurist, sentences LeFevour to 12 years in prison, which is lenient. He is eligi-ble for 300.

July 12, 1951

Late in the afternoon, Gov. Adlai Stevenson calls out the Illinois National Guard. About 300 members of the 129th Infantry Regiment, 33rd Division, leave summer training and head to Cicero. Each guardsman is issued two rounds of ammunition and told not to shoot unless ordered. Joined by 100 or so state and local police, they form a perimeter around 6139 W. 19th Street, a three-story, 20-unit apartment building where earlier in the week Harvey E. Clark, a Black CTA bus driver and World War II vet, had tried to move with his family—wife Johnette, daughter Michelle, eight, and son Harvey III, six. They would have been the first Black family to live in Cicero.

Tuesday night, rioters smashed windows in the building while Cicero cops stood by and did nothing. Wednesday, locals broke in and trashed the apartment, tossing the Clarks' furniture into the street. Today's battle lasts about two hours. Some 4,000 rioters hurl bricks and rocks. A police car is set on fire. The guardsmen use tear gas. Police make 60 arrests. Nineteen people are injured, including six guardsmen and four rioters cut by bayonets.

"I didn't think there were people like we saw last night," one guardsman marvels the next morning.

July 13, 1903

Manufacturing automobiles is expensive. The new company is less than a month old and has already burned through the $28,000 put up by its initial dozen investors. Now they're down to $223.65 in the bank.

So today's bookkeeping entry of $850 from Chicago dentist Ernest Pfennig is a welcome infusion into the fledgling Detroit firm. The income is written into the ledger, making it official: the Ford Motor Company has sold its first car, though the car itself is the 11th vehicle manufactured by Henry Ford. A two-cylinder, eight-horsepower Model A automobile, in red—the only color available—with a top speed of 30 miles per hour. It will be delivered to 18 Clybourn Avenue in two weeks.

July 14, 1966

Dawn will not come. The minutes crawl by in deathly silence. Corazon Amurao, a student nurse, hides under the bed. For hours. Too terrified to move. She hears the 5 a.m. alarm go off. She slowly begins to untie the sheets binding her hands and feet. She emerges, shakily stands, peers into the hallway, enters it. She sees a body in the bathroom. Heading to her own bedroom, she steps over three more bodies, drenched in blood. She climbs atop her bunk bed, opens the window, and starts to scream. "They are all dead! They are all dead! My friends are all dead!" For five minutes. No one replies. She crawls out the window and screams for 20 more minutes until someone finally comes, another nursing student from a nearby townhouse. The story begins to radiate across the city and world.

Eight student nurses murdered on the Southeast Side. A killer on the loose. Amurao, who survived by rolling under a bed, remembers the killer's "Born to Raise Hell" tattoo, which leads authorities to suspect Richard Speck, a boozy, wandering sailor already being questioned for a string of murders and attacks. Five days later he'll attempt to kill himself, slashing his wrists, then change his mind and seek help. At Cook County Hospital, one of Amurao's nurse friends tends to Speck. A doctor notices his tattoo.

July 15, 1832

Gen. Winfield Scott is American's go-to military man. He has been since the War of 1812, and will be until the Civil War. So of course President Andrew Jackson would dispatch him westward to get rid of Chief Black Hawk who, tired of constant encroachment on his land, is raiding the countryside with a band of followers.

Scott dutifully assembled a force and headed west, but ran into a foe even more elusive and deadly than the Sauk leader. Today he shares the bad news.

"Sir," begins Scott's letter to Gov. John Reynolds, from "Headquarters N.W. Army Chicago," "to prevent or correct the exaggerations of rumor in respect to the existence of cholera at this place, I address myself to your Excellency."

Scott came from Buffalo on the steamer *Sheldon Thompson* with three other ships carrying six companies of artillery and two companies of infantry. They crossed Lake Erie, heading for Detroit. But the fast-moving disease was a stowaway, and made short work of the men. On the morning of the 8th, "all on board were in high health and spirits," Scott writes. "The disease rapidly spread over the next three days." By the time they reached Chicago, a quarter of his men were dead and more than a third sick. Thirty bodies were thrown overboard during the last leg from Mackinac Island to Chicago. On shore, the men died so fast that they were buried in pits without coffins, "without notice and without remembrance."

Gathering what men can still walk, Scott will march his band to Prairie du Chien, only to find out that Black Hawk's forces had been destroyed a few days earlier. Cholera will plague Chicago for decades, a terrifying illness where victims can wake up healthy and be dead by nightfall. If Chicagoans seem unusually fixated on clean water, leaving a water tower in the middle of their showcase street, cholera is one unspoken reason why.

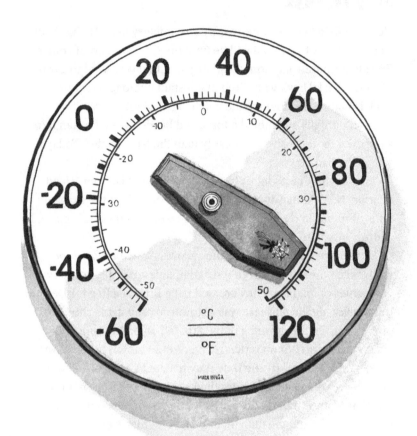

July 16, 1995

The temperature peaks at 94 degrees, the coolest high in five days. Five brutally hot, humid, deadly days, including one that hit 104 degrees.

"This is an unprecedented disaster in the history of the city of Chicago," Cook County medical examiner Edmund Donoghue said, after only 56 heat deaths had been confirmed, with at least as many bodies waiting to be examined, and more arriving all the time. As the tragedy unfolded, the city was maddeningly slow on the uptake.

"It's hot out there," squeaked Mayor Richard M. Daley, master of the obvious. "It's very very very hot."

Over these five days, 739 Chicagoans die—twice as many as perished in the Great Chicago Fire. The city will be reluctant to acknowledge what is happening, even as local meatpackers send refrigerated trucks—nine in all—to the medical examiner's office on Harrison Street to store bodies in the parking lot. Chicagoans, including the media, cling to the notion that Donoghue must be grandstanding, must be calling every person who dies in Chicago during the heat wave a heat death.

"You can't attribute it all to heat," Daley sputters when confronted with the facts. "You can't. It's impossible."

But it is possible: poor, mostly Black, often elderly Chicagoans who lack air conditioning, are isolated, and have no ability to escape the furnace. The Chicago heat wave remains the worst heat-related disaster in American history.

July 17, 1866

The Chicago River is narrow. Originally about 50 feet across. While the Hudson River is more than half a mile wide passing between Manhattan and New Jersey. Even after being dredged, the Chicago River is only 300 feet wide at Michigan Avenue. Its banks are low. A bridge over the river clears the water by 20 feet. Which means for ships to pass along the river, the bridges must open. The more ships ply the river, the more bridges are open, the more tangled downtown traffic becomes. So the common council votes today to finance and dig a tunnel under the river at Washington Street, and, further, that the Board of Public Works be ordered to construct a second tunnel, going north, at State Street.

"As we cannot much longer go over the river, we must go under it," the *Tribune* observes. Easier said than done. The effort, once started, will run out of money and be abandoned. And when the work *is* done, the tunnel will collapse and have to be begun anew. Finally, the 1,605-foot-long tunnel opens in 1869. (It's that long because a horse and buggy have to be able to go up and down a gentle slope.)

July 18, 1980

A Ukrainian bus driver, in this country six months, walks into the 14th District police station and, well, let Sgt. Leo G. Rojek describe the situation, in his report to the Youth Division: "Mr. Michael Polovchak stated his daughter Natalie enticed Walter Polovchak (son) to run away from home rather than to return to Russia with the family and she was hiding him in the home of their cousin."

The police and the elder Polovchak go to the cousin's house and arrest Walter, 12, taking him to Area 5 Youth Division as a runaway. There the boy tells police that he refuses to return with his parents to the Soviet Union. The cops shrug, call the State Department, and the international media lets out a whoop and hurries over to watch. Moscow says the boy—sister Natalie, 17, is old enough to make her own decisions, apparently—has been kidnapped, tempted away from his family and homeland with "a bicycle and Jell-O."

That's actually true, kind of. His cousin had dug a bike out of the basement, won years earlier on Bozo's Circus, and given it to Walter. A "real American bike," as Walter later enthuses. "As real to me as the stars and stripes of the American flag." With "shiny chrome fenders, big flaring handlebars, and a sturdy frame." Walter loves the bike. And he loves Jell-O, too. "When I first arrived, all I could think of was Jell-O."

The next day Walter announces his intention to defect, not due to the dual allure of his bike and Jell-O, but based on faith. He is a Baptist, he says, and will face persecution back in the atheistic Soviet Union. Edwin Meese's Justice Department runs out the clock and five years later the case is dropped as moot. Polovchak becomes a US citizen, days after his 18th birthday.

July 19, 1888

The bosses have the upper hand. Always. They don't just control the railroads and the factories, the money and the politicians. They also have the spies, the Pinkertons, and a glance at their letterhead hints at what a potent force they truly are: Pinkerton's National Detective Agency, founded by Allan Pinkerton in Chicago in 1850, with offices across the country—Chicago, Denver, Philadelphia, New York, Boston—all "CONNECTED BY TELEPHONE." They have a fearsome reputation embodied by their logo, an open eye above the slogan "WE NEVER SLEEP." They employ operatives such as M. D. J., who can slip in and out of union offices and meetings. His report for Thursday, July 19, 1888, relays:

> The operative called at the National Hotel at 8:30 a.m., but did not see any one he knew, so went to 119 Fifth Ave., where he met engineer Scott, Vroman and Carroll from California, Even from Ft. Wayne, and Conners from Cleveland and was introduced from Bowles, the brother of the "squealer" as they call him.

The men talk about the recent trial of saboteurs, convicted of dynamite attacks against railroad property downstate, and what the next step the Brotherhood of Locomotive Engineers might take in its strike against the Chicago, Burlington & Quincy Railroad, whose management rejects even the notion that workers have a right to collectively bargain.

M. D. J. shares the union scuttlebutt: "Carroll said, P. M. Arthur would never be elected this fall if this strike goes against the Brotherhood; the convention will be filled with fire eaters from the coast and all over the West. . . . He also said the men were d—— fools for allowing those 'scabs' to get their engines out; where he was there were two revolvers on every engine and all trouble settled this way."

The strike will be settled the CB&Q way: by failing utterly, the strikers all fired, replaced by scabs, management conscripts, and, yes, Pinkertons.

July 20, 1901

Charlie Fitzmorris arrives at Chicago from the west, by train.

He has been gone exactly 60 days, 13 hours, 29 minutes, and 42.8 seconds. In that time, he has circumnavigated the world.

Charlie is 17 years old, a student at Lake High School.

His adventure began in July, thanks to a stunt cooked up by publisher William Randolph Hearst, who had spent the first months of 1901 abroad, buying medieval tapestries and Renaissance bric-a-brac. A "Round the World Race" among three schoolboys from three cities served by his papers, San Francisco, New York, and Chicago.

The goal: beat the 72-day record set in 1890 by Nellie Bly, a reporter for Hearst's hated rival, Joseph Pulitzer's *New York World*.

Fitzmorris and a handler traveled from New York to Berlin, then on to Moscow. Traversing Russia was the biggest challenge—25 days from Moscow to Vladivostok—then Japan, British Columbia, and back home to Chicago to set the record.

A record improved by Hearst's *Chicago American* cheating on his behalf, hiring express trains, running full throttle on orders from railroad presidents, while the boys representing New York and San Francisco stuck to the rules and credulously relied on regularly scheduled transportation. The fix was in all along for Hearst's newest paper.

On his return today, Fitzmorris is met at Union Station by his parents, the acting mayor, a brass band, and Buffalo Bill Cody, who drives him home to 4623 S. Emerald Avenue in a gilded coach followed by 200 horsemen, the *Daily News* reports, never mentioning Hearst. Fitzmorris wins a job as a "super office boy" at the *American* and a reputation for resourcefulness that will lead to political power: two years later he will become secretary to Mayor Carter Harrison II, then to "Big Bill" Thompson for five years, before becoming the city's youngest police chief ever at 36.

July 21, 1919

Five p.m. approaches. The Illinois Trust and Savings Bank at LaSalle and Jackson is now closed to the public. Under the grand two-story central rotunda, 150 clerks, bookkeepers, telegraphers, and secretaries finish up for the day, checking figures, carrying records to the vault, covering their typewriters. A shadow passes over the domed skylight, then a flash, an ominous single second before a charred body crashes through the glass and slams to the marble floor. The room seems to explode, fire pouring from above.

"Oh my God, it's raining hell!" someone screams.

The Goodyear *Wingfoot Express*, a hydrogen-filled blimp, has exploded over the Loop and crashed into the bank. It is the first major aviation disaster in American history, the news instantly disseminated—fans at the White Sox game at Comiskey Park see the dirigible explode; sports reporters telegraph the news to their papers, which are relaying it to New York before the *Wingfoot* hits the ground. Thirteen people die, 10 bank employees and three of the five aboard the blimp—two survive thanks to parachutes, including one that is aflame on the descent.

July 22, 1934

The lady in red wears orange. Anna Sage tipped off the feds the day before. The Romanian prostitute has information to trade, but wants something first. She is considered an "undesirable alien." She wants a promise she will not be deported.

Sure, sure, an agent said.

Good to her word, there Sage is, in an orange skirt, accompanying Public Enemy No. 1, John Dillinger, into the Biograph Theater on Lincoln Avenue to see *Manhattan Melodrama*. Dillinger, the nation's most notorious bank robber and murderer, the man who broke out of the jail at Crown Point, Indiana, by whittling a piece of wood into the shape of a gun and blackening it with shoe polish, buys the tickets.

After the movie, at 10:38 p.m., Dillinger and Sage exit. Dillinger is gunned down by half a dozen waiting FBI agents. Sage will be deported anyway, past promises swept aside, as is her insistence that she wore orange. History still calls her "the lady in red." History can be funny that way.

July 23, 1941

An abortion costs $50 in Chicago, and though the procedure is illegal, hundreds of doctors know where to send women "in trouble"—the Gabler clinic on the sixth floor of 190 N. State Street.

Keeping Gabler open—over the past decade, it has arranged or performed 18,000 abortions, or about five a day—incurs nonmedical expenses. So Ada Martin, the former receptionist who now runs the place, meets once a month at a tavern on LaSalle Street to slip $100 to state's attorney police officer Daniel Moriarity. In return, he is expected to keep investigations away from her clinic.

But the system breaks down, as will happen when a medical procedure is both in demand and illegal. Federal agents, drawn by the high income earned connecting abortion doctors to eager patients, start poking around. The case is "too hot," in Moriarity's words, even for the $3,000 bribe—more than a year's salary—she gives him to spread around and make this trouble go away. As added inspiration, Martin threatens to take him down with her if she's arrested. That was unwise.

Moriarity, 15 years in the department, thinking to silence Martin, went to her home, pushed past a maid, and emptied his service revolver into what he thought was her sleeping form. It wasn't. Killed was her daughter, Jennifer, 24. The circle of tragedy widens. Moriarity's wife had a nervous breakdown when he was arrested. The youngest of their three daughters is seven.

Today, about 3 p.m., prosecutors wind up their statements in the latest case to come out of the "Million Dollar Abortion Ring" that has already sent out shock waves of anguish. A doctor, Dr. Henry J. Millstone, killed himself after being indicted on felony charges in April. He left a note for his wife, Emily, to "keep her chin up." Instead she drank ammonia and died too. Two assistant state's attorneys were fired, caught in a widening slough of corruption that involves doctors, nurses, druggists, cops.

Moriarity pleads insanity. The state asks for the electric chair.

The jury deliberates for six hours and 25 minutes, with a 40-minute break for supper. They find him not insane, and sentence Moriarity, 40, to life in prison. He'll die in Joliet in 1946. Abortion becomes legal in Chicago 27 years later.

July 24, 1915

Bobbie Aanstad can do something most 13-year-old girls cannot do. She can swim. Her boyfriend Ernie Carlson taught her on vacation in Michigan.

She lives in Logan Square, a Norwegian immigrant enclave, with her widowed mother and little sister. Her uncle Olaaf works at the vast Western Electric works in Cicero, and invited them to come today on the company excursion to Michigan City.

So the family takes an early trolley and arrives at the Chicago River about 6:45 a.m. Five ships await them, but the *Eastland* is to leave first, so they find a spot on the cabin deck.

When the *Eastland* receives its 2,500 passengers—the absolute limit—the gangways are closed. The ship, notoriously unstable, begins listing back and forth, now toward the dock, now the river. For the picnickers, the swaying is a lark; they whoop happily as the boat tilts.

Then the *Eastland* begins to tip toward the middle of the river and keeps going. A refrigerator topples over, sending beer bottles crashing. A piano crushes a boy. The laughter turns to screams as the boat tips on its side and doesn't return.

In what is now a dark, watery cell, Bobbie dog-paddles for her life, then grabs on to a railing, while others die around her. Outside, the surface of the Chicago River is a thrashing, clawing, screaming mass of humanity.

"Most of them, it seemed, could not swim, or were dragged down by those that could not swim," deckhand Harry Miller says later. "Men, women and children, all over that part of the river."

Bystanders toss chairs, ropes, chicken crates, anything they can find, into the river. Along with rescuers come pickpockets and gawkers. The women in the water are doubly doomed—not only have the vast majority never been taught to swim, but they are weighed down by long buttoned dresses that can't be quickly shed. If rescue doesn't come in seconds, it's too late.

Acetylene torches are used to cut holes in the hull to release those trapped inside. But 838 passengers and six crew die aboard and around the *Eastland*, still tied to the pier.

Some things will remain unchanged to the 21st century: the same clock across the river at the red brick Reid, Murdoch Building broods upon the scene. And most girls still cannot swim well enough to save their lives. In her golden years, Bobbie Aanstad will marry the boy who taught her to swim and live to be 90. Her granddaughters remain in the Chicago area and remember her always saying: "It's very important you girls know how to swim."

July 25, 1942

The Douglas Aircraft Company plans to build a factory on 1,347 acres at Orchard Place, a bucolic expanse of apple trees and cornfields south of Des Plaines. Beginning today, farmers start auctioning off equipment and finding new places to live, sometimes by moving their houses miles away. "It's about time for me to quit farming anyway," says Herman Stade, who with his wife farmed a 40-acre spread along Higgins Road for 43 years. A thousand people attend his auction. By autumn, bulldozers will be leveling tomato patches, pulling down barns, and felling apple trees. Orchard Place will be memorialized in abbreviated form as "ORD" on billions of luggage tags, code for O'Hare International Airport, which will rise here after the Douglas plant closes in 1946.

July 26, 2019

Chantell Grant and Andrea Stoudemire, members of MASK—
Mothers Against Senseless Killings—are standing on the corner
of 75th and Stewart, a vacant lot where the group often gathers,
holding barbecues, trying to exert a calming presence on the
Gresham neighborhood and quell periodic violence. Formed in
2015, MASK also fights for greater access to healthy food and
adequate housing.

About 10 p.m. a blue SUV pulls up and someone inside opens
fire. Both Grant, 26, a mother of four, and Stoudemire, 35, a mother
of three, are shot in the chest and killed. Years go by without police
identifying a suspect or making an arrest. Which is not unusual.
Only about half the murders in Chicago result in police ever arresting a suspect. When the victim is white. When the victim is Black,
that figure falls below 25 percent.

July 27, 1919

Five friends hop a produce truck and head east to the lakeshore on a sweltering Sunday afternoon. They retrieve a raft they've tucked away, and take it out on Lake Michigan, halfway between the Black beach at 25th Street, "the race's answer to Atlantic City," and the white beach at 29th Street. As they play, their raft drifts south. Too far south. A young German immigrant standing on the breakwater, George Stauber, starts hurling stones at the raft. Eugene Williams, 17, is hit on the forehead, slips into the water, and doesn't come up.

His friends rush to a lifeguard, then to a white policeman, who refuses to arrest Stauber and prevents a Black officer from doing so. Instead, they arrest some of the Black bystanders, enraging others. Chaos and rumor spread—Blacks tell each other that policemen held back a Black crowd while the whites threw stones; whites tell each other that it was a white teen who died.

Whites attack and Blacks defend themselves. At first. Then general mayhem sets in. Two Black men are shot. A white policeman is shot and wounded. The fighting escalates as people pour into the streets and night falls.

The next day, newspapers fan the flames. In the *Daily News*, the violence is the result of Black mobs rampaging over nothing. The police are quoted saying there isn't a bruise on the drowned teen. No atrocity is too horrific or, it turns out, too untrue for the *Chicago Defender* to breathlessly print on the front page while simultaneously decrying "groups of men whose minds were inflamed by rumors of brutal attacks."

The reality is bad enough: Chicagoans being shot, stabbed, stoned, pulled off streetcars, and beaten. Homes burned to the ground, rampaging mobs chasing victims. Seven days of riots, the worst racial turmoil in Chicago's history. By the end, 23 Blacks and 15 whites are killed.

July 28, 1932

Admission is 25 cents, but attendance is still poor. Between the State Department denying visas to foreigners and the NCAA threatening to ban any college athlete taking part, not half of the predicted thousand participants show up for the International Workers Athletic Meet, sponsored by the Communist Party USA.

Known informally as the Chicago Counter-Olympics, it is a high-water mark in the marriage of radical politics with track-and-field competition. But a modest one. The sports-oriented *Times* limits its coverage to a three-sentence squib, one sentence being "The carnival is sponsored by the Labor Sports union and will run until Saturday." Even coverage in the *Daily Worker* is spotty. Mostly it represents a populist vision of sports that won't take hold, as the next century sees athletics cemented to collegiate life, consumer capitalism, and unblinking patriotism.

They are lucky to have a venue at all. Loyola University originally agreed to host the competition. But Samuel Insull, college trustee and utility magnate, raised a ruckus, and Loyola backed out in May. So the organizers boldly approached Amos Alonzo Stagg, "the Muscular Christian," who was puzzled by the politics of it, but gave use of the University of Chicago's Stagg Field, for free, provided no liquor is served.

"I could not see any harm could come to the university," explained Stagg. Harm, or at least notoriety, does come to the University of Chicago, which takes on a pinkish hue, especially after the president of the Communist Party is invited to chat with students.

July 29, 1938

The simplest question can lead to the most trouble.

"How do you keep in trim during the winter months in order to keep up your batting average?" WGN broadcaster Bob Elson innocently asks Yankee outfielder Jake Powell on live radio during a pre-game interview at Comiskey Park.

"Oh, that's easy," Powell replies. "I'm a policeman. I beat n—— over the head with my blackjack while on my beat."

Elson cuts Powell off and later apologizes to listeners. But outrage will grow. When baseball commissioner Kenesaw Mountain Landis calls Powell into his Chicago office, the slugger "didn't remember saying anything offensive." Which is how some sportswriters of the day view the situation. Landis suspends Powell for 10 days, the first major league athlete sidelined for a racist remark. Yankees manager Joe McCarthy blames the radio station for forcing players to do interviews and suggests the comment was "said maybe only in a joke."

It isn't a joke to Black fans.

"For the good of all," demands the *Defender*, "Jake Powell should be banned from organized baseball" and fired from the Akron Police Department. The latter turns out to be impossible, because he never worked there. It was just a self-aggrandizing lie, spun out of his applying for a job as a policeman, a reminder of the close connection between bigotry and deceit.

Baseball welcomes Powell back, and he will play until 1945. In his own twisted way, he contributes to the integration of the major leagues nine years later by shoving what has been ignored out into the open for all to see. Baseball "has always treated the Negroes as Adolf Hitler treats the Jews," Westbrook Pegler will write. "Powell can argue plausibly that he got his cue from the very men whose hired disciplinarian has benched him."

July 30, 1971

A solid century of operation, plus, from Christmas Day 1865 to tonight at midnight. A square mile of land, from 39th to 47th and from Halsted to Ashland. And livestock in quantities that burst the limits of language. "So many cattle no one had ever dreamed existed in the world," Upton Sinclair wrote in *The Jungle*, one of the most significant novels to come out of Chicago. "The sound of them here was as of all the barnyards in the universe." Visitors to Chicago were obligated to make the pilgrimage to contemplate the stockyards, to see pigs hauled up by a leg and conveyed, squealing and writhing, to where their throats were slit moments before being plunged into a vat of scalding water. Cattle forced down chutes, stunned between the eyes with a sledgehammer, then butchered.

"Hog butcher to the world," in Carl Sandburg's immortal phrase.

The Union Stockyards name refers, not to the North during the Civil War, but to the joining together of slaughterhouses that had been scattered around the city. They consolidated to be near rail transport, and it is the decline of those railroads that sealed their doom. At midnight, the stockyards abandon their location near the river and railroad tracks. On Monday morning a new, much smaller stockyard opens 50 miles away in Joliet, next to a highway.

July 31, 1929

Allen Heinekamp is only three years old. But at 1:45 p.m. he does something that later generations of Chicagoans will never be allowed to do at any age, nor even imagine possible: tour the Mars candy factory at 2019 N. Oak Park Avenue. He is among 11 children who watch sticky masses of sweets palpitated in giant mixing machines, flavored with chocolate, spread over tables, then taken into a cooling room.

The factory was built a year earlier by Frank Mars, who moved his candy company from Minneapolis to be closer to Chicago's transportation hub. He set out to build "the most beautiful" candy factory in America, and the Spanish-style, red tile-roofed structure he came up with certainly looks more like a country club—it was built on 16 acres purchased from the Westward Ho Golf Club—than an industrial operation.

The children watch in "quiet fascination," perhaps because they are chaperoned by three mothers and a policeman, John Sprengel, a 17-year vet of the mounted force. The effort is sponsored by the Illinois Congress of Parents and Teachers, which is trying to give mothers more time on their own and reduce the solitary nature of motherhood by organizing play groups, issuing rules for games, and sponsoring weekly outings to factories. Mars will continue its open-door policy until 1934, when Frank Mars dies and his heirs retreat behind the unfortunate curtain of secrecy that enshrouds most candy companies in Chicago. The factory will operate quietly for nearly a century until 2022, when Mars announces that it will close in two years.

AUGUST

Aug. 1, 1897

"FREE BABY DAY" reads the classified ad in today's *Tribune*.
"At the BEATRICE TONNESEN PHOTOGRAPHIC STUDIO."
The 26-year-old Wisconsin native is doing something new. Let an
amazed July 7, 1897, *Printers' Ink* magazine describe the wonder:

> A young woman artist in Chicago . . . who owns a large photograph
> studio on Michigan Avenue, has, in connection with portrait work,
> developed model photography. She uses models just as any artist
> uses his models, only in place of brush and paint she uses the camera
> and such accessories are needed to make the picture. In this way,
> beautiful art pictures are made. Besides this purely artistic use of
> models, there is also a practical commercial use, which is at the same
> time artistic. That is to say, these pictures are used in advertising.

Tonnesen pioneered the commercial modeling agency. "When
I am walking along the street or am in a store and see a person
who strikes me as particularly desirable for a model, I usually stop
her right on the spot and tell her what I want," she told a reporter.
"Of course, I have to use a little discretion, but I am almost never
refused."

A client requesting 100 photos of 100 babies, half smiling, half
frowning, is a bigger challenge. Too many babies to snag one by one
in the street. So Tonnesen runs her advertisement, hoping that the
promise of a free photograph of their children will draw mothers
with babies to her studio at 1301 S. Michigan. It does.

Aug. 2, 1965

Chicago promised to desegregate schools. But the city is taking its time about it. To give it a nudge, Dick Gregory, comedian and political activist, leads a march from City Hall to Bridgeport, demanding the Chicago Public Schools get rid of superintendent Benjamin Willis, who's been happily packing Black students into makeshift trailer classrooms.

"First we will go over to the snake pit," Gregory says. "When we leave there, we will go to the snake's house."

They are met near the mayor's home at 3536 S. Lowe by a mob of about 350, shouting racial hate, spitting, hurling raw eggs and rocks. Rather than arrest the assailants, however, police ask the demonstrators to leave. When they refuse, the police arrest 65 and charge them with disorderly conduct.

The Illinois Supreme Court will uphold the arrests. But in *Gregory v. City of Chicago* (1969), the US Supreme Court overturns the conviction, ruling unanimously that the protesters were arrested for demonstrating, not for failing to obey police orders to disperse.

Chicago's disorderly conduct laws are a "meat-ax ordinance" that do not overrule constitutionally protected rights, Justice Hugo Black writes. Allowing the arrest of demonstrators due to the actions of bystanders would amount to a heckler's veto. Nor do American freedoms depend upon the snap judgments of any given policeman in any given situation.

"Under our democratic system of government," Black writes, "lawmaking is not entrusted to the moment-to-moment judgment of the policeman on his beat."

Aug. 3, 1795

"A treaty of peace, between the United States of America and the Tribes of Indians called the Wyandots, Delawares, Shawnoes, Ottawas, Chipewas, Puttawatimis, Miamis, Eel River, Weeas and Kickapos," the draft begins. "To put an end to a destructive war, to settle all controversies, and to restore harmony and a friendly intercourse between the said Indian tribes and the United States . . ."

The Treaty of Greenville, signed today by Gen. "Mad Anthony" Wayne and the tribes he defeated at the Battle of Fallen Timbers, won't do any of that. It's one of countless pacts solemnly signed then promptly ignored in the relentless expansion of settlers, pushing Native Americans from their land.

But it does place under the authority of the future US government "One piece of land six miles square at the mouth of Chikago River, emptying into the south-west end of Lake Michigan, where a fort formerly stood."

Aug. 4, 1830

It's all so familiar. Nearly 200 years later, "A map of the town of Chicago" by James Thompson could still be used to navigate downtown. The Chicago River in the center, of course, dividing into a North Branch and South Branch. The rest of the map filled by orderly numbered lots between straight, horizontal streets: South Water, Lake, Randolph, Washington. Intersected by north and south streets, Market, Franklin, Wells, LaSalle, Clarke (eventually sanded down to "Clark").

The map was created because the state had authorized a canal from the Illinois River at Ottawa to Chicago. To pay for the canal, the state will plat and sell the land. But to do that, they need a map. The Illinois and Michigan Canal Commission hired Thompson, a well-respected surveyor. He surveyed Ottawa first, then Chicago.

The streets are made 66 feet wide because that is the length of a surveyor's chain. They are still that wide today. Thompson not only laid out the streets, he named them. Some names are personal— he's from Randolph County. Some are practical. Lake is the usual route to Lake Michigan. Canal because that's what this is all about. The map is bordered by State, on the right, and Madison along the bottom, though those aren't named. Seventy years later those two streets will be used as the starting point for the city grid system because they border this map.

As payment for his work, the committee offers Thompson the choice of two acres in Chicago or $300 in cash. He takes the money.

Aug. 5, 1966

The Rev. Martin Luther King Jr. steps out of a car.

"Kill him! Kill him!" screams the mob. They've been waiting in Marquette Park for hours. Waiting for civil rights marchers protesting against real estate companies that refuse to show Black Chicagoans homes in all-white neighborhoods like Chicago Lawn and Gage Park.

They scream "White power!" and "Up with the KKK!" and "Go home, you apes!" and worse. Waving Confederate flags, they hurl firecrackers at the marchers, whom they outnumber 10 to 1. They throw rocks and bottles at the police and the police surge at them, nightsticks drawn.

King makes it about 20 paces before he is hit in the back of the head by a large rock. The blow drives him to one knee. But he stands up and keeps going.

"I have never seen such hate, not in Mississippi or Alabama," King says. At a rally afterward, he thanks his parents for teaching him not to hate. "Stones are not going to stop us," he says. "Our numbers will grow larger. We are going back, because we are in the right."

Aug. 6, 1912

Teddy Roosevelt bursts through a curtain of policemen like a star tenor striding onto an opera stage, and the 12,000 faithful packing the Chicago Coliseum go berserk. The wild cheering, singing, and general delirium goes on for almost an hour. "We want Teddy!" the crowd chants. Men weep. Suffragettes in their yellow "Votes for Women" sashes wave red bandanas, a symbol of Roosevelt's Rough Riders. They stand on their chairs and shout. Jane Addams is lifted bodily into the air and passed over the press section to meet the former president, who shakes her hand and smiles.

"This is more than politics," Sen. Joseph Dixon observes. "It is almost a religion."

Roosevelt has formed his own political party, the Progressive or "Bull Moose" Party ("moose men" are calling "moo-oo! moo-oo!" during the pandemonium). The party is in favor of votes for women—half the crowd today is female. And a minimum wage. And strong unions. And child labor laws, government oversight of industry, and wilderness conservation. And more.

There is one issue, however, where their passion for justice wavers. It isn't mentioned in Roosevelt's written speech but is already having repercussions. Jane Addams was to have delivered a seconding speech, but when she learned of Roosevelt's stance, she pulled out, shocked.

A delegate, perhaps a plant, in the front yells out what is on everyone's mind: "How about the negro question?"

Roosevelt takes up the challenge. "Wait a moment, wait a moment!" he says. "Nobody can ask me a question I'm afraid of."

Mississippi sent two delegations to the convention. One included Blacks. The other was "lily white." The Progressives recognized the latter.

"I think," Roosevelt begins, "that the American people is a mighty good people to lead, and a mighty poor people to drive. I regret that everybody who has been to a Republican National Convention knows that the character of the colored delegates has been such as to discredit the party and disgrace the race. We are standing against the brutality of the Democrats and the hypocrisy of the Republicans on this question."

If that equivocation seems dubious and garbled now, it seemed dubious and garbled then. The *Chicago Examiner* summarizes Roosevelt's stance this way: "The Colonel proceeded to state at some length and with much obvious embarrassment that he was all for letting in Northern negroes and all for keeping out Southern negroes. Just why, he failed to make clear to many of those present, but it was plain that he was not to be shaken on the subject."

Roosevelt will poll heavily in the South and beat the incumbent, President William Howard Taft, nationwide. But the Democratic challenger, Woodrow Wilson, crushes them both.

Aug. 7, 1915

Nothing drives you to excel like a rival on your tail. Or better, slightly in front of you. Which happens again and again as Dario Resta, in his Peugeot, and Earl Cooper, in a Stutz, battle each other over 50 laps of the two-mile wooden-plank Chicago speedway before 38,000 spectators in Maywood. "These two ran wheel-to-wheel for 80 miles at 104 miles per hour," pants *The Automobile*. The four-car field is rounded out by racing legend Barney Oldfield, whose new 4.5-liter Delage hasn't been tuned up properly, and Bob Berman in another Peugeot. Oldfield drops out early, but not before breaking the course record, clocking five laps at 110.15 mph.

The race ends with Resta crowned "World Speedway Champion." He receives a purse of $2,500, having done something no race car driver has ever done: finished 100 miles in under an hour—58 minutes and 54 seconds—for an average speed of 101.86 miles per hour.

Aug. 8, 1988

Storm warnings send the Goodyear blimp, which has been cruising low over the rooftops of Wrigleyville, hurrying back to base. Tom Skilling, veteran WGN weatherman, promises it won't rain until after midnight. But meteorology, like baseball, is half inexact science, half imperfect art. There is a thunderclap at 8:15 and a minute later the rain begins, during the fourth inning of Wrigley Field's first night game, with the Cubs up 3–1.

Play is halted. A dozen of the 39,008 fans present risk arrest by jumping onto the field and sliding across the watery tarps protecting the infield. Four Cubs players shrug and join them.

The rain keeps falling. Rules require five *full* innings of play for a game to count. So, after a two-hour-and-10-minute rain delay, the game is called, and tonight's contest is wiped away. Ryne Sandberg's homer—he also hit the last home run in Wrigley before the ballpark submitted to the fad of artificial illumination—will also be negated, and all those 8/8/88 t-shirts are suddenly in need of an asterisk. Which is in keeping with the mysterious koan that is baseball: it's the first night game, except it isn't. Pitcher Rick Sutcliffe says the rain is the will of God, who prefers baseball in sunlight.

Cubs fans, weaned on disappointment, take this one philosophically. Everyone adjourns to the bars to wait until tomorrow, when they'll try again.

Aug. 9, 1937

Chicago was born in land speculation, and for nearly two
centuries the buying and selling of real estate has never stopped.
But today there is a transaction that might be unique. The estate
of Marshall Field, owner of the Times Building, 211 W. Wacker
Drive, swaps that structure for the Central Life Insurance
Company building at Michigan and Superior. "Not a dollar will
change hands," the *Tribune* notes. "No brokers figured in the
transaction, so no commissions will be paid." Which explains why
it was done: by simply swapping, the parties keep about $100,000
extra in their pockets.

Aug. 10, 1928

Not everyone who gets polio is paralyzed. Johnny Weissmuller contracted the disease when he was nine, took up swimming to strengthen his legs, and swam his way into history. He never lost a competition, and his triumphs become so predictable that a certain sarcasm creeps into accounts of them. A 1927 *Daily News* story begins, "Ho hum! Johnny Weissmuller has hung up another world's record and won another gold medal." He earned three Olympic gold medals in Paris in 1924, and two more in Amsterdam, where today he qualifies, of course, for the 100-meter freestyle, setting an Olympic record of 58.6 seconds, breaking his own record of 59.0 from 1924. Tomorrow he'll do "what he was expected to do" and win the event. He'll retire next year, and become a durable film star, first in 16 Tarzan movies, then 13 Jungle Jim films.

Someday Chicago's Intercontinental Hotel, which has a lovely Olympic-sized pool on its 14th floor, will start referring to it as "the Johnny Weissmuller pool." Countless guidebooks imagine the Olympic star "training" in it. But training for what? By the time the hotel, built as the Medinah Athletic Club, is completed in mid-1929, Weissmuller will have stopped swimming competitively and be bumming around Los Angeles, modeling swimwear. He might take a dip there during the five years before Medinah goes bankrupt in 1934.

Aug. 11, 1948

"August 11, 1948! I am eighty-seven today, an old man," Dr. James Herrick writes in his autobiography, *Memories of Eighty Years*. "I see it in the mirror, feel it in bones and muscles, am conscious of it in the unreliable and uncertain activity of the brain."

Maybe. Though that might just be his natural humility. His mind still seems sharp. Herrick, on the staff at Cook County and Presbyterian hospitals, begins his life's story with his earliest recollection, of seeing Abraham Lincoln's funeral cortege pass by, and includes his travels abroad, and meetings with famous surgeons.

What he only mentions glancingly is sickle cell anemia, for years called Herrick's Syndrome. He first described the disease in 1910 after seeing the distinctive crescent shapes in the blood of Walter Clement Noel, a 20-year-old Black dental student from Grenada. That discovery would distinguish any physician for a lifetime. But Herrick has one more achievement up his sleeve: a paper, published in 1912, that suggests patients can survive a heart attack. His research is so ahead of its time that the paper "fell flat as a pancake." As any pioneer must, Herrick shook off his "disappointment and despair" and kept pushing until the medical community caught up with him.

Aug. 12, 1939

Sleep and Wakefulness is published by Dr. Nathaniel Kleitman, a University of Chicago physiologist who is not only creating sleep science—this book will be the definitive text for half a century—but publicizing it. His 40-day sojourn the previous year into the eternal night of Kentucky's Mammoth Cave was both the perfect sunless setting to study sleep cycles—he theorized a 28-hour day as ideal— and a masterstroke coup de théâtre, drawing world attention to the heretofore arcane study of circadian rhythms. Otherwise, he could have conducted the research more conveniently in the basement of Harper Memorial Library.

In 1953, Kleitman and graduate student Eugene Aserinsky will revolutionize our understanding of the human condition with a two-page paper revealing that sleep is not a passive dormant state, like a switched-off light, but a dynamic condition characterized by periods of rapid eye movement, or REM, sleep.

Aug. 13, 1927

"There he comes!" the PA announcer cries at Soldier Field as 20,000 in attendance look skyward and cheer themselves hoarse. A small, silvery Ryan NYP monoplane appears, first as a speck, then larger and larger. It banks abruptly and heads south, then cuts west, then north, flying above Clark Street, seeming to just clear the skyscrapers, circling the Loop three times. The noise below is deafening—car horns, fire truck sirens, streetcar bells, "L" train whistles, police gongs, and a general howl of humanity, including newsboys pointing up and yelling "Yo yo yo yo!"

A few minutes later the *Spirit of St. Louis* touches down at Municipal Air Field, at 63rd and Cicero, piloted by Col. Charles Lindbergh, whose arrival, three months after his historic flight from New York to Paris, touches off "what stunned old-timers say unreservedly is the greatest welcome that Chicago has ever tendered any one at any time." Lindbergh refuses to leave the airfield until the plane is safely stowed in a hangar, out of reach of the grabby public. Then he is driven past 10 miles of waving crowds to Comiskey Park, where 35,000 more people wait. "Men, women and children climbed and clawed over each other and the hollow stands rocked with the mighty surge of cheers." He stops at home plate, where the chief of police pins a gold star on Lindbergh's leather flying coat. Then it's off to Soldier Field, and another 40,000 people.

"Citizens of Chicago!" the slim, modest, youthful hero says. "Chicago has been in the position to observe the development of aviation as has probably no other city in the United States or in the world."

He proclaims that Chicago has perhaps the best airfield in the world, too, though it needs to be closer to downtown.

"Commercial aviation needs airports," Lindbergh says.

Aug. 14, 1812

Captain Nathan Heald faces a delicate task: tomorrow he plans to march his 66 men and nine women, plus 18 children in two wagons, out from the protection of Fort Dearborn. They'll be reinforced by a paltry band of 15 friendly Miami warriors.

Heald has been ordered to abandon the fort because his superiors believe they can no longer keep it supplied. The tides of war are turning against the United States. The War of 1812 broke out that June, and the garrison at Mackinac had to be surrendered the month before. Heald's orders are to burn the arms and munitions, using what supplies are left to placate the Native Americans, who are being riled up by the British. Or, if he can, hire them as an escort. The goal is to get to Fort Wayne, a 170-mile walk across Indiana.

They'll never make it.

Heald has been trying to parlay with the Potawatomi. There is miscommunication. Translations are fatally inexact. The Native Americans believe they are not only getting the weapons and the ammunition, but liquor and a large sum of money. Tonight, a Potawatomi named Mucktypoke—Black Partridge—returns his medal of friendship from the US government to Heald. "I will not wear a token of peace while I am compelled to act as an enemy," Black Partridge says. That's something of a tip-off.

Heald burns the arms and ammunition, and pours the liquor down the well, setting the stage for what happens about 9 a.m. tomorrow.

His procession of soldiers, women, and children will travel about a mile and a half from the fort, on the dunes along the shore of Lake Michigan, approximately where Michigan Avenue and Roosevelt Road intersect today. There some 500 Potawatomi wait in ambush. The encounter goes down in history as "The Fort Dearborn Massacre," but later it will be viewed as more of a battle that went very badly for the vastly outnumbered soldiers, who charged first. A third of those who left the fort that morning are bludgeoned to death. The rest are captured. Some die in captivity, others are ransomed. The fort is burned to the ground, but rebuilt in 1816. Its contours will be marked in the pavement in bronze at the intersection of Michigan and Wacker.

Aug. 15, 1967

What the hell is it? A woman's head? An Afghan hound? A seahorse? A baboon? The *Tribune* calls it a "predatory grasshopper." Gwendolyn Brooks, who reads a celebratory poem, privately thinks it looks "stupid." Mayor Richard J. Daley also doesn't like it, though publicly declaring that he sees "the wings of justice."

It looks like a vulture to Alderman John Hoellen, and he introduces a resolution in the city council to replace the sculpture with one honoring Cubs first baseman Ernie Banks.

The work has no title. Chicagoans call it "The Picasso." That name sticks and is the whole point. We have a massive work by the world's most famous artist—his only monumental sculpture—in the heart of our city, constructed out of the same sheets of COR-TEN steel as the building behind it.

Two journalistic icons mingle in the crowd gathered for the 11 a.m. dedication: Mike Royko and Studs Terkel. Royko will capture the shock when Daley pulls a white ribbon, sending a turquoise percale shroud tumbling away.

"A few people applauded," he writes. "But at best, it was a smattering of applause. Most of the throng was silent."

Hugh Hough, from the *Sun-Times*, hears "cheers and applause." Not Royko.

"The silence grew," he writes. "Then people turned and looked at each other. Some shrugged. Some smiled. Some just stood there, frowning or blank-faced. Most just turned and walked away." Royko stares at the "big, homely metal thing" and sees "a long stupid face" that "looks like some giant insect that is about to eat a smaller, weaker insect. It has eyes that are pitiless, cold, mean." Royko sees the faces of slum owners, brutal cops and mobsters, corporate polluters and corrupt city officials.

The voices that speak into Studs Terkel's portable tape recorder are thick with accent and attitude.

"At first glance, it looks rather grotesque . . . ," ventures one.

"You got something like this, 99 percent of the people don't know what it resembles," observes another.

"A nightmare," adds a third.

"A *woman*!?" marvels a man, told what Picasso in fact intended it to be. "A woman, yes, definitely, now it makes some sense. At first, when they had no idea what it was, I didn't think too much of it. But now I like the idea of a woman being placed at the civic center. It seems like the woman has to do with everything in life, and this has to do with the good things in life. This is a civic center and the goodness of a woman. That's my idea."

Aug. 16, 1926

Simple question: why does the Museum of Science and Industry have a coal mine? You might be tempted to answer, "Because of the importance of coal to the Illinois economy." You'd be wrong. When Sears chief executive and philanthropist Julius Rosenwald went to Germany with his family, he was impressed by Munich's Deutsches Museum, which has a coal mine. So the wonders to be featured at the new museum, Rosenwald announces today at a lunch at the Union League Club, include locomotives, airplanes, and a coal mine, just like Germany's. The museum will be located in the old Palace of Fine Arts, a relic from the Columbian Exposition in Jackson Park. Rosenwald donates $3 million. The press assumes, incorrectly, that the museum will therefore be called the Julius Rosenwald Museum. It won't be, though for decades proud Chicago Jews will call it simply "The Rosenwald." Almost a century later, the richest man in Illinois donates $125 million to put his own name on it, making it the Kenneth C. Griffin Museum of Science and Industry, at the rate of $8,333,333 per letter.

Aug. 17, 1970

"You gotta be crazy," everyone tells Don Cornelius. Even his own wife. "He said, 'I'm going to be a Black Dick Clark,'" Delores Cornelius later recalls. "And I said, 'You're crazy.'"

Black people are hardly even *seen* on TV, maybe a token couple dancing discreetly in the corner of Clark's *American Bandstand*, never mind going around and creating their own shows. Even Black stars don't do well with their TV programs—Nat "King" Cole's lasted a little over a year, Sammy Davis Jr.'s three months. But the management of WCIU has already carved out a niche with Black programming, so they told Cornelius to go ahead, and even gave him the rights to the show.

A lucky break. But then Cornelius has had his share of good fortune. Graduating from DuSable High School, he joined the Marine Corps and was sent to Korea just in time to miss the war. Back home, he ground through 15 jobs in 10 years: driving a cab, selling tires, autos, insurance. He became a cop, and in 1966 ticketed Roy Wood, the news director from WVON (which stood for "Voice of the Negro"), for speeding. Wood told Cornelius he had a great voice and invited him to stop by the nation's biggest Black radio station for an audition.

After going into radio, Cornelius remained restless for something bigger. Seed money for his television show came from the Motown record label in Detroit. Sears Roebuck committed to running commercials. It helps that Chicago is a source of popular dance crazes: the Bird, the Monkey, and the Watusi all originated here.

Filmed on the 43rd floor of the Chicago Board of Trade building, of all places, *Soul Train*—or should that be "*Sooooouuuuuul* Train!*"—pulls out of the station for the first time today at 4:30 p.m. "A daily live hour of soul music and dancing." The next year the program moves to Los Angeles and goes weekly and national, featuring every significant act from Michael Jackson to James Brown, Marvin Gaye to R. Kelly, not to forget a crowd of regular kids dancing aboard a streamlined express of music and motion and proud uninhibited cool barreling into homes coast-to-coast every Saturday morning for 35 years.

Aug. 18, 1835

For almost two years, they camped in and around the new village of Chicago, "old warriors might be seen sitting smoking under every bush," Charles Joseph LaTrobe notes in *The Rambler in North America*. Thousands of Potawatomi "palavering, or 'powwowing,' with great earnestness."

Then at last, their treaty ratified, the agreed-upon cash and merchandise delivered, the Native Americans take their leave, a final war dance through the streets of Chicago.

"They appreciated that it was their last dance on their native soil," writes eyewitness John Dean Caton, a future chief justice of the Illinois Supreme Court. "A sort of funeral ceremony of old associations and memories."

They gather north of the river, at Rush and Kinzie, some 800 men, "foreheads, cheeks or noses covered with curved stripes of red or vermillion, which were edged with black points, and gave the appearance of a horrid grin."

Striking clubs and sticks together, beating on drums, they cross the river at Kinzie. The whoops and grimaces put fear into onlookers.

"It seemed as if we had a picture of hell itself before us," Caton writes, "and a carnival of the damned spirits there confined."

Aug. 19, 1972

New buildings bring new problems. No matter how architects ponder and engineers calculate, they can still be blindsided. When the massive skyscrapers went up downtown in the late 1960s and early 1970s, little thought was given to how they would interfere with television broadcasts. But they do. The Sears Tower is two years from completion, and already is offering local TV stations $5 million to relocate to their building, while engineers rush to figure out if it will support the weight of the antennas and communications equipment required. Nor is it alone.

"There are serious ghosting problems on Channel 7, caused by the new Standard Oil Building," the *Daily News* notes today. "These problems would virtually disappear if Channel 7, now located atop Marina City, moves to either Sears or the Hancock."

The Standard Oil Building isn't completed either, and will soon have problems far greater than blocking television signals. The 82-story square tower just east of Michigan Avenue is clad entirely in white Carrara marble, thanks to new technology that allows the 43,000 panels covering its steel frame to be cut very thin: about 1½ inches thick.

Too thin, as it turns out, for Chicago weather. On Christmas Day 1973, a 350-pound slab will detach itself and fall onto the roof of the Prudential Building next door. Over the next 15 years, engineers will find that 30 percent of the panels are bowing out more than half an inch. Cracks send more marble crashing to the street. Due to the wide temperature swings—27 below in winter, 102 in summer—the marble is losing strength, and has to be braced with steel straps.

In the early 1990s, the entire skin of the building will be replaced with panels of white North Carolina granite, two inches thick, at a cost of more than half the price tag of constructing the building in the first place. Most of the old marble panels will be crushed into gravel and used as landscaping at Amoco's refinery in Whiting, Indiana.

Aug. 20, 1965

An "L" train pulls into the 35th Street station.

"This is beautiful Comiskey Park," the conductor announces over the intercom. "Where you'll see the Beatles." The passengers, mostly women and girls, stream out.

The Beatles play three consecutive years in Chicago, 1964, 1965, and 1966, but the concerts today at Sox Park—there are two shows—are the ones people recall most, not the pair of performances sandwiching this, at the International Amphitheater.

The Chicago police asked the group not to use O'Hare. So the Beatles arrive at Midway Airport, at 3:13 a.m., to cut down on crowds. They go directly to where they're staying, the O'Hare-Sahara Motel on Mannheim Road in Schiller Park.

The Fab Four's shows are at 3 p.m. and 8 p.m. Tickets are $2.50, $4.50, and $5.50. Each is a single 45-minute set. The screaming is so loud that the songs can barely be heard.

At the press conference between shows, a reporter asks what the band thinks about the comment that they could be great songwriters someday, if only they wanted to be.

"Well," says Paul McCartney, 23. "We write what we feel like at the moment, like Cole Porter did. People will like us a lot more when we're older, just you watch."

Aug. 21, 1950

The Elgin, Joliet & Eastern Railway is a 238-mile ring, also known as the Chicago Outer Belt Line, circling the city, shuttling raw materials and finished steel bars from Waukegan to Porter, Indiana.

Unless it's on strike. No trains mean no ore to transform into steel. Nor freight cars to bear finished beams away. With that prospect looming, Carnegie-Illinois Steel starts to bank the blast and open-hearth furnaces today at its huge South Chicago and Gary works, preparing for a "token" five-day rail strike set to start tomorrow.

The first of 10 Gary blast furnaces goes dark at 4 p.m. Twenty-seven thousand workers are laid off. The coke works in Joliet, too, though the ovens are kept warm so it won't take so long to resume operations. The shutdown is intended to draw attention to a labor dispute that has been going on for a year and a half. The issue: workers want their 48-hour workweek reduced to 40 hours at the same pay. The strike, by the Brotherhood of Railroad Trainmen and the Order of Railway Conductors, has already hit Cleveland, St. Paul, and Louisville.

The unions urge President Truman to seize the railroads, as he did in June when the Chicago Rock Island and the Switchmen's Union were at loggerheads, and promise they'll stay on the job if he does. The president, worried about the army getting all the steel it needs for tanks in Korea, will do exactly that on Friday, with the federal government running the railroads for the next 21 months.

Aug. 22, 1991

George Anderson is charged with first-degree murder in the killing of Jeremiah Miggins. Three teenagers, 15 to 13, were selling drugs on a West Englewood corner the day before when Anderson came by and demanded payment for use of the corner. The teens refused. Anderson opened fire, and they fired back. Miggins, 11, helping clean a neighbor's backyard nearby, was struck in the chest. A minister's son, the youngest of five, he died on the spot, under a tree in the backyard, one of 121 people murdered in Chicago this month, making August 1991 the bloodiest month of the second bloodiest year in Chicago history, with 922 murders. Though one of the other drug-dealing teens fired the fatal shot, Anderson will be found guilty of the murder of Miggins—his confession extracted by torture, he will later allege—and sentenced to life in prison. Thirty years later, he's still there.

Aug. 23, 1988

"These documents smack of socialistic tendencies," says Rufus Taylor at a press conference today. "They are an attempt to dictate to the residents of the city of Chicago what they can do on their lakefront."

What Taylor and his friends at the Lincoln Park Gun Club can do, and would like to continue doing, is fire shotguns at clay targets propelled over the lake. The club began in 1912, started by P. K. Wrigley and Oscar Mayer and their chums, and has seen its share of highlights, such as John Philip Sousa conducting a concert. (Taylor calls opposition to the club "elitist," which takes chutzpah.) The percussive pops of the shotguns are a summertime soundtrack in the park. Now the Chicago Plan Commission is taking aim at the gun club, as well as Meigs Field. The Environmental Protection Agency gives the club the thumbs-down too. There isn't much shot that goes into the lake, relatively, but it is lead, and the poison adds up over the years. The plastic shell casings also wash up on beaches. In 1991, the attorney general will sue the club, and the Park District will unceremoniously demolish its buildings at Diversey and the Lakefront.

Aug. 24, 1943

George Herbert Walker Bush qualifies as a carrier pilot. One of 15,000 airmen who do so by taking off at Glenview Naval Air Station and landing either on the USS *Sable* or the USS *Wolverine*, two coal-fired, paddlewheel steamers refitted as aircraft carriers and anchored off Navy Pier.

Or not landing on them. Perhaps a hundred World War II–era planes still rest on the bottom of Lake Michigan, thanks to novice airmen missing their mark. The future 41st president, the youngest pilot commissioned in the navy, will have opportunity to practice ditching at sea under less ideal circumstances, bailing out of two planes during action in the Pacific, the second one afire. He'll fly a torpedo bomber on 58 combat missions and earn the Distinguished Flying Cross.

Aug. 25, 1932

Nettie Dorsey goes into labor. Her husband, Thomas, the father of gospel music, is out of town, performing a few concerts in St. Louis. They live with his uncle Joshua, and he rushes Nettie to Provident Hospital. They've already paid for her to deliver at the "black medical mecca" near their home. But the hospital has only 75 beds to serve a population of 200,000 Black Chicagoans, and today those beds are all full. So Nettie goes home, where the next day she gives birth.

Dorsey will receive a telegram. "HURRY HOME! YOUR WIFE IS VERY SICK." He'll phone, and be told Nettie is dead. Choir director Augustus Evans joins him on the long drive to Chicago in numb silence. Dorsey walks into the house, crowded with friends and relatives, and faints. He meets Thomas Andrew Dorsey Jr., born alive and healthy. But the baby dies in the night. Mother and child are buried in a single casket.

A prodigious composer of jazz, blues, and gospel songs, Dorsey toured with Ma Rainey and battled depression before finding salvation in faith. Now he isn't sure. "God had been unfair. I felt that God had dealt me an injustice," he later says. He is ready to quit. "I didn't want to serve Him anymore or write gospel songs."

That mood lasts until Saturday, when he'll find himself in front of a piano. Dorsey pours out his anguish in a new kind of song, a gospel blues song. Suffering rendered directly into words and music. It instantly becomes a beloved standard, to be recorded by singers from Elvis Presley to Beyoncé. "Take My Hand, Precious Lord" becomes Rev. Martin Luther King's favorite song. Mahalia Jackson will sing it at his funeral.

Aug. 26, 1968

Protesters aren't allowed near the International Amphitheatre, where the Democratic National Convention is taking place. So they gather in Grant Park, across from the Conrad Hilton where Hubert Humphrey has his headquarters on the 24th floor and many conventioneers are staying. About a thousand protesters march around the hotel, chanting "Dump the Hump!"

The police have been arresting protesters all day, just to show they are "not going to screw around." After organizer Tom Hayden is grabbed in the park, Rennie Davis leads hundreds to police headquarters, where they link arms and chant, "Pig, Pig, Oink, Oink, soo-ee, soo-ee." A young man climbs high atop the statue of General Logan; in hauling him down, police break his arm. There are skirmishes throughout the day. Protesters gathering, police wading in with nightsticks.

Over at International Amphitheatre, the mood is grim for those who can get into what is dubbed "Fort Daley." The place is hot and "stunk like a hippie's armpit." Surrounded by fences and barbed wire, crawling with security so overbearing they refuse entry to a New York delegate for carrying a copy of the *New York Times*. The only drama there is whether Humphrey, the "subdued practitioner of the politics of happiness," will immediately clinch the nomination, or whether an anti-war longshot like Eugene McCarthy or even George McGovern might slow the inevitable.

Toward evening, thousands of demonstrators take over the streets of Old Town, throwing bottles, hopping on car hoods. "Monday night, the city was washed with the air of battle," Norman Mailer writes.

About 10 p.m., thousands of protesters gather in Lincoln Park. They're met by thousands of police, in baby-blue helmets and gas masks, wielding nightsticks and firing tear gas. After 11 p.m. the police begin to clear the park, enforcing the curfew that is suddenly very important to the city of Chicago. "The Park is closed," police announce, through loudspeakers. Shortly after midnight, the battle is on. What is happening on the convention floor suddenly doesn't seem that important anymore.

Aug. 27, 1930

At 8 p.m., 1000-watt experimental television station W9XAP begins broadcasting from the 26th floor of the Daily News building, 400 W. Madison. "Radio gets its eyes tonight," notes the paper.

Along with another Chicago station, W9XAO, run by manufacturer Western Television, they'll be among the first TV stations offering regularly scheduled entertainment. Only the picture is broadcast on W9XAP, with sound synchronized on radio station WMAQ. Programming has to suit the vast majority of listeners who can't see the pictures, but also viewers at times when WMAQ isn't offering the accompanying sound.

The TV station broadcasts 90 minutes each day of lectures, news, sports, cartoons—drawn live by a cartoonist, not animation—and drama, including *Their Television Honeymoon*, which some consider the first television drama. The next year, Hollywood film cosmetics pioneer Max Factor will create the first TV makeup for a W9XAP play, *The Maker of Dreams*.

A new vocabulary needs to be decided upon. What to call the audience? The *Daily News* tries "television lookers-in." What are they watching? The paper floats both "sight-and-sound programs" and "talking pictures of the air." On September 2, the *Daily News* will hit upon a winner, running a standing notice in the radio listings: "WMAQ programs to be seen on W9XAP are designated by the word 'televised.'"

A few minutes into today's televised offering, a filter condenser blows in the transmitter, cutting reception for Chicago's several hundred TV sets. While engineers struggle to get back on the air, viewers, not realizing the problem is elsewhere, fuss with their controls. When the program "developed to show the possibilities and problems of the new medium" goes live again, their sets aren't configured to catch the signal—receivers have to be hand-tuned to 2800 kilocycles and then the image framed, all to view a picture two inches square.

Aug. 28, 1929

They wait all day. People from 100 miles away, filling every parking space downtown, men in straw boaters and women in cloche caps, sitting on newspapers in Grant Park, eating boxed lunches. Thousands gather at Soldier Field, thousands more fill the windows and roofs of downtown office buildings, passing the time tossing out paper, which rains "like a summer snow storm."

Nature itself joins in. Rain so severe the weather service tries to wave off the much-anticipated visitor, which has traveled around the entire globe, almost, to be here. But mere weather defers to the modern wonder, hurrying offstage just before 5:20 p.m., when the great silver airship LZ 127 *Graf Zeppelin*, surrounded by a retinue of some two dozen private aircraft, sails into view.

The zeppelin is on the last leg of a world tour that started three weeks before: Lakehurst, New Jersey, to Germany, Germany to Russia, Russia to Tokyo, then the first nonstop air crossing of the Pacific. Across the continental United States. This morning it was over Texas. Tomorrow it'll reach Lakehurst, setting a world circum-navigation record of 11 days, 23 hours, and 14 minutes, cutting 15 days from the old record, set by US Army fliers in 1924.

Now it passes above the Loop from the southwest, slicing through the haze over Grant Park to "a mighty roar"—yells, car horns, train whistles, tugboats on the lake. Those present are reminded of Armistice Day.

Drivers stop and stand next to their cars, doors flung open, gazing upward. They climb on their running boards, on hoods, roofs, shouting at the sky. Police blow their whistles and try to get the traffic moving, unheeded. They finally give up and look skyward too.

Aug. 29, 1911

Alexander von Babo is granted US Patent #1,001,800 for a Trunnion Bascule Bridge. He didn't invent the distinctive drawbridges that dominate Chicago's riverfront, but rather improved them, this second-generation design putting the rack-and-pinion mechanism *inside* the leaf element, giving it a cleaner look, and eliminating the need for overhead bracing, so vehicles of any height can cross. But you don't have to imagine what that means. Go look at the Washington Boulevard Bridge, the first constructed with this design in 1913—builders being careful to sink concrete supports so its weight would not crush the Washington Street tunnel underneath. The tunnel was closed in 1953, but the bridge remains, a rare piece of pre–World War I engineering still in daily use in the heart of a major city.

Aug. 30, 1847

Cyrus McCormick and his partner, future Chicago mayor Charles
M. Gray, buy three lots on the north bank of the Chicago River,
about 300 feet from the current Michigan Avenue Bridge, to build
their reaper works. A reaper is a complicated mechanism of metal
threshers and spinning wheels, so it may be hard to envision, or to
fathom just how revolutionary "Chicago's first great machine" really
is. Presented at the London Crystal Palace Exhibition in 1851, it gets
mocked by the *Times of London* as "a cross between an Astley's
chariot, a wheel-barrow and a flying machine." Though the "extrav-
agant Yankee contraption" still takes the Grand Prize.

The McCormick reaper revolutionizes agriculture around the
world. Before, grain was harvested with scythes and sickles, as
it was in the Bronze Age. By doing the work of dozens of men
wielding hand tools, the reaper helps free up Northern farmers to
fight the Civil War. The fortune it earns for McCormick allows him
to scatter largesse throughout the city: the McCormick Theological
Seminary, the Brookfield Zoo, the Art Institute. The *Chicago
Tribune*'s most famous publisher for 30 years will be Cyrus's great-
nephew, Col. Robert McCormick—well, every gift, no matter how
generous, contains a drawback.

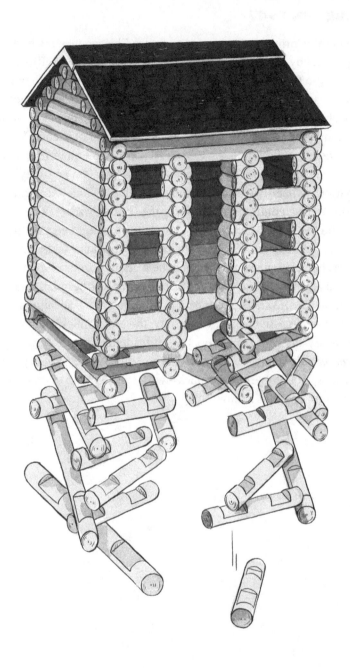

Aug. 31, 1920

Frank Lloyd Wright learned architecture by playing with wooden blocks as a child. His son, John Lloyd Wright, learned wooden blocks by playing with architecture as an adult. Specifically, accompanying his father to Tokyo to observe the construction of the elder Wright's Imperial Hotel. Japan has earthquakes, so Wright used an interlocking beam design to reinforce the building. And indeed, after the devastating 1923 Kanto earthquake, Wright's hotel was one of the only large buildings left standing.

Back in Chicago, John Wright, inspired by the success of the new Tinkertoys created by an Evanston stonemason in 1914, came up with his own construction set, Lincoln Logs, which he started selling in 1916 and patents today. A smart move, though he'll eventually sell the brand for a song—$800—in 1943, a decade before the frontier craze, spurred by popular interest in Daniel Boone and Davy Crockett, makes the simple notched wooden dowel forts and cabins and ponderosas part of the landscape of American childhood. The logs were made of wood in 1916 and still are, more than a century and 100 million sets later.

SEPTEMBER

Sept. 1, 1930

At 11 a.m. Walter J. Kohler, Wisconsin's "Flying Governor," lands in his Ryan Brougham and taxis to a stop in front of the grandstand at Curtiss-Reynolds Airport in Glenview.

"Any people who lag behind in the development of air transport must, in a measure, lose their place in the march of progress," he says in his speech, marking the final day of the National Air Races. Such aviation contests "make a tremendously important contribution to the development of America's aeronautical progress."

He's right—engineers develop the air-cooled radial engine, trying to power souped-up planes circling 30 feet off the ground at 200 miles per hour at the "Olympiad of Aviation." Ten days, 44 events, including a Los Angeles to Chicago derby won by Wiley Post in a Lockheed Vega. Just about anything that flies shows up: navy biplanes in V-formation, gliders, fluttering autogyros—a helicopter/airplane hybrid. One race is open to only women. There is a parachute-jumping contest and a "dead-stick" landing competition—an important skill, since hastily rebuilt engines routinely fail.

Three pilots die during the fun, and a concessionaire is burned to death on the ground by an exploding gas tank. The final fatality is in the capstone event, the first 100-mile Thompson Trophy, a closed-course race around 50-foot red-and-white-checked pylons. Charles "Speed" Holman lives to win the race in a Laird Solution that was still being assembled earlier that afternoon.

Sept. 2, 1955

The Panama Limited arrives at Central Station. Mamie Bradley runs across three sets of tracks to the baggage car.

"My darling! My darling!" she cries. "I would have gone through a world of fire to get to you!"

A pine coffin is unloaded and set on the platform. Bradley falls to her knees, supported by clergymen.

"You didn't die for nothing," she promises, in a harsh whisper.

Two weeks earlier, Bradley had sent her 14-year-old son, Emmett Till, south to stay with relatives in Money, Mississippi. After he visited a small grocery store with friends, the owner, Carolyn Bryant, a white woman, claimed the boy whistled at her. Early the next morning, her husband, Roy, and another man kidnap, torture, and shoot Till through the head, dumping his body in the Tallahatchie River tied to a blast wheel from a cotton gin fan. Three days later, his body was found by a teenager fishing in the river. Authorities were about to bury Till in a shallow grave when Till's relatives claimed the body and had it embalmed and shipped home to Chicago.

His mother accompanies the casket to the A. A. Rayner & Sons Funeral Home, where she insists that the lid be kept open during the wake.

"Open it up," she says. "Let the people see what they did to my boy."

Thousands come to witness. Bradley delays the funeral until Tuesday so they have the chance to file by. The gruesome photos of Till's battered, bloated face will be featured in *Jet* magazine and distributed across the county. The awful sight galvanizes the civil rights movement. His mother was right: he didn't die for nothing.

Sept. 3, 1979

Labor Day is typically sleepy around Daley Plaza, the courts and government offices being closed, along with many Loop businesses.

Which make the three-day weekend a perfect time for the place to be invaded by the army. Plus firetrucks, police cars, and the entire rolling circus of *The Blues Brothers* film production, which has two helicopters in the sky and three Sherman tanks on the ground.

Two hundred real National Guardsmen.

How did this happen? Well, Richard J. Daley had to die first, along with his aversion to moviemaking, which tends to slander Chicago, in his view, by suggesting that crime occurs here. But Jane Byrne will agree to just about anything fun. She smiled at how nervous John Belushi was when he came to her office to stammer out his request. The $50,000 donation to her favorite charity didn't hurt, nor does the fact that George Dunne, the president of the Cook County Board, has a son, Murphy, who is the keyboardist in the Blues Brothers band.

It's good to have friends. Watch the movie, and at the end you'll see a young mustachioed man, eating a sandwich, ostensibly the clerk in the Cook County tax assessor's office. That's film director Steven Spielberg.

Sept. 4, 1975

The name of the program debuting today is direct, bordering on simplistic: *Opening Soon at a Theater Near You*. It is broadcast just once a month, on the backwater of local public television, WTTW. The hosts are a pair of corduroy-clad newsmen: an obese alcoholic, Roger Ebert of the *Chicago Sun-Times*, looking un-dapper in his eyeglasses, sweater vest, and helmet of brown hair, and a high-toned Yale toff, Gene Siskel, of the *Chicago Tribune*, with his porn-star mustache and hardly any hair on his head at all. Neither was interested in doing a television program with the other. The pilot episode was cringingly awful.

Yet it works, eventually. The hosts develop chemistry. They clash, they argue, they agree, they are a matched set, the salt and pepper shakers of movie criticism, the thin one and the fat one, soon to go biweekly, then weekly, then nationally in syndication, perched next to Johnny Carson, parodied in *Mad* magazine. They become famous, rich.

The show will have enormous impact, and not only on movies. It injected the "thumbs up/thumbs down" dichotomy into popular usage. Ebert will become a cultural force. A technophile, he also leads the charge online, and profits from it, as an early investor in Google. After developing salivary gland cancer and losing part of his lower jaw, Ebert's frank writing about his condition—he'll pose for a full-face portrait in *Esquire*—helps acclimate the public to seeing and thinking about people with disfigurements. He writes about walking in London and about cooking rice even though he cannot himself eat. He'll also write a stellar autobiography, *Life Itself*. Oh, and on a date at the Hamburger Hamlet, Ebert will encourage a young TV personality just starting her own namesake television show in Chicago to think seriously about syndication. Oprah Winfrey will take his advice.

Sept. 5, 1984

If you've never heard a galvanized steel garbage can dragged across a concrete driveway at dawn, the world-bending importance of this might elude you.

But in the Eighth Ward today, the first wheeled garbage cart in Chicago is tipped into the first garbage truck equipped with a lift. Four other wards are also taking part in the pilot program.

For decades, Chicago garbage collection was a notorious mess of patronage, inefficiency, and almost unfathomable squalor. Before World War II, apartment dwellers routinely threw garbage out the windows, as in medieval times. They had to be threatened with fines to do otherwise.

In the 1940s, half the alleys were "lined with open piles of filth." Only about 15 percent of garbage found its way into a metal can with a lid. The rest? A third of the trash was heaped in "old washtubs, battered baskets and boxes." A quarter was left in open piles of garbage, with the last quarter dumped into large concrete containers. Garbagemen went at the piles with shovels.

In the 1950s, Chicago made several vigorous pushes to promote garbage can use. In 1957 the Citizens Committee for a Cleaner Chicago set up a gilded garbage can on a float at Wacker and Wabash. In the 1970s, 55-gallon oil drums were popular, but those could take two or even three men to tip into a truck.

Enter "the garbage collection system of the future," already introduced to a handful of smaller cities like Atlanta, Milwaukee, and Tempe, Arizona. In 1984 Harold Washington welcomed the "supercarts"—90-gallon wheeled cans with attached lids.

Change always threatens someone. The program was to have begun April 1. But aldermen, fighting to preserve the tradition of doling out trash cans in return for votes, resisted. A survey in March 1984 found that an astounding 98 percent of Chicagoans did not want the new cans; 96 percent are unwilling to even try them. "It could mean we would have to sell our home," said a resident of the 39th Ward.

"Fear of change is the most disturbing fear," said Alderman Roman Pucinski, who held meetings in his ward to let constituents air concerns, which included worries the wheels would break, the carts would be impossible for elderly widows to roll, or they would be stolen or vandalized.

But being better in every way—cleaner for the homeowner, easier for garbagemen—creates its own momentum, and once started, the radically better system eventually catches on.

Sept. 6, 1874

Father Vincent Barzynski, a priest from Lublin, Poland, arrives in Chicago, via Rome and Texas, to serve as pastor of St. Stanislaus Church. He has been to the city before and witnessed the Great Chicago Fire. Now he is back, heading the most important church of a community at war with itself.

The church had split in two, Holy Trinity peeling off due to crowding, but now the factions are fighting over a range of issues, from who owns particular properties to the assignment of priests.

Despite the divisions, Barzynski will set up a school and a nunnery, a bank—the Bank Parafialny—and the first Polish high school in the United States. He also will co-found the Polish Roman Catholic Union, and build St. Stanislaus into the largest Catholic parish in the country. All the while coping with serial schisms that in the mid-1890s led to riots and even more fracture: some parishioners will break off to join what is now the Polish National Catholic Church.

Yet St. Stanislaus Kostka remains one of the most prominent churches in Chicago, not only because it is "the mother church of Polonia in the United States," but for a much more mundane reason: the Kennedy Expressway skirts the parish rectory by about three feet. Original plans were for the Kennedy to run west of the church, cutting it off from its parish, or even go through it, requiring its demolition. Popular myth credits Rep. Dan Rostenkowski, the powerful Ways and Means chairman from the fifth district, where the church is located, with saving it. But the truth is, before Rostenkowski was elected to Congress, State Rep. Bernard Prusinski, a civil engineer, worked out a plan to relocate the expressway. The hundreds of thousands of drivers who pass every day aren't quite attending mass at St. Stanislaus Kostka. But close.

Sept. 7, 2010

The City Hall press conference is supposed to be routine; some staffing announcement.

Instead, there is Richard M. Daley, surrounded by his beaming wife, Maggie, and their children. "Today, I am announcing that I will not seek a seventh term as mayor of the City of Chicago," says Daley. "Simply put, it's time. Time for me, and time for Chicago, to move on."

Interesting choice of words, "move on." What you struggle to do after a loss, or a tragedy, or a breakup. What is done when something unpleasant must be jettisoned, left behind to drift into the past and be forgotten. The goal when one party can't bear the other. But who is breaking up with whom?

Never as despised as his father was, but not beloved either, Daley and his father have run Chicago for 42 of the past 55 years. Why take his ball and go home? Failure to snag the 2016 Olympics—Chicago had been out-grafted by Rio. Burned by the disastrous parking meter deal he forced on the city; humiliated and angry to be called out, like a junkie caught selling his grandmother's silver service. The sale filled an urgent need at the moment; regret came later. His approval rating hovers at 35 percent. His wife is dying of cancer—Maggie, unlike him, is sincerely admired; she will die 13 months later. Had it been his father announcing his retirement in 1975, sycophants would have lined up to beg him to stay. Nobody does that now. The tug-of-war over his office curtains begins immediately.

Sept. 8, 1977

The Mirage, at 731 N. Wells Street, is an ordinary bar, for the most part, with a jukebox and a pinball machine. It opened in mid-August, quietly, to get the kinks out. But today the place is having its "Grand Opening" from 5 p.m. to 1 a.m., an attempt to draw a crowd. Beer is 25 cents, well drinks 75 cents. "A new tavern in the heart of antique row," the sign says.

Maybe not so new. The building certainly isn't. There are problems: faulty wiring, leaky plumbing, collapsed ceilings, rotted floorboards. Though repairmen in coveralls are here all the time, nothing ever seems to get fixed. No matter. As little as $5 and city building inspectors look the other way. And sometimes, in the rare cases where there's nothing wrong, palms must be greased anyway to stave off false reports. Accountants encourage fraud and pinball operators offer kickbacks. This is Chicago, after all.

Plenty of bar and restaurant owners complain about city shakedowns and payoffs. The mayor always scoffs, "Where's your proof?"

It's coming. Because in one way, the Mirage is indeed extraordinary: the bar is owned by the *Chicago Sun-Times*, which runs it along with the Better Government Association. The Mirage is opened for the sole purpose of documenting corruption by inspectors and officials. Norty the bartender is reporter Zay Smith. The repairmen are photographers Jim Frost and Gene Pesek, with cameras in their toolboxes, climbing up into a hidden loft in the back to shoot through view holes in the walls, the jukebox turned up to cover the clicking of their cameras. The Mirage Tavern stays open four months, spawning an eye-opening 25-part series written by Smith and Pam Zekman, who came up with the whole idea, that'll begin in January.

Sept. 9, 1937

Ludwig Mies van der Rohe drives up from Chicago to visit Frank Lloyd Wright at his Wisconsin home in Taliesin. Since the former director of the Bauhaus speaks little English, he brings along fellow architect Bertrand Goldberg—the future designer of Marina City—to translate.

Just being permitted an audience with the great man is itself a compliment; Wright generally detests European architects; when Walter Gropius and Le Corbusier tried to make the same pilgrimage, Wright rebuffed each with exquisite rudeness. But Wright likes Mies, as much as he can like anybody other than himself. Told that Mies wanted to meet him, Wright replied, "I should think he would."

The visit goes well. Next year, when Armour Institute of Technology holds a ceremonial dinner for 400 guests at the Palmer House to welcome Mies as its new director, he will request that Wright introduce him, and the reliably caustic genius will agree.

"Ladies and gentlemen, I give you Mies van der Rohe," begins the "irritable and bored" Wright, before taking full credit. "But for me there would be no Mies—certainly none here tonight. I admire him as an architect, respect and love him as a man. You treat him well and love him as I do. He will reward you."

Mies does, designing his first half-dozen buildings for Armour, which later became the Illinois Institute of Technology, then creating such Chicago landmarks as 330 North Wabash (formerly One IBM Plaza) and the Dirksen Federal Building.

At the Armour dinner, Wright won't stick around to hear Mies's speech. Perhaps just as well, as it is delivered in German, untranslated.

Sept. 10, 1900

Nearly a quarter of a million pupils show up for the first day of school in Chicago, or 5,000 more than there are classroom seats to accommodate. Students are responsible for getting themselves to the school door; they arrive on foot, by streetcar, or, if their parents are well off, by carriage. Those who can't walk can't attend, except for a few carried by older siblings. One enterprising legless boy pushes himself in a wheeled cart he constructed.

With such pupils in mind, Chicago is trying something new: a school especially for students with disabilities, three classrooms on the second floor of the Crippled Children's Home at Ogden and West Madison. That is a public school first, as are the two horse-drawn omnibuses ferrying those who live within a three-mile radius to class for free.

Less than a dozen such children show up today, "owing to a general misunderstanding," says the *Daily News*. Many more will come tomorrow.

The new school does not yet have a name, but several older students make a request: they would prefer "that the word 'crippled' be omitted from any title given the institution." In 1907, the Chicago Public Schools will open the first separate school building dedicated entirely to children with physical and mental challenges. CPS will call it the "Spalding School for Crippled Children."

Sept. 11, 1961

He is not the star. Time tends to obscure that fact. Yes, the show
is called *Bozo's Circus*, but Bozo himself does not even appear in
person on today's debut. Rather, the cast is an ensemble, if that isn't
too high toned a word for an entertainment built upon the three Ps:
pratfalls, plates twirled on sticks, and pies in the face.

The Bozo franchise—there are Bozo shows in cities all over the
country—started slowly in Chicago, with Bob Bell in Bozo getup host-
ing a half hour of cartoons from a cramped set in 1960.

At noon today that changes, as the 13-piece Big Top Band at WGN's
Studio One strikes up the Bozo theme. The 200 lucky kids in the
audience shriek. To be honest, today's first show is "a disaster"—WGN,
always looking to the bottom line, thought the Bozo aspect could be
safely and economically limited to the showing of Bozo cartoons, a
cut-rate late 1950s insult to the art of animation. The station quickly
learns from its mistake, however, and Bob Bell will be in greasepaint,
greeting the kiddies, for the second broadcast.

When Bozo is onscreen, joined by Cooky the Cook and Wizzo
the Wizard and Oliver O. Oliver and the rest, viewers know his nose
is red, his nimbus of stiff hair orange, because the show is broadcast
in glorious color. WGN began "colorcasting" in 1956 and is now up to
almost four hours a day, triple the color programming of 1958.

But the show is still best experienced in person. That's the only way
a kid can hope to be chosen to play the Grand Prize Game, tossing
ping-pong balls into a series of six ever-more-distant buckets for six
increasingly fabulous prizes. Fifty thousand fans attend the first year. By
1962, the waiting list will be four months long. Couples apply for Bozo
tickets when they get married, it is said, for their as-yet-unconceived
children. In 1980 producers of the show will stop offering tickets, having
given them all away for the next decade. In 1990, WGN opens up a Bozo
hotline for five hours. Even though it costs $3 to place the call—the
money goes to charity—35,000 call in. The show will run until 2001—
Joey D'Auria, the last Chicago Bozo, knows something is up when
WGN, true to form, is reluctant to pay for the annual cleaning of Bozo's
wig. The last program will be filmed in June 2001, just shy of the show's
40th anniversary.

Sept. 12, 1992

Sometimes you have to leave Chicago to realize just how much you love the place.

Fifty-seven million horsepower of thrust kick the space shuttle *Endeavor* into orbit at 10:23 a.m. from Cape Kennedy, Florida. In some ways, it's just another routine foray into space—the 50th space shuttle mission. But every spaceflight makes history in some fashion, and the weeklong Mission STS-147 is not only a cooperative scientific flight—on board is a Japanese chemist experimenting with carp eggs. Also among the seven-member crew is mission science specialist Mae Jemison, the first female African American astronaut, who grew up in Woodlawn and Roseland, and was inspired to go into space by the unflappable, elegant, and proudly Black Lt. Uhura on *Star Trek*.

A dancer, Jemison brings with her a poster from the Alvin Ailey Dance Troupe, as well as a photograph of Bessie Coleman, the Chicago beautician who became the first female African American pilot in the early 1920s.

"About 90 minutes into the flight, someone called me to the window and the very first thing I saw, clear as a bell, was Chicago," Jemison later recalls. "Right then, I realized just how strongly I was attached."

Sept. 13, 1998

Moe Mullins catches the ball, but doesn't keep it long. He tucks his mitt under his arm and uses both hands to clutch the ultimate ballhawk souvenir: Sammy Sosa's 62nd home-run ball, a pivotal moment in the Great Race of 1998, pitting the Cubs' Sosa against the St. Louis Cardinals' Mark McGwire. Both trying to top Roger Maris's 1961 feat, breaking Babe Ruth's revered 60-home-run record by a single four-bagger.

"I got it! I got it!" Mullins cries, and does have it, for one second before he is flung to the pavement of Waveland Avenue and the ball ripped from his hands. Brendan Cunningham comes up with it, but this isn't over. The police shrug and say whoever has the ball is the owner. Mullins will file a lawsuit, but balk when a judge requires he put up a $50,000 bond to cover Cunningham's legal expenses in case he is eventually determined to be the true owner. Cunningham ends up giving the ball to Sosa.

A milestone moment in the way that money, drugs, and celebrity degrade baseball. Every star athlete suspects that the grinning kid shyly holding up a ball for him to sign will turn around and sell it on eBay. The Sosa-McGwire duel will be spat out of baseball's soul, if not its collective memory, because of the steroid scandal. But not before McGwire's 70th-home-run baseball sells for $3 million. Sosa donates this 62nd-home-run ball to the Baseball Hall of Fame at Cooperstown, which puts it into storage. Out of sight, out of mind.

Sept. 14, 1932

Samuel Insull is in Paris, attending the wedding of a subordinate at the Peoples Gas, Light and Coke Company, one of his many, many business interests.

Dwight Green is in Washington, DC. The US attorney for the Northern District of Illinois, Green is conferring with the attorney general.

And Illinois State's Attorney John Swanson is in Chicago, meeting with his staff, discussing this newly released auditor's report on Insull Utility Investments. The loss could be $2 billion. Stockholders will be "wiped out entirely."

Insull came to this country as Thomas Edison's personal secretary. He used that position to build an electrical empire—he started the Commonwealth Electric Light & Power. He also owns the gas company, and part of most commuter railroads. He started Chicago's first radio station, KYW, in 1921, and built the Civic Opera House in 1929. Insull was heavily leveraged, though, and his fortune evaporated in the 1929 Crash.

Green will soon charge Insull with fraud. Insull will flee to Europe, be arrested in Istanbul, and be brought back to Chicago to face Green, who sent Capone to prison.

The government will marshal 2,500 exhibits, arrayed in a 22-foot-long bookcase, custom-built, plus 200 witnesses. The evidence will require seven weeks to present, while the jury needs but two hours to acquit Insull, who will return to Paris, free but ruined. He'll die of a heart attack in the Metro in 1938, with 30 centimes—84 cents—in his pocket. The body will be identified by a laundry ticket.

Sept. 15, 1982

They are just teachers. Six staffers from Bowen High School. Why would they bother trying to create a museum in honor of Mexican culture? Why now? Maybe it's because of Reginald Mays, 16, stabbed to death in the hallway last spring. Someone asked Carlos Tortolero why he wasn't crying and he said, "I stopped crying a long time ago."

Maybe it's the shock of leaving the classroom. The week before, Tortolero traded teaching history for the chaotic cat-herding of the Board of Education headquarters at Pershing Road.

Maybe because the books they're forced to use are so atrociously bad. "Beyond bad. The misinformation was unbelievable," Tortolero recalled. "No one knew about Mexican culture. The students, young people, don't know the impact of Mexico. All the great things. They know nothing about it."

The six teachers form a board and hold their first meeting. Why today? For the date's symbolic value, as the evening before Mexican Independence Day, "El Grito," the anniversary of Father Miguel Hidalgo ringing his church bell and calling for the Spanish to be driven out. "The Cry of Dolores"—the perfect day to start a revolution.

"Time for us to preserve our culture," said Tortolero. "To share our culture too."

There have been attempts before. But now the moment is right. The election of Harold Washington was a catalyst for the African American community, but Latinos are energized too. If they don't respect and draw attention to their own culture, who will? It takes time. That first year they'll raise $900. In 1989, $2 million. Five years later they have a building in Pilsen. Not that the art world, which is supposedly so progressive, welcomes them, at first. They are just teachers, remember, mostly Mexican teachers at that. Still, they create the National Museum of Mexican Art, considered the premiere institution showcasing Mexican, Latino, and Chicano art and culture in the United States, in all its bright, joyful, sorrowful, political, personal, dramatic, wry complexity. Admission is free.

Sept. 16, 1977

They are just parents. Moms, mostly, in Pilsen. Why would the Chicago Board of Education listen to them? It didn't. Not at first. And not that all of them would have understood the board's response, had one come. Some of the parents could barely speak English. But they could sign petitions. That was in 1972. As parents they saw no reason why their children had to cross gang territory to go to Harrison High School, a mostly Black high school in South Lawndale. Where Spanish-speaking students were put in the learning-disabled class by default. Pilsen deserved better than that; it deserved its own high school. They petitioned again. The school board said no, again. "When are you people going to learn to speak English?" one member asked.

In 1973, they boycotted the Pilsen branch of Froebel High School, then occupied it for three days. They protested. The school board again said no.

In 1974, they picketed the Board of Education. Holding signs, "They NEED a new HIGH SCHOOL." A coffin emblazoned "The education in our barrio is dead." They marched through the Loop. This time, the school board approved $8.9 million for a new high school.

Close. But not there, yet. The money was approved. But not spent. In 1975, parents kept their kids home for the first five days of school. They suspended their strike only so the parents would be free to picket the Board of Education again. The next day, the Illinois Capital Development Board gave almost half the money the new school required.

Pilsen residents chose the name Benito Juarez Community Academy, for the president of Mexico during its own Civil War— not that American students are taught much about this, but they will be, here—that took place just before the US Civil War.

The building is designed by Mexico's top architect. Decorated with paintings and murals of Latino history. Today, not by coincidence, is Mexican Independence Day, and the school's official opening. Music, dancing, and Mayor Michael Bilandic, waving a Mexican flag.

Sept. 17, 1920

George Halas wrote to each of the young football teams in various cities, suggesting the need for a professional league, if only to keep everybody from stealing each other's players. They meet today in Canton, Ohio, at the car dealership of Ralph Hay, who owns the Bulldogs there. Sitting on the running boards of Hupmobiles are owners of the Cleveland Indians, Dayton Triangles, Akron Professionals, Massillon Tigers, Chicago Cardinals, and of course Halas, who owns the Staleys, the factory team of a starch company in Decatur. Plus teams from Rochester, Rock Island, Muncie, Racine, and Hammond. In two hours, the American Professional Football Association is formed and Jim Thorpe, Hay's partner in the Bulldogs, is named president because he's famous. Franchises cost $100. Not that anybody fronts the money, which they can't spare. Yet.

Sept. 18, 1889

The bullfight broke her trance. Jane Addams had been drifting through Europe, studying with her particular friend, Ellen Gates Starr, when the pair found themselves at a *corrida* in Madrid. Addams watched five bulls slain, marveling at the medieval magnificence of the pageant, while Starr and the rest slipped away, revolted. Later, Addams was surprised to find them "stern and pale with disapproval of my brutal endurance, and but partially recovered from the faintness and disgust which the spectacle itself had produced upon them."

Right there, she had her epiphany.

"It was suddenly made quite clear to me that I was lulling my conscience by a dreamer's scheme," she would write in her memoirs, "that a mere paper reform had become a defense for continued idleness."

Not willing to become "the dupe of a deferred purpose," she fled Europe, after pausing for several months in London to hone her skills at Toynbee Hall. The new year saw Addams and Starr giving speeches in Chicago while scouring the city for a suitable place, which they found in the form of a pillared mansion "battered by its vicissitudes" with offices and storeroom and a factory in the back. The home's owner, Helen Culver, offered it for free, and the settlement was called "Hull-House" because the building was built in 1856 by real estate tycoon Charles J. Hull.

Addams and Starr move in today, and in a few days will begin their first book group. Next month, the city's first kindergarten will open in the drawing room, and decades of social action combined with physical and cultural uplift follow. The city's first playground will be built here, and Hull-House will host art exhibits and musical concerts, social clubs, and union meetings, advocating for workers' rights and against child labor.

Sept. 19, 1910

The gaslight in the hall is off. The Hillers always keep the hall light lit at night in their home at 1837 W. 104th Street. Clarence Hiller, alerted by his wife, goes to investigate just after 2 a.m. He meets an intruder. They struggle, falling down a flight of stairs. Hiller, a railroad clerk, is shot twice. His wife screams, neighbors come running, then police, who find two lead slugs and, on a freshly painted rail outside the kitchen window, four fingerprints.

Half an hour later, Thomas Jennings is spotted four blocks away, heading to the streetcar. His coat is torn and bloody. A loaded revolver is in his pocket. Police question him and learn he was released from prison six weeks earlier on a burglary conviction. None of this is a crime, however. But there is that freshly painted rail. First used by the British in India in the mid-19th century as a way to conclusively identify those signing documents, fingerprinting is part forensic science, part eugenics, a symptom of the early 20th-century passion for measuring people. The fingerprints on the Hillers' window frame match Jennings's.

What does that prove? At his trial, the defense will solicit fingerprints from the public, trying to establish that they are not all unique. But fingerprints *are* unique, and a jury will convict Jennings, the first such conviction in the United States. An appeals court will uphold the new scientific principle. Jennings will hang.

Sept. 20, 1992

The secret is balance, with bridges and just about everything else. The drawbridges in Chicago have a counterweight that sinks into a waterproof pocket. Because the steel leaf going up and the weight going down are equal, it doesn't take much force to open a bridge.

But bridges, like everything else, can become unbalanced, go out of whack. Something goes wrong today on the Michigan Avenue Bridge, which is being renovated. As the northern half closes after opening to let a sailboat pass, the southeast span flips up, sending a 40-ton crane tumbling, its boom falling across Michigan and Wacker, trailing steel cable, snapping a light pole, and smashing its 285-pound ball hook into the rear seat of a blue Ford Escort parked on Lower Wacker Drive. The driver in the front seat is startled but unhurt. A CTA bus is pelted by debris, and six people are injured, none seriously, not due to projectiles but from the mad crush toward the back of the bus. The bridge is out of service for a month, and engineers will later determine that the accident was due to the surfacing being stripped off, severely unbalancing the bridge.

The Michigan Avenue Bridge deserves more respectful treatment than to focus on one moment of dysfunction in a century of service: it was in the original 1909 plan of Chicago, and its opening in 1920 helped Pine Street, a quiet residential boulevard, transform into the shoppers' paradise of North Michigan Avenue. Though the bridge does know how to startle: in 1922, a classic movie stunt, clichéd even then, was reproduced in real life when safecracker Vincent "Skimmer" Drucci, a member of the Dean O'Banion gang, was being chased by two detectives. He sped his touring car through the lowered warning gates as the bridge began to rise, and jumped his sedan over a three-foot gap. Alas for him, the police jumped an even wider gap and arrested him on the other side.

Sept. 21, 1927

The Boeing Air Transport Company brings two men to Chicago from San Francisco by air today.

That's it, that's the story.

Two men. *By air*. Spectators for the big event tomorrow. The *Daily News* runs the story on the front page, along with the National Air Transport Company flying in *seven* passengers, four from Oklahoma City, three from Kansas City.

The wonder is conveyed to establish just how big tomorrow's fight between heavyweight champion of the world Gene Tunney and challenger Jack Dempsey will be. When sportswriters tire of calling it "the fight of the century," they try out "the spectacle of the ages."

All available prohibition agents—at least 100—from Milwaukee to Indianapolis are in town to try to stanch what is expected to be a tsunami of illegal booze. Chicago hotels are packed. One reporter writes a story about trying to get a room; it's suggested he try hotels north of Lawrence Avenue, about six miles from the Loop. Top celebrities gather in an array the wattage of which has not appeared in Chicago before or since. From Hollywood: Charlie Chaplin, Gloria Swanson, Douglas Fairbanks, Tom Mix, Al Jolson. From the East Coast: George M. Cohan, Irving Berlin, Condé Nast, Joseph Pulitzer, Walter Chrysler. Titans of industry. The presidents of the nation's six largest railroads. Nine US senators and 12 congressmen. Ty Cobb is here, and ring legends Jim Corbett, Jack Johnson, and Jim Jeffries, who writes a column explaining why Dempsey will win.

Everyone is rooting for the underdog, Dempsey, who lost to Tunney last year but won fans' hearts after his wife asked him what happened and he answered: "Honey, I forgot to duck."

Everyone loves the Manassa Mauler and hates Tunney, who conspicuously reads books, is friends with British playwright George Bernard Shaw, and loftily corrects newsmen if they call what is to occur in the ring tomorrow "a fight." Rather, it is a "boxing contest."

Dempsey will knock Tunney down in the seventh round tomorrow night, but fail to go to his corner, as the rules require. The ref doesn't begin counting until he does. The 14-second "Long Count" is among the most famous moments in sports history, and allows Tunney to get back up. After the 10th round he is declared the winner, though fans' hearts remain with Dempsey. Next year, Tunney will seal his doom by delivering a lecture on Shakespeare at Yale, alienating what few "people who hadn't hated him up to that point," his son, Jay Tunney, will remember. Winning can be overrated.

Sept. 22, 1959

"Get the children's shoes together," says Morris Barazani, as he and his wife, Gail, stand at their screen door, and the two artists listen to the vibrating wail of the city's air raid sirens.

It's 10:30 p.m. Forty-five minutes earlier, the White Sox beat the Indians to clinch the American League pennant. But that was in Cleveland, and connecting the win to the sirens in Chicago is "too ludicrous to believe," according to Gail.

For five minutes, the sirens shriek, like they did over the radio during World War II, a terrifying sound that Chicagoans associate with bombs, searchlights sweeping the sky, and cities in ruin.

Switchboards are flooded at newspapers, at radio, TV, and police stations. People hide in their basements, hold each other, pray. They pour into the street, some in their pajamas, and scan the skies for planes. The Barazanis huddle around their transistor radio. Is this the end?

The sirens were ordered by fire commissioner Robert J. Quinn, also the acting civil defense director. The next day there will be fallout of a nonradioactive kind. At first Quinn blames Chicagoans for not tuning to the Civil Defense radio stations. "We've been instructing them for years to stand by for orders from CONELRAD. I see this doesn't do any good. There was no need to complain."

That won't wash.

"If Mayor Daley did this, he should be ashamed," says Mrs. Anne Paluch, of 2857 Fletcher, who woke her kids up and herded them into her basement.

The mayor did do it, and he is not ashamed. Quinn tries to take responsibility, like a good soldier. But Daley spills the beans: "We had hoped no one would be aroused or inconvenienced," he says. Then he sort of apologizes before blaming the city council, which did indeed pass a resolution the week before: "Be it further resolved that bells ring, whistles blow, bands play and general joy be unconfined when the coveted pennant has been won by the heroes of 35th Street, the Chicago White Sox."

For a few days, the letters-to-the-editor sections of the papers are a chorus of disapproval. "Our air raid warning system," Harry W. Arndt writes the *Daily News*, "is hardly a party noisemaker to be used at the whim of some simple-minded sports fan."

But Quinn keeps his job: he'll retire in 1978 and the fire academy will someday be named for him. The Sox go on to lose to the newly transplanted Los Angeles Dodgers in the first World Series played on the West Coast.

Sept. 23, 1917

"You Can Have Beautiful Eye-Brows and Lashes," announces a frugal little display advertisement atop page eight in section five of today's *Chicago Examiner*, along with a drawing of a woman whose eyes are unsettlingly raccoonish, at least by future standards.

The product is Lash-Brow-Ine, a kind of mascara, which still merits explanation in the press. "Mascara is a black matter used to bead the eyelashes," noted the *Tribune*'s "Ask Me! Ask Me!" column in June. Two years earlier, Thomas Lyle Williams, then 19, noticed his sister Mabel applying a mixture of Vaseline and coal dust to her eyebrows and lashes, or so the story goes, and thought he could improve upon her concoction and sell it. Mabel accounts for the first part of his company's name, "Maybell Laboratories," that scientific second part hoping to counteract the aura of danger around cosmetics in the days before consumer product safety was fully taken up by the government. "Guaranteed absolutely pure and harmless," the makers feel compelled to promise. Another concern is reflected in the line "Used and endorsed by thousands of society women and actresses," a subtle plug for the acceptability of makeup, which in some quarters is still seen as a product exclusive to brothels and the stage, two realms that only recently have begun to diverge in the public mind, the latter rising somewhat in acceptability.

Williams will be sued in 1920 over the Lash-Brow-Ine name by a competitor, Lashbrow Laboratories. Williams will lose, fortunately, forcing him to rename his product. He settles upon "Maybelline."

You Can Have Beautiful Eye-Brows and Lashes

Sept. 24, 1901

Two weeks ago, Emma Goldman, "the high priestess of anarchy," was arrested after President William McKinley was shot at the Pan-American Exposition in Buffalo.

Now she sits in the Cook County Jail.

Asked why he did it, Leon Czolgosz claimed to be a disciple of Goldman. He had heard her speak in Cleveland and "she did not believe in government or in rulers." So he bought a gun from Sears and shot the president.

Goldman was in St. Louis when news swept the nation that she is wanted as the "arch conspirator." She immediately boarded a train to Chicago. Her plan was to give an exclusive interview to the *Tribune* in return for $5,000, and use that to pay for legal defense, which she is obviously going to need, then turn herself in. But police got to her first. A dozen cops broke into the home where she was staying while she was taking a bath. She put on a kimono.

At police headquarters, Goldman was grilled for more than eight hours by Chicago's finest.

"You was with Czolgosz in Buffalo, I saw you myself!" one copper yelled, in Goldman's account. "Better confess, d'you hear!"

Nine other Chicago anarchists were also taken into custody, but attention focused almost exclusively on Goldman, who captivates the press. The *Daily News* describes her this way: "Emma Goldman has a face which once seen is never forgotten. Her eyes are a blue that flashes fiercely with an impetuous temper. Her forehead is high. She looks like a leader. One might imagine her in the place of Joan of Arc."

"She was like a caged lion," said Mary K. Keegan, the police matron at Harrison Street, of Goldman's first night in jail.

After two weeks, however, actual evidence of any kind of plot is not forthcoming. Czolgosz seems unhinged, rambling, with Goldman more an object of his fascination than a confederate. A judge orders the anarchists released. Goldman is sprung today.

Asked her plans, she replies that she "will earn my living lecturing and writing, as I always have, and I do not expect anybody can object to that."

They can and do. Goldman is driven by carriage to a friend's house. There, eighth graders from a nearby school are waiting to pelt her with stones.

Sept. 25, 1856

A devout 19-year-old Dwight Moody sits down, pen in hand, and tells his mother back in Massachusetts about his arrival. "I reached this far-famed city of the West one week ago to-night," he writes. "I went into a prayer-meeting last night, and as soon as I made myself known, I had friends enough." The shoe salesman immediately hires a pew in a church, as is the custom, and buttonholes young men in the street, or in bars, inviting them to join him in praise of the Lord.

For the next half century, Moody preaches the Gospel, the first of a long line of flamboyant midwestern evangelicals that will include Billy Sunday, who finds God as an outfielder for the Chicago White Stockings, and Billy Graham, whose first ministry will be in a basement in Western Springs before he bursts into public awareness during a revival at the Auditorium Theater in 1943. Moody will build the Young Men's Christian Association into an organization that includes gymnastic equipment, "a Christian clubhouse" to supplement the allure of the Lord. His influence is felt around the country. In 1890 in Denison, Texas, Ida Eisenhower will pick her son's middle name in honor of Moody, naming him David Dwight Eisenhower. Though the future president will eventually flip those first two names around.

Sept. 26, 1960

"There goes another knee," Richard Nixon quips, ramming his right one into the limousine doorframe as he exits at the WBBM studios at 630 N. McClurg Court for his debate with John F. Kennedy. A month earlier he had bashed his left knee in Greensboro, North Carolina, requiring an 11-day stay at Walter Reed Hospital. The vice president is still pale and drawn.

Chicago was chosen to host the first televised presidential debate because the location fit with the candidates' campaign schedules. The debate runs for an hour on all three networks, ABC, NBC, and CBS; the CBS studio was picked for the debate by drawing slips out of a hat.

The topic, domestic policy. Kennedy projects "sureness, alertness, dexterity of mind, and swiftness of retort," in the words of syndicated columnist Sydney J. Harris.

Nixon, on the other hand, looks bad. A five-o'clock shadow across his jowls. You can see beads of sweat on his face. Even his smile has "a kind of fixed grimness," notes Harris.

That said, few minds are changed. Chicagoans who talk to the *Daily News* afterward still support the candidates they supported beforehand, though Nixon fans worry he might be ill. His mother phones to see if he's all right.

The indifferent, as usual, remain indifferent.

"They are both no good," says Mike McPhillip, who would have preferred to watch an old movie. "I ain't going to vote."

Sept. 27, 1925

The lights are turned brighter in Department 6325, manufacturing receiver coils at Western Electric's mammoth Hawthorne Works in Cicero. Just one variable in a National Academy of Sciences effort to see how the 40,000 employees turning out most of the telephones and switching equipment in the country respond to various changes in illumination. Other aspects of their jobs are also fiddled with—wages, breaks, scheduling, even humidity. The experiment is a bust—how well lit the workrooms are hardly seems to matter when it comes to output. None of the variables do.

But AT&T will persist into the 1930s, bringing in Harvard Business School social scientist Elton Mayo to oversee the project. His researchers eventually decide that workers perform better just by participating in a study, being given attention, observed, talked to, and asked about their circumstances. This revelation— that workers are not cogs to be manipulated but humans to be consulted—will become a mainstay of social science, and in 1958 the tendency of experimenters to affect their subjects will be dubbed "The Hawthorne Effect."

Sept. 28, 1920

"I refused to pitch the ball until I got the money," pitcher Eddie Cicotte tells the grand jury, which indicts eight baseball players on a charge of conspiracy. "It was placed under my pillow in the hotel the night before the first game of the series."

"They promised me $20,000," says Shoeless Joe Jackson. "All I got was $5,000 that Lefty Williams handed me in a dirty envelope."

The 1919 World Series is baseball's blackest eye. Knuckleballer Cicotte hit the lead-off batter in the first inning, a signal that the fix is in. The Sox lost to the inferior Cincinnati Reds 2–1 in the first game, and went on to lose the nine-game series. Two players today make what the prosecutor calls "a full, free and complete statement" verifying that eight members of the team accepted money to lose.

Much that is generally believed about the "Black Sox Scandal" is untrue: the team wasn't underpaid by skinflint Comiskey. Players approached gamblers about fixing the game, not the other way around. And there probably wasn't any little boy who tugged on Jackson's sleeve and implored, "Say it ain't so, Joe," just a creative *Chicago Herald* reporter trying to embellish a story that had devolved into an endless chain of courtroom appearances. A jury will clear the White Sox organization itself of wrongdoing in 1921, but Kenesaw Mountain Landis, the famous judge brought in to clean up baseball, will ban the eight players for life. And beyond, into eternity.

Sept. 29, 1982

"Mary, are you okay?"

Dennis Kellerman hovers by the bathroom door. He saw his 12-year-old daughter go inside. Then a thud.

She had woken up feeling unwell—a scratchy throat—and her parents said she could stay home from school. Her dad knocks again. "Mary, are you okay?"

He opens the door. It's about 7 a.m.

Adam Janus, 27, an Arlington Heights postal worker, is also staying home with a cold. At noon he picks up his children from preschool and stops by Jewel to grab some medicine. He goes home and has lunch.

"I'm going to take two Tylenol and lie down," he says.

About 3:45 in Winfield, Mary Reiner is home with her four children, the youngest a week old. Her husband comes home to find her collapsed on the floor.

An hour later, the family of Adam Janus is planning his funeral. His brother, Stanley, who has a bad back, asks his wife to get him something. She takes two red-and-white capsules for him from a bottle in the bathroom. And two for herself. He takes them. And so does she. He crumples to the floor. She does too.

At 6:30 p.m., Mary McFarland is at work, at an Illinois Bell store in Lombard. She has a headache. . . .

Arlington Heights public health nurse Helen Jensen is called in to help figure out what is going on. She goes to the Janus house, where she sees the bottle of Extra-Strength Tylenol. She takes it with her to Northwest Community Hospital, where doctors and police are frantically puzzling over what is happening.

"Maybe it's the Tylenol," she says, setting the bottle down.

They phone the Cook County medical examiner's office. Edmund Donoghue tells them to smell the bottle. They do. Almonds. A strong scent. The telltale odor of cyanide.

Johnson & Johnson yanks the drug from shelves the next morning. Police drive slowly down residential streets, in that pre-internet age, using loudspeakers to warn residents not to take the popular painkiller. A few days later, all Tylenol bottles—31 million of them, worth $100 million—are recalled.

Seven people die in the Tylenol murders. There will also be hundreds of copycat crimes—acid in eye drops, strychnine in capsules. From now on, medicines will come in bottles with tamper-proof caps, or blister packs. A man will be convicted of trying to extort $1 million from Johnson & Johnson, but no one is ever charged with the killings.

Sept. 30, 1914

Ezra Pound sits down in London to write a letter to Chicago. He acknowledges to the editor of *Poetry Magazine* the 18 pounds, 10 shillings received, complains at length about the play he is working on as only a playwright can, then gets down to business.

"I was jolly well right about Eliot," he writes to *Poetry* founder Harriet Monroe. "He has sent in the best poem I have yet had or seen from an American. PRAY GOD IT NOT BE A SINGLE AND UNIQUE SUCCESS. He has taken it back to get it ready for the press and you shall have it in a few days."

There is no rush. Though Pound sends the poem in October with a nudge—"Hope you'll get it in soon."—Monroe will spend months puzzling over T. S. Eliot's wander through narrow streets while gathering his courage to eat a peach. "Do get on with that Eliot" Pound will write, prodding her in April, the cruelest month. Finally, in the June issue of *Poetry*, "The Love Song of J. Alfred Prufrock" will make its debut.

The same day that Pound, who has already helped steer James Joyce toward publication, is raving about his latest discovery, Eliot is coincidentally also writing a letter to their mutual friend Conrad Aiken, who had introduced him to Pound. In it, Eliot describes his older benefactor as "rather intelligent as a talker: his verse is well-meaning but touchingly incompetent."

OCTOBER

Oct. 1, 1932

The bleacher bums do what bleacher bums do: they boo. They heckle Babe Ruth for just standing in the outfield at Wrigley Field, waiting to muff the next easy fly ball. Someone tosses a lemon that hits Ruth in the leg. Watch the legs, pal, they're fragile, Ruth says, or words to that effect. A portly 37, he taps his head. Hit me here, where it's thicker.

Nothing can dampen Ruth's good mood. It's the third game of the World Series. The Yankees are on top, two games to zip. The Cubs fans are frantic. Ruth is eager to grind their faces in it. He never lets up.

"Hey, mugs!" Ruth yells into the Cubs dugout after batting practice. "You mugs are not going to see the Yankee Stadium any more this year. This World Series is going to be over Sunday afternoon. Four straight."

Then he turns and repeats his boast. "Did you hear what I told them over there?" he asks fans in the stands.

As he runs the bases following his first-inning home run, Ruth blows raspberries—the famous Bronx cheer—at the Cubs.

He almost hits another home run in the third inning, and fully expects to go long in the fifth.

"Wait, mug, I'm going to hit one out of the yard," Ruth taunts Guy Bush, a Cubs pitcher standing in the dugout. He points his bat at center field.

There will be controversy over whether Ruth actually predicts the home run deep to center, but that's ridiculous. He isn't Nostradamus. He's been issuing a string of boasts all day. This one just happened to come true. And Westbrook Pegler is here to fan the flames of myth. The next day Pegler insists Ruth did "call his shot," glorifying the brag-made-real as "the most gorgeous display of humor, athletic art and championship class any performer in any of the games has ever presented."

Sure, why not? History often is, as Napoleon said, a lie agreed upon. No more reliable a witness than Supreme Court Justice John Paul Stevens will someday testify to the miracle, having sat 20 rows back on the third-base line and witnessed it himself. Of course, he's only 12 at the time.

Oct. 2, 2009

Thousands gather at Daley Plaza to celebrate the big moment. The International Olympic Committee will cull the four cities contending for the 2016 Games—Chicago, Rio de Janeiro, Tokyo, and Madrid—down to two. Chicago will be one of them. We know it. Then there will be a second vote. We'll win that too.

Orange Olympic t-shirts and "CHICAGO 2016" signs are handed out by organizers, who spent four years and $50 million on the effort. The water in the fountain is dyed orange, the bid's official color. President Barack Obama flew to Denmark to plead our case. The First Lady too. And Oprah Winfrey.

"My Kind of Town" squawks confidently from loudspeakers. The big Jumbotron screen conveys the latest from Copenhagen, where the decision will be announced. Occasionally chants of "Chi-ca-go! Chi-ca-go!" break out. The Picasso statue, relic of a previous clutch at global significance, has an enormous Olympic medal around its neck. We've already won.

Now we just await the word. Official confirmation. Fistful of confetti in one hand. Horn to our lips in the other, our civic breath drawn in, filling our lungs, collectively held, waiting for the sign that we may explode in joy.

Yes, public opinion is split. Rich Daley, in his tradition of pushing through dubious deals, promised that he wouldn't put taxpayers on the hook for any financial losses, then did exactly that. Okay. What glorious achievement isn't greased by a few strategic lies?

The news flashes. We didn't even make the first cut.

Dead last, fourth of four: 18 of 94 votes. Jaws drop. Tears roll. Blame flies like spittle. Later it will be whispered that Rio bribed the committee, which somehow makes it worse. Beaten at our own game. Or would make it worse, if anybody cared. Which we don't. Not anymore, all interest having leaked away, like air blatting out of a collapsing balloon at that stillborn victory party. Shoulders slumped, confetti dribbling from slack fingers, not looking at one another, we shuffle out of Daley Plaza, back to our ordinary lives.

Oct. 3, 1918

Sneezing is now a crime in Chicago; at least doing so without covering your mouth. Coughing too. The first offense gets a warning; the second a $1 fine. Interim police chief John H. Alcock will send out a "spitting detail"—spitting is also banned—part of the city's scattershot attempt to battle influenza, the lethal Spanish flu detected at the Great Lakes Naval Base in mid-September and now raging across the city and nation.

In an order issued today, health commissioner John Dill Robertson instructs police officers to tap offenders on the shoulder and demand to see their handkerchiefs, asking, "Where is it? Let me see it."

The order will be enforced in theaters, schools, and churches, but such gatherings are not banned. Actors get their noses and throats ceremonially disinfected before shows, while the virus rages unchecked; 397 new cases are reported in Chicago today, with 23 deaths from flu and 51 from pneumonia. An enormous Liberty Bond parade will be held October 12, city streets "jammed to the point of suffocation with cheering crowds."

Some are in denial. Midway through the lethal October, *Daily News* columnist Frank Crane weighs in with his opinion: the Spanish flu is a fad, possibly a delusion, certainly no different from bugs of the 1890s, and "if we all take reasonable care of ourselves and by simple rules of health fortify ourselves against bad colds we shall not be in serious danger." The next day, 317 people in Chicago die of the flu.

Some minds snap. Even though the flu is fatal in only about 2 percent of the cases, it can seem a death sentence. After his family becomes sick, Peter Marrazzo, a laborer living on South Morgan Street, cuts his own throat and the throats of his wife and four children. Only he survives.

The death toll surges during October—a month that sees 200,000 Americans die—peaking on October 17, a day with 524 flu and pneumonia deaths in Chicago. All told, 100,000 Chicagoans will fall ill: at one point, so many telephone operators are out sick that Illinois Bell makes a public plea to limit phone calls.

Oct. 4, 1931

He was supposed to be a modern version of Sherlock Holmes. The deerstalker hat swapped for a snap-brim fedora. But the same sharp nose for clues, the same determined jaw. The idea came the previous May to Chester Gould, an artist for the *Chicago Daily News* who draws other people's comics and illustrations of oriental rugs. All these headlines about gangsters murdering each other, only to go smirkingly free. Law-abiding citizens are fed up. Criminals ought to be caught. Gould drew up some sample strips of what he called "Plain Clothes Tracy" and sent them off to the Tribune Syndicate—his 61st comic idea submitted over the past decade. On August 13, he received a telegram. "Your Plain Clothes Tracy has possibilities. Would like to see you when I go to Chicago next." Two days later, he was in Joseph Medill Patterson's office. "I think the name is too long," Patterson said, promptly solving the problem himself. "John Tracy . . . Fred Tracy . . . *Dick* Tracy. Let's call this fellow 'Dick Tracy.' They call detectives 'Dicks.'" Patterson also suggested the backstory: the murder of his fiancée's father prompts Dick to join the force. That plotline runs today in the debut Sunday strip, kicking off a saga that will continue unbroken for 90 years, spawning radio spin-offs, movies, toys. The comic becomes famous for its rogues' gallery of villains whose appearance reflects their criminality: Pruneface, Flattop, Wormy. And of course that prescient two-way wrist radio. Gould will keep this first strip framed on his office wall for the rest of his life, along with the telegram delivering the good news.

Oct. 5, 1979

Even popes need to sleep.

It's 10:30 p.m. An enormous throng has gathered outside John Cardinal Cody's residence, 1555 N. State Parkway.

"Viva il Papa!" they shout.

Pope John Paul II, the first pope to visit Chicago, the largest Roman Catholic archdiocese in the country, has already had a very long day. Mass for 1.5 million or so. Enough that the Park District, during the scramble to get ready, felt compelled to pile concrete blocks as a test, to make sure the Grant Park lawn wouldn't collapse into the subterranean parking garage under the weight of the faithful.

The pope folds his hands against his ear and tips his head, the universal sign for "bedtime."

"I'm grateful for your presence," he tells the crowd. "Now you must go to sleep. I give you my blessing for a good night and a pleasant sleep."

John Paul II turns to go, then comes back out on the balcony, and leads everyone in singing "Alleluia, alleluia." He smiles. "Repeat," he says, spreading his arms. "Good night." He ducks inside.

Oct. 6, 1921

A small town like Decatur can't support a professional football team. "Why don't you take the team to Chicago?" A. E. Staley explained to a flabbergasted George Halas. "I think football will go over big there."

The starch factory owner offered the young man $5,000 to get the team going, so long as he calls it "The Staley Football Club" for one more season and advertises the company in its program. The contract they sign today terminates in 1922, when Halas will need a new name. He'll consider "The Chicago Cubs" in honor of William Wrigley and Bill Veeck, who have been so much help to him. There is a tradition of naming a city's pro football franchise after its existing baseball team—that's how New York ended up with a Giants football team and a Giants baseball team. But Halas notes "that football players are bigger than baseball players; so if baseball players are cubs, then certainly football players must be bears!" Thus the Chicago Bears will be born. Their colors, orange and blue, since the Staley's colors are orange and navy blue, taken from the colors of Halas's alma mater, the University of Illinois, where he graduated from in 1918.

Oct. 7, 1853

The morning session of the First Convention of the Colored Citizens of the State of Illinois begins at Warner's Hall with a prayer by the Rev. R. H. Cain. "The colored man eloquent," Frederick Douglass, is warmly welcomed, and makes a few "happy and appropriate remarks which were enthusiastically received by the convention."

The recording secretary, alas, does not preserve Douglass's words. But their nature can be hinted at by the 37 resolutions later adopted. The first three reject the idea that Blacks should return to Africa as ultimately designed "to perpetrate the wicked and horrible system of slavery."

"We will plant our trees in American soil, and repose in the shade thereof," one declares, before moving on to the need to create businesses, build homes, and establish schools because "wealth and education are the great levers by which we hope to improve ourselves."

They conclude by penning a lengthy plea to "intelligent Anglo-Saxon minds" in Illinois, a state that has just passed laws forcing runaway slaves who reach here to be returned South.

"We are Americans by birth," the convention says in a statement signed by its five officers, "and we assure you we are Americans in feeling; and in spite of all the wrongs which we have long and *silently* endured in this country, we would yet exclaim, 'with a full heart, Oh, America, with all thy faults, we love thee still!'"

Oct. 8, 1871

A fire breaks out just after 9 p.m. in a barn at the back of the Patrick and Catherine O'Leary residence on DeKoven Street, on the near Southwest Side. That much is true. As is the fact that the fire department is exhausted from fighting a big blaze the night before. It was a dry and fire-filled summer, and a windy early autumn. The first week in October averaged four fires a day in Chicago.

And there is a cow in the barn, without question. Five cows, actually. The business about the cow kicking over a lantern, however, is certainly fiction cooked up by a newspaperman in an era when reporters would frequently embellish or simply manufacture their stories. A seed of anti-Irish calumny, planted while the fire was still burning, one that would sprout and put down deep roots over the years, outliving the bias that spawned it.

The streets were wooden blocks. The sidewalks, planks.

A thousand stories could be told. But perhaps, to counterbalance the stain of the O'Leary slander, it should be noted that while most Chicagoans flee—to the safety of the river, or the cool of the cemetery in Lincoln Park, carting or carrying what possessions they could save—at the *Tribune* office, the reporters file their stories even as the building fills with smoke. At the *Times*, as the flames advance, the staff sets the news in type: "THE VERY LATEST! The entire business portion of the city is burning up and the Times building is doomed." That is not a fabrication, but entirely true, the self-reference forgivable. They write the edition, set the type, even as the building catches fire. The presses roll. The newsmen, some carrying bundles of papers, flee at the last second and the building is consumed along with 3.3 square miles of the city.

Oct. 9, 1871

Around 6 a.m., the fire that began the evening before spreads by flying embers and whirling vortexes—"fire devils"—to the dressmaker shop run by an Irish immigrant named Mary Harris Jones.

This is not the first time tragedy has touched her life. In Memphis, Jones nursed her four small children as they died, one by one, in the yellow fever epidemic of 1867 that also took her husband.

"I sat alone through nights of grief," she'll later write. "No one came to me. No one could."

When the flames reach her shop, destroying it, and her home, and everything she owns, Jones flees to the lakefront.

"The fire made thousands homeless. We stayed all night and the next day without food on the lakefront, often going into the lake to keep cool. Old St. Mary's Church at Wabash Avenue and Peck Court was thrown open to the refugees and I camped there until I could find a place to go."

Next door, the Knights of Labor hold meetings. While Jones waits for whatever is coming next, she attends those meetings. Her life changes.

"From the time of the Great Chicago Fire I became more and more engrossed in the labor struggle and I decided to take an active part in the efforts of the working people to better the conditions under which they worked and lived."

She'll become a familiar figure at union rallies and strikes, a fiery orator, always dressed in black in memory of her lost husband and children. Workers call her "Mother Jones."

Oct. 10, 1944

Read the newspaper thoroughly, the city editor told Terry Colangelo when she came on board the *Chicago Times*; a spunky, sports-oriented photo tabloid, no relation to Wilbur Storey's *Times*, thank you very much. If someone isn't barking at her to go somewhere or do something, she is expected to keep up on the news.

So she does, starting with the news section, editorials, financial, and sports. She even scans the classified ads, those tiny-type offers of apartments to rent, cars for sale. One today stands out: "$5,000 Reward for killers of Officer Lundy on Dec. 9, 1932. Call Gro. 1758, 12–7 P.M."

Why, Colangelo wonders, is someone interested in a 12-year-old murder? She points out the ad to her editor, who puts a pair of more experienced reporters on the case.

At that phone number is Tillie Majczek, 60, working nights downtown as a cleaning woman at Commonwealth Edison. The money she earns scrubbing floors is put toward a reward because her son, Joe, is serving a 99-year sentence at Stateville prison for murder. That's a human-interest story right there: Woman Scrubs Floors to Free Killer Son.

Unlike most mothers of convicted felons who believe in their sons' innocence, however, she seems to be right. The more the *Times* pulls the thread, the more the case unravels: cops desperate to solve the slaying of one of their own, a single witness hoping to be let off for bootlegging, faked police reports, a drunken defense attorney, a passive judge.

That August Joe Majczek will be pardoned and given $24,000 in compensation by the legislature—a bounty an Illinois state rep promptly tries to steal. The case also becomes a classic noir film, *Call Northside 777*, starring Jimmy Stewart and Lee J. Cobb.

Oct. 11, 1947

Two dozen good-sized advertisements, plus a full page facing the back cover, are scattered throughout this week's edition of *The Bill-board*, all announcing the same thing: "Nudgy," the big exciting pinball machine breakthrough that Bally is, umm, ballyhooing. A game with a "new, SHIFTING playfield" operated by a "Nudge Lever" that allows "PLAYER-CONTROLLED action"—you can shift the entire field that ball is tumbling down back and forth an inch.

Close. Very close. But no cigar.

Lost amid all that advertising real estate is a tiny teaser ad atop page 132, a few square inches offering a four-word question: "What is Humpty Dumpty?"

Humpty Dumpty is Gottlieb's new pinball machine that will dropkick Bally's vaunted achievement into oblivion. The very first pinball machine featuring its own novel gimmick allowing player control: electric flippers.

For 50 years, the practice of playing games where balls are sent cascading down inclined planes, bouncing off metal pins, has been battling laws against gambling, and losing, in cases such as *People v. One Pinball Machine*, the 1942 decision allowing Illinois to ban such machines.

The irony is that in the 1930s Chicago became a center for the industry—first Gottlieb, then Bally, then Williams, and finally Stern. Chicagoans can make them and sell them, but not play them. Pinball won't be legal in public here until 1977, when the city council follows New York's lead and permits the machines.

Being able to control stout rubber-rimmed flippers that bat the ball back upward into play is crucial to nudging the machines from games of chance to games of skill. Less like slot machines—also invented in Chicago, by Ideal Toy in 1890—and more like bowling. Bally, despite its stumble with "Nudgy," will become a slot machine and casino behemoth. Williams will merge with other gambling device makers. Gottlieb vanishes, but not before leaving a legacy of all those nickels, dimes, and quarters in the form of Gottlieb Memorial Hospital. And Stern continues, to this day.

Oct. 12, 1912

Mrs. F. Cameron-Falconet of Minneapolis, having hurried to Chicago to rescue her daughter, confronts the teen near the rooming house where she lives on Grand Boulevard near East 41st Street. She pleads with her: leave Jack Johnson right now. Heartbroken, she promises the girl she will take care of her and protect her from the shame of having taken up with a man of another race, if only she returns home to Minnesota.

But Lucille Cameron, 19, is adamant. She will stay with Johnson, the heavyweight champion of the world, and while he has not yet proposed in words, they will certainly marry.

Failing, Cameron-Falconet stifles her pride enough to "call that black man up."

That doesn't work either.

Convinced that Johnson has a hypnotic influence over her daughter, who is not the blushing innocent portrayed in the press, but a prostitute, Cameron-Falconet swears out a complaint at the Clark Street station and Lucille is arrested. Johnson too.

"I don't care whether he is white or black, I love him," she will tell federal officers as they transfer her to the jail at Wheaton. Her bond is $25,000; Johnson's is $800.

The city council denounces Johnson and unanimously demands the mayor revoke the license for his saloon, Café de Champion. Tomorrow, when Johnson arrives at a bank at Dearborn and Monroe to get his bond back, a crowd of hundreds will gather, shouting "lynch him!" and "kill him!" Johnson flees in a taxicab, and Chicagoans will have to settle with hanging him in effigy. The lovers marry in December.

Oct. 13, 1983

Exactly one week ago, the Federal Communications Commission approved an operating license requested by Ameritech Mobile Communications, making Chicago the first area in the nation to offer cellular telephone service.

Such a momentous development demands a hokey public relations stunt, so the flacks at Burson-Marsteller arrange for a footrace today in the parking lot of Soldier Field—15 technicians running to activate the mobile cellular telephones within the trunks of 15 convertibles, to choose who has the privilege of making the first consumer cellular phone call (and win free service for a year, no mean prize, as it costs $50 a month plus 40 cents a minute).

As will happen in hastily arranged hoopla, something goes wrong: the winning car has a dead battery. And while the battery charges, and longtime radio announcer Jack Brickhouse, today's master of ceremonies, fills time telling old baseball stories, we can explain why this is happening here and not somewhere else. Motorola began in Chicago in the 1930s selling car radios—its name a mash-up of Motor and Victrola. In the 1960s, when Japan began to take over the market for inexpensive electronics, it and Zenith sought refuge in niche, higher-end products, like police radios, which begat cell phones.

In the late 1970s, Chicago had the first large-scale experimental cell service. Last March, it introduced the DynaTAC 800X, the first truly portable phone. But that weighs over two pounds, costs $4,000, and service is lousy compared to the more powerful car phones. Now Ameritech is rolling out service to the public called the Cellular Mobile Telephone System: about 1,000 customers have phones, which cost only $1,000 and are "mobile" in the sense a car is mobile: they weigh 80 pounds and their electronics are bolted in the trunk. Ameritech predicts that by 1990 they'll have 100,000 customers. As it turns out, a million people sign up for cellular service in 1990 alone.

Oct. 14, 1908

Detroit catcher Boss Schmidt is having a miserable series—just one hit in 14 at-bats. Blame a sore finger. His 14th effort is a feeble grounder that the Chicago catcher scoops up and throws him out at first.

That play ends the game. The Cubs are world champions for the second year in a row, and Schmidt is the only player in baseball history to represent the final out in two World Series—he popped up the year before.

There is little sense of drama. The West Siders are the dominant team in baseball, and their victory is practically foreordained. During the season there were constant grumblings that the Cubs are so good it's somehow wrong. They shouldn't be allowed to win again "for the good of the league." All the umpires' calls seem to go against them (though not, crucially, three weeks before, in the deathless play that came to be known as "Merkle's Boner," which ultimately handed the Cubs the pennant).

Today's win seems more mundane than momentous—the Cubs take the Tigers four games to one. Only 6,210 Detroit fans attend, the lowest attendance in World Series history.

But some malign fate enters the Cubs' story after today. Silently, without fanfare, like the most devoted fan ever, Bad Luck works his way down the front row and settles into a primo box seat, starts shelling peanuts, and simply will not leave. The Cubs will play in seven World Series over the next 37 years and lose them all. One hundred eight years will pass before they become world champions again.

Oct. 15, 1921

Immigrants come to this country and struggle to learn English, then their children struggle to learn their parents' mother tongue. Jennie Moy and Virginia Wong are featured today in the *Daily News*'s "Wide-Awake Club for Boys and Girls," bows in hair, pens in hand, curled over their work.

The pair, the newspaper explains, are "Chinese girls born in the United States, who have American names and who go to school in the daytime as other boys and girls do. But this fall they are attending an evening school such as few boys and girls in Chicago have ever seen."

They are learning Chinese, walking that tightrope between assimilation and cultural endurance, between embracing their new home and preserving old ways, a calculus every immigrant group grapples with.

"Unlike their fathers and mothers, these boys and girls will be able to speak and write two languages, for they are going to master both English and Chinese," the *Daily News* notes. "You can't go shopping in Chinatown unless you know some Chinese."

Oct. 16, 1891

At 2 p.m. the audience, mostly young women, settles in. The Chicago Orchestra strikes up the first notes of its first performance, the otherworldly tuba and strings opening of Richard Wagner's "A Faust Overture," a daring choice, though natural for German musical director Theodore Thomas.

Every town in America worth the name has a band, or a chamber orchestra, plus a band shell to put it in. Last year, Chicago needed a full symphony orchestra, and already had a magnificent space, the Auditorium Theater. The hunt was on.

Thomas had been the director of a renowned touring orchestra based in New York. Approached by a Chicago businessman who asked if he would consider relocating here, Thomas gave the legendary reply "I would go to hell if they gave me a permanent orchestra." (Actually, he had just about done that, after his orchestra arrived in Chicago to play a performance scheduled for October 9, 1871. When their train stopped at the 22nd Street station and Thomas was told they couldn't go on, because the city had burned to the ground, he ordered his musicians to grab their instruments and luggage and marched them off the train, into the smoky chaos. He wasn't about to miss a gig. Only when he determined that the opera house where they were to perform had indeed been reduced to rubble, along with the fine hotels, did his orchestra return to the train.)

How does the first concert go? "An artistic triumph," the *Daily News* reports, ". . . in every way an auspicious beginning."

"The body of the tone produced is superb," the *Tribune* agrees, "possessing a vitality, a fullness, and volumed such as has been heard by no orchestra ever before in Chicago."

To show just what a force Thomas is, after his death in 1905 from an illness worsened by rehearsing in the new, damp, and chilly Orchestra Hall, the trustees will rename the group the Theodore Thomas Orchestra. It is not until 1913 that it will be dubbed "The Chicago Symphony Orchestra."

Oct. 17, 2007

The attention of Roger Gunderson, owner of RPN Sales & Auction House, was caught by an old-fashioned steamer trunk with stickers of exotic locations. So he bid $260 for the contents of five lockers at Metro Self-Storage, put up for sale for nonpayment of fees.

Included among the books, bills, and papers are a thousand photographs, another thousand rolls of undeveloped film, and 100,000 negatives. The creative output of an elderly woman named Vivian Maier. He almost throws out the negatives, which are usually worthless.

But what the heck. He breaks up the lots, art books, and other possessions, and turns around to sell them—two sales, today and November 7. And so the legend of the genius nanny street photographer begins. Maier minded children while prowling grubby neighborhoods with her Rolleiflex, chronicling "the folly of humanity . . . the bizarreness of life, the unappealingness of human beings." But never sought success or even tried to market her work. Four years later the photos are the subject of an exhibit at the Chicago Cultural Center, then become an international sensation, her work celebrated and analyzed in shows and books, prized by collectors and galleries.

Oct. 18, 1892

The first long-distance phone call from Chicago to New York this morning is a test.

"Hello, Chicago," someone in the Manhattan offices of American Telephone says.

"Well, what is it, New York?" is the reply.

"Are you all right?"

Hmm, good question. The telephone works fine. Right now.

Not so much at 4 p.m., for the main event, intended to be a moment of high historic drama: Mayor Hempstead Washburne—a Republican, served two years, not exactly in the pantheon of mayoral greatness—sitting in the American Telephone and Telegraph office on Quincy Street, exchanges greetings with New York mayor Hugh J. Grant, or at least tries to. Inventor Alexander Graham Bell, also on the call, reminisces about the 1876 Philadelphia Exposition debuting the device. The copper line between the two phones, it is determined, weighs 200,000 pounds. The service will not be cheap; a five-minute call costs $9, almost a week's pay for factory workers assembling sleeper cars in Pullman. Forty Chicago police stations were invited to share the great moment, and their presence on the line considerably weakens the signal. Later it will be revealed that while Chicago could hear New York perfectly, New York could barely hear a word from Chicago. Which is about par for the course.

Oct. 19, 1917

With men rushing to fight the Great War in Europe, industry in Chicago needs workers, and women want those jobs. So the government today creates an employment exchange to pair heavy industry with eager female laborers. Mrs. Raymond Robins, president of the National Women's Trade Union League, is also chair of the committee of woman and children in industry for the Council of National Defense.

"The problem is serious," she says. "We are facing difficulties where technical skill is necessary to rightly place these workers. Picturesque and strenuous work appeals strongly to the new recruits. We are besieged with women who wish to do munition work, perform out-of-door tasks and even handle freight."

For years, Robins has been saying young women are "mentally and spiritually equipped to lead" while pushing for a raft of reforms. Starting with paying women the same as men if twhey are performing equal work and the eight-hour day, to one day off out of every seven and the idea that factory work should be done exclusively by adults.

But are men mentally and spiritually ready to understand her message? Not yet. In tomorrow's *Examiner*, the news will be headlined "U.S. TO GIVE AMAZONS WAR WORK."

Oct. 20, 2014

On the dashcam video you see squad cars, one, two, three of them. You see Laquan McDonald, 17, walking down the center of Pulaski Road, a little hop in his step before Officer Jason Van Dyke, within two seconds of exiting his car, gets into his shooter's stance and fires 16 shots into the teen, who spins to the ground. In the subsequent report, the police claim that McDonald attacked them. In the video, you see McDonald moving away before he is shot. In the report, Van Dyke says he steps back. In the video, you see Van Dyke step forward, firing and firing. And firing. And firing. Sixteen shots. You can see the puffs of smoke on McDonald's clothes as he lies there, receiving bullets. The city will pay McDonald's mother $5 million and the video will be buried, until a journalist sues to see it. The shooting becomes national news, and Van Dyke will become the first Chicago police officer in 35 years to be charged with first-degree murder in connection to a duty-related shooting. He is convicted of second-degree murder and sent to prison. Rahm Emanuel, the former Obama White House chief of staff who grabbed the mayoral chalice dropped by Rich Daley, insists he never saw the video until the public did. He will decide not to run for re-election, in keeping with his life strategy of never playing a game he isn't certain he's going to win.

Oct. 21, 1976

Saul Bellow wins the Nobel Prize in Literature, part of an unprec-
edented sweep. Seven Nobel laureates are Americans; two are
University of Chicago professors, Bellow and economist Milton
Friedman.

The opening sentence of Bellow's *The Adventures of Augie
March* is perhaps the epitome of Chicago literary swagger: "I am
an American, Chicago born—Chicago, that somber city—and go at
things as I have taught myself, free-style, and will make the record
in my own way: first to knock, first admitted; sometimes an innocent knock, sometimes a not so innocent."

Bellow, like Nelson Algren, will gnaw on his plaudits, testing
their authenticity, and find them lacking, certainly not equal to his
self-estimation. He'll complain that his hometown doesn't love him
enough, then decamp. Like Algren, Bellow will head east late in life,
seeking fresh flattery and more enthusiastic applause. Accolades
are as addictive as anything else; even the high of a Nobel Prize
dissipates quickly.

"Better watch out for Saul Bellow today; he's in a bad mood," a
longtime friend will caution his colleague in later years. "The Nobel
Prize is being announced, and you can't win twice."

Oct. 22, 1963

Only 100 of the 2,000 students enrolled at DuSable High School come to class this morning. At Dunbar Vocational High School, 30 of 2,400 students show up, part of a massive Freedom Day boycott to protest segregated, inferior schools for Black students. The stats are shocking: most Black students are crowded into Black schools; 80 percent of African American students attend Chicago public schools that are 90 percent Black or more, reflecting the extreme segregation of housing in the city. Their schools are big: the average white elementary has 700 students; the average Black, 1,200. Their classes are 25 percent larger than white classes. Some go to school in double shifts. The schools are underfunded too; students share textbooks.

Not today. Today the school board estimates that 225,000 students march, or attend some 200 "Freedom Schools" set up in churches, union halls, and community centers, teaching the workings of democracy and Black history not taught in public schools.

They skip school, despite threats of flunking assignments given that day and of their parents being fined or even sent to jail. Thousands of those parents protest downtown, carrying signs reading "Our kids are receiving inferior education" and "Give our children a chance," "25% LESS spent in Chicago to teach a NEGRO CHILD" and "Willis must go."

That last sign is a reference to CPS superintendent Benjamin C. Willis. Lauded in the press as "a model of efficiency and competence," he scorns educators "swayed by the winds of uninformed public opinion," aka considering the perspective of parents.

His solution for overcrowding is to put temporary classrooms in trailers that are immediately dubbed "Willis Wagons" and seen as emblematic of the neglect Black students suffer. Demonstrators burned one in August. It is the board's refusal to accept his resignation—tendered after a power struggle—that prompts the protest. (One organizer explains that the "Freedom Day" refers to "final freedom from Dr. Willis.")

"Boycott a Thumping Success!" the *Defender* exults on its front page. Sort of. Yes, nearly a quarter of a million kids stayed home from school. But the demonstration will accomplish little. Segregation not only continues, it gets worse, as whites flee to the suburbs and religious schools while city schools deteriorate. Willis will not retire until 1966. In 1987, US Secretary of Education William J. Bennett will call Chicago schools the worst in the nation and suggest CPS parents consider private education for their children.

Oct. 23, 1950

"Don't move! Change TV programs from your easy chair," orders the debut ad in *Time* magazine announcing Zenith's "Lazy Bones," the first TV remote control. The device has a long wire and two buttons—one for volume, one to change the channel. It is not cheap: $30, about 15 percent of the price of the set itself. The cord is considered unsightly and viewers trip over it, and by 1955 Zenith replaces it with the "Flash-Matic" cordless remote.

Why the name "Zenith"? R. H. G. Mathews and Karl Hassel were radio fans who met at the Great Lakes Naval Training Station during World War I and went into business together as Chicago Radio Laboratory in 1918. One of their first devices was the longwave radio transmitter the *Tribune* used to skip traffic on the congested Atlantic cable, beating its competition on reports from the Versailles treaty talks by up to 24 hours. The pair set up a factory on the lakefront, with room for an amateur radio station, whose call letters 9ZN became a trade name, Z-Nith, which became Zenith. The company pioneered a number of breakthroughs forgotten today. For instance, up until 1926, radios required messy and cumbersome wet batteries. Zenith engineers found a way to plug radios into AC wall current.

Oct. 24, 1924

There's a new product in today's cluttered Walgreen's advertisement in the *Tribune*. The 21-cent box of Kleenex offers the classic tale of figuring out how to sell something you've already got cluttering up a warehouse. When the Great War ended, Wisconsin papermaker Kimberly-Clark was left with lots of cellu-cotton crepe—used in filters for gas masks that were no longer needed. They first sold it as a feminine product, Kotex. That was slow to catch on—women were embarrassed to ask for it—and the company tried selling the stuff in sheets. But what are the sheets to be used for? "A soft, velvety tissue for removing cold cream from face," Walgreen's ventures, still years away from suggesting customers might sneeze into a Kleenex tissue. Right now, reassurance is in order. "It is safe, sanitary and inexpensive. Use it once and throw it away."

In the same spirit of product repurposing, notice, on the right of the ad, "Walgreen's Double-Rich Malted Milks." Malt syrup was an essential staple at any pharmacy, mixed with noisome medicines to make them more palatable. Walgreen's has long been trying to sell the stuff directly, hawking jumbo "Hospital Size" canisters of malt powder. Their soda fountains began mixing a tablespoon of malt powder with milk and chocolate syrup as a kind of early energy drink.

In 1922, a Walgreen's soda jerk, Pop Coulson, added two scoops of ice cream and invented the malted milkshake, or so the company claims. The chain certainly popularized it, with lines out the door of customers eager to plunk down two dimes for a malted, complete with a pair of vanilla cookies from the Walgreen's bakery. They also sell it in frozen bricks, pushing it with full-page ads, trying to remove any stigma of serving guests from an icy block purchased at a drugstore. "At gatherings and summer parties, it is more than appropriate—it is just *the* thing."

Today's ad mentions Walgreen's "53 drug stores," 50 in the city, with three others in Evanston, Oak Park, and Hammond. Another is opening tomorrow at Roosevelt and St. Louis. The company's rapid growth is still being directed by Charles R. Walgreen, who founded the chain in 1901. The child of Swedish immigrants, Walgreen is the best-known Swede in a city that once boasted the largest Swedish enclave outside the mother country. Or didn't boast it. While the four larger groups, the Poles and the Irish, the Germans and the Italians, battle it out in politics and culture, the Swedes never projected a similar high profile, Walgreen's notwithstanding. By 2021, it'll have more than 9,000 stores nationwide, with 574 in Illinois.

Oct. 25, 1974

Alexander Calder likes circuses. So Chicago boosters decide a circus parade is the best way to honor the 78-year-old artist, whose 53-foot-tall *Flamingo* is unveiled at noon in Federal Plaza. The gold and white Schlitz Circus Bandwagon pulled by 40 draft horses conveys Calder, joined by clowns and a marching band, to the site. A limo later takes him to the Sears Tower, where he flips a switch activating a moving abstract mural he names *Universe*.

Despite his childish whimsy, Calder is still a professional and a perfectionist. This morning he is given a preview of the Museum of Contemporary Art's retrospective of his work. He asks for pliers, and adjusts a dozen wire mobile and stabile sculptures, some more than 40 years old. Using a pair of hammers, he flattens the corners of a 1932 piece, *Little Ball with Counterweight*. He also asks that a copy of a motorized sculpture, *Bicycle*, be turned on. It's pointed out that the work's owner, New York's Museum of Modern Art, stipulated that the artwork not be activated in agreeing to loan the piece.

"I've never seen it in motion," Calder pleads. The MCA gives in.

Calder also lets it be known he isn't happy with where his *Flamingo* is situated in Federal Plaza. "It's too far back," he complains, wishing it were on the north side of the plaza. That can't be fixed with pliers, however, and the parabolic wading bird of curving red steel stays where it is.

Oct. 26, 1825

At 9 a.m. a cannonade is fired in Buffalo, on the northeastern tip of Lake Erie. The booming tribute continues east across New York State, all the way to Albany on the Hudson, following the 362-mile length of the Erie Canal, marking its official opening. No other occurrence is as significant to the eventual creation of a great city 500 miles to the west, in what today is an abandoned stockade surrounded by a few hovels.

Dismissed as "a little short of madness" by Thomas Jefferson, the canal means that goods from Europe can now, after crossing the ocean by ship to New York City, sail up the Hudson, then be ferried by canalboat west to the shore of Lake Erie, where they are taken aboard smaller schooners to travel southwest across the lake, north up the Detroit River, across Lake St. Clair and the St. Clair River, up Lake Huron following the contours of Michigan State, through the Straits of Mackinac and down choppy Lake Michigan, to be deposited on the as-yet-unbuilt wharves of the as-yet-unborn Chicago.

The next step, obviously, is to keep going: dig a canal from the muddy trickle of the Chicago River—dredged wider and deeper—to the more significant Des Plaines River, leading into the Illinois River, connecting to the Mississippi, flowing all the way down to New Orleans.

To do this, the future Chicago will be mapped in 1830, to facilitate Native American lands being seized, stolen, or swindled away, then platted and sold off to fund the canal. There are fewer than 200 inhabitants in the swampy nowhere at the intersection of the Chicago River and Lake Michigan when the Erie Canal opens in 1825. Twenty-three years later, when the Illinois and Michigan Canal opens, there will be nearly 30,000.

Oct. 27, 1990

Rivals can come together. At least when there is money to be made. The Chicago Mercantile Exchange is the more forward thinking. In today's vote, 98 percent of its membership approves the agreement. The Chicago Board of Trade is more backward looking—it's hard to imagine buying futures (I pay you $1 for a dozen eggs you'll deliver next May) and options (I pay a nickel for the right to pay you $1 for a dozen eggs you'll deliver next May) without traders in colored jackets, waving their arms and shouting at each other, and filling out little cards with their pencil stubs. Only 90 percent of CBOT members approve.

Good enough. The Globex Corporation is formed, a joint venture of the CME, CBOT, and Reuters to run a global electronic trading system using electronic terminals buying and selling after-hours. It takes 15 seconds for an order to process, which is considered a wonder. Three decades later it will take three milliseconds. By then the hexagonal trading pits will be mostly gone, with only a few— trading in Eurodollar options, for instance—remaining.

Oct. 28, 1893

Cities Day at the World's Columbian Exposition, which ends
Monday. The mayors and their staffs show up early at City Hall to
get their badges, a thousand strong, beginning with Alton, Aurora,
and Appleton, as far east as New York City and as far west as Santa
Cruz. At 9 a.m., they march, in their tall silk hats, led by the Second
Regiment Band, then Chicago mayor Carter Harrison and the city
council and various officials, to the special Illinois Central train that
takes them to the fairgrounds.

That is how the day begins. It ends with Harrison at home in his
mansion on South Ashland, relaxing after dinner about 8 p.m. There
is a caller; there often are. Chicagoans are known to walk right into
Harrison's home and confront him, demanding favors. This one,
Patrick Eugene Prendergast, is under the delusion he is to be made
corporation counsel. Harrison comes to the door. Prendergast pulls
out a revolver and fires three times, killing him.

Oct. 29, 1955

Captain Joseph Grant taxies a four-engine TWA Constellation onto the runway at O'Hare Field and takes off at 9:59 a.m., shortly before the ceremonies officially opening the airport to commercial aviation. Bound for Cairo, Egypt, with stops first at Shannon, Ireland, then Paris, Geneva, Milan, Rome, and Athens, it is one of two flights that will leave today.

From such a modest beginning, much is expected. The whole area will become an industrial center, it is predicted, perhaps even with factories situated between the enormous runways.

"The plan looks forward to the day when Chicago is the biggest, most important city in the world," John Justin Smith writes in this afternoon's *Daily News*. It certainly is an ambitious airport: set on 6,393 acres, or almost 10 square miles, O'Hare is 11 times larger than Midway Airport, the busiest airport in the world.

The 10 passengers aboard Capt. Grant's Egypt flight board on a rolling stairway in blustery weather. But that might soon be a thing of the past.

"Perhaps most impressive of all is the amazing new 'landing bridge' on which bids are being prepared by railway car builders," travel editor Lucia Lewis marvels in the *Daily News*. "This bridge, built like the stainless steel cars of a streamliner, will fit flush against an airliner at one end and a terminal entrance at the other."

Made of 30,000 lbs Chocolate.

Standing 38 feet high.

The great World's Columbian Exposition ends today. The last visitors depart with backward glances. Now all that remains is for the world's nations to pack up their displays and send them home. Of course, not all the exhibits are going home. The fair first and foremost served as a celebration of industry, and business certainly was conducted here.

For instance, chocolate. The Germans and the Swiss seized the opportunity to show off their national treat, which is not as popular in this country. In the agriculture building, the Stollwerck Brothers of Cologne built a 38-foot-tall, domed temple out of chocolate, with white cocoa-butter swirls mimicking marble in the fluted columns, topped with Teutonic eagles. In the Industrial Arts Building, J. M. Lehmann ran a full working factory taking raw cocoa beans and turning them into silky chocolate bars.

That operation caught the eye of an eastern candymaker in town to check up on a branch of his Lancaster Caramel Company, opened the year before on West Harrison Street—a necessary move, since freight charges were making it difficult to compete with National Caramel in St. Louis.

"The caramel business is a fad," Milton S. Hershey told the manager of the Illinois plant as they gazed upon the production line. "But chocolate is something we will always have."

Hershey bought the entire Lehmann chocolate factory, down to the last marble roller, and with the fair closed, is shipping it to Lancaster, Pennsylvania.

Oct. 31, 1933

There is a full harvest moon and unseasonably warm weather, so you know trouble is coming. The entire uniformed Chicago Police Department is on the street, but that doesn't keep windows from being broken and wagons burned across the city. An automobile is torched at North and Sheffield. Other cars are stripped, or chalked, and fences are torn down, piled up, and set ablaze. Two hundred twenty fire alarms are pulled, four times the usual, most of them false. Streetcar rails are greased, and overhead wires torn from poles.

This, despite concerted effort to give youth something to do—parties at businesses, bonfires at schoolgrounds, and a parade with thousands of children, many in costume.

Sometimes the presence of police is more an invitation to mischief than a preventative. A well-thrown tomato hits patrolman Dan Leahy of the Woodlawn station squarely in the face at 61st and St. Lawrence. Patrolman John Layendecker, from the Englewood station, is hit by a brick at 73rd and Racine, breaking his right hand. A dozen department-store windows are broken on 47th Street.

Some of the injuries are self-inflicted. William Zimmerman, age seven, of 1430 W. Wellington, is walking atop a picket fence when he slips and falls, impaling himself.

By night's end, Chicago police take hundreds of boys into custody, just to get them off the streets—Oak Park police arrest 300. After a few hours in the tank, their names are recorded, and they are sent home.

NOVEMBER

Nov. 1, 1954

Maria Callas makes her American debut at the Civic Opera House, singing Bellini's *Norma* at the opening of the first full season of the Lyric Opera of Chicago. How did that happen? Lyric co-founder Carol Fox flew to Milan and outbid the Metropolitan Opera's Rudolf Bing by $250 a performance. But the fiery soprano won't really stride onto the world stage, dragging the Midwest's latest attempt at high culture with her, until next year when, still made up from *Madame Butterfly*, she will be served with a subpoena from a former manager suing her for nonpayment of fees. Photographers just happen to be there—maybe to catch her in Cio-Cio San costume, maybe because this is her last performance under contract to the Lyric and impresario Danny Newman sees a potential for publicity in the process server, who has been chasing her around the world. It certainly allows Callas to utter a strong candidate for the most diva line of all time as the papers are served.

"I am an angel," she screams. "You can't do this to me!"

Naturally, she'll blame the city. "Chicago will be sorry for this," she tells Carol Fox. Next season she opens at the Metropolitan Opera in New York.

Nov. 2, 2016

Of course the Cubs have to blow their lead, for old times' sake.

The World Series is tied, three games apiece, with the finale tonight in Cleveland. The Cubs start strong, with the first Game Seven lead-off homer in Series history, a series already historic just for having the Cubs in it for the first time since 1945.

The Cubbies build a 5–1 advantage to carry into the bottom of the fifth, when the Cleveland Indians finally wake up and begin scoring. Still, the Cubs have a 6–3 lead in the bottom of the eighth, when the Indians single, then double, then Rajai Davis hits a home run. Game tied.

Cubs fans fall silent. The glistening nightmare beasts of past collapses—1969, 1984—start to stir in their lairs. The weight of the curse presses on fans' sagging shoulders. Somewhere, a goat bleats.

The Lord God Almighty is not on the official Cubs roster today. Yet someone sends the rain. Before the start of the 10th inning. The Cubs flee to the locker room. "We're the best team in baseball," Jason Heyward tells his teammates. "Stick together and we're going to win this game."

Bad Luck, who has been a season ticket holder for 108 years, for reasons mysterious, now checks his watch, nods once, then stands up, brushing peanut shells off his lap, and departs. The Cubs take the field.

A single, a fly ball, a walk. Then Ben Zobrist hits that clutch double into the left-field corner. They get an insurance run. It's 8–6. Cleveland makes it interesting in the bottom of the 10th, with Rajai Davis driving in another run.

Then the Cubs do something very un-Cubs-like, something they have not done since 1908. The Cubs win the World Series. And there is joy in Chicago.

Nov. 3, 1948

An hour later and it never would have happened. But a typesetter strike pushes up the *Chicago Tribune*'s deadline. Managing editor J. Loy Maloney has to make the call. He consults with his Washington correspondents. It's a done deal. Take it to the bank. The presses roll about 10:30 p.m.

Yes, Thomas E. Dewey is an uninspiring candidate. Formal, frosty, with a thin mustache. The groom atop a wedding cake. His arrival onstage is, in the words of columnist Richard Rovere, like that of "a man who has been mounted on casters, and given a tremendous shove from behind." Yet the dapper if cold New York governor is expected to trounce Harry Truman, hampered by a postwar slump at home, ascendant communism abroad, not to forget Truman's politically reckless support of a civil rights bill and an integrated military.

The new issue of *Life* magazine, already on newsstands, has a full-page portrait of Dewey with the caption "The next president of the United States." Every poll, every pundit, is certain. The final Gallup Poll has Dewey up by five points. Oddsmakers favor Dewey 4 to 1. The *Tribune* editorial page has called Truman a "nincompoop." The head of the Secret Service and five of his men are in New York, taking up position around the presumptive president-elect. The actual president's security entourage is a third of the size: Truman slips away from his Kansas City election headquarters with a pair of agents and drives to Excelsior Springs, a nearby resort town, to spend the night.

"DEWEY DEFEATS TRUMAN" reads the headline across the top of the November 3 edition of the *Tribune*. About 150,000 copies of what will be considered the biggest blunder in 20th-century newspaper history hit the streets. Like the coronation of Dewey in *Life* magazine, it would have been quickly forgotten, along with the vast majority of all journalism. But the next day Truman, taking a train back to Washington, will stop in St. Louis. He'll step onto the back platform to greet the crowd, and someone will hand him a copy of his least favorite newspaper. Truman, beaming, displays it for the gathered photographers, an image that will radiate down the decades.

Nov. 4, 2008

"Daddy," Malia Obama reluctantly observes from the back of the big SUV as it speeds south down Lake Shore Drive toward Grant Park. "There's no one on the road. I don't think anyone's coming to your celebration."

Michelle Obama puts a comforting arm around her 10-year-old daughter. "The people are already there, sweetie," she says. "Don't worry, they're waiting for us."

That they are. A quarter of a million Chicagoans gather in Grant Park to spend election night basking in the unseasonable warmth, the pleasure of each other's company, and the eloquence of Barack Obama, whose meteoric rise from South Side organizer to state legislator to US senator to, now, president-elect was fueled by the perfect blend of hard work, clear vision, penetrating intelligence, calm demeanor, and liberal doses of good old-fashioned luck. He is the right man in the right place at the right time.

"If there is anyone out there who still doubts that America is a place where all things are possible, who still wonders if the dream of our founders is alive in our time, who still questions the power of our democracy . . . ," begins Obama. "Tonight is your answer."

Obama finishes and the crowd disperses, reluctant, lingering. They stroll up Michigan Avenue. People play music, drums. Some dance in the streets. A middle-aged man goes to one knee in front of the old Conrad Hilton and presses his fingertips against the street, as if testing its solidity. "It was right here," he says to his son, "that the protesters sat down and the police beat them." The country, it seems, has finally escaped the wreckage of 1968.

Nov. 5, 1960

John F. Kennedy could have attended the dedication of the highway
that will be named in his honor in a little more than three years.
He was in town last night for a torchlight parade and rally. But with
the presidential election three days away, Kennedy has to hurry
to the East Coast. So, at 11 a.m., Mayor Daley, Gov. Stratton, and
other dignitaries gather to officially open the eight-lane, 15-mile,
$237.8 million Northwest Expressway. The talk is of hours saved in
commuting and the possibility of a 25-minute dash from the Loop to
O'Hare. Nothing is said of the neighborhoods cut in half. Nor of the
superhighway greasing the way for white flight even farther from
downtown jobs. And, this being Chicago, we can't christen a new
road without using it as an occasion for self-flattery. A headline in
this afternoon's *Daily News* will read "World Envies Our Freeway."

Nov. 6, 1864

No Civil War battles were fought in Chicago. Or in Illinois, for that matter. But we came close, maybe. There was a conspiracy, supposedly. A plan, an audacious plan, perhaps. Hatched by the Confederacy, the whispers went, to free the 8,000 Southern prisoners held at Camp Douglas, at Cottage Grove and 31st Street, arm them, unite the rebels with Southern officers who had infiltrated the city, and use them as a de facto battalion to burn Chicago and cut out the heart of the Union's manufacturing center and transportation hub.

Unless there wasn't. Unless it was all baseless gossip and fervid wartime imagination.

There had been rumors before. In August, during the Democratic National Convention, it was believed that Southern officers slipped into town along with McClellan backers, who wanted to defeat Lincoln and make peace with the South. Nothing came of that.

Three months later the commander of the camp, Col. Benjamin Sweet, isn't taking chances. Convinced this time it is real, he released a prisoner whose sympathies had turned to the Union, who confirmed the imminent uprising. So this evening Sweet alerts his superior that the town is filled with "suspicious characters" and he must act immediately. A few hours after midnight, he marches troops into the city.

They surround the homes of former mayor Buckner Morris and Charles Walsh, both Confederate sympathizers. In the latter, they find a supply of loaded revolvers and shotguns. To arm the prisoners. In theory. So, unlike most rumors, this has at least an element of truth. The guns are there. That's enough for the commander of Camp Douglas.

"Seldom have so few men been charged with the protection of interests so great," Sweet will later write, foreshadowing Churchill.

Nov. 7, 1934

The Ford Trimotor airplane carrying avant-garde writer Gertrude Stein and her companion, Alice B. Toklas, to Chicago is loud. So they communicate with notes. Stein's are almost poems:

In a kind of a way
the light up here on
the wing is the most
beautiful thing.

After decades in Paris, at the center of a legendary circle that included Picasso, James Joyce, F. Scott Fitzgerald, and Ernest Hemingway, Stein has returned to the nation of her birth to lecture at Columbia University in New York. Her Chicago fans pay for the famous couple to travel here for the debut of Stein's opera, *Four Saints in Three Acts*, at the Auditorium Theater, a fundraiser for the Vocational Society for Shut-Ins, a charity supplying the disabled with craft materials.

Stein is met by amused, appreciative newsmen, who pepper their stories with her more famous phrases, such as "tender buttons" and "pigeons on the grass." They are surprised to find that, despite her opaque prose, Stein speaks "perfectly understandable English."

"The trouble with you newspaper people is you write about what others say and not what you think," she tells the *Daily News*, whose story subhead, "Noted Woman Author Talks Sanely Enough Here," is rivaled only by the *Tribune*'s "But Noted Author Takes Sunsets Calmly."

Stein, who last visited Chicago in 1893 to see the World's Columbian Exposition, stays just one day, then returns with Toklas to New York. Their notes, scribbled on airline stationery, end up in the Beinecke Rare Book and Manuscript Library at Yale:

An airplane is made for
writers as it is the only
way to communicate.

Nov. 8, 1991

Tony's Famous Pizzeria isn't really famous. Just a humble storefront pizza joint that opened in 1946 at 5149 S. Archer. Today's *Chicago Tribune*, trying to put a bright spin on Anthony DiCrescenzo's obituary, claims he "introduced pizza to the city's Southwest Side."

Maybe so. His son is more realistic.

"He was just a man who liked to make his pizza, to cook and to be in his restaurant," said Anthony DiCrescenzo Jr. "He spoke in broken English and it never got better. He made his pizza his way and either you liked it or you didn't."

The thing with Chicago pizza is, the brightest stars have a way of blotting out the rest. Everyone knows Pizzeria Uno opened in 1943, inventing the distinctive Chicago deep-dish pizza—it's still there, with its cornmeal crust and loitering knot of tourists. Home Run Inn Pizza is in every supermarket freezer section in the city. Lou Malnati came to help run Uno's, and now you can get Malnati's pizza anywhere in the country on two days' notice. It's still great pizza. The tomato sauce. Magic.

Before World War II, pizza was an obscure ethnic Italian dish, served by Italians to Italians in Italian neighborhoods. The *Daily Times* needed to explain pizza in 1935: "Pizza is a sort of pie, the crust of which is filled with such things as tomatoes, cheese, anchovies or shrimps."

Most pizzerias were like Tony's Famous. Not enormous rooms belonging to enormous chains. Not Gino's East or Giordano's or what have you. Solitary, distinctive little eateries—Tony's had six tables to start. Places with quirks. The upside-down bowl pizza of Chicago Pizza & Oven Grinder Company on Clark. The great black disc of caramelized pizza served at Burt's in Morton Grove.

DiCrescenzo came to Chicago at 16 from southern Italy. He learned to bake at a biscuit factory, served in the navy in World War II, then came home to satisfy the bottomless hunger for pizza developed by American servicemen in Italy. His pizza wasn't round, but an elongated oval, like in the old country, cut down the middle. "Every piece an end," said his son. His father also rejected such modern indulgences as delivery.

"His brother always said, 'Let's do carry out,'" said Tony Jr. But his father wasn't about to fiddle with gimmicks. "If they want my pizza, they come to me," he replied.

Nov. 9, 1927

A nightclub singer keeps late hours. So, though it's 10:30 a.m., Joe E. Lewis is still asleep at his room on the 10th floor of the Commonwealth Hotel on Pine Grove Avenue just south of Diversey; he didn't get to bed until 5 a.m. There is a rapping at the door. Lewis had been warned not to open up for anyone, but he does anyway and three men rush in. One takes a .38 and cracks him with it from behind so hard the blow shatters his skull. The latest negotiating tactic in what is in essence a contract dispute.

Lewis was paid $650 a week to perform at the Green Mill, where he had been packing them in for a year. The New Rendezvous Cafe, at Clark and Diversey, offered him $1,000 a week, and Lewis was naïve enough to believe that his contract running out meant he could shift venues. This was unacceptable to one of the co-owners of the Green Mill, Machine Gun Jack McGurn, who encouraged him not to. "You'll never live to open," is how the ruthless killer phrased it. Then came the threatening phone calls. But Lewis ignored these lesser encouragements.

The unconscious Lewis has his throat cut, ear-to-ear, with a hunting knife, but miraculously does not die. He crawls to the elevator, gets to the lobby, where of course they think it's a practical joke, at first. His singing voice is ruined, however, and he becomes a comedian, most notably in Billy Wilder's *Some Like It Hot*. Al Capone, who claims to have been unaware of the attack by his henchman, feigns sympathy, and gives Lewis money to live while he recovers.

Nov. 10, 1834

What you toss away in your backyard eventually shows up in your well water.

This essential environmental lesson is becoming increasingly clear in the newly organized village of Chicago. Or, in the words of Dr. A. S. Martin, an early resident: "Dish water, wash water, and all fluid refuse from the kitchen were generally thrown on the ground in back yards. In time, the water drawn from the wells began to taste—a little brackish, at first, then saltish, and finally it had a perceptible odor, which ultimately became offensive."

This discouraged the use of private wells. Wagons with big barrels at the end back into the lake. Fresh water fills the barrels, and is then sold throughout the town. But that is complicated by the spread of the population away from the lakefront, and the tendency for those living along the lake to pollute the water immediately offshore. Plus sometimes the lake is choppy, making filling the barrels difficult.

One solution would be to dig a well beyond the means of the average homeowner, deep enough that yesterday's dishwater won't show up in unfiltered form tomorrow.

So today Chicago authorizes the expenditure of $95.50 to dig a well at the corner of Cass and Michigan, or what is now Wabash and Hubbard, its first municipal expenditure of money and effort to provide water to its residents.

Nov. 11, 1921

Mary Garden, general director of the Chicago Grand Opera, helps Westinghouse debut a radio station by testing its transmitter from the stage of the Auditorium Theater.

Garden is a star soprano, shining at the center of the city's highbrow cultural life. She "oppressed and horrified" Chicago with her performance of Richard Strauss's *Salome* in 1910, with its passionate kiss of the severed head of John the Baptist, and is controversial enough that a deranged man once tried to shoot her. Now she has settled into the role of beloved patron of Chicago opera, "Our Mary."

For today's test, a tent has been set up around the microphone to reduce echo. Thus the first words to go out over the radio waves from Chicago are "My God, but it's dark in here," followed a short while later by the more formal "This is station KYW, Chicago."

The first program is music from Puccini's *Madame Butterfly*. At the start of the 1921 opera season, there are 1,300 radio sets in Chicago. When the season ends, 10 weeks later, there will be 20,000. The Civic Opera House will be built in 1929 by Samuel Insull, who runs Westinghouse, in part to provide something to put out over the airwaves.

"No longer will it be necessary to dress up in evening togs to hear grand opera," the *Tribune* will observe.

Nov. 12, 1893

The fair is gone, but William T. Stead is here. A few weeks after the World's Columbian Exposition closed its doors, the British reformer—or, if you prefer, "London Sensationalist"—arrived and got busy touring the Levee red-light district and police stations, interviewing madams, barflies, and machinists.

All day today he holds a mass meeting at the Central Music Hall, whose audience is notable in its diversity, from society ladies to streetwalkers. Stead insists his sympathies are with the latter; he will chastise another meeting, the gathered members of the Women's Club, as "self-indulgent" and "worse than any harlot."

Stead discusses what Christ would wish to change if he came to Chicago. The Savior, in his view, is a labor leader who would decry long hours and low pay. Chicago has "done less for the unfortunate than any other city in the Western world."

Unlike many reformers, Stead accomplishes something lasting. His meetings lead to the creation of the Civic Federation. And in February he will leave the city with a parting gift, *If Christ Came to Chicago*, a book that not only offers an unsparing tour of the city's bottom-tier debauchery, but assigns responsibility directly to excess and corruption at the top: poor people suffer because the rich exploit them for profit. Rather than the large-hearted benefactors they fancy themselves and are slavishly depicted as being by the newspapers that profit from their advertising, Marshall Field, George Pullman, and Philip Armour, "the Chicago Trinity," are "supreme money-getters of their day." Field straddles a "pyramid largely composed of human bones," and the harsh business practices of all three destroy competitors and crush employees, all so they can join "the predatory and idle rich." He uses Chicago's supposed Christian faith and its desire to rise to greatness to pry open its eyes and force the city to look around.

Nov. 13, 1961

Robert J. Quinn, the city's fire commissioner and civil defense director, still, despite that business with the sirens two years ago, orders his fire marshals to survey all buildings that could provide adequate fallout shelters for 50 people or more. This in advance of an inspection at the end of the month by the Army Corps of Engineers to decide what sites should be stocked with food, water, medical supplies, and Geiger counters, necessities salted away to sustain the population as it cowers in subterranean darkness after a Soviet atomic attack on the city. A topic on everyone's minds and lips since the summer and President Kennedy's speech on the value of civil defense. What last year was the realm of paranoiacs and "nuts" has become public policy. Chicago's health commissioner, Dr. Samuel L. Andelman, suggests "cave cities" could be kept livable by martial law and the army. This week newspaper advice columnist Ann Landers revisits advice she gave in October to a Michigan mother who asked if she should spend $800 on a family recreation room or a fallout shelter. She said go with the shelter, because "the race should not allow itself to commit mass suicide. We must make an effort, no matter how slim the chances of survival might seem, to save ourselves and our young children."

Hundreds of readers denounced that decision, one calling fallout shelters "the lousiest fraud ever perpetrated on a nation of sheep."

The blowback causes Landers to recant, a little. "I still believe in this advice, but I would not take it myself," she notes, explaining, "I have no desire to survive in a world of maimed and sick people. . . . I would prefer to stay above the ground and try to live each day with dignity—and take whatever comes."

Nov. 14, 1943

Sid Luckman flips a four-yarder to Jim Benton, who makes a spectacular catch for a touchdown against the New York Giants at the
Polo Grounds. Later, Luckman uncorks a 31-yard pass to Connie
Mack Berry, who takes it on the 23 and runs it into the end zone as
the gun sounds, ending the first quarter.

In the second, Luckman cocks back his right arm and throws 27
yards to Hampton Pool, who bobbles the ball in the end zone, but
holds on just as he goes out-of-bounds. There is also a touchdown
run in, the only one of the game.

The half ends.

In the third quarter, Luckman spirals a 33-yarder that Harry
Clarke catches, then dives in the end zone. Then Jim Benton pulls
down a 15-yard pass for a TD.

The third quarter ends.

George Wilson catches a three-yard pass. Then Luckman fires
40 yards to Hampton Pool, again, who snatches the pass from two
defenders and carries both of them three yards across the goal line.

The Bears win 56–7, the third-highest-scoring game up to that
point in NFL history, a day that happens to be "Sid Luckman Day,"
welcoming the former Columbia University star, who once played
football in the streets in Brooklyn. Luckman is the first quarterback
to complete seven passes for touchdowns in a game, and while
seven quarterbacks will tie his record, none have yet thrown eight.
With 453 passing yards today, he is also the first to break 400.

"Well, they didn't score 73 on us," Giants owner Tim Mara cracks,
looking for the bright side. If you don't know what he means by
that, keep reading.

Nov. 15, 2005

The Mills Corporation breaks ground on a development they think will be called "108 N. State Street." What they refer to as "an urban mixed-use destination, located in the heart of Chicago's Loop," unconsciously echoing an earlier, more accurate, and enduring cardiac-themed description of the site as "a permanent wound at the heart of the city." Most people call it simply "Block 37."

"To understand the rise and fall of this one block in some of its daunting detail is to appreciate the city's unique attraction to city lovers and haters alike," the Chicago Encyclopedia observes. "To know Block 37 is to know Chicago."

What is it? Perhaps the most notorious problem block in American urban history. Books have been written about it. Hundreds of millions of dollars have been poured into making something happen on Block 37—named with misplaced whimsy for its original plat designation on Thompson's 1830 map. Bordered by Randolph and Washington streets to the north and south, State and Dearborn streets to the east and west, Block 37 was a hodgepodge of early 20th-century construction until 1989, when it was seized by the city as blighted and razed except for a mid-block Commonwealth Edison power station, in the hope that development would come.

It didn't, for years. The CTA "superstation" built beneath it remained a $250 million subterranean void. Above, a big empty weedy lot. Maggie Daley repurposed it as an exhibit space for youth art. For a while it was a makeshift skating rink.

Eventually buildings of staggering mundaneness were constructed— a four-story retail mall called, with a fist-shake at fate, "Block Thirty Seven." A 690-unit apartment tower. Block 37, like Daniel Burnham's Chicago Plan, is a reminder of the myriad ways that grandiose schemes go awry and are thwarted by practical reality. In a dynamic, shifting metropolis, Block 37 is the empty socket, steps from City Hall, waiting for the shiny new tooth that for decades has eluded it.

Nov. 16, 1947

"Where Your Christmas Dollars Go Further," promises a display advertisement for Montgomery Ward covering most of a page in today's *Tribune*. It touts "Gifts for the Home," such as living-room furniture, a vacuum, or a "brown plastic beauty" of a table radio. In the middle of the page, a shift from adult desires to children's wishes, under the headline "VISIT WARDS TOYLAND," next to a drawing of a reindeer. "Free! Rudolph the Red-Nosed Reindeer push-out action puzzle!"

Giving away something to draw in customers is an old merchandising tactic, and Ward, who created the first mail-order catalogue in 1872, pioneered a number of them, including the money-back guarantee. In the 1930s, his company was handing out coloring books and story booklets. Realizing it was spending a lot of money buying other companies' booklets, the company asked an advertising copywriter, Robert L. May, to come up with a Christmas story, suggesting it be about an animals, based on the success of Ferdinand the Bull. To May, the only animal associated with Christmas are the reindeers from Santa's sleigh, and he concocted a tale of one ridiculed for his shiny, glowing nose, based on the bullying in his own childhood. Borrowing its meter from "The Night Before Christmas," he crafted "Rudolph the Red-Nosed Reindeer." Ward gave away millions of booklets.

After the war, May was approached by record companies interested in the story, and he persuaded Ward chairman Sewell Avery to give him the rights, so a catalogue conglomerate wouldn't be bothered with collecting pennies in royalties. May perhaps surprised them by supervising an explosion of products: not only records, but toys, watches, school bags, radios, umbrellas, cake molds, rugs, flashlights, wrapping paper, and board games, with hit songs and a beloved TV show to come. Today's ad includes a "Big Rudolph Stuffed Toy" for only $2.95.

May will become a millionaire and move to Evanston, though not without the requisite teasing from his six children. "We all know who you work for, mister," one will say. "You work for Rudolph the Red-Nosed Reindeer."

Nov. 17, 1928

The children sing as they march, despite the rain. Four thousand strong, whistling and shouting, while their parents line South Parkway, the future Martin Luther King Drive, clapping and cheering.

They are grouped by playground—Jackson Park, Douglas Park, McCosh, Carter, and the rest—carrying their banners and trophies. Joining them is a procession of automobiles, including one holding Robert S. Abbott, editor and publisher of the *Chicago Defender*, "the World's Greatest Weekly and unsurpassed by any other newspaper."

The children are members of the Bud Billiken Club, created by the paper to attract, engage, and entertain young readers. Today's procession will be formalized this summer into an annual parade; right now, it is the easiest way to get a lot of kids to a big party.

At 47th Street they arrive at the Regal Theater, newly opened that February, for four hours of festivities. The children are given horns, balloons, and chocolate bars. There is a movie, music, and contests, from shoe lacing to boxing, tap dancing to climbing a greased pole. The competitions become an annual tradition. Two years from now the piano contest will be won by Nathaniel Coles, 10, who receives a freshly killed and dry-picked turkey. He'll win the piano contest three years running—his family is grateful for the free turkey—and eventually change his name to Nat "King" Cole.

Nov. 18, 1883

About a quarter to 12, activity slows in the West Side Union Depot. At the offices of the Pennsylvania, the Burlington, the Panhandle, and the Alton railroads, superintendents, dispatchers, and telegraph operators set aside their tasks. Conductors and engineers wander over. All have their pocket watches, an essential tool for a trainman, out and in their hands. At 12 noon, Depot Master Charles Cropsey stops the main terminal clock. The trainmen stop their watches.

Time stops. In Chicago and across the country, a baptism into the modern world without precedent or repetition.

They wait. At 9 minutes and 32 seconds past the previous noon, a signal marking a second noon, according to the new Central Standard Time, clicks over the telegraph wire from the Allegheny Observatory at the University of Pittsburgh. The chief telegraph operator yells, "12 noon!" and the pendulum is set in motion. The watches start up with a collective snap.

Fort Wayne trainmen set their watches back 28 minutes—they are still on Columbus time, which gives a sense of the problem being addressed. At Columbus, 280 miles southeast, the sun is at its zenith—12 noon, local time—19 minutes before it is directly above Chicago. An acceptable system when your town is a small, self-contained unit stranded in the middle of Ohio (Chicago being so wide, solar noon comes to the shores of Lake Michigan a full minute before it arrives at the western border at Harlem Avenue).

But a nation connected by railroads and telegraphs can't work like that. Jewelry stores have long been the source of accurate time, and leading up to today's change, the newspapers consulted them to gauge their reaction.

"I shall certainly change the time if the majority of the principal jewelers do so, and I think it would be the wisest move," said Mr. C. D. Peacock. "There is no use in having two times here in Chicago."

Loop jewelers place signs reading "The New Central Time" under the clocks in their windows. For an afternoon, having the right time becomes a piece of valuable information. Acquaintances meeting in the street ask each other, "Have you the new time?" and if the answer is "No," offer it up.

A few railroads hold out: the Chicago, Milwaukee & St. Paul, the Michigan Central, and the Illinois Central, which is worried about confusing suburban passengers. That lasts exactly one week. Then they too yield to the continual ticking of progress.

Nov. 19, 1937

"Single crystal cardioid element," Benjamin Bauer jots on the top of his notebook, over three schematics of microphone design, with markings like P1 and P2, and symbols for capacitors, inductors, and resistors.

A microphone should capture the performer but not the audience, catch the crooning of Bing Crosby but not the sighing of women in the front row. Which is a problem, because most microphones grab a figure-eight pattern of sound, front and back. The element Bauer is designing at Shure Brothers, 225 W. Huron, takes sound from the back of the microphone, pointed toward the audience, and delays it, using these delayed waves to offset unwanted noises seeping in the front. This creates a heart-shaped, or "cardioid," zone of pickup projecting toward the performer.

The technical details catch professional attention, but it is the style of the Shure Unidyne Model 55 dynamic microphone that embeds itself in popular culture. Introduced in 1939, its curving chrome face inspired by the grill of a 1937 Oldsmobile, the microphone will be so immediately and hugely successful that it becomes *the* iconic singer's microphone. In photos, on postage stamps, having the Model 55 in a static image conveys that a person is singing and not just standing with their mouth hanging open. The Model 55 becomes that rare piece of technology that sails through the decades practically unchanged—not only does the microphone that Shure sells in the 21st century look the same as the one sold in 1939, but its inner workings are nearly identical, except for a few tweaks: for example, the quarter-sized diaphragm inside, glued to a coil of wire that turns sound vibrations into electrical impulses, goes from aluminum to Mylar. The inner windscreen, once cloth, will become foam. And of course the price. List price, $42.50 in 1939. That would be $819 in 2021 dollars. But such marvels will become bargains in the 21st century, and 82 years later the Model 55 will list at $179.99.

Nov. 20, 1848

A delegation of Chicagoans climb aboard a primitive baggage car fitted with seats behind a secondhand wood-burning steam engine. Bought with railroad stock and dubbed "The Pioneer," the locomotive was hauled to the city by ship since there are no rail lines connecting it to anyplace else. That is changing. The men become the first Chicagoans to officially depart the city by rail, traveling from Kinzie Street eight miles due west to the Des Plaines River courtesy of the Galena & Chicago Union Railroad. The tracks they travel upon aren't the full iron rails we associate with trains today, but cheaper "strip rails"—pine covered with 2½-inch strips of iron ¾ of an inch thick.

The "Galena" in the company name is aspirational: they'll need to lay another 170 miles of track to reach the lead-mining town on the Mississippi. Today they reach what will become Oak Park. One passenger, Jerome Beecher, spots a farmer driving a load of hides and pelts and buys them to bring back to the city. Another, Charles Walker, buys a load of wheat. The first freight purchased to be sent to Chicago by rail.

While early agreements left room for rails to be converted to roads, this train business takes off. Next year, 171,365 bushels of wheat will come by rail into the city. The Galena & Chicago will eventually grow into the Chicago & Northwestern Railway. And the destructive hand of history will somehow spare the Pioneer; exhibited at both the 1893 and 1933 fairs, the plucky little engine will find a permanent home at the Chicago History Museum.

Nov. 21, 1911

The Chicago Butter and Egg Board meets and decides that the price of butter will go up a penny, to 33 cents a pound, wholesale, falling in line behind a similar boost from the Elgin Butter Board yesterday. Tomorrow, however, Assistant US District Attorney Albert Welch begins presenting his case that the board should be dissolved precisely because of such machinations. The board "is a body of men operating in the restraint of trade," as evidenced by that lockstep penny hike.

"We are going to try to prove that the board has as its sole excuse for existence the manipulation of prices on butter and eggs," Welch says. "The prices are juggled in favor of the big commission merchants on South Water Street. The buyers for these commission houses contract with creameries surrounding Chicago for their entire output during the year."

The case has already been going on for well over a year and will roll along for another year before the Butter and Egg Board, whose constitution forbids margarine makers from joining, announces that it will abolish its pricing committee. It will still deal in contracts for butter and eggs, as well as produce, until 1919, when it expands its mandate to include other staples and reformulates itself as the Chicago Mercantile Exchange.

Nov. 22, 1950

Two men set fire to the large home in Oak Park that Percy Julian is renovating for his family. They drive away from 515 N. East Avenue in a dark sedan and are never caught. If the arson is supposed to scare off the 1949 "Chicagoan of the Year," it does not. Nor will the dynamite bomb being thrown into a flowerbed two weeks later. Julian takes to sitting in a tree with a shotgun, watching over his home. His son sometimes joins him.

A surprising perch for one of the most respected organic chemists in the country, with a PhD from Harvard, which wouldn't offer him a teaching position because he's Black. Nor in the mid-1930s could he take a job at the Institute of Paper Chemistry in Appleton, Wisconsin, which has a law against people of his hue spending the night. But that attempt, plus his fluent German after studying chemistry in Vienna, prompted Glidden Paint to offer him a job as head of its Soya Products Division in Chicago. That proves a smart move.

Julian will earn 130 patents, extracting everything from firefighting foam to steroids from soybeans, helping countless Americans with conditions from arthritis to infertility.

Oak Park will eventually develop a reputation for diversity, with partial credit due to the shock and shame that some residents feel at the reception the village gives Percy Julian, his wife, and their three children. They are not Oak Park's first Black residents, as some believe—their first prominent Black residents, perhaps—though Percy Julian Jr. will be the only Black among 2,500 students at Oak Park–River Forest High School. Regularly harassed, he will become a well-known civil rights lawyer and live to see, 30 years later, an Oak Park middle school named in his father's honor.

Nov. 23, 1927

The Savoy Ballroom is jumping in Harlem. So the owners branch out to Chicago, opening a Midwestern Savoy at 47th and South Parkway, in a mecca that includes the Regal Theater. "The most elegant, expensive and elaborate entertainment complex ever built in black Chicago." It will not only host stars such as Louis Armstrong, Count Basie, and Dizzy Gillespie, but also present boxing matches and basketball games, briefly boasting its own squad, the Savoy Big Five, whose players mostly come from Wendell Phillips High School. In January, they'll beat a visiting team from Howard University, and start playing Sundays at the Savoy for $25 a game, once facing George Halas's Chicago Bears.

Very quickly—after a pay dispute, according to one account; because the Savoy changed its basketball court into a skating rink, according to another—the team, guided by manager Abe Saperstein, will hit the road as "New York's Harlem Globetrotters." The name is a code, signaling that this is a Black team, the sort of team you'd expect to be from Harlem. The Globetrotters are still based in Chicago, and will be for 50 years.

There are not enough players to permit the luxury of substitution. So at first their showy ball handling and on-court antics are a way to buy time for exhausted athletes to catch their breath. Then the clowning becomes the point of the game. "For trick jigging, dribbling, passing and comedy the Harlemites proved the best attraction that basketball or any other sport has brought here for some time," the *Defender* will note in 1936, calling them "magicians of the maple floor."

You can be both funny and good. With Black athletes barred
from professional basketball, the Globetrotters will attract top
talent, and beat both the US 1936 Olympic basketball team and, in
1948, the Minneapolis Lakers. The Globetrotters showcase for the
National Basketball Association just how good Black players can
be. In 1950, Chuck Cooper will sign with the Globetrotters, before
being snatched away by the Boston Celtics, becoming the first Black
player drafted into the NBA.

Nov. 24, 1887

One hazard of attending college is that a man graduates, eventually, and is cast out into the world, and thus deprived of a certain realm of intercollegiate sport such as sculling, aka rowing boats competitively.

Thank God for the existence of organizations like the Farragut Boat Club, where hale young fellows can interrupt the tedium of their work lives, often in banking and finance, with races and regattas, dividing their time between keeping in shape and challenging their constitutions with food and drink.

For a few months, in the summer, at least. If the weather cooperates. Otherwise there are an endless series of dinners, dances, and entertainments or, as today, just horsing around, enjoying the company of like-minded men.

Today, Harvard and Yale alumni are gathered at the clubhouse. During the obligatory boxing, someone rolls up a boxing glove and throws it at someone else. A third party swings at it with a broomstick. George Hancock, a reporter for the Board of Trade, quickly takes matters in hand.

"Say, boys," history records him suggesting, "let's play baseball."

The glove is wrapped in tape, the broomstick designated a bat, a wrestling mat turned to be a diamond, and softball is invented.

"Its popularity was assured from the very outset," the *New York Times* will note, describing how the game spread from Chicago to other midwestern cities, then around the country, where it was particularly popular among national guardsmen. Their cavernous armories are well suited to the game, which eventually gravitates outside. Its 12-inch version will be played everywhere, the larger 16-inch variety, played without gloves, remaining mostly a Chicago phenomenon.

Nov. 25, 1860

Samuel G. Alschuler is one of many German immigrants who settle in Chicago, amounting to perhaps one-fifth of the population before the outbreak of the Civil War. He came by way of Urbana, where in 1858 the Bavarian Jew photographed a Senate candidate named Abraham Lincoln, loaning him his own black coat because the rough duster Lincoln showed up wearing wouldn't serve for a formal portrait.

Now Lincoln is president-elect, and sits for Alschuler a second time, arching his left eyebrow sardonically and showing off something that had never before appeared in a photograph of him: a beard.

The story is well known. Grace Bedell, an 11-year-old in upstate New York, wrote to Lincoln a few weeks before the election. "I have got 4 brothers," she told the Republican candidate, "and part of them will vote for you any way and if you let your whiskers grow I will try and get the rest of them to vote for you. You would look a great deal better for your face is so thin. All the ladies like whiskers and they would tease their husbands to vote for you and then you would be President."

Lincoln replied to the "dear little miss": "As to the whiskers, having never worn any, do you not think people would call it a piece of silly affect[at]ion if I were to begin it now?" Just days after his election, though, he made up his mind. "Billy," he supposedly told his barber, "let's give them a chance to grow."

Nov. 26, 1927

Downtown hotels are packed, streetlights decorated in the University of Southern California's scarlet and gold, and Notre Dame's blue and gold. Tickets that originally cost $3 to $7 go for $15 or $20.

Two thousand Californians arrived yesterday on special Rock Island trains. In the morning, the USC squad got off at the Englewood station and proceeded directly to Stagg Field to practice. Finding the weather frosty, three dozen sweatshirts were sent for.

In the afternoon, Notre Dame came in on the South Shore line, led by their "master strategist" Knute Rockne who, worried about a wet field, noted with approval the lack of rain or snow.

Today, great crowds make their way toward the lakefront, hours before kickoff at 1:30 p.m., when the Trojans and the Fighting Irish meet under a slate-gray sky at Soldier Field, with 115,000 spectators "massed in a towering wall that stretched without break around the white striped field." Hundreds are perched atop the colonnade roofs, even atop the press box. It is the greatest crowd to ever see a football game up to that point.

Each team makes one touchdown within the first 10 minutes, and neither scores again. But after their touchdown, USC misses the extra point, so Notre Dame wins, 7–6.

Nov. 27, 1975

Halston is going to open a boutique in Water Tower Place, the glittering mecca of elegant shopping fabulousness with its glass elevators and eight-level atrium. "I'm so excited," he tells Peg Zwecker, the *Daily News* columnist who in the mid-1950s introduced him to designer Lilly Daché, giving him a boost into the world of fashion. "It's going to be my first place outside of New York and in Chicago where I started—it will be like coming home."

He's got that right. Dial back 20 years, he was Roy Halston Frowick, a Norwegian milliner, fresh out of the School of the Art Institute, sitting cross-legged on the floor of a beauty salon in the basement of the Ambassador East, making ladies' hats. Now he is the wealthiest clothing designer in the country, with his namesake perfume selling for $60 an ounce and his better dress line, sold in 250 stores, pulling in $16 million a year.

Nov. 28, 1895

The conveyances are so new they don't yet have a name. Or rather, they have many names, but none seem right. "Prize for Motors" was the headline July 9 in the *Chicago Times-Herald*, calling upon "inventors who can construct practicable, self propelling road carriages" while admitting a better term is needed. The public offers up suggestions like "horseless carriage," "vehicle motor," and "automobile."

The *Times-Herald* settles on "Motocycle" for the first automobile race in the United States. The race didn't come off November 2 as scheduled, because only a few vehicles were ready (though there was a "consolation" race that day, with a prize of $500, to reward those who showed up, so that could arguably be considered auto racing's actual debut).

Today is the official race—and Thanksgiving Day. Of the 80 vehicles expected to be there, six actually appear at the starting line, at the lakefront near the Palace of Fine Arts on 55th Street, for the 9 a.m. opening gun. Each vehicle has a driver and an umpire, to keep an eye on things. One entry, running on an immense 1,600-pound lead battery, is called an "Electrobat."

The race was to be to Milwaukee, but the roads aren't good enough. It is decided to go to Evanston and back, 54 miles round-trip, a journey complicated by streetcar traffic and mischievous boys with snowballs—a particular menace since the drivers sit out in the open.

Speed is not the only factor: according to race rules, fuel economy and general appearance and operation of the vehicle will also taken into consideration. As it is, only two cars finish. A Benz, driven by Oscar Mueller, and the winner, a Duryea driven by J. Frank Duryea, who takes the top $2,000 prize.

He completes the race in 10 hours, but time spent breaking for meals and repairs—55 minutes to find a blacksmith to repair steering gear that broke at Rush and Erie—totaling about three hours, is not counted. Duryea, by the way, refers to his machine as a "motor wagon."

Nov. 29, 1879

The *Chicago Daily News* takes its readers to an opium den, Gabe Foster's, in an alley between Monroe and Adams.

"Let's hit the pipe," a friend had suggested, claiming it has become almost as popular an expression as "let's have a drink."

Up a flight of stairs, they are admitted, and find two rooms. In the first, a sideboard, several easy chairs, and a very wide bed. Then an inner room where, on another bed, two men lie, lazily drawing on huge pipes. There is also a room just for ladies.

One man is in a near stupor; the other "began to talk in a highly excited manner, enlarging upon his own greatness and the great wealth soon expected to amass by some speculation on the Board of Trade."

This is the common effect, the reporter notes, the opium eater going on as if "he owned the whole town." Foster offers the reporter a pipe, claiming to have a tea that will efface both the effects and any hunger for more. The reporter declines.

"The habit," he writes, "once contracted, is one of the most difficult to break off from."

Instead, he watches Foster prepare a pipe. The opium, about the size of two peas, is twisted around a knitting needle and cooked over a spirit lamp.

"The best people in town are among my patrons," Foster claims. "They have all been here at one time or another."

The reporter isn't going to be one of them.

"The sight of one at work at the detestable business is most revolting, and fills one with disgust," he writes. "To one looking at it, unbiased by the desire, it seems a most debasing and demoralizing habit."

Of course, sometimes it is only a matter of packaging.

Directly under this front-page exposé is a classified advertisement for Mrs. Winslow's Soothing Syrup, "used for many years with never failing safety and success by millions of mothers for their children." Only 25 cents, its main ingredients are morphine and alcohol.

Nov. 30, 1982

"The Unforgettable Fire," one of the most successful shows at Chicago's new Peace Museum, ends today, having gotten good reviews for its display of drawings by those who survived the atomic bombing of Hiroshima and Nagasaki.

"As chilling an exhibition as anyone is likely to see," the *Tribune* writes.

Supporting the museum, located in a Near North Side warehouse, are celebrities such as Stevie Wonder and Yoko Ono, who donates one of her husband's guitars. Success is elusive, however, and the effort will close its doors in 2007. But not before leaving an impact on the music world. Beloved WXRT DJ Terri Hemmert, volunteering to help assemble a "Give Peace a Chance" show on how folk and rock music influence the peace movement, will feel the material is too stuck in the 1960s, and reach out to the Irish band U2, hoping they'll offer something more contemporary.

She'll meet with band members in a Michigan Avenue coffee shop and, to give them a sense of the museum, bring a catalogue from "The Unforgettable Fire" show, plus another from a show on Martin Luther King.

The band will not only donate items for the museum, such as an autographed electric guitar, but title its next album *The Unforgettable Fire*, including a song about the assassination of Dr. King, "Pride (In the Name of Love)." It is a hit.

DECEMBER

Dec. 1, 1958

A fifth grader sets the fire. Deliberately, on the back stairway in the basement. That won't become public for years. And what does it really matter? However the fire starts, the school goes up "like a cereal box in an incinerator." Dense black smoke fills the building. When firefighters arrive, children are at the windows, screaming for help, jumping to escape the flames lapping behind them as the fire tears through the building, a few minutes before the bell that would have freed them.

A neighborhood school in Humboldt Park. Parents hear the news and come running from all directions, their faces twisted with fear. "Where are they!?" a mother screams. "Where are they?!" Parents fight the police holding them back. A few break through the line, rush toward the building, then stop, confronting the inferno. One father believes he hears his daughter's voice. He runs into the burning school, but can't find her and the flames drive him out. A woman weeps even though her child is safe. "I'm a mother," she explains. "All mothers are crying."

The sirens merge into one wail. Firefighters find bodies jammed by the windows—the younger ones on the bottom, where the older crawled over them. Books still open on the desks. Two-thirds of the survivors are boys. Ninety-two students die at Our Lady of the Angels School, plus three nuns. Another 75 are burned or hurt leaping to safety. Mayor Daley weeps touring the scene. "If we had three more minutes, we could have saved them all," says fire commissioner Robert J. Quinn.

Dec. 2, 1942

Cadmium absorbs neurons, muffling atomic activity. The cadmium control rods inside six tons of uranium stacked on a squash court under the stands at Stagg Field at the University of Chicago keep its atoms from spontaneously breaking apart in a chain reaction.

Until today.

Several dozen spectators gather in a balcony above what has become known as the "Pile"—a rough sphere 27 feet high, made of uranium and graphite lumps. Physicist Enrico Fermi orders the last rod pulled out 13 feet—halfway—from the Pile. The Geiger counters click faster, then level off. The figures are read aloud. Fermi consults his slide rule. After 90 minutes of growing anticipation, there is a crash. A safety mechanism has released one cadmium rod suspended above the Pile. That stops the reaction. The Geiger counters fall silent.

"Time for lunch," Fermi announces. His associates return the control rods and lock them in place. They troop over to Hutchinson Commons.

Leaving time, while the scientists eat, to ask a question not often raised when this story is told: Why is this happening *here*? Why set off the first controlled self-sustaining nuclear reaction—fission, splitting the atom, the basis of the radical new bomb that will end World War II—in the middle of a crowded college campus in the nation's second-largest city?

Several reasons. Recent attempts at other universities, such as Columbia, failed, thanks to impurities in the uranium. The plan had been to perform this experiment 24 miles west, in the seclusion of Argonne Forest. But the building being constructed there is delayed due to a labor strike. The scientists can't wait. There's a war on.

The physicists return from lunch and start removing the rods. At 3:25 p.m., Fermi orders the last rod drawn out another foot.

"This is going to do it," Fermi says. "Now it will become self-sustaining."

It does. Instead of leveling off, the rate of reaction increases on its own. The Pile goes critical, uranium atoms splitting apart, each freed neutron knocking off several others, splitting those apart too, in an ever-expanding chain reaction. The Geiger counter clicks blend into a continuous whine.

"We're cookin'!" Richard Watts pencils in the ledger, alongside a row of numbers.

The cascade of disintegrating atoms proceeds for almost half an hour. Then a warning bell sounds. The rods are returned, and the reactor shut down. Chianti is passed around in paper cups. But nobody toasts; their minds are on the enormous power now in human hands. Lab director Arthur Compton phones a coded message to the head of the National Defense Research Council. "The Italian navigator has just landed in the New World," he says.

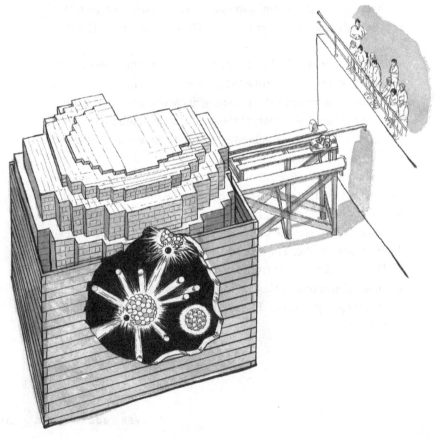

Dec. 3, 1926

William Wrigley did not need to own a baseball team. He was plenty busy with his chewing-gum company, not to mention construction of its new Michigan Avenue skyscraper and various side projects, such as creating a beach at Oak Street.

But Charles Weeghman, "The Quick Lunch King," was overextended, and brought in meatpacker J. Ogden Armour as a partner, who invited Wrigley to be a minority investor in the Chicago Whales, playing in the Federal League. The team would go through a variety of names in that less formal era—Colts, Orphans—before newsmen settled on "Cubs," in part because of its headline-friendly brevity. Weeghman brought the team from its West Side home to the North Side, building a ballpark at Clark and Addison. Weeghman could not run the team as efficiently as he runs his chain of cafeterias, however, and in 1919 sold out to Wrigley, who first called their home "Cubs Park." But who was he fooling? Modesty did not get Wrigley where he is today, the day his ballpark starts going by the name "Wrigley Field," which, worn smooth by the sands of time, just doesn't seem as mercenary and wrong as "Guaranteed Rate Field." But the idea's the same.

Dec. 4, 1969

Shortly before 5 a.m., 14 police officers, plus Cook County State's Attorney Ed Hanrahan himself, creep up to a two-flat at 2337 W. Monroe. They are here, ostensibly, to serve a search warrant for weapons supposedly stockpiled by the Black Panthers.

The Panthers are much in the news, for good works—running breakfast programs—and a militant aggressiveness and belief that guns and violence are the way to improve the lot of Black America. Two police officers were killed three weeks earlier after an encounter with Black Panther members, prompting the *Tribune* to insist that police officers "should be ordered to be ready to shoot when approaching Black Panther suspects," in an editorial headlined "No Quarter for Wild Beasts."

None is given this morning. The officers burst into the apartment and start firing, killing Black Panther chairman Fred Hampton and his subordinate, Mark Clark.

The story given to the press is of a "wild gun battle." The *Tribune* "EXCLUSIVE" displays photos of the holes from bullets fired at police. Acting on a tip, the *Sun-Times* will send a reporter and photographer to look at these alleged bullet holes and find they are in fact unplastered nail heads. A grand jury will eventually indict Hanrahan and the police officers for murder, but the case is dismissed. The Hampton and Clark families sue the government and receive $1.8 million in damages. Hanrahan will not be re-elected in 1972.

Dec. 5, 1962

"Here's an indecent woman . . . ," Lenny Bruce muses, displaying
a pinup calendar on stage at the Gate of Horn nightclub. "You're
kidding? How can that pretty woman be indecent? . . . It's God, your
filthy Jesus Christ made these tits, that's all."

Five couples walk out during his performance. A trio of Chicago
police officers stay. They arrest him, Bruce will later insist, not for the
sexual aspect of his routine, but for his remarks about the Catholic
Church and the Pope.

Bruce isn't the only one taken into custody. Police also arrest
the club owner, the bartender, and a 25-year-old comedian named
George Carlin. Bruce is charged with giving a lewd performance.
Carlin with disorderly conduct, for refusing to show his ID.

Bruce will ask for a trial and be found guilty of obscenity, fined a
thousand dollars, and sentenced to a year in prison. The sentence is
upheld by the Illinois Supreme Court. But the US Supreme Court,
ruling on a different matter in 1964, throws out the practice of
balancing social value against obscenity, deciding that any political
content is redemptive. This prompts the Illinois Supreme Court
to grudgingly overturn its previous ruling, noting in sorrow that
despite "the gradual deterioration of its moral fabric that this type
of presentation promotes, we must concede that some of the topics
commented upon by defendant are of social importance."

"They're really saying that they're only sorry the crummy
Constitution won't permit them to convict me," Bruce observes.

Dec. 6, 1918

The Friday afternoon concert at Orchestra Hall kicks off with "The Star-Spangled Banner." Then Sergei Prokofiev performs the American debut of his "Concerto for Pianoforte No. 1 in D Flat." After intermission, "Scythian Suite" is also heard for the first time.

Prokofiev has come to Chicago—the first of four visits—after meeting Cyrus H. McCormick Jr. in Petrograd in the summer of 1917. The young composer's name meant nothing to the president of International Harvester, there with a State Department mission to Russia. But Prokofiev, whose late father was a farm manager, was familiar with agricultural equipment, and certainly knew McCormick's. The reaper heir ends up not only paying to publish "Scythian Suite," but sending several scores to the Chicago Symphony Orchestra's musical director.

The music causes a stir. "Russian Genius Displays Weird Harmonies" is the headline in the *Chicago American*. "The music was of such savagery, so brutally barbaric," Henriette Weber writes in the *Herald and Examiner*, "that it seemed almost grotesque to see civilized men, in modern dress with modern instruments performing it. By the same token, it was big, sincere, true."

The director of the Chicago Opera suggests a commission, and Prokofiev remembers "a strangle little divertissement," called *Liubov' k trem apel'sinam*—"The Love for Three Oranges."

That too will premiere in Chicago, at the Auditorium Theater in 1921. After it is performed in New York, Prokofiev notices a difference in the two cities' receptions. "In Chicago, they did not understand everything, but still defended 'our' production," he writes. New York critics are "a pack of dogs let out from behind the gate to bite my trousers to shreds," whose "competitive feelings toward Chicago were aroused." Their thinking seems to be: "You want to show us something we didn't think of putting on ourselves? So take that!"

Dec. 7, 1921

The Drake opened just last year, and is among the fanciest hotels in town. But the several hundred men who gather for dinner in the ballroom tonight find the long tables bare. No table settings. Nothing to eat. Not even tablecloths.

"We have been invited to meet each other and to dine together," begins Jacob K. Loeb, businessman and philanthropist, active on the Chicago Jewish Relief Committee. "We have met, but there is no banquet spread, no food prepared."

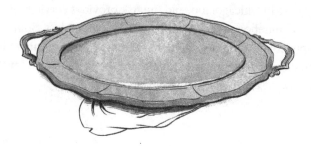

World War I left Europe broken, and people are starving as winter approaches. In Russia. In Poland. In well-fed Chicago, each ethnic group leaps to care for their own, and Jews are no different, perhaps bringing an extra flourish of marketing savvy to the endeavor, with a variety of urgent slogans like "Suppose you were starving." Jewish organizations such as the Standard Club get involved, and leaders including Julius Rosenwald dig deep. Still, more is needed.

Were food set out, Loeb explains, the cost would be $3,500, an "unwarranted extravagance and, in the face of starving Europe, a wasteful crime. Thirty-five hundred will feed the starving, clothe the naked, and heal the sick. What right have we to spend on ourselves funds that have been collected for them?"

Not only does skipping dinner save money, Loeb says, but "The Foodless Banquet," as it came to be called, helps those gathered understand what their money will combat.

"For you, the disappointment, temporary and passing," Loeb says. "For them, permanent and lasting."

The stunt does not set a trend, unfortunately, though over the years uncounted dinner goers, yawning as the hours unfold, will shift in their chairs and wish it had, wondering why not just collect the money and skip the rubber chicken, silent auctions, and tired musical acts who were semi-famous a quarter century earlier.

Although one organization will reinvent the practice. There are needy Jews in Chicago, too, and the Ark provides services: warm meals to homebound elderly, shelter for the homeless. Some years they sponsor a "dinnerless dinner," sending supporters an invitation, a bit of chocolate, and a pledge card. But no need to wait for that; you can donate right now at arkchicago.org.

Dec. 8, 1940

Think of today's game as one of the great technological mismatches in history: the English archers mowing down the French with their longbows at the battle of Agincourt. The British with their rifles and Gatling guns facing Zulu warriors with cowhide shields and short spears. And Chicago, armed with the T formation, going up against Washington for the National Football League championship at Griffith Stadium.

The Bears gain 372 yards rushing. The Redskins gain three. The Bears make 11 touchdowns. So many balls are kicked into the stands that officials asked the Bears to pass or run in their post-touchdown extra points, because they are running out of footballs.

Or view it as the ultimate example of why it's important to never trash-talk an opponent. Three weeks earlier, after beating the Bears in a regular-season game, Washington owner George Marshall called the Chicago team "crybabies" and "quitters."

"We were just fired up," 270-pound team captain George Musso explains after the game. "We went out there to kick the pants off them."

The game would have been historic whatever the score. It is the first championship football game broadcast nationally on radio, on the Mutual network, and the last one where a player, Dick Plasman, takes the field without a helmet.

The 36,000 fans at Griffith Stadium sit "stunned and stricken at the spectacle of the most crushing defeat ever administered in a championship game in either professional or college football," the *Daily News* will report the next day. More than 80 years later, the record stands. Final score: 73–0.

Dec. 9, 2008

Shortly after 6 a.m., Robert Grant, the head of the FBI's Chicago office, calls the emergency line to the governor's residence. It rings and rings. So he dials Rod Blagojevich's personal cellphone. We have federal agents outside your house, he tells the governor, please open the door, "so we can do this quietly."

"Is this a joke?" Blagojevich replies.

Yes, in a sense, it is. A bad joke: the governor of Illinois, required to fill the open US Senate seat vacated by Barack Obama upon his being elected president, did not consider who might most benefit the state whose well-being is supposed to be his primary concern. Instead, he shopped the vacancy around to see what he could get for himself. Into an open federal wiretap. That he either knew was there, or ought to have known was there.

His wife, Patti, lets the agents in. As the feds handcuff Blagojevich, he turns to her and asks, "How does my hair look?"

That is Blagojevich in a nutshell. A vain, dimwitted man, who had a career in politics only because his father-in-law, Alderman Dick Mell, gave it to him like a set of his old golf clubs. The fourth Illinois governor to go to prison out of the previous eight, and the worst of the lot. The other jailbird governors weren't arrested until after they left office. Since Blagojevich is such a pitiful figure, some people pity him. But remember: Blagojevich also shook down sick children, then sought to punish them when their caregivers didn't pony up, trying to claw back an $8 million state grant to Children's Memorial Hospital because its trustees didn't contribute to his campaign.

He'll never apologize, nor seem to grasp he has done anything wrong. He deserves everything he got. Except the pardon.

Dec. 10, 1924

God bless the bureaucracy. Sometimes it permits progress through its trademark blend of inertia and incuriosity. Post office employee Henry Gerber gathers six friends willing to add their names— that process took a year—pays the $10, and nobody at the Illinois Secretary of State's office notices anything objectionable about their "Society for Human Rights," a group whose stated goals are "to promote and to protect the interests of people who by reason of mental and physical abnormalities are abused and hindered in the legal pursuit of happiness which is guaranteed them by the Declaration of Independence, and to combat the public prejudices against them by dissemination of facts according to modern science among intellectuals of mature age."

Above which some anonymous official scribbles "OK."

And so the first group dedicated to improving the lives of homosexuals is chartered in Chicago. More than 30 years will pass before there is a second. Gerber will be arrested, his papers destroyed, and the post office will fire him as "not a suitable person." The address listed on the charter approved today, 1710 N. Crilly Court, will eventually be designated a National Historic Landmark.

Years later, Gerber will point out that no one from the state "seemed to have bothered to investigate our purpose." A rare instance of bureaucratic indolence serving the greater good.

Dec. 11, 1921

Thomas O'Connor is among several prisoners exercising under the gaze of a single guard in a fourth-floor bullpen in the Cook County Jail. Why a man sentenced to hang Thursday *needs* exercise on Sunday is one of the many unanswered questions about this day. Another is who slipped a nickel-plated revolver to "the most cold-blooded, unscrupulous criminal in Chicago," nicknamed "Terrible Tommy" for his three murders, the most recent being of a police officer, Patrick "Paddy" O'Neill.

O'Connor and four other prisoners jump a guard and beat him unconscious. Two other guards come running, one with the keys to the jail. Still other prisoners start to sing to cover the ruckus. A conveniently placed ladder allows the escapees to scale a 20-foot wall. O'Connor leaps onto the running board of a car on Clark Street. "I'm Tommy O'Connor and I've just escaped from the County Jail. Drive like hell!" he announces. The driver does.

Here O'Connor vanishes from history, last seen heading northwest on Clybourn. Three guards are suspended. "It's all bunk about O'Connor escaping," complains police superintendent Charles Fitzmorris. "He was turned loose as definitely as if he was escorted out the front door. For all I know, he was."

The scaffold on which O'Connor is to hang stays in the basement of the Cook County Jail for the next 56 years, waiting for Terrible Tommy. But he is never found.

Dec. 12, 1938

"Visit Evanston" reads a tiny ad in today's *Daily News*, "and DINE pleasantly at The OLD DOMINION ROOM, 501 Davis Street, says ye 'adventurer in good eating.'—Duncan Hines."

Who is Duncan Hines that he should tell anybody where to eat? Not a chef, not a restaurateur, but a traveling salesman. In the 1920s, he was based in Chicago, hawking promotional gewgaws for printing companies: key chains, erasers, fans, pens, and pencils emblazoned with a company logo. He would leave his apartment on Cornell Avenue and drive around the Midwest, selling his line. His challenge was always to find a place to eat, a task he took very seriously, keeping careful notes. Good food was something to be lauded. Bad food was a "personal insult" to be denounced.

In his spare time, he'd take road trips with his wife, Florence, seeking out new places to try. It was a game, almost a quest. Hines might drive to Detroit for lunch. He developed a reputation. People he hadn't met would phone to say, "I'm off to Nashville—where should I eat?" Then, in 1934, a newspaper reported on Hines and his unusual hobby. After that, the phone never stopped ringing.

Trying to regain a little peace and quiet, in November 1935 Hines drew up a list of the 167 best restaurants he and Florence had found and gave it a title, "Adventures in Good Eating." He printed 1,000 copies on heavy blue paper and sent the list in their Christmas cards to everyone they knew.

But that only made the problem worse. Now friends of *those* friends started requesting a list. Hines's charging $1 for the list did nothing to stem the tide. In 1936, he self-published a 96-page booklet. The places he recommended, like the Old Dominion Room, began to publicize his endorsement, which in turn publicized Hines. His book sold enough that he soon moved back to his home in Kentucky, where he'll affix his name to his truly lasting contribution to American cuisine: cake mix. A month after Duncan Hines Cake Mix is introduced by Nebraska Consolidated Mills in June 1951, it'll account for almost half the local cake mix sales. Betty Crocker is a marketer's fantasy, but Duncan Hines was real.

Dec. 13, 2015

Midway through the first quarter, Patrick Kane, the National Hockey League's leading scorer, assists on Duncan Keith's power-play goal. There is such a long time between the pass and the goal—more than 10 seconds—that Kane worries the officials will decide he didn't have a role in the puck going into the net after all, and call the assist back. But they don't, meaning that Kane extends his points streak to 26, breaking Sidney Crosby's 25-gamer set in 2011 and making it the longest streak in 22 years. The Blackhawks shut out the Canucks, 4–0, in front of 21,711 fans at the United Center, thanks to Ronnie Crawford's 30 saves. Kane will stop at 26, just above half of Wayne Gretzky's 51-game streak at the start of the 1982–1983 season. But still the all-time record for an American-born player.

Dec. 14, 1877

The train stops with a jerk at Chicago, nearly sliding A. H. Wylie
to the floor. He has been traveling for more than a year—London
to Agra, across India, around Australia, to China, Japan, and a 16-
day sail from Yokohama to San Francisco, where the Englishman
is horrified at American table manners. "They are far more like
animals than human beings."

Then a five-day train trip from San Francisco to Chicago, surrounded by the harsh babble of American voices and vocabulary.
"They never think, but always 'guess' or 'calculate.'" Nevertheless,
Wylie finds Chicago "a wonderful town," where "everybody was
very civil." He visits at least three places: the Chicago Club, where
he is gratified to find all the English papers, except *The Times*. The
Board of Trade, discerning not a single word among the "shouting
and shrieking." Then to the obligatory stockyards pilgrimage, de-
parting, as many do, a changed man.

"Killing and dressing twelve pigs a minute was a sight quite new
to me," he writes. "The unfortunate beasts have hardly finished
squealing, before they are split and hung up as carcasses. I think
the poor animals suffer but little; and, so far as I could judge, the
butchers, and all connected with the work, were very expert, from
the highest to the lowest. . . . I looked at all the cooling-rooms,
packing rooms, and meat-cellars, and they certainly were a marvel
of cleanliness, and the mammoth proportions of them all could not
fail to strike a stranger. Nevertheless, it must be a long time before
I can partake in Mr. Pig; my recent visit to this establishment will
prevent my eating him in any shape or form."

Wylie records his observations in a 1879 book, *Chatty Letters
from the East and West*, which is exactly that: conversational dispatches of an educated gentleman as he circumnavigates the globe.
Though as he does, a mystery gathers for the reader. Wylie never
drops a hint who he is or why he is traveling around the world,
which he concludes is barbaric and inferior to England. He uses
the word "uninteresting" again and again, and is overjoyed to return
home and find himself once more "amongst cultivated human beings—a class one seldom meets abroad." He left no other trace.

Dec. 15, 1908

At midnight, "Bathhouse" John Coughlin, sporting a lavender cravat
and a red sash across his ample belly, stands in the center of the
jam-packed Coliseum, spreads his pink kid-gloved hands wide, and
utters a garbled cough that sounds like "hep!"

And so the grand march begins. Coughlin is joined by hoodlums
and slum girls, dope fiends, plug-uglies, pickpockets and policemen
in street clothes, brothel keepers, Board of Trade members, college
boys on a lark, and wide-eyed mechanics. Sixteen abreast, some
masked or in elaborate costume, others half nude, they slowly tour
the floor, the smoke so thick you can hardly see across the room,
ringed by boxes where men in evening clothes observe the 15,000
revelers who managed to get in. "A howling, pushing, drinking,
carousing mob" that doesn't so much move as undulate in waves, in
the words of the *Examiner*, which sent a minister to cover "the 11th
annual insult to the people of Chicago." Two brass bands provide
what can be called music, and people dance, or hold each other
up anyway, the women, "painted, powdered, marcelled and false-
haired."

The First Ward, north of 22nd Street along the Chicago River,
is home to the infamous Levee, one of the greatest concentrations
of vice and criminality ever produced by any city anywhere ever.
The First Ward Ball is part celebration, part scam. Every brothel,
gambling den, and strip show that doesn't want to find itself raided
must sell blocks of tickets. Coughlin is the alderman, along with
Michael "Hinky Dink" Kenna, at a time when each ward has two,
before the number is cut in half in a bold stroke to reduce municipal
corruption by 50 percent.

But the activists are coming. The Anti-Cigarette League and the
Law and Order League thundered against the ball, and cooked up
but did not implement a scheme to set cameras at the entrances so
as to shame those revelers who might yet feel shame. The *Tribune*
threatened to publish the names of those attendees whose names
could still be sullied. Lawsuits were filed and dismissed. The day

before the ball, someone threw a dynamite bomb at the Coliseum, the shards of which police label "Bomb No. 27" and place on what the press calls its "shelf of mysteries."

Change is in the air, literally, our more temperate, calibrated, and controlled future present here at the Coliseum in the form of Dr. J. F. Biehn, of the health department, a meek little man who neither drinks nor dances, but goes about the ball collecting air samples in glass mustard bottles, which are then corked, so he can later analyze the germs within.

Dawn arrives to find "an amazing spectacle of thousands of empty and shattered bottles, great pools of odorous liquids, cigar and cigarette stumps, broken tables and chairs and great piles of soiled debris," according to the *Daily News*, including piles of bent serving trays—sold to the waiters, who bend them across the bar when alcohol sales are cut off at 3 a.m. so the same trays cannot be sold to them again next year.

But there will be no next year. The city, fed up with tolerating a debauch, will revoke the ball's liquor license, and while Coughlin and his cohorts will stage a sedate, dry classical music concert in 1909 as mockery and protest, attendance is a fraction of tonight's, and the arid festivities will end at 11 p.m.

Dec. 16, 1959

The carpet is still being nailed down. The audience arrives shortly before 7 p.m. to what until recently has been a Chinese laundry, Wong Cleaners and Dyers, at 1842 N. Wells. Now it is a cafe featuring an improvisational comedy troupe known as "The Second City," the latest of a series of ensembles that bloomed and wilted throughout the 1950s—University Theater, Playwrights Theatre Club, the Compass Players—this one supercharged with a heady draught of good old-fashioned now-or-never desperation.

"We were tired of the start-up-in-hope-and-go-down-in-flames cycle," co-founder Bernie Sahlins later explained. "We were pushing 30."

"We" is Sahlins, manager at the Gate of Horn, plus Paul Sills, flipping burgers in the kitchen that night, and Howard Alk, the club's lighting man.

About 120 of the curious pay $1.50 to get in to see the first review, *Excelsior! And Other Outcries*. The lights come up on Barbara Harris, in pearls. She sings:

Everybody's in the know but me
Knows who Eisenhower has to tea . . .

Three months later they are lauded in *Time* magazine: "the declining skill of satire is kept alive with brilliance and flourish." Harris goes to Broadway and wins a Tony. A parade of talent starts marching through Second City: from Alan Arkin and Joan Rivers to Tina Fey and Stephen Colbert. For a while a teenage David Mamet buses tables listening to the staccato, improvised dialogue.

The company moves to larger quarters at 1616 N. Wells in 1967, and its most notorious alumni, John Belushi, is hired in 1971, at age 22, after auditioning as a samurai.

Dec. 17, 1938

When you represent the folks kicking $18 million into a project, candor is your privilege.

"At last Chicago has awakened from its Rip van Winkle sleep," begins Secretary of the Interior Harold Ickes, to thousands of Chicagoans gathered on State Street, across from Holy Name Cathedral, to break ground on a subway system. Quite late, relatively. New York City began their subway in 1900. Ickes recounts the Samuel Insull traction wars, chiding a city that "has taken decades to do what might have been accomplished in a few short years of concentrated co-operation among men of good will."

Ickes's "imposing list of disinterested and patriotic citizens who fought for their city without a selfish thought, without hope of personal reward" does not include Mayor Ed Kelly. But Kelly, standing next to him, gets off light compared to *Tribune* editor Col. Robert McCormick, this "ill-natured rear-guarder . . . in his impregnable tower looking down upon this gathering with jaundiced eye." (Opposed to Roosevelt in general and Ickes in particular, the *Tribune* editorialized that, subway or not, "The elevated loop will remain as an eyesore and a nuisance, and little will be accomplished to reduce congestion in the streets" until it is torn down. Chicago will manage to stumble forward into the next century with the "L" in place.)

Ickes and Kelly do join forces long enough, at 3:41 p.m., to flip the switch on a silver-plated jackhammer and break ground for the subway line, which will take five years to complete.

"The Chicago subway is now started!" Kelly cries.

Dec. 18, 1969

Freedom is seldom achieved in one leap, but approached by a series of steps forward and slips back.

A month ago—Nov. 20, "Black Thursday" to some—seven members of the National Organization for Women burst through the door of the men-only standup bar attached to the Berghoff, the 19th-century German restaurant at 17 W. Adams.

"It was like invading a shower room," one later remembered. Winifred Gandy ordered a shot of the venerable institution's 14-year-old bourbon. The bartender objected that, being female, the women could not be served. So they stood there, taking up room at the bar. Someone handed the manager a copy of the Chicago anti-discrimination ordinance. "We can't refuse it," the manager said, shrugging, ordering liquor to be poured for them.

The headline that ran over a smirking story in the *Daily News*, "Girls 'Integrate' Male-Only Bar," hinted that the battle might not yet be over, and it isn't. When not present in force, women are still turned away at the Berghoff.

So the National Organization for Women returns today for a second round.

"Intense, straight-haired, University of Chicago types" is how Mike Royko describes the participants. With picket signs, and a camera to record any bartender who might rebuff them. The camera offends a patron, there's a tussle, and a visitor from Texas truly named John Jolly steps in to help. In the resulting melee, a woman bites "a chunk" out of his hand. Police are called.

"Somebody's got to stand up against this kind of stuff. It's a men's sanctuary," Jolly later says, after a tetanus shot.

Eventually the Berghoff will put in stools for the ladies, whose delicate constitutions, the management assumes, do not permit them to belly up to the bar and stand like a man. The original Berghoff will close in 2006, a ploy to fire the union waitstaff, and almost immediately reopen in a new form, a faux Berghoff, a kind of imitation of itself, the bar rebranded a "brewery." No matter. Nobody who knows better goes there anymore. Miller's Pub is right around the corner.

Dec. 19, 1975

John Paul Stevens is sworn in by Chief Justice Warren Burger as an associate justice of the US Supreme Court. He'll become the third-longest-serving justice, weighing in on numerous important cases. Though a Republican, he'll become known as a liberal, in an era when that kind of thing could happen, even on the high court.

As son and grandson of the founders of the Stevens Hotel, the future Conrad Hilton on Michigan Avenue, Stevens has already had an incredibly full life before ascending to the Court, from meeting such luminaries as Amelia Earhart and Charles Lindbergh, to his first job, as a wandering raisin-tart salesman at the 1933 Century of Progress World's Fair, to being a navy cryptographer during World War II.

Stevens joined the law firm of Poppenhusen, Johnston, Thompson & Raymond—the future Jenner & Block—when it had 24 attorneys, and they docked his pay for the day he traveled to Springfield to be sworn into the Illinois bar. He became an avid pilot to ease his visits to clients around the country.

But perhaps the greatest wonder of Stevens's career, in retrospect, is the Senate nomination process. The Judiciary Committee approved him 13–0. Two days before his swearing in, he was confirmed by the Senate by a vote of 98–0 after five minutes of discussion.

Charles Percy, Republican of Illinois, praised the Senate's "nonpartisan sense" in handling the nomination. "Judge Stevens is clearly a man of great integrity," said Sen. Birch Bayh, Democrat of Indiana.

Dec. 20, 1976

Richard J. Daley concentrates power unto himself. He is the mayor of Chicago and the chairman of the Cook County Democratic Party and the Democratic Committeeman of the 11th Ward, a role he kept throughout his life, which ends today.

You do not relinquish power. You aggregate it, to yourself, except for the slivers you delegate to build loyalty, magnifying your authority. You make the decisions. You are the boss, the title Mike Royko gave to his best-selling biography of the mayor who, despite his mangled syntax and shrugging unvoiced racism and botching of the 1968 Democratic National Convention, is still considered among America's greatest mayors, and not without reason: his policies helped Chicago escape the doom that befell midwestern cities such as Detroit and Cleveland and Milwaukee.

Now he himself is at the office of Dr. Thomas J. Coogan Jr., his personal physician, complaining of chest pains. Coogan is making arrangements to get him to a hospital when Daley collapses and dies of a heart attack, age 74.

For all the vehemence of the opposition, the response of friend and foe alike is shock, almost disorientation. There had been no preparation; Daley suffered a slight stroke in 1974, but seemed to recover. Power does not look beyond itself to its own end. No successor was chosen to replace him. He had always been mayor; there were no mayors before. Not one Chicagoan in 100 can name the mayor who preceded Daley (sigh, Martin Kennelly).

Many aspire, of course. But no one has been groomed. The next five Chicago mayors will serve, on average, less than three years apiece until his son, Richie, takes up the mantle, beats the old man's record of 21 years by serving 22, then promptly quits.

Dec. 21, 1978

John Wayne Gacy is suing the Des Plaines Police Department for harassment—they keep following him in the street, illegally poking around his house, violating his civil rights, destroying his reputation. He's asking for $750,000 in damages.

But the hunt for a missing 15-year-old Maine West High School sophomore keeps pointing toward the contractor and part-time birthday clown. This morning police see Gacy hand a container of marijuana to a gas-station clerk and arrest him. Judge Marvin J. Peters grants police another search warrant, and they return with Gacy to his unincorporated Norwood Park Township home and threaten to tear up the floor. Gacy tries to distract them, leading them to a body buried under the floor in his garage; a man killed, Gacy claims, in self-defense.

But police also find the hatch to a crawl space, where the sump pump has been unplugged, flooding the low room. Police plug it back in. The device whirs. The water lowers. Evidence technician Daniel Genty gets down into the space and begins digging. Within minutes he comes up with rotten flesh and a human arm bone. He yells up to investigators: Go ahead and charge Gacy with murder.

Tomorrow Gacy will confess. Authorities will find the remains of 33 teens and young men: 27 in the crawl space, two under the garage and driveway, and four more in the Des Plaines River. That April the county will demolish the house. Nothing comes of the lawsuit.

Dec. 22, 1904

Chicago is broke. Well, the city does have $10 million in the bank. Cash does go out; just last night $448,000 was paid to eastern banks as interest on the city's crushing debt. But there are no funds that can be legally used to pay the December salaries of city workers.

"SORRY CHRISTMAS IN THE CITY HALL" reads a headline in today's *Tribune*. "HOPE IS ALMOST GONE."

A last-minute bookkeeping dodge—tapping the water system improvement fund—is struck down this morning by the Illinois Supreme Court. From the mayor—who has $833.33 coming—to the humblest clerk, there will be no pay for anyone who works for the City of Chicago.

"The only way out would be for Santa Claus or some other Christmas loving soul to give us the money outright," says comptroller Lawrence E. McGann, throwing up his hands. "And I'm afraid there isn't any great prospect of this."

But a city with $10 million in the bank must have credit somewhere, and City Treasurer Ernst Hummel heads over to LaSalle Street and borrows $700,000 from seven banks, personally guaranteeing the loans. His staff works all night, 20 clerks counting out the cash and putting it into 6,000 envelopes. They finish at 4 a.m.

At 6:57 on the morning of Christmas Eve, City Hall doors will be thrown open and payment will begin. Cheering clerks, secretaries, and stenographers parade inside, carrying banners—"Hurrah for Hummel"—in time to a man beating on a bass drum. Hundreds of uniformed firemen wait, under the watchful eye of police. The firefighters grow unruly, yelling and cheering and jostling the policemen, until the fire commissioner comes out and has a word with them, and all is in order again. The old pay wagons, long in disuse and headed for the junkyard, are spruced up and sent to deliver cash to far-flung police stations and firehouses.

"It was a day of true rejoicing in the City Hall," the *Daily News* notes.

Dec. 23, 1919

"Be it known that I, JAMES LEWIS KRAFT, a citizen of the United States, residing at Chicago, in the County of Cook, in the State of Illinois, have invented certain new and Improved Processes of Sterilizing Cheese. . . . The chief object of the invention is to convert cheese of the Cheddar genus into such condition that it may be kept indefinitely without spoiling . . ."

James Kraft knows spoiled cheese. Born into a Mennonite farming family in Canada, arriving in Chicago by way of Buffalo as the agent of a New York cheese concern, he quickly noticed that small grocers flocked to South Water Street every morning to buy their day's supply of cheese. He saw an opportunity, bought a horse and wagon, and made rounds delivering cheddar, which came in enormous discs that could weigh 80 pounds. In cutting off wedges, there was crumbled cheese and wastage, not to mention the rinds, which nobody wants to pay for. It could be hard to do on the fly. So he would cut the cheese into portions ahead of time, wrapping it in foil, placing it in glass jars. Meanwhile, he experimented with rendering cheese into a more permanent state.

". . . and to accomplish this result without substantially impairing the taste of the cheese."

You have to admire the candor of that "substantially." While Kraft cheese food—even in 1919 Kraft couldn't get away with simply calling it "cheese"—might not have the tang of a good gouda, it didn't go bad, and you could easily slice it.

"As a new article of manufacture, a hermetically sealed, completely sterilized package of cheese of the Cheddar genus."

Kraft first got the patent in 1916—today it is being reissued—and a lot has happened for Kraft in the past three years. Most significantly: the US Army placed an order for 25 million four-ounce tins of his cheese food product to feed soldiers going overseas in the Great War. Kraft's company will grow on variants on that theme: Velveeta (developed by another company that Kraft purchased), Cheez Whiz, Macaroni and Cheese, and in 1965 the apex, individually wrapped Kraft Singles, a kind of tribute to Kraft's original business model of finding a better way to keep, slice, and wrap cheese or, when that is impractical, an adequate imitation of cheese.

Dec. 24, 1954

A "boisterous crowd" gathers in front of the Martin home at 707
S. Cuyler Avenue, drawn by predictions by the lady of the house,
Dorothy Martin, that tonight she and her followers will be lifted up
to heaven by spacemen. The world had failed to end Tuesday, as
expected, so now they gather in her living room and sing Christmas
carols while waiting for the flying saucers. The crowd outside
grows restive. Oak Park will threaten to charge Mrs. Martin with
inciting a riot, and she will be placed under psychiatric care to avoid
that. There are even more long-lasting ramifications. Unbeknownst
to Martin, her group of faithful Seekers has been infiltrated by
University of Minnesota psychologist Leon Festinger, plus several
colleagues and students, taking advantage of the era's looser standards of research to conduct a close-up study of the psychology of
cults. Their book, *When Prophecy Fails*, will introduce the concept
of "cognitive dissonance," the tendency of some people, who
strongly define themselves by their beliefs, to cling to those beliefs
even tighter when confronted by evidence of their falsity—such
as the world not ending as expected, nor any spacemen arriving to
escort them to heaven. Dorothy Martin will live to be 92, her belief
unshaken.

Dec. 25, 1945

The soldiers have been mustering out for months. But that barely dents the 12 million Americans in uniform. The arrival of the first peacetime Christmas in five years only intensifies the rush to get them home as quickly as possible.

There are so many, and they keep coming. Today alone, 20 troopships arrive in eastern ports, and on the West Coast, California has 150,000 demobilized troops waiting for rides. The trains are full—the Southern Railroad estimates that 94 percent of passengers are military vets. Hundreds of civilians simply give up their reservations for veterans. Chicago train officials say Christmas breaks a passenger record. Though some trains are eight hours late, they all depart, eventually. Six marines grab a cab in San Diego and hire it to take them to New York City. Illinois servicemen who borrowed a furniture van in Denver are spending today snowbound in Kansas City.

As the nation's rail hub, Chicago hosts an occupying army of stranded vets. The city's four servicemen centers host 132,000 uniformed soldiers, sailors, marines, and airmen for the holidays. One sees boxer Joe Louis arrive at Municipal Airport, on his way to visit his daughter, ill at Children's Memorial Hospital. In asking for an autograph, the vet explains he's been marooned at the airport for two days. The champ reaches into his pocket, removes a Chicago–to–New York ticket, and gives it to the soldier. "Here, take this," he says. "And have a merry Christmas with your folks."

Those who can't go home phone instead. Bell Telephone reports that all its long-distance operators are on duty, a first. In part, because the pricy calls are being given away. One thousand wounded vets recovering at the Great Lakes Naval Hospital each get a five-minute call home, paid for by the Phone Home Fund, financed by readers of the *Chicago Times*.

Compounding the chaos, Chicago, like much of the Midwest, is glazed by ice, the worst since records have been kept. A navy plane carrying nine sailors east lands at Municipal Airport but can't take off again.

Dale Drew and June Kemper, two young ticket agents for Consolidated Airlines, see the Pacific vets sulking around the airport this morning. They phone their mothers, who are already preparing Christmas dinners for 11 and eight, respectively. What's a few more? The sailors are split up and sent to their homes, where presents materialize under the trees. After dinner, they gather at the Drew home, where friends of the two agents arrive. The carpets are rolled back, and there is dancing and singing.

Before they leave, the nine sailors draw up a resolution: "This has been a wonderful Christmas for us," it reads. "One just like you read about in books or see in the movies. We thank you from the bottom of our hearts." They all sign.

Dec. 26, 1944

The Glass Menagerie opens on a snowy night at the Civic Theater after two weeks of stormy rehearsals. Hopes are dim for this claustrophobic saga of the tragic trio of Wingfields. "Well, it looks bad, baby," author Tennessee Williams confided in his diary after a rehearsal. Pushed by his leading man to revise the play, he snapped, "I can't find the tranquility in Chicago to write." At least Williams did not give the producer the happy ending he asked for. Laura Wingfield, with her brace and her mother's dream of "gentleman callers," remains as fragile as her easily shattered animals. The play's reception is . . . odd.

"It was a strange night," cast member Eddie Dowling will recall. "There was no applause for anybody, no applause on entrances, nothing. It was bitter cold. The audience, it seemed to me in the first part of it, were all huddled like people trying to get close to each other to try to keep warm." But the reviews will be warm enough, and the play moves to Broadway in March.

Dec. 27, 1978

About noon, J. Patrice Marandel, curator of early painting, sculpture, and classical art, looking as pale as a Renaissance virgin, sticks
his head into the office of Larry Chalmers Jr., director of the Art
Institute of Chicago.

"I hate to be the one to tell you this . . . ," says Marandel, in his
heavy French accent. "But I think we have had a theft of three
Cézanne paintings."

Worse. The three paintings—*Madame Cézanne in Yellow
Armchair, Apples on a Tablecloth*, and *House on a River*—may
have been stolen, or may have simply been misplaced. Right now,
all that's known is: they're gone.

When? Sometime over the past month.

Where? The three paintings were not taken off the walls. Nor
from a vault. But from a . . . and this might be the worst part . . .
locked storage room where they were carelessly stashed while the
gallery where they usually hung is used for a treasures of Pompeii
exhibit. A closet, really. A messy closet where cleaning supplies are
stored. A broom closet, basically.

The museum estimates the loss at $3 million. During the inven-
tory that follows, the Art Institute assesses how many employees
had access to the key to the small room. That figure: 300.

But luck smiles on the museum. One of those 300 employees, Laud Spencer "Nick" Pace, who works in the packing and shipping department, was noticed around the storeroom five days earlier by a guard, at 6 a.m., hours before Pace was due on the job. Pace was later seen leaving with a painting-shaped package under his arm.

Police will ask him what he had been doing.

"I wasn't there," Pace says. He'll refuse to take a lie detector, but permit police to search his apartment. They find his writing about robbing art from the museum—fiction, Pace insists. He offers other explanations for the museum Plexiglas and books about Cézanne found in his apartment.

Five months later, Pace will be arrested in a hallway at the Drake Hotel, where he arranged to pick up a $250,000 ransom. The paintings are recovered from a hotel room, unharmed, and returned to the Art Institute in time to be featured at a 100th-anniversary celebration the next day. Pace will spend four years in prison, mostly because he was carrying a gun when he went to pick up the money.

Dec. 28, 1966

"Why do you call me Clay?" the champion bristles. "You know my right name is Muhammad Ali."

The usual prefight interview, announcing a February 6 match in Houston, in front of television cameras at Madison Square Garden, presided over by ABC sportscaster Howard Cosell. Typically, the boxers would scowl at each other, trade boasts, and maybe stage a punch for the cameras. But nothing is being staged now.

"I know you as Cassius Clay," replies Ernie Terrell. Both fighters live in Chicago. They've indeed known each other since they were teenagers, competing in the Golden Gloves tournament in the late 1950s.

"That's an Uncle Tom name," says Ali. "That's a slave name, a white man's name."

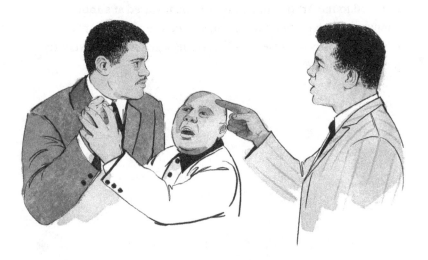

It's certainly the name that white newspapers across the country insist on using. But Ali changed his after joining the Nation of Islam in 1964.

"I respect you as a man," says Terrell.

"So why don't you call me by my right name?" says Ali. "You are acting just like another old Uncle Tom, another Floyd Patterson. I'm going to punish you."

They nearly come to blows right there, Ali slapping Terrell's arm and ripping off his jacket. "Let's have at it right now!" he yells.

Terrell lunges for Ali, but their handlers hold them back.

They will finish this conversation in Houston, "a vicious, ugly, horrible fight," where Ali mauls Terrell, breaking a bone in his face and damaging his eye, all the while shouting, "What's my name? Uncle Tom! What's my name?"

Dec. 29, 1903

The twin millstones that are Time grind us all into uniform powder, into dust. To be blown away. Even a person as lovely and talented, famous, and significant as Hazel Lavery. Fated to vanish and be forgotten, even in her own hometown, as if she were one of us lesser mortals.

Celebrated by W. B. Yeats, no less, who name-checks her in "The Municipal Gallery Revisited":

Hazel Lavery living and dying, that tale
As though some ballad-singer had sung it all.

How to begin? Today the *Tribune* leads its society page with "one of the most beautiful weddings of the year." The bride, "noted not only for her beauty and popularity but also for her artistic taste in all things," was wed yesterday to Dr. Edward Livingston Trudeau Jr. of New York City, where his parents are setting up the couple in a furnished apartment at 772 Park Avenue. The bridesmaids wear wreaths of gold leaves.

Hazel Trudeau would have probably never been lauded by poets—Yeats being not the only bard who will sing her praises. Nor would her face have gazed placidly from Irish banknotes for half a century. The glorious marriage is actually a disappointment, to her. She has a passion for art—instead of the standard diamond ring, she asked for an etching press. As a teen, she studied art in Europe under several masters, including Belfast-born painter John Lavery. He was 24 years older, but teacher and student became close, causing her mother to spirit her back to Chicago.

Here, fate plays a hand. Trudeau will die in May. Hazel will race back to the side of Lavery. They'll marry, and he will paint her portrait, again and again. The painter is deeply involved in the establishment of the Republic of Ireland, and the new nation turns to him in search of a woman to put on its currency. He offers up Lady Lavery. There's more—she will be friends with George Bernard Shaw, and teach her neighbor, Winston Churchill, how to paint. She will be the lover of Kevin O'Higgins, leader of the Irish Free State, which some believe she had a direct hand in creating. Her blood-soaked letters are found on freedom fighter Michael Collins after his assassination. Maybe sincere, maybe a code.

Hazel Lavery's portrait will also be among the compatriots who will all but make Yeats renounce his own writing. He ends his poem:

You that would judge me, do not judge alone
This book or that, come to this hallowed place
Where my friends' portraits hang and look thereon;
Ireland's history in their lineaments trace;
Think where man's glory most begins and ends,
And say my glory was I had such friends.

Dec. 30, 1903

Eddie Foy looks ridiculous. That's his job. The popular comedian is dressed in women's clothes and a wool wig, ready for the "Old Woman Who Lived in a Shoe" number in *Mr. Bluebeard*, the holiday extravaganza on stage before a standing-room-only matinee crowd packing the new Iroquois Theater. More than 1,800 people are in attendance, far more than fire codes allow, mostly women and children.

Foy is the star of the show, but not onstage when accident and neglect conspire to create disaster. Sparks from a faulty spotlight ignite drapery, and the oiled ropes and painted scenery burst into flame. The firefighting equipment backstage is useless. Performers somehow keep singing and dancing as the fire spreads. When the audience does turn to flee, panicked, en masse, they can't find the exits, many unmarked or hidden behind curtains so as not to detract from the beauty of the interior. Even if they find an exit door, it's often locked—to prevent those in the balcony from coming down and taking a better seat. Ushers outside ignore their pleas to open the doors. Those doors that are unlocked open inward, and are blocked by the crush of people. Patrons who make it out the upper-balcony fire escapes find no ladders have been installed, and many fall or leap to their deaths in the alley.

In the middle of all this, Eddie Foy does not panic or run. After making sure his six-year-old son Brian, watching from the wings, is taken outside by a stagehand, he returns to the middle of the stage to try to calm the audience. As he does, the crew flings open the doors at the back of the theater, and the influx of icy oxygen supercharges the fire. Foy flees at the last moment. About 600 Chicagoans out for a holiday entertainment die in the Iroquois, not only the worst theater death toll in American history, but the most lethal fire in any kind of structure before 9/11. The building, though scorched, will be basically unharmed. In 1926, it will be replaced by a movie palace, the Oriental Theater, which in 2019 will be renamed the Nederlander. You can still see a show sitting in the exact spot where those people died, the afterglow of the fire preserved in the clearly marked, well-lit, fiery red exit signs.

Dec. 31, 1914

The Essanay employees stride busily around, holding sheaves of paper, more like bank clerks than people engaged in a creative endeavor such as the making of a motion picture. He hasn't gotten the $10,000 bonus he was promised. His fellow actors tend to gape at him. And it's cold in Chicago.

Charlie Chaplin, arriving two days before Christmas, will last exactly 23 days here, and make one silent movie—titled *His New Job*, and yes, Chaplin made it to poke fun of his new employers. Then it'll be back to California to kiss the warm, fragrant ground.

At least he has a place to stay near the Essanay studios, for free, with "Broncho Billy" Anderson, the movies' first cowboy star, and his wife, Mollie, at their apartment at 1027 W. Lawrence Avenue. Here there is holiday spirit and family warmth, complete with a baby daughter, Maxine. Chaplin, whose parents separated when he was an infant, revels in it. "A baby, a Christmas tree," he marveled. "It's wonderful."

To welcome in 1915, the couple takes Chaplin to the $5-a-plate dinner at the chic College Inn in the basement of the Sherman Hotel. Mollie has to dig up cufflinks and a decent suit for Charlie, and when they get into the car, she notices he is wearing his pajama bottoms around his neck as a muffler.

A number of theatrical stars are there, big names like Henrietta Crosman and Mabel Taliaferro. And the great movie comedian John Bunny. One of the Howard brothers recognizes Chaplin, and makes him stand on a chair to be introduced. "Ladies and gentlemen," his admirer cries out, "I want to introduce to you the funniest man in moving pictures . . . Charlie Chaplin."

Later their party is confronted by an angry patron.

"Do you mean to tell me," the man fumes, "that this *boy* is the funniest comedian in moving pictures? Do you know that John Bunny is in the audience tonight?"

ACKNOWLEDGMENTS

This book was conceived by Timothy Mennel, an executive editor of the University of Chicago Press, and Levi Stahl, the Press's marketing director, inspired by Mychael Barratt's *London: Map of Days*. I am grateful they saw that book, saw my blog, everygoddamnday. com, and thought to juxtapose the two.

My longtime agent and friend, Susan Raihofer, of the David Black Literary Agency, skillfully handled the business side of the book. Artist Lauren Nassef created whimsical illustrations, which were paid for through the generosity of Cari and Michael J. Sacks.

Thanks as well to all the copy editors, proofreaders, graphic designers, and publicists who worked on this book at the University of Chicago Press.

These vignettes were researched and written entirely during the first year of COVID-19 lockdown, and I am grateful to all the librarians who kept their stacks open. Research was conducted at the Newberry Library, where I am honored to be a scholar-in-residence, at the Chicago History Museum, the Northbrook Public Library, the Wilmette Public Library, the *Chicago Sun-Times* library, and the Harold Washington branch of the Chicago Public Library, where Michelle McCoy, senior archival specialist in Special Collections, was particularly helpful.

Thanks as well to Nicholas Alen, reference specialist at the British Library, Julia Bachrach, longtime Chicago Park District historian, Derek Marinello at the Milwaukee Public Library, Liz O'Connell-Thompson at the Poetry Foundation, and Michael Wells at the Kansas City Public Library. Insight was provided by Peter Cole at Western Illinois University, Katherine M. Leo at the Millikin University School of Music, Whit Sadusky at the Gerber/Hart

Library and Archives, Thomas Haskell Simpson at Northwestern University, and Lindsey Wurz at Intuit: The Center for Intuitive and Outsider Art.

Businesses do not always leap to assist in a project like this, and I appreciated everyone in the corporate world who took the time to help. Thanks to Anita Liskey, senior managing director at the CME Group, Courtney McAlpine, senior digital archivist at the Ford Motor Company, Tom Panelas at Encyclopædia Britannica, and Michael Pettersen at Shure Microphone.

Thanks too to Bill Hillman, an expert in the life and work of Edgar Rice Burroughs, to Bob Dylan experts James Ziegler and Richard Thomas, to Michael McCoyer, who shared his research on Mexican immigrants, and to bridge expert James Talbot.

Whenever possible, I approached Chicagoans involved in these events, and they often spoke with me. Thanks to that treasure of the Chicago stage, Mike Nussbaum, who shared the story about Joe Mantegna that everyone in Chicago knew but me. Thanks as well to Jo Ann De Klerk, Robert Falls, Jeanne Gang, Barry Gross, Terri Hemmert, Rich Melman, Nicolás Medina Mora, Jesse Saunders, Dread Scott, Robin Loewenberg Tebbe, and Carlos Tortolero. Jay Tunney not only spoke about his father, Gene, but tipped me off to the existence of Hazel Lavery.

This book would not have been possible without the NewsBank online archive of historical newspapers—101 years of the *Chicago Daily News* at your fingertips, as well as the *Chicago Sun-Times*, *Chicago Sun*, and *Chicago Times*. The *Chicago Tribune* and *New York Times* online archives were also useful. The Library of Congress tried to track down the *Chicago Examiner* for summer 1900, when it sponsored Charlie Fitzmorris's jaunt around the world. But every library that appears, online, to have those issues in reality does not. It is tragic that months of that lively newspaper seem to have vanished. Those runs that the Chicago Public Library have preserved of the *Chicago Examiner* and the *Chicago Inter Ocean* are a reminder of just how vital it is to have multiple voices not only to journalism, but to history. Google Books served up portions of out-of-print texts, and Amazon let me buy them for cheap.

This is my third book for the University of Chicago Press, and that fruitful connection came about due to Northwestern University professor Bill Savage, who has been unfalteringly supportive and introduced me to a wonderful cast of devoted Chicago scholars such as Robert Loerzel. Bill was an academic reviewer of this book, as was Ethan Michaeli, and their close reading of the text flagged many mistaken, awkward, or ill-advised passages. Though any errors that survived this process are my responsibility alone.

I've been on the staff of the *Chicago Sun-Times* for 35 years and am fortunate to have meticulous editors in John O'Neill and Suzanne McBride. I must give individual shout-outs to interim editor-in-chief Steve Warmbir, director of human resources Angela Johnson, tech services manager Erin Wheeler, and photographer Ashlee Rezin. There are too many other cherished coworkers there to thank them all by name, but I appreciate my valued colleagues, past and present.

During the pandemic, exactly three friends risked eating lunch with me: Eric Zorn, Rick Kogan, and Kasey Madden. Thanks, guys.

Thanks to Rick Telander and all the crew at the Lake Superior Philosophical Society, particularly Rory Fanning, of Haymarket Books, who was right about everything. If this book is even a little attuned to the struggle of workers and the yawning disparities of class, that owes much to his patient instruction.

A writer wants to be in a circle of writers, and while I don't want to put on airs, I value knowing Sara Bader, Lee Bey, Rich Cohen, S. E. Cupp, Thomas Dyja, Jonathan Eig, Adam Gopnik, John Scalzi, Marc Kelly Smith, Gene Weingarten, and my lifelong friend and former landlady, Carol Weston, and her husband, playwright Robert Ackerman.

My world would be poorer without Ted Allen, Lori Cannon, Esther J. Cepeda, Justine Fedak, Robert Feder, Tony Fitzpatrick, Jim Kirk, Mark Konkol, Ron Magers, Bob Reiter, Karen Teitelbaum, and John Williams. Not to forget great neighbors, Terry and Ray Garcia, Mike and J. J. Hart, David and Tanya Kesmodel, Bill and Carla Martens, Craig and Gayle Rosenberg, and Kay Stein. Special thanks to Catherine Barron, whose enthusiasm was particularly appreciated.

My blog is enhanced by the unique worldview of Caren Jeskey, and supported from its inception by Marc Schulman, of Eli's Cheesecake. If you don't have Eli's in your freezer, you're not a Chicagoan.

One of these vignettes was discovered with the help of a tailless kitten, Boo, belonging to my younger son, Kent. She knocked over a watering can I brought into my office to irrigate my Chicago hardy fig, sending a sheet of water toward a stack of books piled on the floor in a corner. In snatching the books out of harm's way, I noticed *Sweet Tooth: The Bittersweet History of Candy*, by Kate Hopkins, which tipped me off to Milton Hershey's epiphany over chocolate at the 1893 fair. Serendipity can be a valuable friend to a writer.

My oldest friends are my rock, beginning with my former boss and shipmate, Michael Cooke. Plus Robert Leighton and Val Green, Mark and Thip Paine, Cate Plys and Ron Garzotto, Kier and Cathleen Strejcek, Didier Thys, and my hometown friends Jim and Laura Sayler, who challenged me to try to make this book as fun to read as it was to research. Thanks to Larry and Ilene Lubell, and Sandi and Lise Schleicher.

In books past, I'd thank each of the various Goldberg/Sackett clan members by name, but as the family grows, year by year, for brevity's sake, love to all, and let's simply join together in welcoming the next generation, Lola and Campbell, since the rest of us are but their admirers and support staff anyway.

The most enthusiastic listener to these vignettes as I was writing them was my mother, June Steinberg; thanks to her, my father, Robert, my brother Sam, sister Debbie, and my hero and confidant, cousin Harrison Roberts, and the rest of our wide and loving family.

Saving the best for last, thanks to my wife, my world, Edie, who makes each day a catalogue of joy. This book is dedicated to our boys, Ross and Kent, because, well, you know.

SOURCES

None of these vignettes come from a single source, but I have highlighted a main reference or two for each, for those who want to explore further, or have cited the source where quotes were found:

Jan. 1, 1920: "Raid Reds Here: Seize 150," *Chicago Tribune*, Jan. 2, 1920, p. 1; unsigned report published in *The New Majority* [Chicago] 3.2 (Jan. 10, 1920), p. 2.

Jan. 2, 1900: "Great Canal Is Opened," Jan. 2, 1900, *Chicago Daily News*, p. 1.

Jan. 3, 1974: "Arts at Large: Dylan's Wand of Words Casts Its Magic Spell," by Thomas Willis, *Chicago Tribune*, Jan. 9, 1974.

Jan. 4, 1872: "The Grand Ducal Levee," *Chicago Tribune*, Jan. 5, 1872, p. 2.

Jan. 5, 1973: "Hijack War at O'Hare," *Chicago Sun-Times*, Jan. 6, 1974; "Airlines Will Begin Tight Security Today," by Tom Buck, *Chicago Tribune*, Jan. 5, 1973.

Jan. 6, 1970: "Wrapping It Up, Poetically," by Roy Larson, *Chicago Sun-Times*, p. 3.

Jan. 7, 1954: "Boasting and Braying," in the *Encyclopedia of Great Popular Song Recordings*, vol. 1, by Steve Sullivan (Scarecrow Press, 2013).

Jan. 8, 1901: "Gossip of the Bowlers," *Chicago Daily News*, Jan. 8, 1901, p. 6.

Jan. 9, 1902: "William Wrigley Jr.: The Man and His Business," by William Zimmerman Jr. (privately printed, 1935).

Jan. 10, 1836: "Yesterday and Today: A History of the Chicago and North Western Railway System," by William H. Stennett, 1910.

Jan. 11, 1873: "Chicago Daily Drovers Journal: Year Book of Figures Relating to the Live Stock Business" (*Chicago Daily Drovers Journal*, March 1902).

Jan. 12, 1949: "The Burr Tillstrom Documentary Project," recorded shortly before his death in 1985, found on YouTube.

Jan. 13, 1979: "Snowpocalypse Then: How the Blizzard of 1979 Cost the Election for Michael Bilandic," by Whet Moser, *Chicago Magazine*, Feb. 2, 2011.

Jan. 14, 2014: Press release, US Department of Justice, US Attorneys Office for the Northern District of Illinois, "H. Ty Warner Sentenced To Probation After Paying $80 Million in Taxes and Penalties for Tax Evasion on Funds Hidden in Secret Swiss Bank Accounts."

Jan. 15, 1984: The aphorism of the relationship between cold and death is from "The Icy Miracles," by Sandy Rovner, *Washington Post*, Jan. 26, 1984.

Jan. 16, 1902: "Will Wed at First Sight," *Chicago Tribune*, Jan. 16, 1902, p. 1; "Wed after Mail Courting," *Chicago Tribune*, Jan. 17, 1902.

Jan. 17, 1920: *Get Capone: The Secret Plot That Captured America's Most Notorious Gangster*, by Jonathan Eig (Simon & Schuster, 2010).

Jan. 18, 1896: Thorstein Veblen to Sarah McLean Hardy, University of Chicago Centennial Catalogues.

Jan. 19, 1935: "Tighty-Whities First Hit the Market 80 Years Ago Today," by Laura Clark, *Smithsonian Magazine*, Jan. 19, 2015.

Jan. 20, 1984: *House Music: The Real Story*, by Jesse Saunders (Publish America, 2007).

Jan. 21, 2017: "Thousands Fill Loop after Women's March Rally in Chicago Draws Estimated 250,000," by Duaa Eldeib and Marwa Eltagouri, *Chicago Tribune*, Jan. 21, 2017.

Jan. 22, 1914: *Theodore Dreiser, Letters to Women: New Letters, Volume II*, edited by Thomas P. Riggio (University of Illinois Press, 2009).

Jan. 23, 1951: "How Clint Got Going on Weather," by Jack Mabley, *Chicago Daily News*, Jan. 24, 1951, p. 49.

Jan. 24, 2020: "Woman, 60, Is First Chicago-Area Coronavirus Patient," by Stefano Esposito and Nader Issa, *Chicago Sun-Times*, Jan. 24, 2020.

Jan. 25, 1890: "It Is Time to Call a Halt," by T. Thomas Fortune, BlackPast, Jan. 29, 2007.

Jan. 26, 1986: "As a Rule, Defense Did Rule—Exceptional Bears Dominating from the Very Beginning," by Brian Hewitt, *Chicago Sun-Times*, Jan. 27, 1986, p. 135.

Jan. 27, 1967: "Suburbs Isolated by Storm," by Arthur Gorlick, *Chicago Daily News*, Jan. 27, 1967, p. 3.

Jan. 28, 1910: "Society Girl Leper? Oak Park Is Terrified," *Chicago Examiner*, Jan. 29, 1910, p. 3.

Jan. 29, 1968: "Film Censorship Here Isn't Dead," *Chicago Daily News*, Jan. 31, 1968, p. 24.

Jan. 30, 1931: "Mason Attends 'Chanticleer,'" by Edward Moore, *Chicago Tribune*, Feb. 1, 1931, p. 17.

Jan. 31, 1910: *The Social Evil in Chicago: A Study of Existing Conditions* (Vice Commission of the City of Chicago, 1911).

Feb. 1, 1900: *Notable American Women 1607–1950: A Biographical Dictionary*, edited by Edward T. James (Harvard University Press, 1971).

Feb. 2, 1925: *From Main Street to Mall: The Rise and Fall of the American Department Store*, by Vicki Howard (Penn, 2015).

Feb. 3, 1876: *America's National Game: Historic Facts Concerning the Beginning, Evolution, Development and Popularity of Baseball, with Personal Reminisces of Its Vicissitudes, Its Victories and Its Votaries*, by Albert G. Spalding (American Sports Publishing, 1911).

Feb. 4, 1977: "The 'L' Crash of 1977: A Slow-Motion Horror," by Elizabeth Greiwe, *Chicago Tribune*, Feb. 4, 2017.

Feb. 5, 1924: *Pops: A Life of Louis Armstrong*, by Terry Teachout (Houghton Mifflin Harcourt, 2009).

Feb. 6, 1984: When I asked Mike Nussbaum, perhaps the oldest working stage actor at 95 and among the best at any age, about that opening night, he said of course there is the story that about Joe Mantegna going blank, but everyone knows that. I didn't, and filled in his account with press interviews in the 1980s with both Mantegna and William L. Petersen about that moment.

Feb. 7, 1968: "Blast Toll Rises to 8," *Chicago Daily News*, Feb. 8, 1968, p. 1.

Feb. 8, 1959: *Waylon: An Autobiography*, by Waylon Jennings with Lenny Kaye (Warner Books, 2009).

Feb. 9, 1947: *History of the American Academy of Oral Pathology, 1946–1987*, by Hamilton B. G. Robinson, p. 10.

Feb. 10, 1969: "U.S. Court Finds CHA Bias; Calls for Action on Remedy," by Fred Fraily, *Chicago Sun-Times*, Feb. 11, 1969, p. 3.

Feb. 11, 1952: "Chicago Rebels Against Filly de Mignon," *Life*, Feb. 11, 1952, p. 32.

Feb. 12, 1901: "For Hatchet Brigade," *Chicago Daily News*, Feb. 13, 1901.

Feb. 13, 1882: "Oscar Wilde: The Esthetic Apostle Greeted by an Immense Audience," *Chicago Tribune*, Feb. 14, 1882, p. 7.

Feb. 14, 1929: *The FBI Laboratory: 75 Years of Forensic Science Service*, by Kim Waggoner (FBI Forensic Science Communications, October 2007).

Feb. 15, 1933: "The Scariest Moment of a Presidential Transition: Six Gunshots Fired at FDR," by Ronald G. Shafer, *Washington Post*, Nov. 13, 2020.

Feb. 16, 1912: "Five Murderers Pay Penalty of Death; Court Appeals Fail," *Chicago Daily News*, Feb. 16, 1912.

Feb. 17, 1989: Dread Scott's website contains a collection of photos, news clippings, and ledger comments from his most notorious work. He spoke with me too.

Feb. 18, 1970: "Not Guilty of Conspiracy; 5 Guilty on Riot Charges," by James Kloss and M. W. Newman, *Chicago Daily News*, Feb. 18, 1970.

Feb. 19, 1909: *Block v. City of Chicago*, 239 Ill. 251 (1909), on Caselaw Access Project.

Feb. 20, 1967: "That Time Chicago Sent a Trainload of Snow to Florida," by Logan Jaffe, WBEZ, Jan. 15, 2016. Also "Our Snow Sends Florida Girl, 13," by Lloyd Green, *Chicago Sun-Times*, Feb. 21, 1967, p. 2.

Feb. 21, 1947: If you seek out only one book in these notes, *America Day by Day*, by Simon de Beauvoir (University of California Press, 1999), should be it, if only for her observations on race (p. 95), which are sadly as true today as they were 75 years ago.

Feb. 22, 1983: "Washington Wins, Aides, Foes Agree," by Basil Talbott Jr., *Chicago Sun-Times*, Feb. 23, 1983, p. 1.

Feb. 23, 1905: "Discover—The History of Rotary," Rotary website. The Rotarian magazine also writes occasionally about the efforts win over critics, including visiting Sinclair Lewis at home and hiring H. L. Mencken to write for them. The lawsuits are from press reports.

Feb. 24, 1870: *Crosby's Opera House: Symbol of Chicago's Cultural Awakening*, by Eugene H. Cropsey (Associated University Presses, 1999), p. 254.

Feb. 25, 1861: "One, Two, Three, and Up She Goes!," *Chicago Tribune*, Feb. 26, 1861, p. 1.

Feb. 26, 1987: "Jordan Bags 58 to Set Record," by Mark Vancil, *Chicago Sun-Times*, Feb. 27, 1987, p. 96.

Feb. 27, 1979: "Close! But Byrne Apparent Winner," by Basil Talbott Jr., *Chicago Sun-Times*, Feb. 28, 1979, p. 1.

Feb. 28, 1984: "Chicago Gambler Buried in Cadillac-Style Coffin," *Jet Magazine*, March 19, 1984, p. 22.

Feb. 29, 1960: "A Bunny Thing Happened: An Oral History of the Playboy Clubs," by Bruce Handy, *Vanity Fair*, April 22, 2011.

March 1, 1784: *How the States Got Their Shapes*, by Mark Stein (HarperCollins, 2008).

March 2, 1908: *The Lazarus Averbuch Mystery*, by Michael Feldberg, American Jewish Historical Society.

March 3, 1914: *Henry Ford: Mass Production, Modernism and Design*, by Ray Batchelor (Manchester University Press, 1994).

March 4, 1837: *Laws and Ordinances Governing the City of Chicago*, compiled by Joseph E. Gary (Myers and Chandler, 1866).

March 5, 1962: "Key to Good Living Moves In . . . With Aid of Mayor," *Chicago Daily News*, March 5, 1962, p. 18.

March 6, 1940: *Richard Wright: The Life and Times*, by Hazel Rowley (University of Chicago Press, 2001), p. 193.

March 7, 1918: "Billy Sunday Takes a Few Practice Shots," by Ben Hecht, *Chicago Daily News*, March 7, 1918, p. 1.

March 8, 1963: "The Rise and Fall of Vee-Jay Records," on NPR, Jan. 15, 2008. The Silver Dollar survey comes up on websites like WorthPoint.

March 9, 1943: *Endgame*, by Frank Brady (Crown, 2011).

March 10, 1894: "Stole All but the Cellar," *Chicago Record*, March 5, 1894. The *Tribune* cites the culprit as Lubonski, the *Record* as Lubouski, and alas neither mentions how the case was disposed. See also Perry R. Duis, *Challenging Chicago: Coping with Everyday Life 1837–1920* (University of Illinois Press, 1998).

March 11, 2016: "Trump Speaks Out After Postponing Chicago Rally: 'I Don't Want to See People Hurt,'" by Veronica Stracqualursi, ABC News, March 11, 2016.

March 12, 1906: Letter from Upton Sinclair to Theodore Roosevelt, March 10, 1906, National Archives identifier 301981; "Partial Ban on 'The Jungle,'"

Chicago Daily News, April 14, 1906, p. 2. "Mud Slingers Mark for the President," *Chicago Daily News*, April 14, 1906, p. 1.

March 13, 1913: "When Is Art Art? When Wicked?," *Chicago Tribune*, March 14, 1913, p. 3.

March 14, 2012: *The Great EB: The Story of the Encyclopædia Britannica*, by Herman Kogan (University of Chicago Press, 1958).

March 15, 1937: "Dr. Bernard Fantus: Father of the Blood Bank and Researching Chicago Medical History, Nov. 1, 2004 through Feb. 7, 2005," Exhibitions in the Special Collections Research Center, University of Chicago.

March 16, 1900: "Circuit Talk on Today," *Chicago Daily News*, March 16, 1900, p. 6.

March 17, 1864: "The Lake Tunnel: Commencement of the Work—Ground Broken by the Mayor," *Chicago Tribune*, March 18, 1864, p. 4.

March 18, 1957: "Robie House Still Standing," by Natalie Friedberg, *Chicago Maroon*, Feb. 17, 2015.

March 19, 1928: *The Adventures of Amos 'n' Andy: A Social History of an American Phenomenon*, by Melvin Patrick Ely (Free Press, 1991).

March 20, 1975: "Bare Police Spying on 5 Civic Groups," by Barry S. Felcher, *Chicago Daily News*, March 20, 1975, p. 1.

March 21, 2000: *The Bridge: The Life and Rise of Barack Obama*, by David Remnick (Knopf, 2010).

March 22, 1958: The Illinois Digital Archive has the entire 15,000-page Vivian Girls saga online, plus Henry Darger's autobiography, which is more readable than you might expect, and his 10-year daily weather diary. Jessica Yu's 2004 documentary *In the Realms of the Unreal* lays out Darger's difficult upbringing.

March 23, 1901: "Show Vehicles at Best," *Chicago Tribune*, March 24, 1901.

March 24, 1981: UPI Report, by Jack Lesar, March 25, 1981.

March 25, 1967: "Vietnam War a 'Blasphemy,' King Tells Peace Rally," by Jerry DeMuth, *Chicago Sun-Times*, March 26, 1967, p. 1.

March 26, 1905: The Jane Addams Digital Edition.

March 27, 1997: "Snappled!," by Neil Steinberg, *Chicago Reader*, May 29, 1997, p. 1.

March 28, 1980: "Steel Mill Shut, May Not Reopen," *Chicago Sun-Times*, p. 4.

March 29, 1675: *Early Narratives of the Northwest: 1634–1699*, edited by Louise Phelps Kellogg (Scribner's, 1917), p. 268.

March 30, 2003: "Meigs Now No-Fly Zone," by Robert C. Herguth, *Chicago Sun-Times*, March 31, 2003, p. 1.

March 31, 1952: "Population of Chicago Estimated at 3,665,792," *Chicago Tribune*, April 1, 1952, p. 19.

April 1, 1918: "Illness Halts Trial of 114 I.W.W. Men," *Chicago Daily News*, April 1, 1918, p. 1.

April 2, 2019: "Who Is Lori Lightfoot? Get to Know Chicago's Mayor-Elect," NBC 5 Chicago, May 19, 2019.

April 3, 1979: "Jane Byrne Scores a Record Win," by Basil Talbot Jr., *Chicago Sun-Times*, April 4, 1979, p. 1.

April 4, 1917: "The Chicago Flag," Chicago Architecture Center. Description of the flag's symbolism is in Wallace Rice Papers, "Works, Miscellaneous, Flag Specifications for City of Chicago," Box 5, Folder 115, Newberry Library collection. "The Story of Chicago's Four-Star City Flag," blog post by Robert Loerzel, April 4, 2017, Medium.com@RobertLoerzel.

April 5, 1955: "Mayor-Elect to Seek 2,000 More City Cops," by Thomas Buck, *Chicago Tribune*, April 6, 1955, p. 7.

April 6, 1915: "Oscar De Priest and the Jim Crow Restaurant in the U.S. House of Representatives," by Elliot M. Rudwick, *Journal of Negro Education* 35.1 (Winter 1966).

April 7, 1968: "Amid the Rubble, They Went to Church," *Chicago Daily News*, April 8, 1968, p. 3; "Shoot to Kill . . . Shoot to Maim," by Christopher Chandler, *Chicago Reader*, April 4, 2002.

April 8, 1889: *Ambassadors in Pinstripes: The Spalding World Baseball Tour*, by Thomas W. Zeiler (Rowman & Littlefield, 2006).

April 9, 1969: "8 Deny Guilt in Riots at Convention," *Chicago Tribune*, April 10, 1969, p. 3.

April 10, 1928: "Votes Cast Exceed 800,000," by Warren Phinney, *Chicago Daily News*, April 10, 1928, p. 1.

April 11, 1973: *Sears in Chicago: A Century of Memories*, by Val Perry Rendel (History Press, 2019), p. 122.

April 12, 1983: "Washington Elected," by David Axelrod, *Chicago Tribune*, April 13, 1983, p. 1.

April 13, 1992: "Leak Drains Loop," by Tom McNamee and Neil Steinberg, *Chicago Sun-Times*, April 14, 1992, p. 1.

April 14, 1956: "The Videotape Recorder Turns 50," *TV Technology*, April 12, 2006.

April 15, 1955: *Grinding It Out: The Making of McDonald's*, by Ray Kroc (St. Martin's, 1977).

April 16, 1913: "A Mixed Reception for Modernism: The 1913 Armory Show at The Art Institute of Chicago," by Andrew Martinez, *Art Institute of Chicago Museum Studies* 19.1 (1993): 30.

April 17, 1943: Charles Kikuchi original diary, vol. 31, p. 89, University of California at Los Angeles Library Special Collection, Charles E. Young Research Library.

April 18, 1950: US Patent and Trademark Office, Patent Full Text Database. Also, the *New Yorker* produced a lovely documentary film, *Eddy's World*.

April 19, 1861: "Illinois to the Rescue," *Chicago Tribune*, April 19, 1861, p. 2; *A History of Chicago*, vol. 2, *From Town to City, 1848–1871*, by Bessie Louise Pierce (Knopf, 1940), p. 275.

April 20, 1951: "Evanston Auto Plant Turning Out a Car a Day," by Anthony Wirry, *Chicago Tribune*, April 20, 1951, p. C5.

April 21, 1855: *The Great Chicago Beer Riot: How Lager Struck a Blow for Liberty*, by John F. Hogan and Judy E. Brady (History Press, 2015), p. 85.

April 22, 1872: "Chief's Relatives Want Land Back," by Mark Konkol, *Chicago Sun-Times*, Feb. 9, 2010, p. 15.

April 23, 1884: *Candy: A Century of Panic and Pleasure*, by Samira Kawash (Farrar, Straus & Giroux, 2013). A spokeswoman for the National Confectioners Association said that nobody there knows anything about their own origins, which is just sad.

April 24, 1933: "Five Loop Banks Besieged by Teachers," *Chicago Daily News*, April 24, 1933, p. 1.

April 25, 1917: *Journal of Negro History* 4.3 (July 1919): 332.

April 26, 1973: "Maturing CBOE Confident at 20," by William B. Crawford Jr., *Chicago Tribune*, April 26, 1993.

April 27, 1959: "Ballet High, Burlesque Low?," *Chicago Sun-Times*, April 27, 1959, p. 3.

April 28, 1919: "Hirsch Defends Loyalty from Temple Pulpit," by Rev. W. B. Norton, *Chicago Tribune*, April 28, 1919, p. 17; *Chicago Transformed: World War I and the Windy City*, by Joseph Gustaitis (Southern Illinois University Press, 2016), p. 278.

April 29, 1983: "Mayor Harold Washington Inaugural Address, 1983," Chicago Public Library.

April 30, 1916: *Lost Chords: White Musicians and their Contributions to Jazz, 1915–1945*, by Richard M. Sudhalter (Oxford University Press, 2001), p. 11. *Who Wrote Those "Livery Stable Blues"? Musical Ownership in* Hart et al. v. Graham, by Katherine M. Maskell, *Musicology*, The Ohio State University School of Music.

May 1, 1893: "Opened the Fair," *Chicago Record*, May 2, 1893, p. 1; "He Is Coming Back," *Chicago Inter Ocean*, May 2, 1893, p. 1.

May 2, 1950: When Gwendolyn Brooks sat down with the American Folklore division of the Library of Congress for a recorded interview in 1986, she got one fact wrong. Asked about her Pulitzer Prize, she said that Jack Starr from the *Sun-Times* called her to tell her she had won and "it would be announced the next day." Which didn't make sense, particularly after seeing there was only the most glancing mention of her receiving the honor. The mystery is cleared up by her handwritten journal, provided by the Poetry Foundation, which correctly places the call on the afternoon of May 1, shortly after the prizes were announced in New York City.

May 3, 1932: The scene was created from accounts in the *Chicago Daily News*, *Tribune*, *Times*, and *New York Times*, particularly "Capone Speeds to Atlanta," by Chesly Manly, *Chicago Tribune*, May 4, 1932, p. 1.

May 4, 1886: *Second City Sinners: True Crime from Chicago's Deadly Street*, by Jon Seidel (Lyons Press, 2019), p. 3.

May 5, 1905: *The Defender: How the Legendary Black Newspaper Changed America*, by Ethan Michaeli (Houghton Mifflin, 2016), p. 20.

May 6, 2004: "The Third School," by Lynn Becker, *Chicago Reader*, May 4, 2006.

May 7, 1902: "Big Barge Sticks on Tunnel," *Chicago Daily News*, May 7, 1902, p. 1; "Barge Yakima Still Fast," *Chicago Daily News*, May 8, p. 3.

May 8, 1921: "New Museum Thrills 'Em," *Chicago Daily News*, May 3, 1921, p. 3.

May 9, 1937: "Labor Rally," flier, Library of Congress Internet Archive, identifier nby_26266-4.

May 10, 1894: "The Lions of Michigan Avenue," by Paul Jones, Art Institute of Chicago, Nov. 21, 2018.

May 11, 1988: *David K. Nelson, Jr., Plaintiff-appellee, v. Allan Streeter, Dorothy Tillman, and Bobby L. Rush, defendants-appellants*, 16 F.3d 145 (7th Cir. 1994), on Justia Legal Resources.

May 12, 1926: "New Chicago-Dallas Air Mail Is Launched," *Chicago Daily News*, May 26, 1926, p. 4.

May 13, 1894: "Chided by a Pastor," *Chicago Tribune*, May 14, 1894, p. 1.

May 14, 1912: "Edgar Rice Burroughs Bio Timeline: 1910–1919," compiled by Bill Hillman and Danton Burroughs, ERBzine. Photo of MS page.

May 15, 2006: "Supreme Bean," *Chicago Tribune*, RedEye edition, May 16, 2006, p. 6.

May 16, 1988: "$70 Million Bank Theft Foiled; Four Held," by Maurice Possley and Laurie Cohen, *Chicago Tribune*, May 19, 1988.

May 17, 1900: "The Wonderful Wizard of Oz" auction notes, Christie's, Dec. 2, 2010.

May 18, 1860: The perhaps anecdotal quote from Lincoln is from *Abraham Lincoln*, by Ellis Paxson Oberholtzer (George W. Jacobs, 1904), p. 143.

May 19, 1875: *The Last Lincolns: The Rise and Fall of a Great American Family*, by Charles Lachman (Union Square Press, 2008), p. 190.

May 20, 1882: "Ghosts," by Michael Meyer, in *Ibsen Plays: One* (Bloomsbury Academic, 1980), p. 15; Det virtuelle Ibsensenteret, "Inserat av Helga Bluhme-Jensen i Skandinaven i Chicago 20. mai 1882 (No. 119, 16de Aargang) i forkant av premieren på Gengangere i Aurora Turner Hall."

May 21, 1924: *For the Thrill of It: Leopold, Loeb and the Murder That Shocked Jazz Age Chicago*, by Simon Baatz (Harper, 2009).

May 22, 1935: "Jane Addams Mourned; Endeared to All World," *Chicago Daily News*, May 22, 1935, p. 1.

May 23, 1895: *American Bee Journal* 35.21 (May 23, 1895), Cornell University Library Digital Collections, identifier hivebees6366245_6500_021.

May 24, 1955: *Willie Dixon: Preacher of the Blues*, by Mitsutoshi Inaba (Scarecrow Press, 2011), p. 149.

May 25, 1979: "The Ghosts of Flight 191," by Bryan Smith, *Chicago Magazine*, May 7, 2019. "The Legacy of Flight 191," by Lauren Zumbach, *Chicago Tribune*, May 23, 2019.

May 26, 1934: "Zephyr Sets Mark of 112 Miles an Hour Speeding from Denver to World's Fair," by Gene Morgan, *Chicago Daily News*, May 26, 1934, p. 1.

May 27, 1933: "Midway Seen as World's Greatest Show," by John Drury, *Chicago Daily News*, May 27, 1933, p. 7.

May 28, 1950: TV listings, *Chicago Tribune*, May 28, 1950, p. W12.

May 29, 1962: "Cubs Hire Negro for 11th Coach," *Chicago Daily News*, May 29, 1962, p. 28.

May 30, 1937: *America's Film Legacy: The Authoritative Guide to the Landmark Movies in the National Film Registry*, by Daniel Eagan (Bloomsbury, 2009).

May 31, 2020: "18 Murders in 24 Hours: Inside the Most Violent Day in 60 Years in Chicago," by Tom Schuba, Sam Charles, and Matthew Hendrickson, June 8, 2020.

June 1, 1970: "Judge Lets Fathers into the Delivery Room," *Chicago Tribune*, June 2, 1970, p. A5; interview with Barry Gross.

June 2, 1928: *Mexican Hometown Associations in Chicagoacán: From Local to Transnational Civic Engagement*, by Xóchitl Bada (Rutgers University Press, 2014).

June 3, 1863: "The Chicago Times Establishment Taken Possession of by the Military Authorities," *Chicago Tribune*, June 4, 1863, p. 4.

June 4, 1927: *Mister Jelly Roll—The Fortunes of Jelly Roll Morton, New Orleans Creole, and "Inventor of Jazz,"* by Alan Lomax (University of California Press, 2001), p. 150.

June 5, 1946: Illinois Fire Service Institute, Firefighter Record—Eugene Freemon.

June 6, 1901: Memo to the Chicago Historical Society from Mary B. Brennan, Aug. 1, 1958.

June 7, 1857: *As Others See Chicago: Impressions of Visitors, 1633–1933*, by Bessie Louise Pierce (University of Chicago Press, 1933), p. 166.

June 8, 1893: The University of Rochester has created a beautiful and engaging website—https://maybragdon.lib.rochester.edu/—devoted to 10 years' worth of diaries of May Bragdon, "a single working woman set free by the bicycle and enlivened by friendships, the Kodak, the theatre and a connection with the natural world." Her entry for June 8 is far longer than I feature, all in that same breathless rush.

June 9, 1930: *Capone: The Man and the Era*, by Laurence Bergreen (Simon & Schuster, 1994), p. 377.

June 10, 1971: "Rich Melman," by Bill Zehme, *Chicago Magazine*, July 6, 2017; interview with Rich Melman, March 2021.

June 11, 1964: *Life*, by Keith Richards (Little, Brown, 2010), p. 157.

June 12, 1920: *Warren G. Harding*, by John W. Dean (Times Books, 2004), p. 63.

June 13, 1986: "A Big Thank You!," by Tom McNamee and Andrew Herrmann, *Chicago Sun-Times*, June 14, 1986, p. 2. Also "Cheers, Tears and 'Welcome Home,'" by Robert Davis and Patrick Reardon, *Chicago Tribune*, June 14, 1986, p. 1.

June 14, 2018: "Zeppelins, Monorails and, Now, Rahm's Rich Folks Underground Railroad," by Neil Steinberg, *Chicago Sun-Times*, June 14, 2018.

June 15, 1921: *Queen Bess: Daredevil Aviator*, by Doris L. Rich (Smithsonian Institution Press, 1993), p. 26.

June 16, 1996: "Jordan's '95–'96 Chicago Bulls and the Best Starting 5 in Each Team's History," by Ryan Comstock, *Bleacher Report*, March 3, 2011.

June 17, 1918: "German Street Name Changes in Bucktown, Parts I and II," by Jack Simpson, Newberry Library, Nov. 1, 2011.

June 18, 1959: "Chicago Movie Censors Face a Court Fight," *Chicago Tribune*, July 2, 1959, p. 2.

June 19, 1984: "Apologetic Bulls 'Stuck with Jordan,'" by Bernie Lincicome, *Chicago Tribune*, June 20, 1984.

June 20, 1966: "Jose Cruz' Troubles in the 'Golden Land,'" by Robert Gruenberg, *Chicago Daily News*, June 20, 1966, p. 1.

June 21, 1920: *Murder City: The Bloody History of Chicago in the Twenties*, by Michael Lesy (Norton, 2008).

June 22, 1937: Did the nearly illiterate Joe Louis really think, "I have a responsibility to them . . ."? The words are there in *Joe Louis: My Life* (Harcourt, 1978), written with Edna and Art Rust. Are they accurate? Or just what Louis imagined, years later, he ought to have thought? An embellishment by his collaborators? We'll never know. At some point, history is going with what you've got, bearing in mind the contraindications, which in this case are found in lines penned by Richard Wright: "Now you can look at Joe / But sure can't read his mind."

June 23, 1960: *The Birth of the Pill: How Four Crusaders Reinvented Sex and Launched a Revolution*, by Jonathan Eig (Norton, 2015).

June 24, 1942: "The Story of Chicago's Nazi Spy," by Ron Grossman, *Chicago Tribune*, May 20, 2012.

June 25, 2011: "New Poetry Building's Lyrical Joys Unfold Gradually," by Blair Kamin, *Chicago Tribune*, June 26, 2011.

June 26, 1833: *The First Presbyterian Church*, by Philo Adams Otis (Clayton F. Summy, 1900), p. 228.

June 27, 1970: "A Brief History of Chicago's Pride Parade," by Emmet Sullivan, *Chicago Magazine*, June 24, 2015.

June 28, 1940: *Radio Network Contributions to Education*, by Carroll Atkinson (Meador, 1942), p. 59.

June 29, 1889: "A Big Day for Chicago," *Chicago Daily News*, July 1, 1889, p. 1.

June 30, 1870: *A Farm Philosopher: A Love Story*, by Ada S. Kepley (Worman's Printery, 1912), p. 55.

July 1, 1910: "July 1, 1910: The 'Baseball Palace of the World' Opens," by Bob LeMoine, Society for American Baseball Research website.

July 2, 1932: "Roosevelt Arrives Here," *Chicago Daily News*, July 2, 1932, p. 1.

July 3, 1899: "Justice for the Child: The Beginning of Juvenile Court in Chicago," by David S. Tanenhaus, *Chicago History* 27.3 (Winter 1998–1999): 4.

July 4, 1909: *Plan of Chicago*, by Daniel H. Burnham and Edward H. Bennett (Commercial Club, 1909). The gorgeous volume is available online. If some of the illustrations look familiar, one of the artists, Jules Guérin, also created the Aida Grand March on the fire curtain at the Civic Opera House.

July 5, 1894: "Fun for All Ages," *Daily Inter Ocean*, July 4, 1894, p. 8.

July 6, 1959: "Throngs Hail Elizabeth in Wild, Noisy Greeting," *Chicago Daily News*, July 6, 1959, p. 1; *Boss: Richard J. Daley of Chicago*, by Mike Royko (Dutton, 1971), p. 110.

July 7, 1931: *Steel Barrio: The Great Mexican Migration to South Chicago, 1915–1940*, by Michael Innis-Jimenez (New York University Press, 2013), p. 139.

July 8, 1926: "Radio Connects Engine and Caboose of Train," *Chicago Daily News*, July 8, 1926, p. 3.

July 9, 1893: *The Man Who Touched His Own Heart: True Tales of Science, Surgery and Mystery*, by Robb Dunn (Little, Brown, 2015), p. 10; *The Evolution of Cardiac Surgery*, by Harris B. Schumacher (Indiana University Press, 1992), p. 12.

July 10, 1926: "Memorial Planned for Radio Martyr," *Radio News*, Aug. 1, 1926, p. 3.

July 11, 1985: "LeFevour Accusers Blistered," by Maurice Possley, *Chicago Tribune*, July 12, 1985, p. 1.

July 12, 1951: "Governor Orders Troops to Cicero," *Chicago Sun-Times*, July 13, 1951, p. 3.

July 13, 1903: Ford Motor Company Ledger, 1903–1904, ID #64.167.85.7, p. 202, Henry Ford Museum, Dearborn, MI.

July 14, 1966: *The Crime of the Century*, by Dennis L. Breo and William J. Martin (Skyhorse, 1993).

July 15, 1832: Letter from Scott to Governor Reynolds, July 15, 1832, in the *Louisville* (Kentucky) *Advertiser*, July 27, 1832, and reprinted in *The History of Peoria County, Illinois* (Johnson & Co., 1880), p. 133. Also *Agent of Destiny: The Life and Times of General Winfield Scott, by John D. Eisenhower* (University of Oklahoma Press, 1997), p. 128.

July 16, 1995: *Heat Wave: A Social Autopsy of Disaster in Chicago*, by Eric Klinenberg (University of Chicago Press, 2002).

July 17, 1866: *History of Chicago: From the Earliest Period to the Present Time*, vol. 2, *From 1857 Until the Fire of 1871*, by A. T. Andreas (1885), p. 64. Also "Common Council," *Chicago Tribune*, July 18, 1866, p. 4.

July 18, 1980: *Freedom's Child: A Courageous Teenager's Story of Fleeing His Parents and the Soviet Union—To Live in America*, by Walter Polovchak with Kevin Klose (Random House, 1988), pp. 2, 4, and, for the Jell-O, 235.

July 19, 1888: Files of the Chicago, Burlington & Quincy Railroad, containing reports on union activities from the Pinkerton National Detective Agency. Newberry Library, #CB&Q 33 1880 9, Box 108.

July 20, 1901: "Around the World in Sixty Days," *The American Almanac, Year-Book, Cyclopedia and Atlas*, p. 6 (W. R. Hearst, 1903).

July 21, 1919: *City of Scoundrels*, by Gary Krist (Crown, 2012).

July 22, 1934: *Second City Sinners: True Crime from Historic Chicago's Deadly Streets*, by Jon Seidel (Lyons Press, 2019).

July 23, 1941: "Moriarity Gets Life for 'Abortion Slaying,'" *Chicago Tribune*, July 24, 1941, p. 1.

July 24, 1915: Bobbie Aanstad's story was told to me by her granddaughter, Barbara Decker Wachholz, co-founder of the Eastland Disaster Historical Society. See also *The Sinking of the Eastland: America's Forgotten Tragedy*, by Jay Bonansinga (Citadel Press, 2004). Aanstad is also listed as a survivor—though her age is given incorrectly—in *"Eastland": Legacy of the Titanic*, by George W. Hilton (Stanford University Press, 1995).

July 25, 1942: "Planes to Roar Off Last Year's Fertile Acres," *Chicago Tribune*, Sept. 20, 1942, p. 1.

July 26, 2019: "Police: 2 Chicago Moms Killed in Shooting Likely Not Targets," by Don Babwin, United Press International, July 30, 2019.

July 27, 1919: *American Pharaoh: Mayor Richard J. Daley, His Battle for Chicago and the Nation*, by Adam Cohen and Elizabeth Taylor (Little, Brown, 2000), p. 35.

July 28, 1932: "Playing for the People: Labor Sport Union Athletic Clubs in the Lake Superior/Iron Range 1927–1936," by Gabe Logan, *Upper Country: A Journal of the Lake Superior Region* 4.1 (2016): 44.

July 29, 1938: "Bigot Unwittingly Sparked Change," by Steve Wulf, ESPN, Feb. 14, 2014.

July 30, 1971: "Requiem for a Slaughterhouse," by William Braden, *Chicago Sun-Times*, Aug. 1, 1971.

July 31, 1929: "Children See Candy Made at Great Factory," by Carol Willis Hyatt, *Chicago Daily News*, Aug. 1, 1929, p. 7.

Aug. 1, 1897: Classified ad, *Chicago Tribune*, Aug. 1, 1897, p. 41; "Tonnesen Models," *Printers' Ink*, July 7, 1897, p. 5.

Aug. 2, 1965: *Gregory v. City of Chicago*, 394 U.S. 111. Decided March 10, 1969. Justia, US Supreme Court.

Aug. 3, 1795: "Treaty of Greenville," DocsTeach, National Archives.

Aug. 4, 1830: "James Thompson," by Lauren Kiehna, the Randolph Society.

Aug. 5, 1966: "I'll Lead Marchers Again, King Pledges," by Edmund Rooney and Jack Levin, *Chicago Daily News*, Aug. 6, 1966, p. 1.

Aug. 6, 1912: "T. R. Will Be Nominated Today with Johnson," *Chicago Examiner*, Aug. 7, 1912, p. 1.

Aug. 7, 1915: *The Automobile*, Aug. 12, 1915, p. 294.

Aug. 8, 1988: "The Big Washout—Rainout Delays Debut of Cub Lights Era," by Joe Goddard, *Chicago Sun-Times*, Aug. 9, 1988, p. 92.

Aug. 9, 1937: "Two Skyscrapers Change Owners in Realty Swap," by Al Chase, *Chicago Tribune*, Aug. 10, 1937.

Aug. 10, 1928: "U.S. Swimmers Qualify," *Chicago Tribune*, Aug. 11, 1928, p. 15.

Aug. 11, 1948: *Memoirs of Eighty Years*, by Dr. James Herrick (University of Chicago Press, 1949).

Aug. 12, 1939: "If You Get Up Early, You're a Born Milkman," *Chicago Tribune*, Aug. 13, 1939, p. 9.

Aug. 13, 1927: "City Cheers Lindy Welcome," *Chicago Daily News*, Aug. 13, 1927, p. 1.

Aug. 14, 1812: "The True Story of the Deadly Encounter at Fort Dearborn," by Geoffrey Johnson, *Chicago Magazine*, Jan. 4, 2010.

Aug. 15, 1967: "Studs Terkel Comments and Presents Picasso Unveiling Ceremony," Studs Terkel Radio Archive, WFMT.

Aug. 16, 1926: "City to Get Great Museum," *Chicago Tribune*, Aug. 17, 1926, p. 1; "Museum Head Lauds Rosenwald Plans," *Chicago Daily News*, Aug. 17, 1926, p. 5.

Aug. 17, 1970: *A Critical History of Soul Train on Television*, by Christopher P. Lehman (McFarland, 2008).

Aug. 18, 1835: *The Chicago Massacre of 1812*, by Joseph Kirkland (Dibble Publishing, 1893), p. 203.

Aug. 19, 1972: "An 'Eiffel Tower' Here?," by Tony Fuller and Norman Mark, *Chicago Daily News*, Aug. 19–20, 1972, p. 4; *Why Buildings Fall Down: How Structures Fail*, by Matthys Levy and Mario Salvadori (W. W. Norton, 1992), p. 187.

Aug. 20, 1965: "Teens Out-Yell Beatles," by Will Leonard, *Chicago Tribune*, Aug. 21, 1965, p. 1.

Aug. 21, 1950: "Rail Tieup Will Idle 27,000 in Big Steel Mills," *Chicago Sun-Times*, Aug. 22, 1950, p. 3.

Aug. 22, 1991: "Violence Spares No One, Not Even a 'Good Guy,'" by Teresa Wiltz and Jerry Thornton, *Chicago Tribune*, Aug. 23, 1991, sec. 2, p. 1.

Aug. 23, 1988: "Gun Club Hits 'Elitist' Plan to Shut Facilities on Lakefront," by Barry Cronin, *Chicago Sun-Times*, Aug. 24, 1988, p. 5.

Aug. 24, 1943: *Lake Michigan's Aircraft Carriers*, by Paul M. Somers (Arcadia, 2003).

Aug. 25, 1932: *The Rise of Gospel Blues: The Music of Thomas Andrew Dorsey in the Urban Church*, by Michael W. Harris (Oxford, 1992), p. 216.

Aug. 26, 1968: *Battleground Chicago: The Police and the 1968 Democratic National Convention*, by Frank Kusch (University of Chicago Press, 2008), p. 70.

Aug. 27, 1930: "Thousands See 1st Television Program Here," *Chicago Daily News*, by K. A. Hathaway, Aug. 28, 1930, p. 26.

Aug. 28, 1929: "Zep Soars over Chicago," *Chicago Daily News*, Aug. 28, 1929, p. 1.

Aug. 29, 1911: "In(to) the Loop," by James Talbot, *Modern Steel Construction*, December 2013.

Aug. 30, 1847: "Cyrus McCormick Moves to Chicago," by Jon Anderson, *Chicago Tribune*, Dec. 18, 2007. Also "Agricultural Machinery Industry," by Fred Carstensen, Encyclopedia of Chicago, Newberry Library.

Aug. 31, 1920: *Timeless Toys: Classic Toys and the Playmakers Who Created Them*, by Tim Walsh (Andrews McMeel, 2005), p. 31.

Sept. 1, 1930: "Kohler Holds Air Transport Aid to Progress," *Chicago Daily News*, Sept. 1, 1930, p. 3.

Sept. 2, 1955: "Slain Boy's Body Arrives Here; Sets Off Emotional Scene at Depot," *Chicago Sun-Times*, Sept. 3, 1955, p. 4.

Sept. 3, 1979: "Plaza Window Gets the Blues," by James Warren, *Chicago Sun-Times*, Sept. 2, 1979, p. 5.

Sept. 4, 1975: "Remembering Roger Ebert," by Neil Steinberg, April 4, 2018, everygoddamnday.com.

Sept. 5, 1984: "Good News Is Always Rolling by Us, if We Notice," by Neil Steinberg, *Chicago Sun-Times*, Aug. 11, 2016.

Sept. 6, 1874: "The Early Years of Wincenty Barzynski," by T. Lindsay Baker, *Polish American Studies* 32.1 (Spring 1975): 29–51.

Sept. 7, 2010: "'I've Given It My All'; Mayor Calling It Quits after 21-Year Stint," by Fran Spielman, *Chicago Sun-Times*, Sept. 8, 2010, p. 2.

Sept. 8, 1977: "Our 'Bar' Uncovers Pay-Offs, Tax Gyps," by Pamela Zekman and Zay N. Smith, *Chicago Sun-Times*, Jan. 8, 1978, p. 1; "It Wasn't Just a Bar, It Was a Mirage," *Chicago Sun-Times*, Jan. 8, 1978, p. 5.

Sept. 9, 1937: *Mies Van Der Rohe: A Critical Biography* by Franz Schulze (University of Chicago Press, 1985), p. 211.

Sept. 10, 1900: "Big Jam at Schools," *Chicago Daily News*, Sept. 10, 1900, p. 6; "The Development of the Home and Hospital Program of the Chicago Public Schools, 1899–1985," by Vivian E. Rankin (1993 dissertation, Loyola University, Chicago), p. 12.

Sept. 11, 1961: *The Golden Age of Chicago Children's Television*, by Ted Okuda and Jack Mulqueen (Southern Illinois University Press, 2004), p. 162.

Sept. 12, 1992: "Jemison Feels Down-to-Earth in Chicago," by Minette McGee, *Chicago Sun-Times*, Oct. 15, 1992, p. 3.

Sept. 13, 1998: "A Vicious Scrum, a Lawsuit, Lingering Anger: The Fight over Sammy Sosa's 62nd Home Run," by Kevin Kaduk, *USA Today*, Sports, June 14, 2020.

Sept. 14, 1932: "Insull Developments Cause Swanson to Order Inquiry," *Chicago Tribune*, Sept. 15, 1932, p. 4.

Sept. 15, 1982: Interview with Carlos Tortolero, June 20, 2020.

Sept. 16, 1977: "How Pilsen's Founding Mothers Built a High School," by Cloee Cooper, WTTW.

Sept. 17, 1920: *Papa Bear: The Life and Legacy of George Halas*, by Jeff Davis (McGraw-Hill, 2006), p. 53.

Sept. 18, 1889: *Twenty Years at Hull-House*, by Jane Addams (Macmillan, 1920), p. 85.

Sept. 19, 1910: "Slain in His Home as He Defends Daughter," *Chicago Daily News*, Sept. 19, 1910, p. 1.

Sept. 20, 1992: "Bridge Is Out: Detour Ahead—Michigan Ave. Accident Hurts 6, Will Stall Traffic," by Neil Steinberg and Minette McGee, *Chicago Sun-Times*, Sept. 21, 1992, p. 1.

Sept. 21, 1927: "Crowds Pour into City for Fight," *Chicago Daily News*, Sept. 21, 1927, p. 1; "Brains vs. Brawn: 90 Years Ago, Dempsey-Tunney Shocked Soldier Field," by Neil Steinberg, *Chicago Sun-Times*, Sept. 22, 2017.

Sept. 22, 1959: "Sirens for Sox Stir Citizens to Anger," *Chicago Daily News*, Sept. 24, 1959, p. 8.

Sept. 23, 1917: Lash-Brow-Ine advertisement, *Chicago Daily News*, Sept. 23, 1917, part 5, p. 8.

Sept. 24, 1901: "The Mental Status of Czolgosz," by Walter Channing, *American Journal of Insanity* 59.2 (October 1902): 23; *Living My Life*, by Emma Goldman (Cosimo Classics, 2011), p. 300.

Sept. 25, 1856: *The Life of Dwight L. Moody*, by William R. Moody (Revell, 1900), p. 47.

Sept. 26, 1960: "Nixon Bangs Other Knee on Car Door," by Sydney J. Harris, *Chicago Daily News*, Sept. 27, 1960, p. 1.

Sept. 27, 1925: "Hourly Output Dept. 6325 Receiver Coils, Illumination Study, 1926," Harvard University Baker Library, West Electric Company Hawthorne Studies Collection.

Sept. 28, 1920: "Comiskey Suspends 7; Cicotte and Jackson Tell the Jury All," *Chicago Daily News*, Sept. 28, 1920, p. 1; "Jackson's Story," *Chicago Tribune*, Sept. 29, 1920, p. 2.

Sept. 29, 1982: "Revisiting Chicago's Tylenol Murders," *Chicago Magazine*, Sept. 21, 2012.

Sept. 30, 1914: *Selected Letters of Ezra Pound: 1907–1941*, edited by D. D. Paige (New Directions, 1950), p. 40; *The Letters of T. S. Eliot, Volume 1: 1898–1922*, edited by Valerie Eliot and Hugh Houghton (Yale University Press, 2001), p. 63.

Oct. 1, 1932: Before he was a shrill right-wing fusspot, caviling FDR and sneering at civil rights, Westbrook Pegler was a decent sports columnist. His "The Called Shot Heard Round the World" originally ran in the *Chicago Tribune*, Oct. 2, 1932; you can find it, as I did, in *From Black Sox to Three-Peats: A Century of Chicago's Best Sports Writing*, edited by Ron Rapoport (University of Chicago Press, 2013).

Oct. 2, 2009: "Quick Exit Stuns Revelers," *Chicago Tribune*, Oct. 3, 2009; "Not Even the Second City—First-Round Knockout Stuns Chicago, Ends 3-Year Quest for Games," by Lisa Donovan, *Chicago Sun-Times*, Oct. 3, 2009, p. 9.

Oct. 3, 1918: "Police to Get You If You Sneeze or Cough," *Chicago Daily News*, Oct. 3, 1918, p. 3.

Oct. 4, 1931: *Chester Gould: A Daughter's Biography of the Creator of Dick Tracy*, by Jean Gould O'Connell (McFarland, 2007), p. 79.

Oct. 5, 1979: "A City Nestles in the Hands of a Gentle Pilgrim," by M. W. Newman, *Chicago Sun-Times*, Oct. 6, 1979, p. 3.

Oct. 6, 1921: *Halas by Halas: The Autobiography of George Halas*, with Gwen Morgan and Arthur Veysey (McGraw-Hill, 1979).

Oct. 7, 1853: "Proceedings of the First Convention of the Colored Citizens of the State of Illinois," Colored Conventions Project, Center for Black Digital Research, Penn State University.

Oct. 8, 1871: *Chicago's Great Fire: The Destruction and Resurrection of an Iconic American City*, by Carl Smith (Atlantic Monthly Press, 2020).

Oct. 9, 1871: *The Autobiography of Mother Jones*, by Mary Harris Jones (Charles H. Kerr, 1925), p. 21.

Oct. 10, 1944: *Deadlines & Monkeyshines: The Fabled World of Chicago Journalism*, by John J. McPhaul (Prentice-Hall, 1962), p. 191.

Oct. 11, 1947: "What Is Humpty Dumpty?," display ad, *The Billboard*, Oct. 11, 1947, p. 132.

Oct. 12, 1912: "'Jack' Johnson Deaf to Plea of a Mother," *Chicago Daily News*, Oct. 17, 1912, p. 1.

Oct. 13, 1983: "FCC Approves Ameritech's License for Mobile-Phone Service in Chicago," *Chicago Tribune*, Oct. 7, 1983, p. B2.

Oct. 14, 1908: "Oct. 14, 1908: Cubs Win World Series for Second Year in a Row," by Mike Huber, Society for American Baseball Research.

Oct. 15, 1921: "Going to School in Chinatown," *Chicago Daily News*, Oct. 15, 1921, p. 11.

Oct. 16, 1891: "125 Moments: 125 First Concert," Chicago Symphony Orchestra, CSO Sounds & Stories.

Oct. 17, 2007: *Vivian Maier: A Photographer's Life and Afterlife*, by Pamela Bannos (University of Chicago Press, 2017), p. 8.

Oct. 18, 1892: "Connection with New York," *Chicago Daily News*, Oct. 18, 1892, p. 1; "Mayor Grant Could Not Hear," *Chicago Tribune*, Oct. 19, 1892, p. 10.

Oct. 19, 1917: "U.S. to Give Amazons War Work," *Chicago Examiner*, Oct. 20, 1918, p. 8.

Oct. 20, 2014: *16 Shots: The Shooting of Laquan McDonald*, podcast produced by Jenn White with WBEZ and the *Chicago Tribune*.

Oct. 21, 1976: *Bellow: A Biography*, by James Atlas (Modern Library, 2002), p. 477.

Oct. 22, 1963: "Boycott a Thumping Success!," *Chicago Defender*, Oct. 23, 1963, p. 1.

Oct. 23, 1950: "Lazy Bones," *Time*, Oct. 23, 1950, p. 16; "Zenith Electronics Corporation History," *International Directory of Company Histories*, vol. 34 (St. James Press, 2000).

Oct. 24, 1924: *America's Corner Store: Walgreen's Prescription for Success*, by John U. Bacon (Wiley & Sons, 2004), p. 68.

Oct. 25, 1974: "Soaring Salute for Calder," *Chicago Daily News*, Oct. 25, 1974, p. 1.

Oct. 26, 1825: *Wedding of the Waters: The Erie Canal and the Making of a Great Nation*, by Peter L. Bernstein (Norton, 2005), p. 31.

Oct. 27, 1990: *For Crying Out Loud: From Open Outcry to the Electronic Screen*, by Leo Melamed (Wiley, 2009), p. 17.

Oct. 28, 1893: "Many Mayors Are Here," *Chicago Daily News*, Oct. 28, 1893, p. 1.

Oct. 29, 1955: "Plants to Soar at Field," by John Justin Smith, *Chicago Daily News*, Oct. 29, 1955, p. 14; "Here Is O'Hare," by Lucia Lewis, *Chicago Daily News*, Oct. 29, 1955, p. 15.

Oct. 30, 1893: *Hershey: Milton S. Hershey's Extraordinary Life of Wealth, Empire and Utopian Dreams*, by Michael D'Antonio (Simon & Schuster, 2006).

Oct. 31, 1933: "Pranksters Give Police Force a Busy Halloween," *Chicago Tribune*, Nov. 1, 1933, p. 3.

Nov. 1, 1954: "Callas Sang Here; Remembering a Great Love Affair in Our Musical History," by John von Rhein, *Chicago Tribune*, Feb. 9, 1997, p. 10.

Nov. 2, 2016: "108 Years and 10 Innings Later, It's Over: Cubs Win World Series!," by Gordon Wittenmyer, *Chicago Sun-Times*, Nov. 2, 2016.

Nov. 3, 1948: *Truman*, by David McCullough (Simon & Schuster, 1992), p. 718.

Nov. 4, 2008: *Becoming*, by Michelle Obama (Crown, 2018), p. 279.

Nov. 5, 1960: "World Envies Our Freeway," by Horton Troutman, *Chicago Daily News*, Nov. 5, 1960, p. 3.

Nov. 6, 1864: "The Plot to Burn Chicago," by Stephen E. Towne, *New York Times*, Nov. 3, 2014.

Nov. 7, 1934: "Road Show: An Airplane Is Made for Writers," by Nancy Kuhl; Beinecke Rare Book & Manuscript Library, Dec. 19, 2020, https://beinecke.library.yale.edu/article/road-show-airplane-made-writers.

Nov. 8, 1991: "Anthony DiCrescenzo Sr., 80; 'He Made His Pizza His Way,'" *Chicago Tribune*, Nov. 8, 1991, p. D-B11; interview with Anthony DiCrescenzo Jr., Oct. 5, 2021.

Nov. 9, 1927: *The Joker Is Wild: The True Story of Joe E. Lewis*, by Art Cohn (Random House, 1955).

Nov. 10, 1834: "Report of the Sanitary Investigations of the Illinois River and its Tributaries" (Illinois State Board of Health, 1901), p. 109.

Nov. 11, 1921: "Opera Carries 1500 Miles by Radio Phones," *Chicago Tribune*, Nov. 12, 1921, p. 13.

Nov. 12, 1893: "When Stead Came to Chicago: The 'Social Gospel Novel' and the Chicago Civic Federation," by Gary Scott Smith, *American Presbyterians* 68.3 (Fall 1990): 193–205.

Nov. 13, 1961: "CD Shelter Hunt Begins in Chicago," *Chicago Sun-Times*, Nov. 14, 1961, p. 17.

Nov. 14, 1943: "56,691 See Bears Rout Giants 56–7," *Chicago Sun*, Nov. 15, 1943, p. 17.

Nov. 15, 2005: *Here's the Deal: The Buying and Selling of a Great American City*, by Ross Miller (Knopf, 1996); "A Brief History of Block 37," by Whet Moser, *Chicago Magazine*, April 11, 2012.

Nov. 16, 1947: "Gifts for the Home," advertisement, *Chicago Tribune*, Nov. 16, 1947, p. N11.

Nov. 17, 1928: "4,000 at Party," *Chicago Defender*, Nov. 24, 1928, p. A3.

Nov. 18, 1883: "Standard Time," *Chicago Tribune*, Nov. 14, 1883, p. 6; "Standard Time," *Chicago Tribune*, Nov. 19, 1883, p. 1.

Nov. 19, 1937: *The Unidyne Story: 1939–2014*, by Michael Pettersen and Greg DeTogne (Shure, 2014).

Nov. 20, 1848: *A History of Chicago*, vol. 2, *From Town to City*, by Bessie Louise Pierce (Knopf, 1940), p. 35.

Nov. 21, 1911: "Butter Goes Up; U.S. May Stop It," *Chicago Tribune*, Nov. 22, 1911, p. 1.

Nov. 22, 1950: "Foil Plot to Set Afire Dr. Julian's New Home," *Chicago Daily News*, Nov. 23, 1950, p. 49.

Nov. 23, 1927: *Elevating the Game: Black Men and Basketball*, by Nelson George (University of Nebraska Press, 1992), p. 41; "Canadian Fans Rave over Harlem Globe Trotters 5," *Chicago Defender*, Feb. 29, 1936, p. 14; *Chicago Jazz: A Cultural History 1904–1930*, by William Howland Kennedy (Oxford, 1993), p. 162.

Nov. 24, 1887: "Game of Indoor Baseball," *New York Times*, Nov. 26, 1900, p. 8.

Nov. 25, 1860: "A Beard Is Born," by Adam Goodheart, *New York Times*, Nov. 24, 2010.

Nov. 26, 1927: "115,000 Bedeck Football Arena," by John W. Keys, *Chicago Daily News*, Nov. 26, 1927, p. 1.

Nov. 27, 1975: "Bramson's Chain Sold," by Peg Zwecker, *Chicago Daily News*, Nov. 27, 1975, p. 78.

Nov. 28, 1895: "The First Automobile Race in America," by Russell H. Anderson, *Journal of the Illinois State Historical Society* 47.4 (1954): 343–59.

Nov. 29, 1879: "Gabe Foster's Opium Den," *Chicago Daily News*, Nov. 29, 1879, p. 1.

Nov. 30, 1982: "Tales from Behind the Mike: Terri Hemmert," *U2 Interference*, Dec. 27, 2005. Plus notes from Terri Hemmert.

Dec. 1, 1958: *To Sleep with the Angels: The Story of a Fire*, by David Cowan and John Kuenster (Ivan R. Dee, 1998); *Remembrances of the Angels: 50th Anniversary Reminiscences of the Fire No One Can Forget*, by John Kuenster (Ivan R. Dee, 2008).

Dec. 2, 1942: Perhaps I'm falling for the hype. David Schwartz in *The Last Man Who Knew Everything: The Life and Times of Enrico Fermi, Father of the Nuclear Age* (Basic Books, 2017) calls the demonstration "contrived," pointing out that Fermi could have just as easily split the atom "with no audience at all . . . But Fermi also clearly understood the drama of the occasion and rose to it." My father was a nuclear physicist at NASA, so I know that sometimes a scientist needs to put on a dog-and-pony show to let the boss see where the money's going.

Dec. 3, 1926: "A Day in Wrigley Field History: December 3, 1926," by Al Yellon, *Cubs Nation*, Nov. 16, 2013; "Boys in the Hoods," by Andy Oakley, *Chicago Reader*, Sept. 26, 1996.

Dec. 4, 1969: "Those 'Bullet Holes' Aren't," by Joseph Reilly, *Chicago Sun-Times*, Dec. 12, 1969, p. 1.

Dec. 5, 1962: *How to Talk Dirty & Influence People: An Autobiography*, by Lenny Bruce (Da Capo, 2016), p. 149.

Dec. 6, 1918: "When Prokofiev Came to Chicago," by Phillip Huscher, Chicago Symphony Orchestra, CSO Sounds and Stories, Oct. 4, 2013; *Sergei Prokofiev: A Biography*, by Harlow Robinson (Plunkett Lake Press, 2018).

Dec. 7, 1921: *The Jews of Chicago: From Shtetl to Suburb*, by Irving Cutler (University of Illinois Press, 1996), p. 110.

Dec. 8, 1940: "Redskin Owner Pays 'Half Share' Players," by Howard Roberts, *Chicago Daily News*, Dec. 9, 1940, p. 22.

Dec. 9, 2008: "The Day They Came for the Governor," Daniel Cain and Patrick Murphy, *Chicago Magazine*, Dec. 3, 2018.

Dec. 10, 1924: *Out in Chicago: Society for Human Rights*, film, Chicago History Museum.

Dec. 11, 1921: "Tommy O'Connor Flees Jail," *Chicago Tribune*, Dec. 12, 1921, p. 1.

Dec. 12, 1938: Duncan Hines display advertisement, *Chicago Daily News*, Dec. 12, 1938, p. 3; *Duncan Hines: How a Traveling Salesman Became the Most Trusted Name in Food*, by Louis Hatchett (University Press of Kentucky, 2014).

Dec. 13, 2015: "Patrick Kane Extends Streak, but Corey Crawford Steals Show in Hawks' Win," by Chris Hine, *Chicago Tribune*, Dec. 14, 2015.

Dec. 14, 1877: *Chatty Letters from the East and West*, by A. H. Wylie (Sampson Low, 1879).

Dec. 15, 1908: "Orgy Records Smashed at First Ward Ball," by Rev. R. Keene Ryan, *Chicago Examiner*, Dec. 15, 1908, p. 1; *Lords of the Levee: The Story of Bathhouse John and Hinky Dink*, by Lloyd Wendt and Herman Kogan (Bobbs-Merrill, 1943).

Dec. 16, 1959: *Ensemble: An Oral History of Chicago Theater*, by Mark Larson (Midway Books, 2019).

Dec. 17, 1938: "Chicago Subway Started; Ickes Shovels First Dirt," by William H. Fort, *Chicago Daily News*, Dec. 17, 1938, p. 1.

Dec. 18, 1969: "Battle of Sexes Gets a Bit Rough," by Mike Royko, *Chicago Daily News*, Dec. 23, 1969, p. 3.

Dec. 19, 1975: "It's U.S. Justice Stevens Now," by Glenn Elsasser, *Chicago Tribune*, Dec. 20, 1975, p. W2.

Dec. 20, 1976: "Daley Dies!," *Chicago Daily News*, Dec. 20, 1976, p. 1.

Dec. 21, 1978: "Timeline: Suburban Serial Killer John Wayne Gacy and the Efforts to Recover, Name His 33 Victims," by Kori Rumore, *Chicago Tribune*, Dec. 17, 2018.

Dec. 22, 1904: "Sorry Christmas in the City Hall," *Chicago Tribune*, Dec. 22, 1904, p. 1.

Dec. 23, 1919: *Fancy Cheese: A Practical Treatise on the Popular Soft Cheeses*, by Walter W. Fisk (Olsen, 1925), p. 68.

Dec. 24, 1954: *When Prophecy Fails: A Social and Psychological Study of a Modern Group That Predicted the Destruction of the World*, by Leon Festinger, Henry W. Riecken, and Stanley Schachter (University of Minnesota Press, 1956).

Dec. 25, 1945: "It Can Happen in Chicago: Storybook Yule for Sailors," by Virginia Marmaduke, *Chicago Sun*, Dec. 26, 1945, p. 3.

Dec. 26, 1944: *Tennessee Williams: Mad Pilgrimage of the Flesh*, by John Lahr (Norton, 2014), pp. 11–13.

Dec. 27, 1978: "The Worst Heist in Art Institute History," by Phoebe Mogharei, *Chicago Magazine*, May 15, 2019.

Dec. 28, 1966: "Clay, Terrell Put on a 'Show' for Writers," *Chicago Sun-Times*, Dec. 29, 1966, p. 99.

Dec. 29, 1903: "In the Society World," *Chicago Tribune*, Dec. 29, 1903, p. 7.

Dec. 30, 1903: *Tinder Box: The Iroquois Theater Disaster 1903*, by Anthony P. Hatch (Chicago Review Press, 2003).

Dec. 31, 1914: *Flickering Empire: How Chicago Invented the Film Industry*, by Michael Glover Smith (Columbia University Press, 2015); *My Autobiography*, by Charles Chaplin (Simon & Schuster, 1964).